AF400809

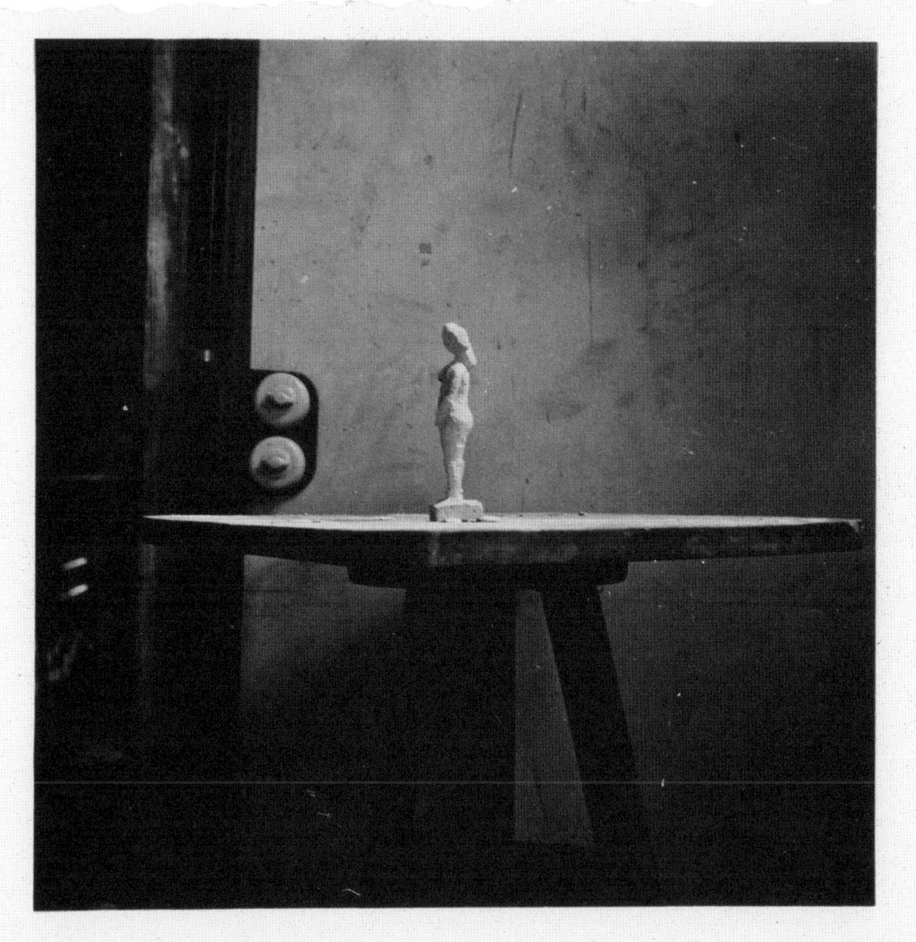

Fig. 1

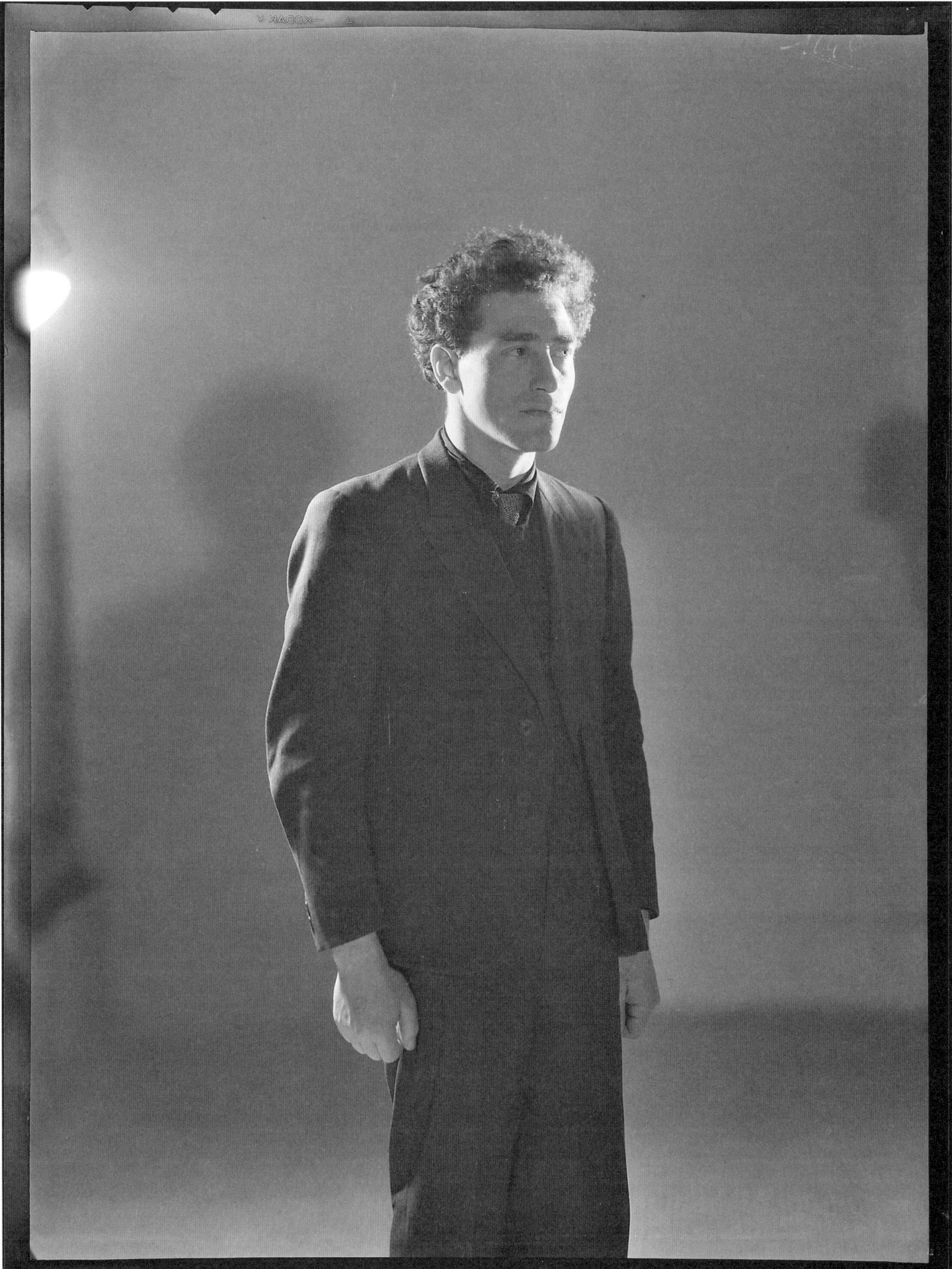

Fig. 2

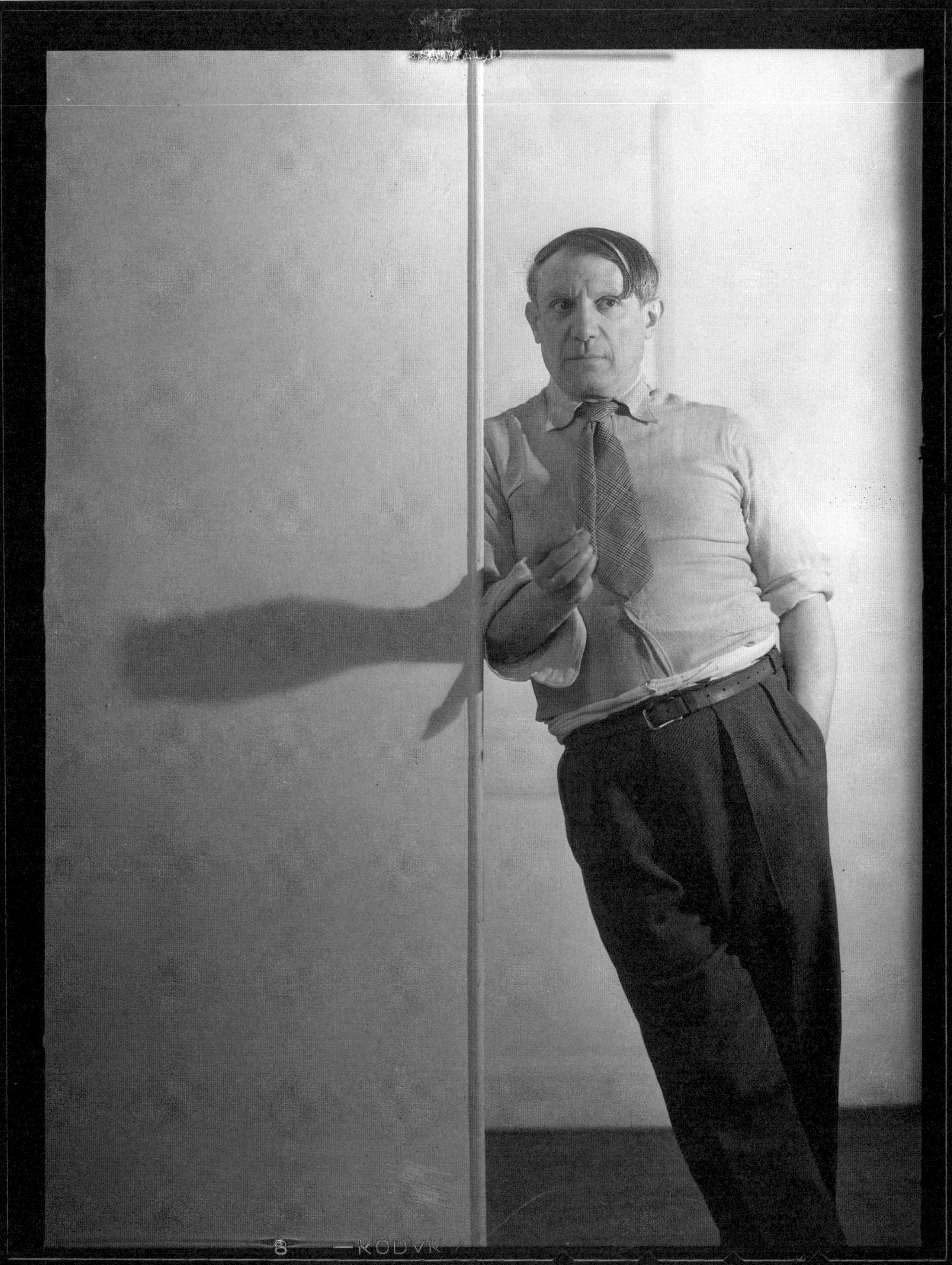

Fig. 3

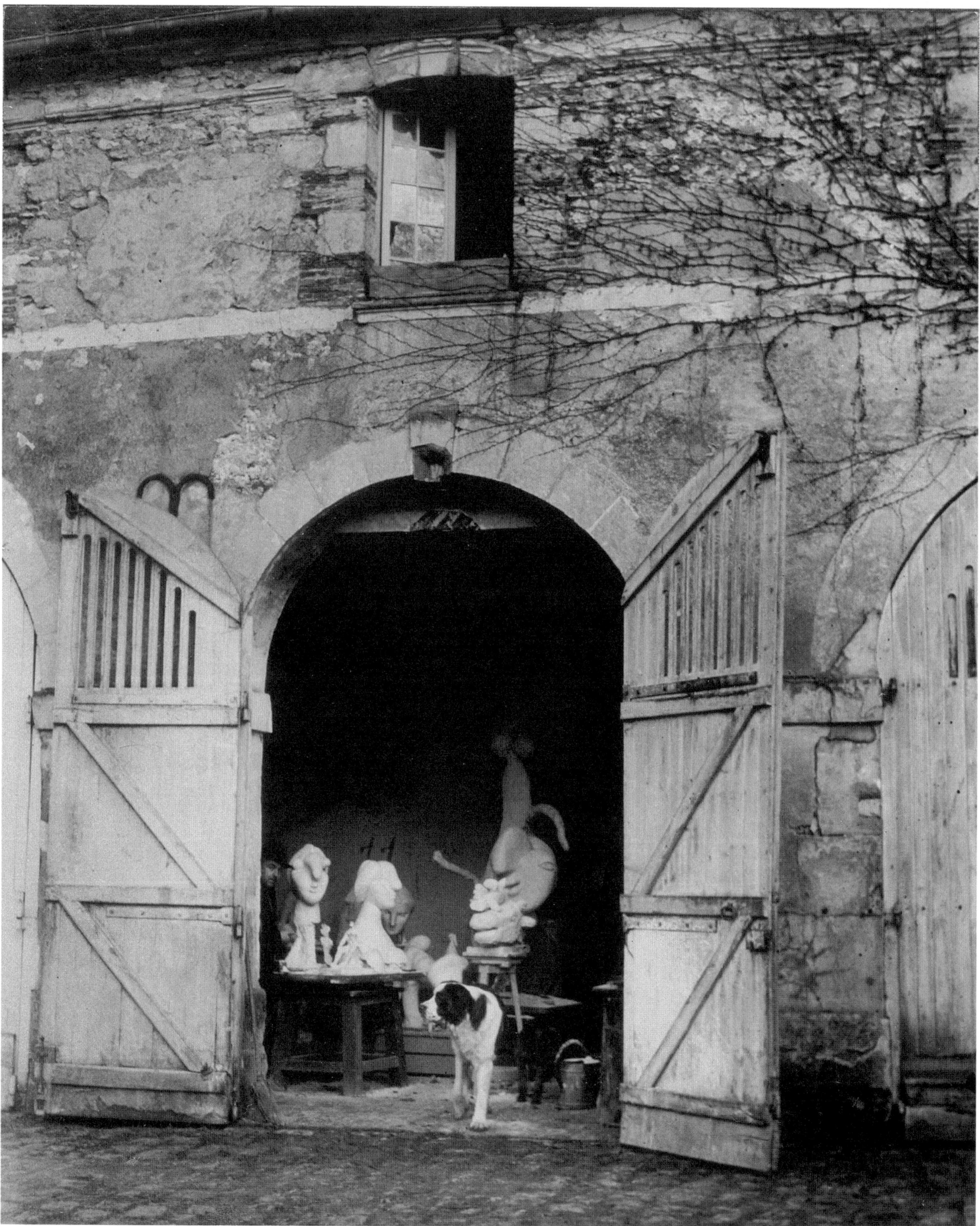

Fig. 4

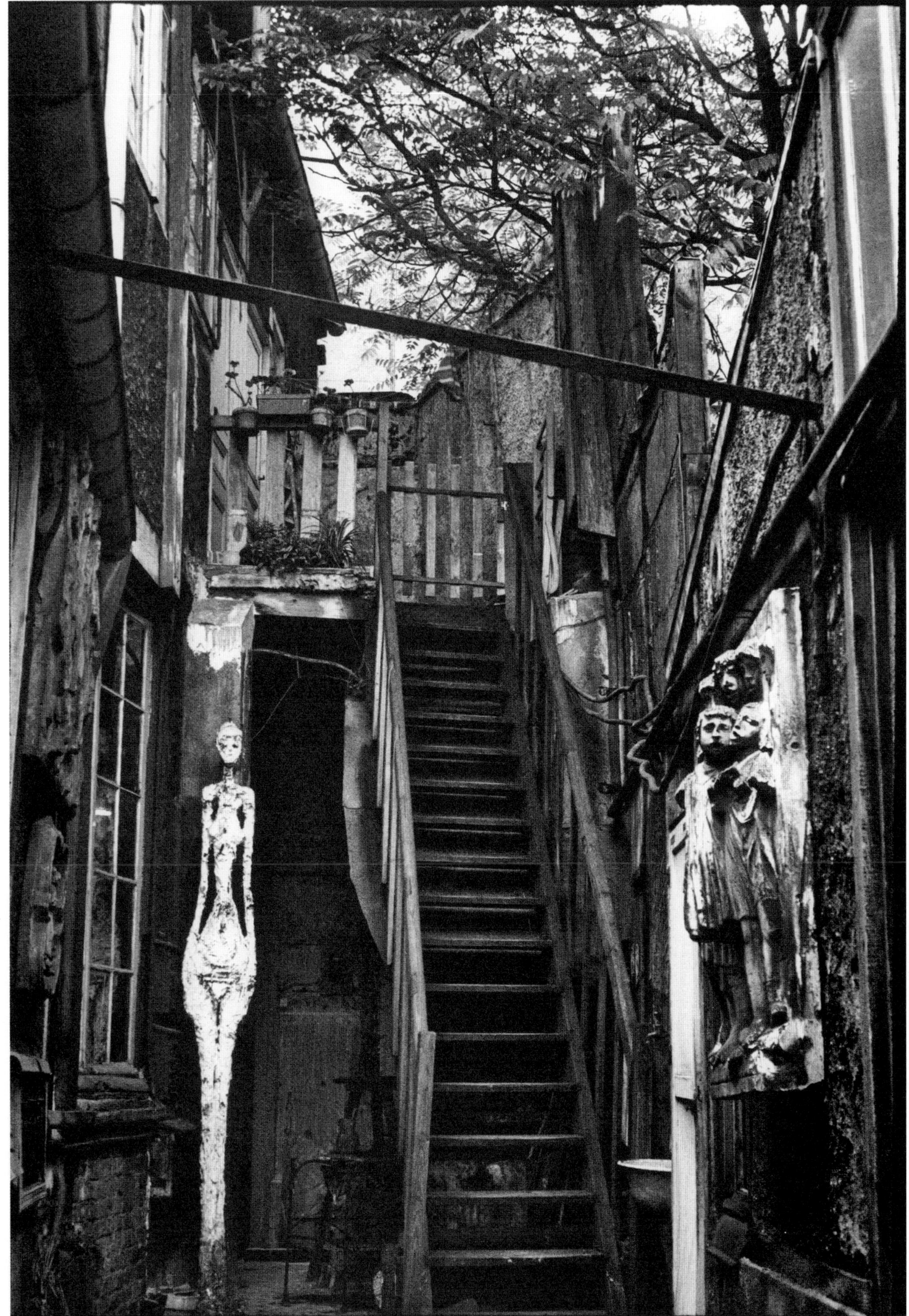

Fig. 5

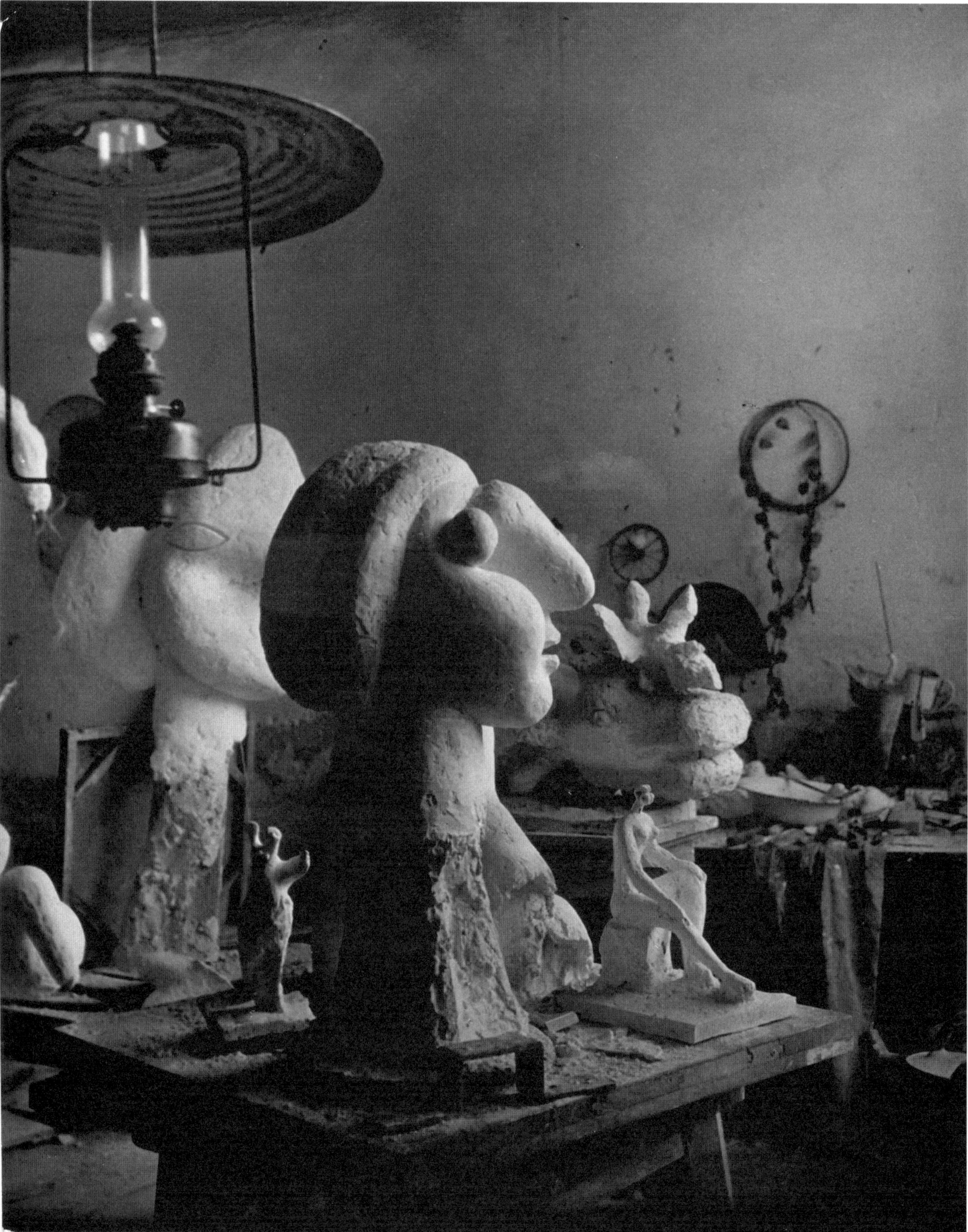

Fig. 6

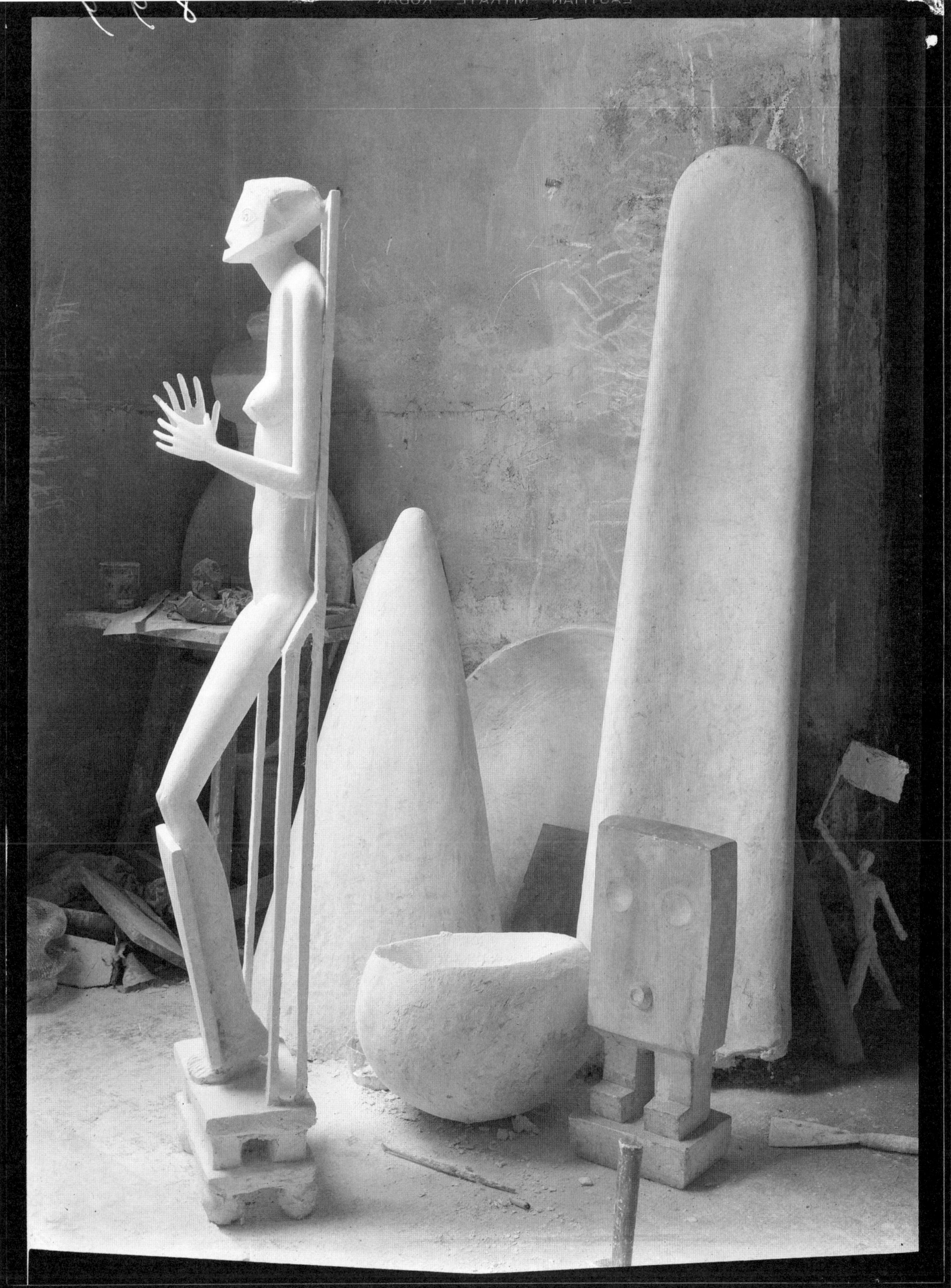

Fig. 7

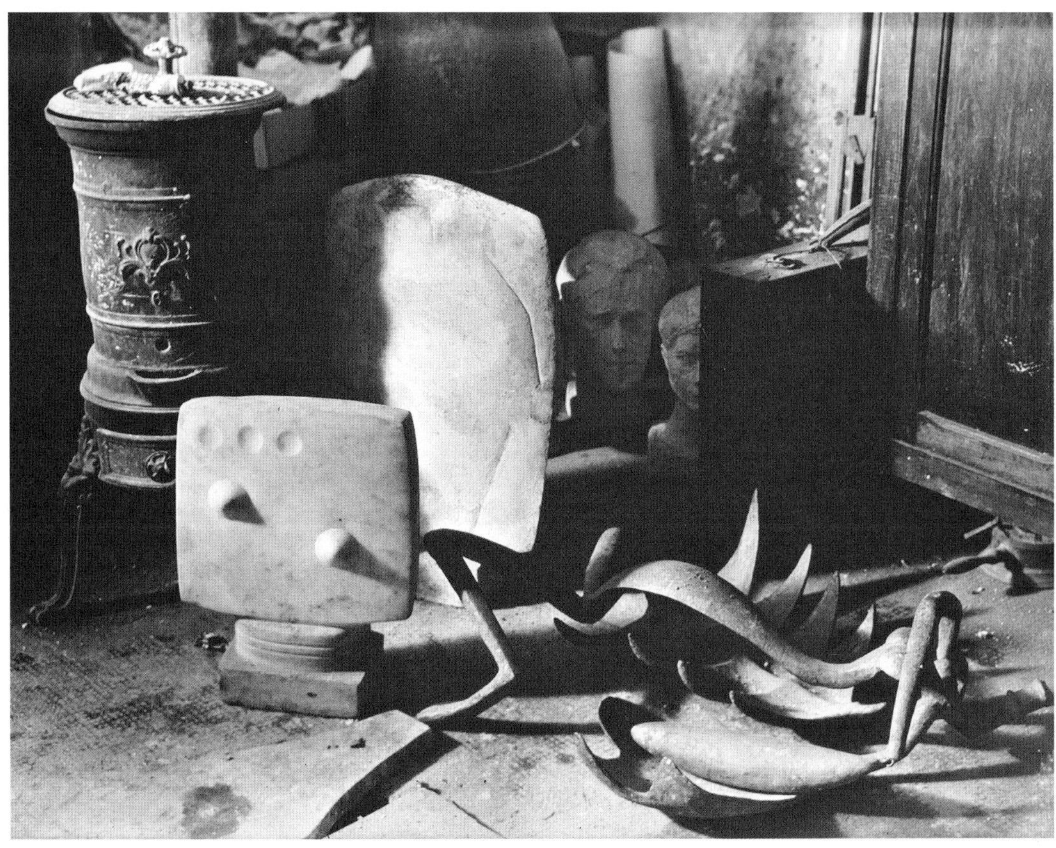

Fig. 8

PICASSO–
GIACOMETTI

In collaboration with the Fondation Giacometti

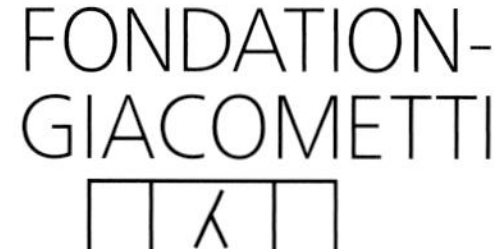

PICASSO–GIACOMETTI

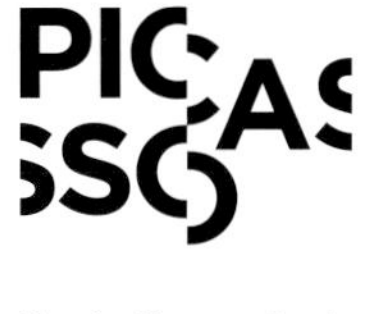

Musée Picasso Paris

Flammarion

Contents

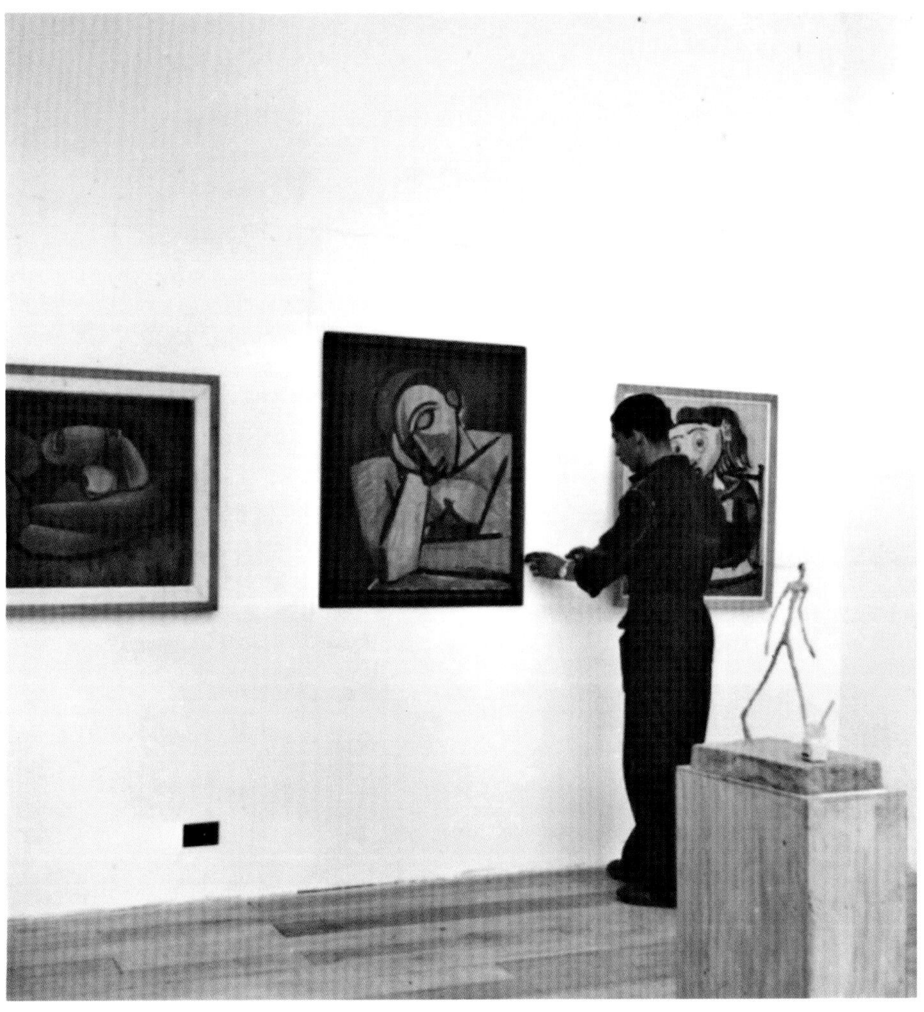

Fig. 9
Peter Scheier (1908–1979)
View of the exhibition space, São Paulo
Biennial, 1951, with Giacometti's
Man Crossing a Square on a Sunny Morning
in the foreground and Picasso's *Bust of a*
***Woman Leaning on Her Elbow* on the wall.**
Silver print
Instituto Moreira Salles, São Paulo

Foreword

The photograph on the facing page shows artworks
by Pablo Picasso and Alberto Giacometti displayed together
at the São Paulo Art Biennial in 1951. The *Picasso-Giacometti*
exhibitions held at the Musée National Picasso-Paris and the
Qatar Museums in Doha are, it would seem, the first shows
dedicated to the relationship between the two artists.

Laurent Le Bon
President of the Musée National Picasso-Paris

Picasso and Giacometti,
Two Monsters of Art

Catherine Grenier

In 1957, Alberto Giacometti renewed contact with Igor Stravinsky, who asked him about his friendship with Picasso and their frequent encounters from 1930 to 1934, which had become almost daily in 1940 and 1941. He responded with a single and rather personal comment: 'He amazes me; he amazes me as a monster would.'[1]

At the time this conversation took place, Giacometti was no longer friends with Picasso; they had grown apart several years earlier. The sculptor no doubt felt a sense of resentment over the circumstances that led to the cooling of their relationship, since Stravinsky's use of the word 'friendship' triggered the following caustic and sceptical remark: 'Well, you know, friendship with Picasso . . .' He failed to mention their reunion after the war, Picasso's visits to his studio on Rue Hippolyte-Maindron and the many dinners with the small circle of friends formed by Alberto and Annette Giacometti, Pablo Picasso and Françoise Gilot, and Michel and Louise Leiris. From 1930 to the early 1950s, the two artists saw each other regularly and, both before and after the war, enjoyed a genuinely warm friendship—despite the fact that they did not seem destined to become close or develop the sort of bond that unites peers.

Giacometti was twenty years younger than Picasso, and when he arrived in Paris in 1922, the Spaniard was the most famous of the avant-garde artists. The Swiss youngster, only twenty-one years old, went to study at Antoine Bourdelle's studio at the Académie de la Grande Chaumière. His first network of friends, his father's influence and the teaching he received all kept him on the margins of the Modernist movements, at least to begin with. With the gap of a generation separating them, the sculptor set out on the same journey as the inventor of Cubism—the journey of a precociously talented artist gradually espousing modernisation and the radicalisation of his aesthetic vocabulary. Once Giacometti had mastered academic and naturalistic representation, he then went on to adopt the new structural model introduced by Cubism, resulting in his assemblages of 'compositions' and the evolution of his 'flat figures', followed by the development of a more idiosyncratic vocabulary of forms and references. This was the stage Giacometti had reached in his work when he first came into contact with Picasso. Until then, the leading light of the School of Paris had done no more than act as a magnetic force on his young fellow artist, arousing in him both the attraction exerted by a liberator and the repulsion felt by a proud spirit when faced with an incomparable master.

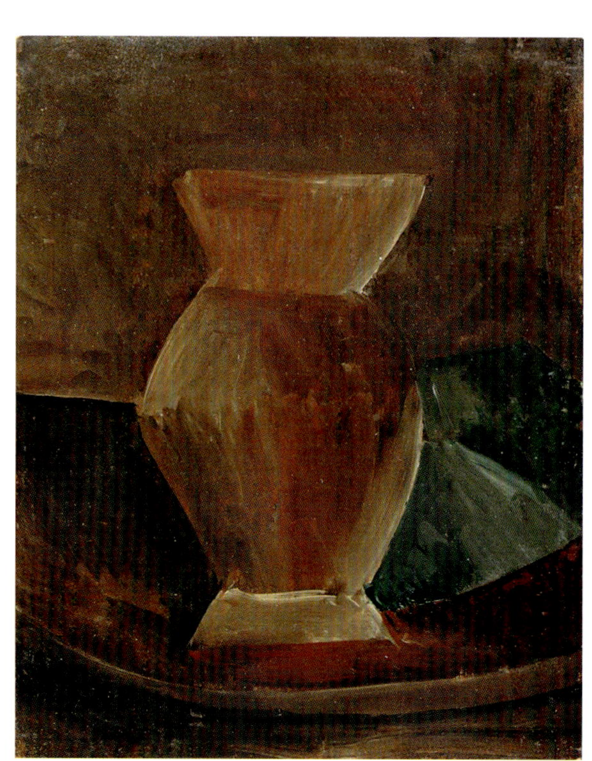

—
Fig. 10
Pablo Picasso
Still Life with Vase and Green Cloth
1908
Oil on wood, 27.1 × 21.3 cm
(10 ⅝ × 8 ⅜ in.)
Musée National Picasso-Paris
Dation Pablo Picasso, 1979. MP27
—

—
1   Extract from the filmed archives used in János S. Darvas' film *Igor Stravinsky: Composer*, Metropolitan Munich, 2001.

Even though Giacometti did not move in avant-garde circles when he first arrived in Paris, he was aware of the different movements thanks to the publications he read and the salons he attended. For Giacometti, as a young artist joining the fray after the intensive aesthetic battles that marked the beginning of the new century, the artistic panorama seemed like a 'tower of Babel' where it was hard for him to find his bearings and fathom where he fitted in.[2] However, his interest was captured by a name that shone like a beacon: Picasso. The first works he saw on display were not Cubist, but the neo-Ingresque paintings of the 1920s along with the Symbolist works from Picasso's Blue Period and Rose Period, then enjoying renewed relevance as the focus shifted back to the subject. The reviews he read provided him with an informed understanding of Cubism, as did the teaching he received from Bourdelle, who, despite being poles apart from the Cubist aesthetic, championed the movement's anti-academic position. Picasso, plural and impossible to categorise, along with the resolutely heterogeneous nature of his work and his unpredictable about-turns, thus served as the model of a modern artist for the young man. Giacometti's correspondence with his parents bears witness to his ambivalent relationship with each of his model's new propositions. He was sometimes shocked by forms whose innovative approach he then went on to assimilate, and was always interested in an artist who shattered the conceptual framework he had been working within until then. He did not hide his pleasure in being able to recount his encounter with Max Jacob—'one of the first to launch Picasso', as he explained[3]—and his pride when the master was the first to write in the visitor's book at Giacometti's first solo exhibition. Another few years went by before they actually met.

Giacometti referred to Picasso as a 'monster', but the term did not have the pejorative connotation that Stravinsky attributed to it. The composer responded to Giacometti by pointing out that Picasso might find such a term offensive. 'Not at all', replied Giacometti. 'Picasso knows that he's a monster.' He himself, with his radical life choices, resolute rejection of the role of successful artist over the long term, and refusal to conform to dominant movements, was an equally extraordinary artist and man. When his artistic journey took off and he embraced the Surrealist movement, he was effectively contributing to the construction of a myth whereby the distance from the norm is the supreme expression of artistic freedom. In his artworks, which

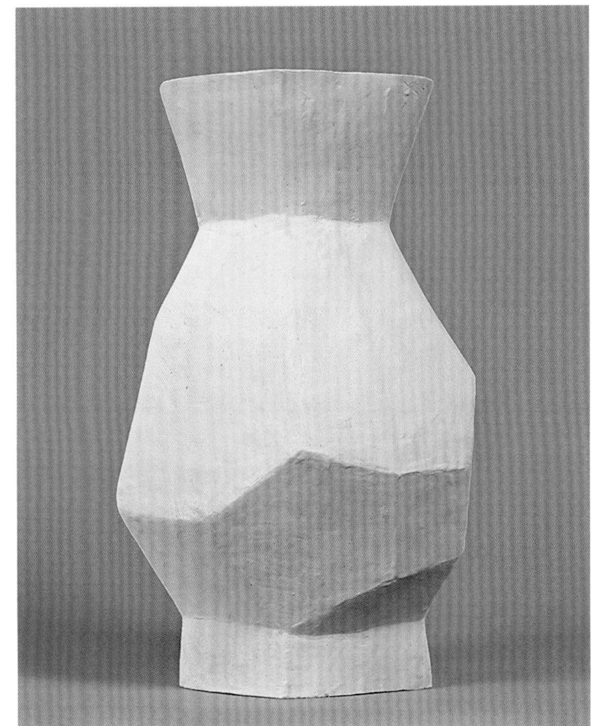

Fig. 11
Alberto Giacometti
Faceted Vase
c. 1934
Plaster, h. 38 cm (15 in.)
Fondation Giacometti, Paris

2 Letter from Alberto Giacometti to his parents, 31 January 1925, Swiss Art Archives, Swiss Institute for Art Research (SIK-ISEA), Zurich, inv.274.A.2.1.46.
3 'Two days ago Max Jacob was at my place [...], a famous writer, one of the first to launch Picasso, a very intelligent man. When he left he told me that 30 years ago he made an "amulet" for Picasso, and that now he would make one for me, and that they were the only two that he made', letter from Alberto Giacometti to his parents, 19 June 1929, Swiss Art Archives, SIK-ISEA, Zurich, inv. 274.A.2.3.22.

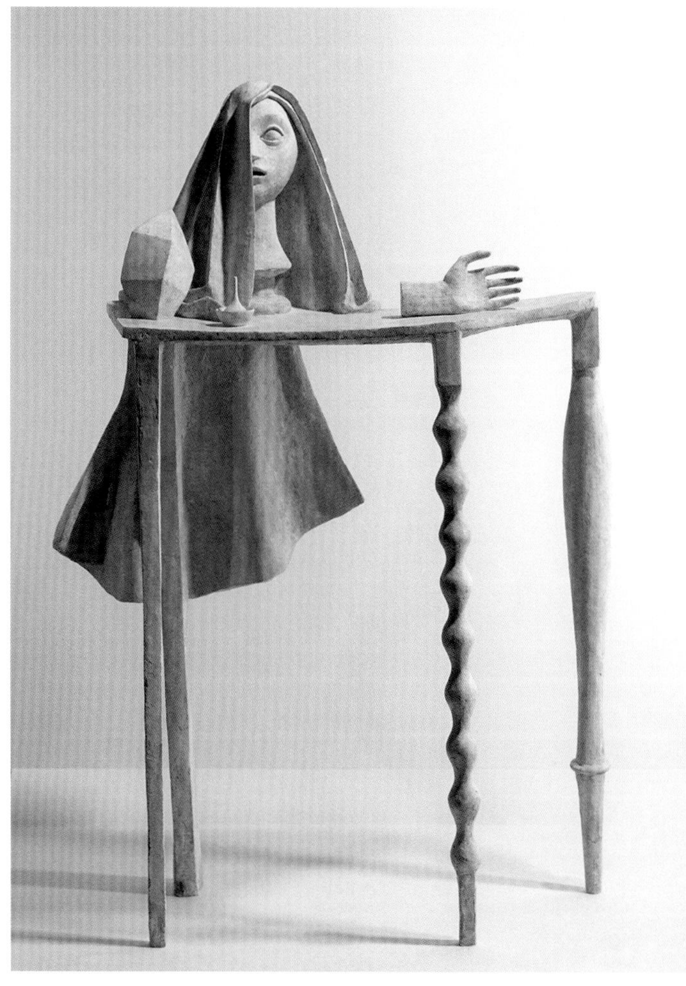

propose the same fusion between Eros and Thanatos as Picasso's works, as well as in his writings, with their provocative depictions of private sadistic fantasies, the young artist revealed an image of himself that carried the risk of the monstrous. In the eyes of his new friends and supporters, Georges Bataille, Carl Einstein, Michel Leiris, André Masson, Salvador Dalí, André Breton, René Crevel, Dora Maar and Picasso, this did not constitute a distortion of the artist's personality, but instead a privilege resulting from an inner experience that escaped the bounds of the norm. Dalí, whom Giacometti saw frequently in the 1930s, constantly built up the legend of his own monstrosity, placing it on the same level as the monstrosity he attributed to Picasso, whom he had immediately recognised as an unsurpassable artist. The fact that Giacometti turned his back on Surrealism and returned to the studio did not mean that he reverted to espousing a more conventional conception of the creative process and the creator's personality. The difficult conditions in which he practised his art at the outset became attributes of the artist's 'persona'. He kept the tiny studio that he had dreamed of leaving in his youth until the end of his life, dedicating himself entirely to his artistic creation to the extent that he developed a form of asceticism. 'That old Indian who comes limping out of his hut, covered in dust, his hair sticking up all over the place, his laughter a little carnivorous, his face steeped in very ancient wisdom—that's Giacometti.' Such is the description offered by Jean Clay, who interviewed the artist in 1963.[4] He thus adopted a counter-model that contrasted with the excessive vitality and assurance that characterised Picasso, radiant and flushed with success. Where Picasso hid his weaknesses and doubts, Giacometti placed them at the very heart of his work as well as his public self. The two artists' mutual recognition no doubt developed not so much in spite of these essential differences, but on account of them, defusing as they did any potential rivalry.

Pierre Daix had talked to Picasso about the importance of the encounter with Giacometti: 'It was always important for Picasso to discover that he was no longer alone, and Giacometti, with his *Couple* in 1930, *Woman Who Dreams* in 1929, *Suspended Ball* and *Disagreeable Object* in 1930 and 1931, catalysed a number of artistic ideas, which had partially been inspired by Picasso.'[5] According to his biographer, Picasso recognised 'the same sexual brutality, the same artistic

---

4 Interview with Jean Clay, 'Alberto Giacometti: Le long dialogue avec la mort d'un très grand sculpteur de notre temps', *Réalités*, no. 215, December 1963, pp. 135–144.
5 Pierre Daix, Picasso: *Life and Art*, New York, Icon Editions, 1994.

violence' in his young colleague. Although their characters were antithetical, they were brought together by a shared space, the space where form capitulated to personal psychology. For both men, artistic creation was being reshaped, sometimes from one work to the next, by the affective dimension. This characteristic was particularly marked between 1935 and 1940 and in the immediate period after World War II, when they both took a renewed interest in realism, finding subjects in their everyday environment. We can thus see specifically psychological factors triggering aesthetic variations in Giacometti's portraits of his wife, Annette, as well as in Picasso's representations of his partners.

'There are moments which one might refer to as a crisis, and they are the only moments that count in life', wrote Michel Leiris in a 1929 article on Giacometti's sculptures. 'I am fond of Giacometti's sculptures because everything he does appears to preserve such a crisis in stone.'[6] The work of both artists is nourished by personal crises. Indeed, their friendship began at a time when both their lives

were affected by a violent shock. However, it was also doubtlessly a crisis that separated them. According to Françoise Gilot, witness to their reunion after the war, their estrangement was the result of a violent argument.[7] Giacometti apparently discovered that Kahnweiler, Picasso's long-time art dealer, had asked Picasso what he thought of Giacometti joining his gallery, and the leading light of the Louise Leiris gallery was said to have opposed his membership. A friendship tarnished by artistic rivalry or an increasing incompatibility of lifestyles, as James Lord claims?[8] Picasso and Giacometti are both such enigmatic characters, and it is this inscrutability that makes this volume so rewarding for readers, lifting the veil further on two remarkable and profoundly different artists who attracted and amazed each other, two 'monsters' who succeeded in forming an impossible friendship.

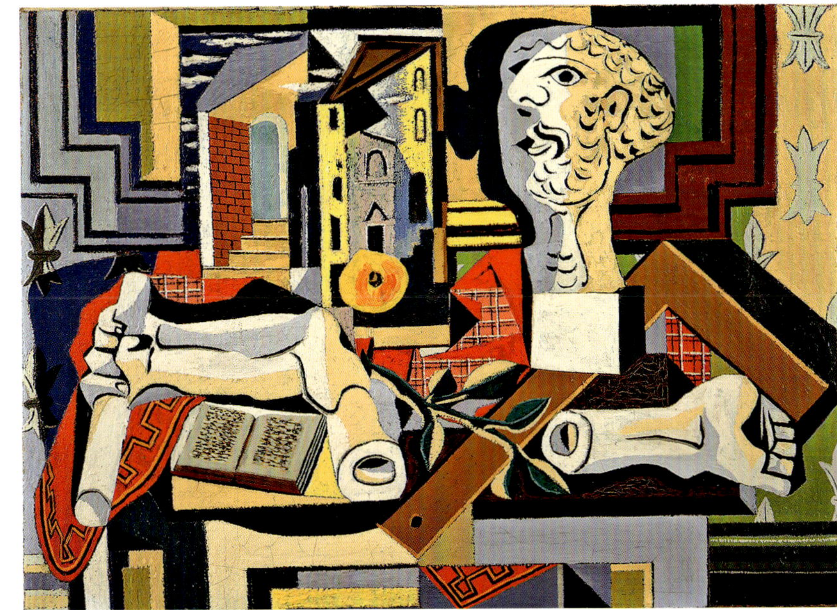

6 Michel Leiris, 'Alberto Giacometti', *Documents*, no 4, September 1929; reprint J.-M. Place, vol. I, 1991, p. 209.
7 Conversation with the author, July 2015. Françoise Gilot remembers having been present when Giacometti, who had just been told about Picasso's selfish response, erupted in anger. The altercation did not put an end to their friendship, but caused it lasting damage. See also Françoise Gilot, *Dans l'arène avec Picasso, entretiens avec Annie Maïllis*, Montpellier, Indigène Éditions, 2004, p. 87.
8 The anecdote concerning Kahnweiler is not included in the art dealer's archives. Lord attributes the breakdown of the two artists' friendship to Giacometti's moral judgement of Picasso's tendency to stardom and to his fickleness as a friend.

Essays

Memories of a Friendship: Picasso through the Eyes of Giacometti

Serena Bucalo-Mussely

On 14 December 1931, Alberto Giacometti was sitting on the terrace of the Parisian café La Coupole writing to his parents: 'After lunch tomorrow, I am going with Miró to visit Picasso, and I'm thrilled at the prospect of meeting him and seeing what he does.'[1] Giacometti was thirty when he met the Spanish artist for the first time. He had come across Picasso's work not long after his arrival in Paris. He was intrigued by the works of art that he discovered in magazines and galleries, and through art dealer and collector friends. The two artists continued to meet on numerous occasions until 1951. What started out as an opportunity to discuss artistic questions went on to develop into a friendship.

Encouraged by his father[2] to acquire formal training, in 1922 Giacometti enrolled in Bourdelle's classes at the Académie de la Grande Chaumière, where he perfected his drawing technique, particularly his ability to perceive and reproduce the human body from a model. This perspective coloured Giacometti's assessment of Picasso's work, as demonstrated by a letter he wrote to his father in 1924: 'I recently visited a Picasso exhibition which I enjoyed enormously. There are six or seven large sitting figures, two or three acrobats and various portraits of women. They are very clear and simple, and very well drawn. They are, besides, based on nature and very much alive. In short, this is an art that does not make a fuss. They are the best modern things I have seen in Paris until now, and he could do something magnificent in this field.'[3] When observing Picasso's works, Giacometti was struck by the immediacy of the subjects represented, the quality of the drawing and how alive the figures looked, figures whose regular forms and conformity to real life pleased him.

But the following year, in 1925, his enthusiasm for the exercises undertaken in class and for Picasso's realistic creations was supplanted by his interest in the major avant-garde movements. Picasso's Cubist works in particular represented a field of study that fascinated him and gave him the answers he needed for his artistic explorations. Giacometti's notebooks from this period (fig. 14) reveal his interest in Cubism and post-Cubism as avenues of creativity.

The human figures that appeared in his drawings, initially formed of lines and facets, evolved to become compositions of angular many-sided blocks. He wrote to his father: 'There are always interesting modern things to be seen, but it's a little like the Tower of Babel: there are so many different things, in every possible direction, and it's difficult to grasp the whole. We see lots of things from Picasso, and even if he changes a good deal, he always remains a good painter.'[4]

Giacometti was ready to soak up everything that enchanted him. The sheer variety of artistic propositions in Paris sometimes left him disorientated, but, just like Picasso, he was not afraid of producing very heterogeneous compositions. He copied the Spanish artist's works that he saw published in art magazines to enrich his creative vocabulary and hone his perception so as to produce new forms and compositions. Giacometti was interested both in Picasso's contemporary works, as indicated by his copy of *Seated Woman* (1927), and the Analytical Cubist compositions of *Woman with Violin* (1911)[5] (fig. 15).

1 Letter from Alberto Giacometti to his parents, 14 December 1931, Swiss Art Archives, Swiss Institute for Art Research (SIK-ISEA), Zurich, inv. 274.A.2.3.35. All letters to his family were written in Italian.

2 Giovanni Giacometti (1869–1933), Swiss post-Impressionist artist.

3 Letter from Alberto Giacometti to his parents, 8 April 1924, Alberto Giacometti-Stiftung Archives, Zurich.

4 Letter from Alberto Giacometti to his father, 31 January 1925, Swiss Art Archives, SIK-ISEA, Zurich, inv. 274.A.2.1.46.

5 *Alberto Giacometti: Dialoghi con l'arte*, Museo d'arte Mendrisio, 2000, pp. 85–86.

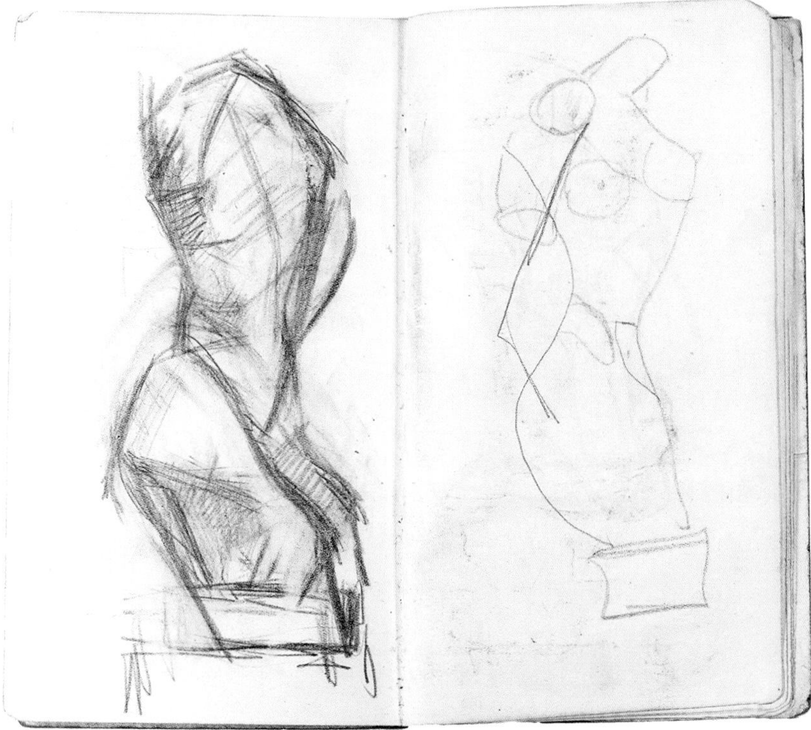

Fig. 14
Alberto Giacometti
Torso Sketches
c. 1925
Pencil on notebook page,
20.7 × 26 cm
(8 ⅛ × 10 ¼ in.)
Fondation Giacometti,
Paris

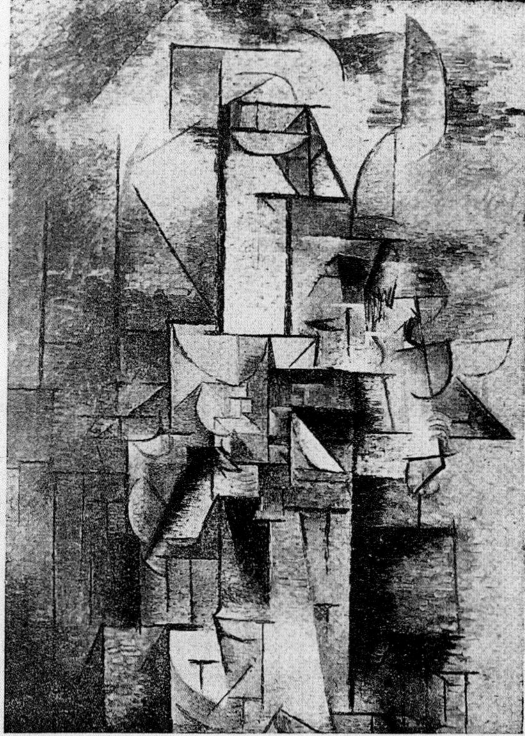

J'avais déjà fait à ce moment, la connaissance de la plupart des artistes français célèbres maintenant et qui sont restés mes amis. Quand j'ai connu Marie Laurencin, elle venait d'exposer sa grande toile « La toilette des jeunes filles ». Je lui ai demandai le prix. Elle m'a annoncé timidement 300 francs. Et, me voyant accepter ce prix : « Mais vous allez vous ruiner, Monsieur. » Je ne me suis pas ruiné, ma chère Marie Laurencin, en achetant votre peinture et celle de vos amis. Au contraire, si je n'avais jamais vendu vos œuvres et celles de Matisse, de Derain, de Picasso, de Vlaminck, de Braque, de Gris, de Dufy, de Rousseau et de Maillol, je serais aujourd'hui un homme formidablement riche.

Malheureusement, je suis devenu depuis marchand et j'ai vendu vos œuvres.

Je suis devenu marchand en décembre 1913. Le jour de Noël j'ai ouvert ma Galerie à Dusseldorf, avec des tableaux de peintres rhénans et quelques artistes allemands habitant Paris et habitués du Café du Dôme que nous avions surnommé les « Dômiers », notamment Rudolf Lévy, Purmann et de Fiori. Rudolf Lévy est mon plus ancien poulain. Son nom me rappelle une vieille histoire, j'avais proposé à des amis de fonder une confrérie des peintres Lévy avec, comme chef, Rudolf Lévy. Je viens d'apprendre que notre ami Léopold-Lévy s'est plaint de ma décision. Tranquil lisez-le, nous lui accorderons la présidence. J'avais naturellement accroché à ma galerie, de la peinture de mes amis de Paris et du douanier Rousseau.

Pendant les événements surnommés guerre, ma galerie fut transformée en hôpital militaire. J'ai appris par les médecins que les tableaux de mes amis de Paris ont réjoui pas mal de malades et guéri plusieurs militaires tombés dans l'état de prostration. Les peintures des cubistes, de Dufy et de Matisse, faisaient la joie et l'amusement des hospitalisés. Il y aurait lieu d'en tirer des conclusions. D'ailleurs je viens d'apprendre qu'un médecin parisien se propose d'écrire une étude sur les vertus médicales des peintures de notre ami Dufy. Qui sait, peut-être on arriverait à guérir par la peinture certaines maladies nerveuses.

J'ai rouvert ma Galerie en 1919, le dimanche de Pâques. Ma première exposition d'après-guerre était faite de tableaux de Vlaminck que Kahnweiler m'avait envoyés à Cologne.

Ce n'est qu'en 1921 que j'ai ouvert une succursale à Berlin. Mais cela c'est de l'histoire contemporaine que vous connaissez.

Ce qui m'intéresse beaucoup c'est la boxe, et sa figure devient si brillante

Picasso. La femme au violon. Coll. Flechtheim.

de joie qu'elle semble transfigurée. Comme André Gide, Flechtheim est un passionné de la boxe. Président — *honoris causa,* — je ne crois pas qu'il pouvait en être autrement, des associations de boxe Macabi, cercle juif et association des sergents de ville de Berlin, il assiste pieusement à toutes les manifestations corporatives et intercorporatives.

— Quel est l'événement artistique, en Allemagne, qui vous a le plus frappé, depuis le début du siècle ?

Flechtheim, allumant encore un gros cigare, dit : « Schmeling, le boxeur. »

CHRISTIAN ZERVOS.

Les Peintres et leur Marchand

La plus franche cordialité règne dans cet Olympe. Le marchand, prisonnier du peintre, sourit sous ses flèches, sourit aux visiteurs, sourit à la galerie. Mme Henry les épousette : c'est elle qui a imaginé de les avoir chez elle, et pour elle seule. Quand elle tourne le dos à l'un, elle cause à mi-voix à son concurrent, toute soucieuse de ne pas trop froisser les convictions ni de dévoiler quelques-uns de ces mystères qui dorent les rues mais qu'on chauffe contre son cœur comme un tuyau de Jockey. Modigliani présente Zborovsky : ce jour là Zboro était poète : car comme les lunes, il a ses heures. Bonnard s'est attaqué à Hessel ; mais Vuillard, piqué au vif présente à son tour Hessel et nous le fournit plus souriant : Vuillard aura donc plus de talent que Bonnard. Mademoiselle Weill, ahurie un peu de tout ce thé mondain, cligne de l'œil : elle ne croit pas un mot de toute cette Union Nationale. Pour ne pas être dupes, les Bernheim Jeune travaillent pas de temps à perdre Bignou rumine : Lurçat l'a peint, vêtu de clair, cravate flamberge au vent ; rêve à Deauville et à son basset.

Deux sœurs jumelles peintes par Gromaire : elles fument la pipe. Quand vous causez à l'une, c'est l'autre qui vous répond. Il faudra les faire bertillonner pour s'y reconnaître.

Marguerite Henry, par Modigliani, c'était suffisant. Vollard par Rouault, Epstein par Gœrg, Van Leer par Billette, Mme Granoff par Friesz, le beau, le plus beau de tous, Jacques Bernheim par Kisling, Léonce Rozenberg par Metzinger et Paul par Picasso.

Madame Guillot par Ramey et quelques autres marchands très illustres par d'autres peintres non moins illustres complètent cette tendre famille.

Il ne reste à Guillaume, Hodebert, Vildrac qu'à faire une exposition particulière de leur effigie par Poiret, Clouet les Le Nain ou Marie : ce sont hommes à qui on ne refuserait rien.

Nous avons regretté l'absence de tableaux tels celui du père Sagot, par Picasso, du Père Tanguy, par Van Gogh, de Vollard - Toréador, par Picasso et de Flechtheim - Toréador, par Pascin.

Fig. 15
Alberto Giacometti
Copy after Picasso's **Woman with Violin**
c. 1927
Graphite pencil on newsprint, *Cahiers d'art* magazine, no. 10, 1927, 31.5 × 24.5 cm (12 3/8 × 9 5/8 in.)
Private collection

Giacometti's interest translated into the works he produced during this period. Examples include the portrait of Flora Mayo (fig. 59), which has much in common with the portraits Picasso produced between 1906 and 1907,[6] and the 1926–1927 Cubist compositions (figs. 62 and 64), wherein he assembles different elements in Synthetic Cubist style. However, despite his evident affiliation with the Cubists, Giacometti did not appreciate being classified as one of them. In 1927, when a journalist from the review *Neue Zürcher Zeitung* described his work as 'Kubistischen Phantasien'[7] (Cubist fantasy), Giacometti was angry and wrote to his father: 'I know that critic from the N. Z. Z., he knows nothing at all, either about painting or about sculpture, and the term "Cubist" doesn't mean anything.'[8] A few months later, at the Salon de l'Escalier, Italian artist Mario Tozzi found Giacometti's compositions overly abstract, oscillating between the formal principles of the Cubists and the Futurists. Rather than the 'entangled planes, overlapping spheres and cones',[9] Tozzi preferred Giacometti's human portraits that drew on 'Negro art', deeming them extremely expressive and powerful.

Giacometti proved to be as attentive an observer of artistic forms of expression from throughout the world as Picasso. Drawings and sketches from the period express the artist's strong interest in the arts that had so significantly influenced the preceding generation. In the late 1920s, art reviews such as *Cahiers d'art* and *Documents* frequently drew a connection between modern art (especially Picasso) and the creations produced by the peoples of the Cyclades, Oceania and Africa. Giacometti tirelessly copied masks, totems and sculptures. The two artists were fascinated not so much by specific works as by their constituent elements. They isolated these elements, assimilated them and reworked them to produce hybrid creations. The foremost work resulting from this process is *Spoon Woman*, produced in 1927 (fig. 73). In 1951, Giacometti declared in a letter to Pierre Matisse that 'the art produced by the Cubists and Picasso contained everything necessary to the birth'[10] of this sculpture. The work, with its evocation of African anthropomorphic spoons, has the same totemic character as Picasso's creations.

In 1929, Giacometti produced his series of flat women (figs. 78, 81, and 82), attracting the attention of art dealers and collectors alike. Michel Leiris wrote the first article on the artist in the review *Documents*.[11] Cocteau was the next to sing the praises of the plaster works, at once 'so solid and so light'.[12] Pierre Loeb then offered him a contract at his gallery and, in December, Tériade included two of his works in an exhibition showcasing the 'best contemporary sculptors'.[13] Captivated by his art, Max Jacob went to see him in his studio, and promised Giacometti an amulet like the one he had made for Picasso.[14] Alberto had become one of the members of the elite Parisian art world, and his works were featured in the most prominent art collections. Full of enthusiasm, he wrote to his family: 'Today at 2 o'clock I was at the home—an actual palace—of the Vicomte de Noailles who was happy to meet me and very nice. They have placed my sculpture in a lovely spot, close to a Picasso and nothing else.'[15]

That same year, André Masson and Jeanne Bucher recommended Giacometti to Daniel-Henry Kahnweiler, Picasso's dealer.[16] The gallery owner went to his studio. He wrote to Masson: 'I went to Giacometti's studio, and he wasn't there. But I nevertheless saw his sculptures as the door was not shut. My first impression (which may of course be revised): the work is very skilful, very sensitive, but a little mawkish, "elegant". The character of it

6 Giacometti created the portrait in the form of a stele, using a penknife to engrave the features on it. The piece is very similar to Picasso's *Head of a Woman (Fernande)*, 1906, on a bronze stele (private collection), and the 1907 *Head* (Musée National Picasso-Paris, MP1990-51).

7 'In your letter, you told us about the Salon [des Indépendants] and promised to send us the papers with the reviews. We have not received anything, and you know how interested we would be in them. In N. Z. Z. [*Neue Zürcher Zeitung*], you were mentioned as "Kubistischen Phantasien"', letter from Giovanni Giacometti to Alberto, 28 February 1927, Fondation Giacometti Archives, Paris.

8 Letter from Alberto Giacometti to his father, 2 March 1927, Swiss Art Archives, SIK-ISEA, Zurich, inv. 274.A.2.1.66.

9 Extract from the journal *La Nuova Italia*, 21 July 1927, sent with Alberto Giacometti's letter to his father, 30 July 1927, Swiss Art Archives, SIK-ISEA, Zurich, inv. 274.A.2.2.33.

10 Letter from Alberto Giacometti to Pierre Matisse, 22 February 1951, Pierre Matisse Gallery Archive, Pierpont Morgan Library, New York.

11 Michel Leiris, 'Alberto Giacometti', *Documents*, no. 4, September 1929, pp. 209–214.

12 Jean Cocteau, *Opium: The Diary of an Addict*, London, New York, Longmans, Green and Co., 1932.

13 *International Sculpture Exhibition*, December 1929, Galerie Bernheim, Paris, invitation.

14 'Two days ago Max Jacob was at my place . . . , a famous writer, one of the first to launch Picasso, a very intelligent man. When he left, he told me that thirty years ago he made an "amulet" for Picasso, and that now he would make one for me, and that they were the only two that he made,' letter from Alberto Giacometti to his family, 19 June 1929, Swiss Art Archives, SIK-ISEA, Zurich, inv. 274.A.2.3.22.

15 Letter from Alberto Giacometti to his parents, 8 October 1929, Swiss Art Archives, SIK-ISEA, Zurich, inv. 274.A.2.1.98.

16 'The other week I met Masson . . . he said that he is already doing everything he can for me . . .

and principally that he will talk to Kahnweiler from the Galerie Simon, and that he will do everything he can so that he has me at his gallery, even if it does not pay much to start with…. And I know that Madame Bucher is also talking about me to the Galerie Simon,' letter from Alberto Giacometti to his parents, 16 April 1929, Swiss Art Archives, SIK-ISEA, Zurich, inv. 274.A.2.1.91.

17 Letter from Daniel-Henry Kahnweiler to André Masson, 24 May 1929, published by Agnès de La Beaumelle in *Louise and Michel Leiris Donation*, Kahnweiler-Leiris collection, Paris, Centre Georges Pompidou, Musée National d'Art Moderne/ Centre de Création Industrielle, 1984.

18 Letter from Alberto Giacometti to his parents, 26 May 1929, Alberto Giacometti-Stiftung Archives, Zurich.

19 Pablo Picasso, *The Bathers*, Dinard, 8 July 1928, Musée National Picasso-Paris, MP1030.

20 Letter from Alberto Giacometti to his parents, 21 January 1929, Swiss Art Archives, SIK-ISEA, Zurich, inv. 274.A.2.1.85.

21 Letter from Alberto Giacometti to his parents, 23 October 1929, Swiss Art Archives, SIK-ISEA, Zurich, inv. 274.A.2.1.99.

22 Alberto Giacometti, 'Copies of Picasso's *Project for a Sculpture*', c. 1929–1930, notebook, Fondation Giacometti, Paris, inv. 2000-0050

23 *Miró, Arp, Giacometti*, Galerie Pierre, April 1930.

24 *Giacometti*, Galerie Pierre Colle, 4–17 May 1932.

25 In French in the text.

26 Letter from Alberto Giacometti to his parents, 6 May 1932, Alberto Giacometti-Stiftung, Zurich.

brings Modigliani to mind. But I need to see the things again.'[17]

As for Alberto, he told his family: 'Last Friday, Kahnweiler, from the Galerie Simon, came to see me at midday. I wasn't there, but as I had left the key in the door, when I got back I found a note on the turntable in the middle of the studio. I met him in the afternoon. He took a great interest in me and told me to call him when I had some new pieces…. He is a very pleasant man … he is also interested in the drawings I recently did.'[18] Kahnweiler did not offer Giacometti a contract, and the two men did not cross paths again until 1950.

Picasso and Giacometti's work regularly featured in the pages of *Cahiers d'art* and *Documents*, giving them the chance to study and get to know each other's creations (fig. 95).[19] In 1929, Zervos dedicated an article to the plans for the sculptures Picasso created in Dinard. Giacometti wrote to his father: 'In the latest *Cahiers d'art* are plans (drawings!) by Picasso

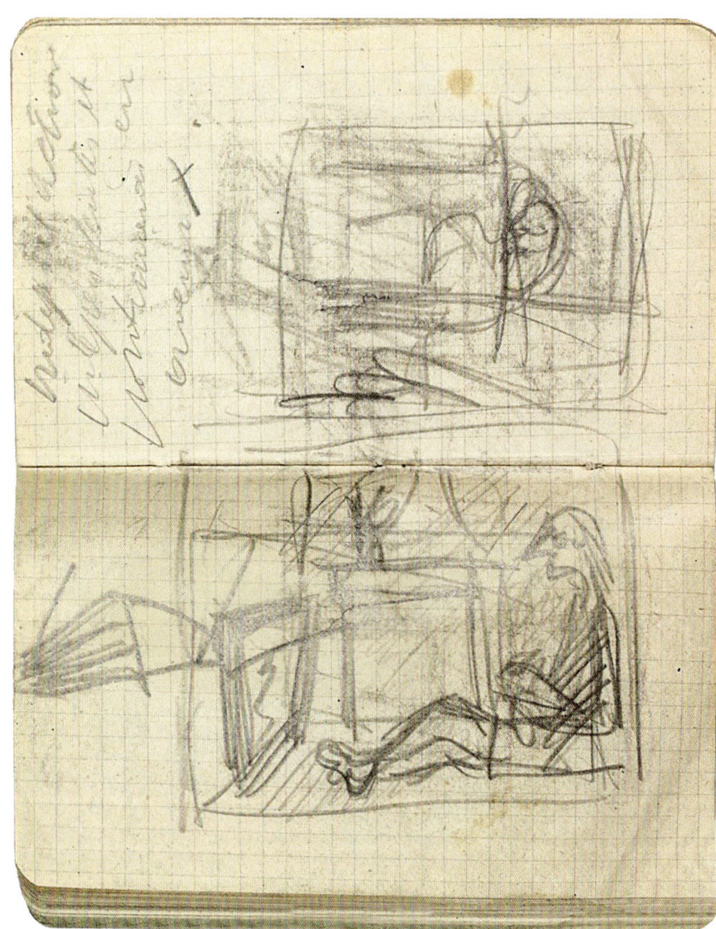

—
Fig. 16
Alberto Giacometti
Copy after Picasso's **The Muse**
c. 1935
Pencil on notebook page,
12.5 × 16.6 cm (5 × 6 ½ in.)
Fondation Giacometti, Paris
—

for some of his sculptures; they even reproduce the drawings for the plans, it's boring, we'll see what the sculptures are like afterwards.'[20] He sometimes seemed critical towards the Spanish artist: 'I saw the reproductions of Picasso's new paintings; they look like sculptures, which I don't like, and he is always so keen to do something new that I end up finding it wearisome.'[21] His criticism had no effect on his desire to analyse Picasso's work, as revealed by his notebooks from that period. Picasso's sculpture plans are carefully copied onto the pages of Giacometti's notebooks, surrounded by sketches of his first Surrealist works (fig. 92).[22] They gave him the inspiration behind the *Project for a Square* and *Suspended Ball* (fig. 100), both pieces displaying the effect of instability expressed in Picasso's oeuvre.

Giacometti presented this work for the first time at the *Miró, Arp, Giacometti*[23] exhibition held by the Galerie Pierre. There is no evidence to say that Picasso saw it during the exhibition. However, we know that Picasso was able to admire it in 1932, at Giacometti's solo show at the Galerie Pierre Colle: he was the exhibition's first visitor (fig. 21).[24] A few days after it opened, Giacometti wrote to his parents, his tone proud but a little disappointed: 'The first person to arrive was Picasso who came at half past midday! He looked and said "*très joli*",[25] like a child,...but he never commits himself, in fact he's known for it.'[26] The *Suspended Ball* clearly influenced Picasso, who used the theme of the encounter between the cleft ball and the crescent in the compositions he produced in the 1930s,[27] particularly in his studies for the *Nude Woman in a Red Armchair* in 1932 (fig. 98).[28]

In the mid-1930s, the two artists established a very strong bond, both artistic and intellectual, which withstood the war and lasted until the early 1950s (fig. 20). [29] At that time, both Picasso and Giacometti were close to Bataille's circle. They used their compositions to express the aesthetic of ugliness, as demonstrated in 'Rotten Sun'.[30] Picasso's paintings showed a terrifying, monstrous ugliness made of distorted images and enormous limbs (fig. 102). In the same way, Giacometti's Surrealist works conjured up 'disagreeable objects', women 'in danger', in the form of insects with menacing spikes and jaws (figs. 103, 108, and 111). Picasso's 'shapeless' figures fascinated Giacometti during the major retrospective at the Kunsthaus Zurich.[31] It is difficult to know if he actually saw the Picasso exhibition, but there is no denying that he carefully copied the works on display (fig. 99) in one of his notebooks,[32] as well as again discussing the multiplicity of Picasso's styles in his correspondence with his father.[33] He does also seem to have visited the Parisian retrospective at the Galerie Georges Petit,[34] mentioning it when he wrote from Hyères: 'There is a major Manet exhibition on at the moment in Paris as well as a Picasso exhibition; I'm very keen to see them.'[35]

In 1934, Giacometti met Dora Maar, who became Picasso's companion and muse the following year.[36] She immortalised *The Invisible Object* in a series of photographs taken in the studio on Rue Hippolyte-Maindron (fig. 7). One of the images was later used to illustrate André Breton's text 'Equation of the Found Object'.[37] The photographs also include a portrait of the artist cut off at the knees (fig. 2), dating from 1934–1936. Giacometti and Dora Maar's friendship withstood the test of time, despite the ending of her relationship with Picasso.[38]

These were the years when they seemed the most unalike, and when Giacometti and Picasso became the most intimate, developing a sustained friendship punctuated with highly productive intellectual and artistic discussions. Many witness accounts relate that Giacometti and Picasso saw each other almost daily at this time, visiting each other's studios or meeting in Parisian cafés, at Lipp, Les Deux Magots and

27 *The Three Bathers. III*, 1934 (Musée National Picasso-Paris, MP2395), *Coupling*, 1934 (Musée National Picasso-Paris, MP1113).

28 Pablo Picasso, 'The Sculptor: Studies of *Nude Woman in a Red Armchair*', 29 January 1932, Musée National Picasso-Paris, MP1990-110(11r).

29 Extract from archives used in János S. Darvas' film, *Igor Stravinsky: Composer*, Metropolitan Munich, 2001.

30 Georges Bataille, 'Rotten Sun', *Documents*, no. 3, 1930, p. 173.

31 *Picasso*, Kunsthaus, Zurich, 11 September–30 October 1932.

32 Alberto Giacometti, 'Copies of Picasso's works', 1932, notebook, Fondation Giacometti, Paris, inv. 2000-0046.

33 Letter from Giovanni Giacometti to Alberto, late 1932, Swiss Art Archives, SIK-ISEA, Zurich, inv. 274.A.1.1.164.

34 *Picasso*, Galerie Georges Petit, 16 June–30 July 1932.

35 Letter from Alberto Giacometti to his father, 19 June 1932, Alberto Giacometti-Stiftung, Zurich. The letter was written in Hyères where the artist was working on a stone sculpture for the Vicomte and Vicomtesse de Noailles.

36 His first contact with the photographer is recorded in his notebook. Since he was not sure of the exact spelling of her name, Giacometti wrote it out several times: 'Dora Mare, Maar, Mare, Dora Mare', notebook, c. 1934, Fondation Giacometti, Paris, inv. 2000-0036

37 *Documents*, 'Surrealist Interventions', no. 1, June 1934, p. 16.

38 A signed note seems to prove the existence of a portrait of Dora Maar by Giacometti: 'I'm giving you a small figure and your portrait and a painting as soon as you want, but you must telephone on Tuesday morning!' Below it can be seen: 'Witnessed by Tzara', signed declaration on paper, 1 February 1947, Café de Flore, Paris, in the auction catalogue *Les Livres de Dora Maar: Manuscrits, documents, photographies*, 29 October 1998, lot 295.

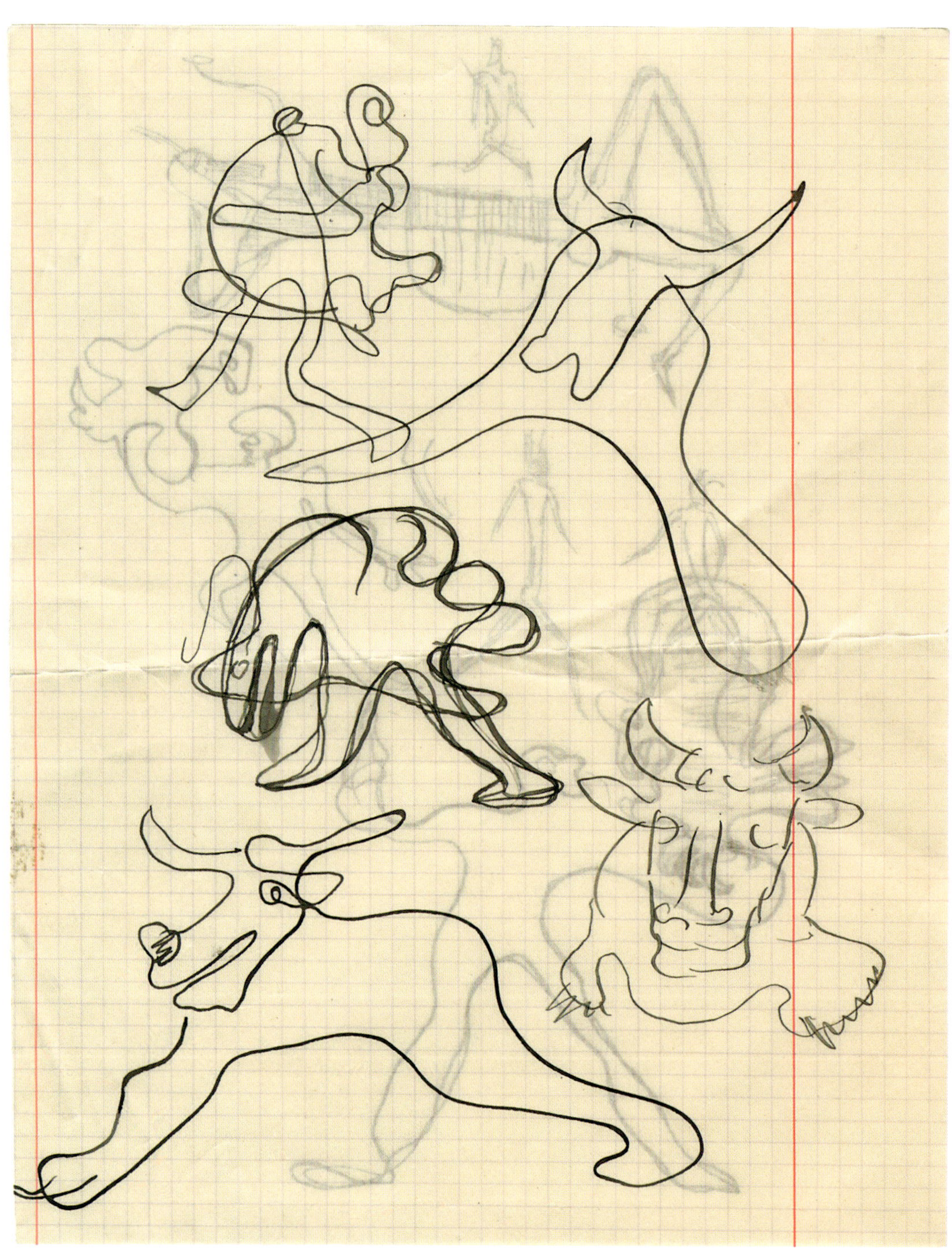

Fig. 17
Alberto Giacometti
Bulls
After 1928
Pen and ink on graph paper,
22 × 16.9 cm (8 ⅝ × 6 ⅝ in.)
Fondation Giacometti, Paris

Le Flore.[39] During the second half of the 1930s, one of the most frequent debates between the two artists was the question of the return of realism in art. Giacometti had begun to distance himself from Breton's movement in 1935, turning back to life drawing and sculpting, and focusing on rendering the reality of the human head and body.

Henry Moore recounted that in May 1937, Giacometti went with him to visit the studio on Rue des Grands Augustins where Picasso was working on *Guernica*. During that visit, the artists spoke about the problem of representing 'reality and fiction in paintings'. Picasso seemed to be making fun of his guests, making sarcastic comments about a subject that had become the obsession of the time.[40] When it came to *Guernica*, Picasso refused to submit to the artistic conventions of historical painting, convinced that the picture's realism resided in the expression of the characters' feelings of despair and anger rather than how the subject itself was rendered. The piece greatly impressed Giacometti, and ten years later he paid tribute to it with his *Head on a Rod*, representing the cry of the men and women suffering at Guernica (fig. 113).

The two artists developed a friendship based on mutual admiration and remained close throughout the 1940s, despite the distance imposed by the war between 1942 and 1945. Picasso paid heed to the advice proffered by his friend and did not scruple to ask his opinion. Françoise Gilot related that, during the creation of *Head of a Woman (Dora Maar)* in 1941, Giacometti often used to visit Picasso and watch him at work. Picasso was trying to break up the classic line of the head by crowning it with a hat, which Giacometti thought was superfluous (fig. 175), sparking a lively debate over the necessity or otherwise of the modest accessory. The sculpture changed several times, until Picasso decided to follow Giacometti's advice.[41]

The Spanish artist greatly valued his colleague's comments, leading him to reflect on his work and, sometimes, reconsider his creative process. Picasso accepted from Giacometti something he disliked in other artists: the capacity to go straight to the heart of the problem without wasting time on useless questions of style. Giacometti was happy to write about his analysis of Picasso's works, as evidenced by his description of *Woman in a Long Dress* in 1943: 'Well, the head is good, but he mustn't leave the rest of it like that. I think it's important for the work to adhere to his principles rather than benefit from accidental success. It would be better to get rid of the happy accident and work until the object is completed in all the purity of its creative power.'[42]

During the 1940s, Picasso took up sculpture once again. Pierre Daix, his biographer, suggests that he did so under Giacometti's influence.[43] The photographs Dora Maar took in the Grands Augustins studio show him working on a small plaster figurine (fig. 175) that brings to mind Giacometti's tiny women. Between 1945 and 1948, when he was in Vallauris, he produced more pottery figurines and heads on rods, some of them cast in bronze. Picasso was certainly very aware of Giacometti's compositions, particularly when they tackled the issue of distance and space. When talking about one of Giacometti's sculptures, Picasso said: 'When he creates these sculptures of a man in the street, moving from one house to the next, you inevitably see them as a reality in the distance. Sculpture, in Giacometti's hands, is what remains when the mind has forgotten all the details. He creates a certain illusion of space, which is far removed from my own conception, but no one had ever thought of it in the same way before. He really embodies a new approach to sculpture.'[44]

In 1941, Picasso asked Giacometti to create a portrait of him.[45] Alberto began to work on

39 'I see Picasso almost every evening and often dine with him, he likes nothing more than when I talk to him about Stampa, its habitants, etc.!', letter from Alberto Giacometti to his family, c. 1938, Swiss Art Archives, SIK-ISEA, Zurich, inv. 274.A.2.1.158. 'We continue to talk to each other and to our friends about sculpture, painting, and so on, and I see Picasso almost every day, it's delightful', letter from Alberto Giacometti to his mother, 15 February 1941, Swiss Art Archives, SIK-ISEA, Zurich, inv. 274.A.2.3.54.

40 Roland Penrose recounts that after lunch one day, together with Henry Moore and his wife, Alberto Giacometti, Max Ernst, Paul Éluard and André Breton, he went to Picasso's studio, in Elizabeth Cowling, *Visiting Picasso: The Notebooks and Letters of Roland Penrose*, London, Thames & Hudson Ltd, 2008, p. 276.

41 Françoise Gilot, *Dans l'arène avec Picasso*, Montpellier, Indigène Éditions, 2004, p. 87.

42 Françoise Gilot and Carlton Lake, *Life with Picasso*, Charleston, S.C., Nabu Press, 2011.

43 Pierre Daix, *Picasso*, London, Thames and Hudson, 1967.

44 Françoise Gilot and Carlton Lake, *Life with Picasso, op. cit.*, on the work *Figure in a Box between Two Boxes Which Are Houses*, 1950 (private collection).

45 'Picasso wants me to do his head, and I have made a start', letter from Alberto Giacometti to his mother, 21 January 1941, Swiss Art Archives, SIK-ISEA, Zurich, inv. 274.A.2.3.52.

46 Letter from Alberto Giacometti to his mother, 1946, Alberto Giacometti-Stiftung archives, Zurich.

47 Alberto Giacometti, 'Sketches of Heads', 1946–1948, notebook, Fondation Giacometti, Paris, inv. 2000-0128.

48 *Alberto Giacometti: Exhibition of Sculptures, Paintings, Drawings*, Pierre Matisse Gallery, New York, 19 January–14 February 1948.

49 'Very important make every effort to finish Picasso bronze for exhibition stop', telegram, 23 October 1947, Pierre Matisse Gallery Archive, Pierpont Morgan Library, New York.

50 Letter from Alberto Giacometti to Pierre Matisse, 27 October 1947, Pierre Matisse Gallery Archive, Pierpont Morgan Library, New York.

51 James Lord, *Giacometti: A Biography*, New York, Farrar, Straus and Giroux, 2001.

52 Françoise Gilot, *Dans l'arène avec Picasso, op. cit.*, pp. 103–104.

53 Recounting his holiday itinerary, Giacometti describes himself as 'incapable of writing the book for Tériade', c. 1957, Fondation Giacometti Archives, Paris, inv. 2000-0084.

54 The gallery's artists at that time were: Fernand Léger, André Masson, André Beaudin, Suzanne Roger, Eugène de Kermadec, Yves Rouvre and Françoise Gilot.

55 In 1965, when Giacometti left the Maeghts, Kahnweiler offered him a contract with his gallery: 'I want to tell you how happy I myself would be if you joined the gallery in 1965, since it is something that has been discussed for many years now. We would never have taken action while you were still with Maeght (you know how fond we are of Clayeux), but circumstances being what they are, we cannot not make an offer,' letter from Kahnweiler to Giacometti, 29 January 1965, Fondation Giacometti Archives, Paris.

56 *Bouquet*, 1953, and *Man with Clasped Hands*, 1957, from the Galerie Louise Leiris.

57 'Since for many years now I have only rarely had any contact with Picasso (for instance, I have been to the Midi several times without visiting him, of which he is aware), it is not possible for me to address him directly. I am totally unfamiliar with everything he has been doing for several years,' letter from Alberto Giacometti to Mario Negri, 16 April 1957, in *Alberto Giacometti, percorsi lombardi*, Sondrio, 2005, p. 282.

it, but was interrupted by the war. Forced to stay in Switzerland, he did not return to Paris until September 1945, when he was happy to find the same group of friends of old: Marie-Laure de Noailles, Francis Gruber, Balthus, Jean-Paul Sartre, Simone de Beauvoir, Albert Camus, Dora Maar and Pablo Picasso. They picked up where they had left off, as though the war had never happened, alternating long conversations in cafés with discussions in studios while observing the works. Picasso and Giacometti had never been so close. In a letter to his mother, the latter wrote: 'Yesterday I spent three hours with Picasso, who produced some very lovely new drawings, and it made me late for lunch with the Vicomtesse de Noailles. Picasso is a very good friend to me, he told me to go to his place whenever I want, and that I can treat it like my own home.'[46]

In his notebooks, Giacometti sketched his friend's head (fig. 18)[47] and the bust appears several times, between 1946 and 1948, among the pieces he set himself the task of working on. Alberto wanted to present it at his New York exhibition at the Pierre Matisse Gallery[48] and tried to finish it in time.[49] However, in October 1947 he decided to abandon the project. In a letter to Pierre Matisse, he explains why the piece would not be part of the exhibition: 'I'm afraid that it will be impossible to include the Picasso. If I had got a little further with the bust, we could have cast it and exhibited it as a study for a Picasso (I believe the bust has certain qualities), but finishing it quickly for the exhibition is not possible. Picasso would be furious with me (in the light of how things went) if I exhibited it without him having seen it, and on the other hand it would be very unpleasant for me if people were to think (and there are people who would think it) that I had exhibited a Picasso as a form of publicity for myself. It would ruin all my pleasure in the exhibition, and

I think you will understand my reasons. But I am sorry that the bust is not in a more advanced state. Besides, when Picasso returns, I'll finish it and nothing will have been lost.'[50] Picasso left Paris in 1948 to set up home at Vallauris and the two artists met with decreasing frequency. Giacometti never finished the sculpture, which was probably destroyed.

Their friendship deteriorated in the early 1950s. In their respective books, James Lord and Françoise Gilot both relate the episode that was possibly a determining factor in the final break. While the former attributes the tensions between the two artists to the way Picasso received his friend on his visit to Vallauris,[51] the latter provides more detailed reasons for the estrangement.[52]

According to James Lord, in November 1951, the Swiss artist and his wife Annette were in Saint-Jean-Cap-Ferrat visiting Tériade. Since he was in the area, he was able to visit Henri Matisse and see his new chapel in Vence, then go and see Picasso in his house in Golfe-Juan, Vallauris.[53] It seems that the Spanish artist greeted Giacometti by reproaching him for being a bad friend who had stopped coming to see him. Giacometti denied it, saying that the frequency of visits was not a measure of friendship. The conversation turned heated and Giacometti stormed out, slamming the door behind him and thus ending their friendship.

According to Françoise Gilot, in 1950 Giacometti was looking for a Parisian gallery; Michel Leiris had suggested that Daniel-Henry Kahnweiler consider him for the Galerie Louise Leiris. At the time, the gallery's rules required that all artists vote for the entry of a new member. When Giacometti's membership was submitted to a vote by the artists,[54] Picasso apparently rejected it, saying: 'No, I don't want him; I like him as a friend, but I don't want him in the gallery.' The negotiation lasted six

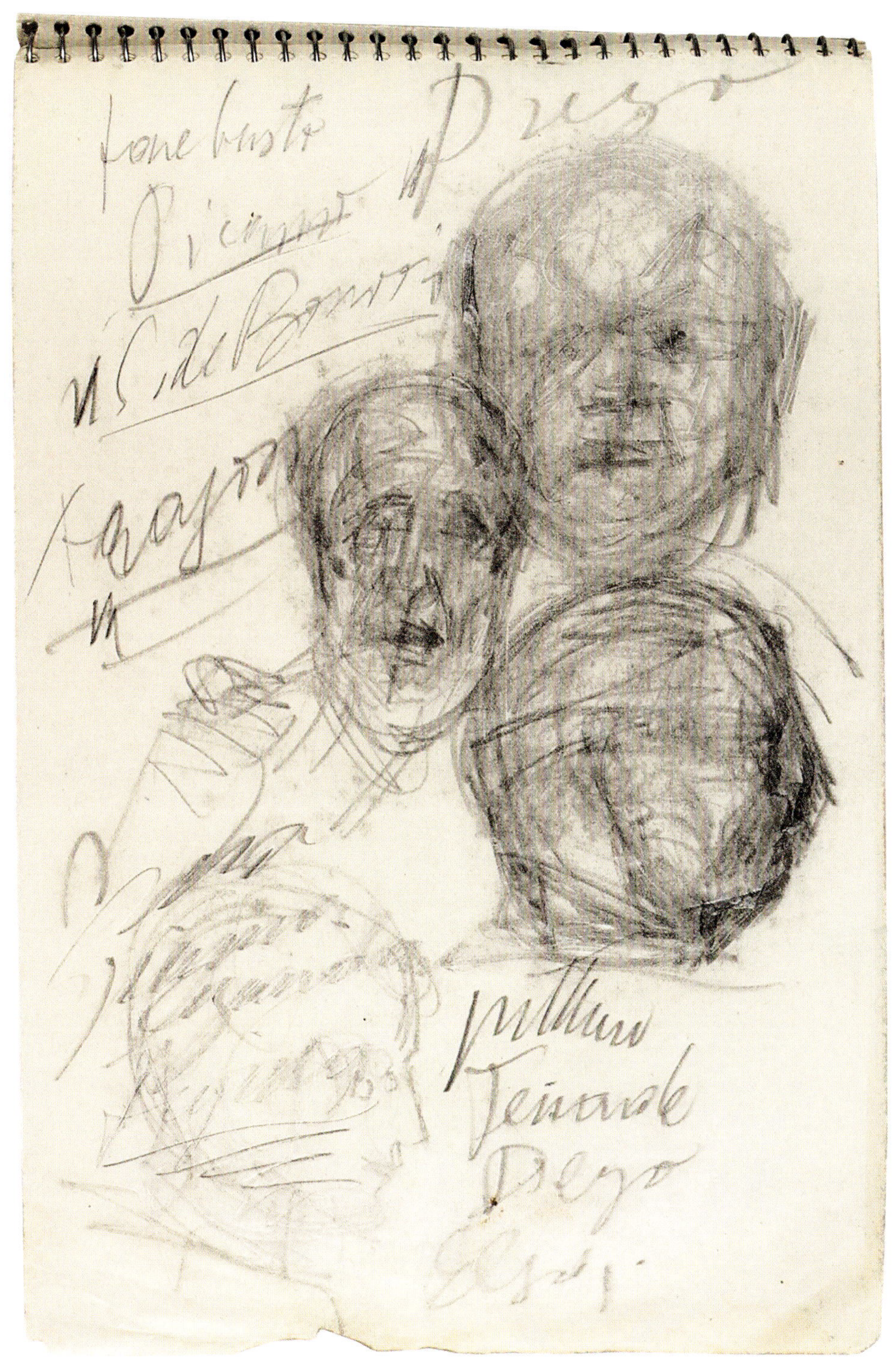

Fig. 18
Alberto Giacometti
Head Sketches
1946–1948
Graphite pencil on notebook page,
21 × 27.2 cm (8 ¼ × 10 ¾ in.)
Fondation Giacometti, Paris

58 Letter from Alberto Giacometti to Mario Negri, 23 January 1957, in *Alberto Giacometti, percorsi lombardi, op. cit.*, p. 280.

59 'You can find more reality in the posters at a cinema entrance than in a Picasso, isn't that so? The distance between a Picasso and a film poster is nothing compared to that which separates Picasso from the real,' in Isaku Yanaihara, *Avec Giacometti*, Paris, Allia, 2014, p. 16.

60 'There is much to say about this, they are possibly not as far removed from each other as one might think,' notebook, c. 1953, Fondation Giacometti Archives, Paris, inv. 2000-0141.

61 Francis Ponge, *L'Atelier contemporain*, Paris, NRF Gallimard, 1977, p. 165.

62 Ernst Scheidegger, *Traces of a Friendship: Alberto Giacometti*, Zurich, Scheidegger and Spiess, 2001.

63 David Sylvester, *About Modern Art*, New Haven, CT, Yale University Press, 2001, p. 33.

64 Ernst Scheidegger, *Traces of a Friendship: Alberto Giacometti, op. cit.*, p. 150.

65 'I saw Picasso and we talked about you, he told me that you are the best sculptor of our times and asked me to greet you when I wrote to you,' letter from Michel Sapone to Alberto Giacometti, 14 May 1959, Fondation Giacometti Archives, Paris, inv. 2003-5197.

66 Alberto Giacometti, interview by Jean-Marie Drot in the film *A Man Among Men: Alberto Giacometti*, 1962.

67 *Du: Kulturelle Monatsschrift*, no. 248, October 1961.

68 Miró, Cocteau, Kahnweiler and Jacqueline Picasso took part. Raphaël Aubert, *Malraux & Picasso, une relation manquée*, Gollion, Éditions Infolio, 2013, p. 91.

69 Alberto Giacometti, *Homage to Picasso [I]*, Musée National Picasso-Paris, MP1981-1.

70 Raphaël Aubert, *Malraux & Picasso, une relation manquée, op. cit.*, p. 91.

months, at the end of which Picasso prevailed. Following this rejection, Giacometti joined the Galerie Maeght, which held his first solo exhibition in June 1951.[55] The resentment created by this event would thus explain Giacometti's attitude when he visited Vallauris and why he criticised Picasso for 'not recognising him at all and wanting to be the only artist in the limelight.' From this moment on, the two artists stopped seeing each other and opportunities for encounters between them became increasingly rare.

In 1957, Giacometti was asked to be part of the organisation committee for the *Scultura All'aperto* exhibition at the 11th Triennale of Milan with Enzo Carli and Mario Negri. The selected sculptures included two works by Picasso.[56] Giacometti did not deal with Picasso for the arrangements but with the Galerie Louise Leiris. In his discussions with Negri, Giacometti said that he had stopped seeing Picasso years before and was completely indifferent to his work.[57] He also criticised Picasso for having stolen other people's ideas.[58] When talking to his close friends, he took an even harsher line. He compared Picasso's paintings to 'pretty posters',[59] 'possibly not as far removed' from Domergue's works,[60] 'virtuous' exercises.[61] The photographer Ernst Scheidegger claimed that one of the reasons for their dispute was Picasso's appropriation of processes used by Giacometti. Following his visits to the studio on Rue Hippolyte-Maindron, apparently the Spanish artist then also began to create painted sculptures, which is why Alberto hid his work when he knew Picasso was planning to visit.[62] Picasso was just as critical of Giacometti, describing his work to Michel Leiris as incredibly monotonous and repetitive compositions.[63] Scheidegger also remembered Giacometti's visit to Vallauris and Picasso's 'secret jealousy' of the other man, 'one of the

rare people among his former friends not to express unconditional admiration for him'.[64] The two artists felt very distant from each other throughout the 1950s, both personally and artistically.

In the early 1960s, tensions between them seemed to abate. A handful of witness accounts unearthed from various archives show that their relationship improved. In 1959, Picasso told Michel Sapone, a tailor and friend of both artists, that he considered Giacometti to be the best sculptor of the period.[65] Giacometti, in turn, when discussing the difficulty of painting or sculpting a head, compared himself to Picasso, who had 'the gift of seeing the characteristics of each head, each beast'.[66] In 1961, for the Spanish painter's 80th birthday, the review *Du: Kulturelle Monatsschrift* produced a special issue in homage to Picasso,[67] asking his friends to contribute verse, memories or images.[68] Alberto created a women's head in profile next to a tree. Below it he wrote: 'Why this design, I do not know' (fig. 146).[69] Alberto Giacometti died aged sixty-five in January 1966 in his native land. In a letter of condolence to his widow, Annette, Jacqueline Picasso recalled 'the great friendship Picasso had, has' for Alberto. Picasso, the elder of the two, outlived him, passing away in 1973. At the end of his life, Picasso told Jean-Claude Noël that, if given the chance, he would have liked to see two people again: André Malraux and Alberto Giacometti.[70]

Fig. 19

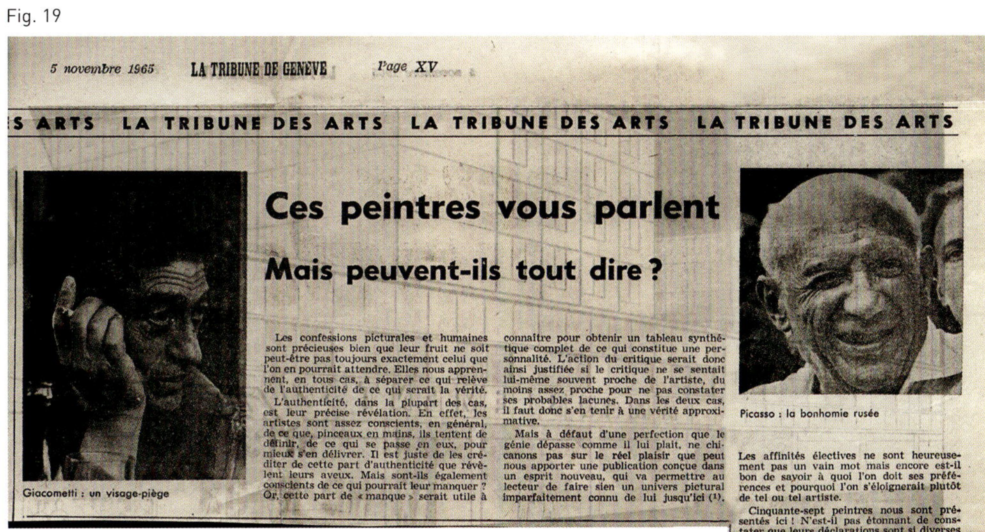

Fig. 20

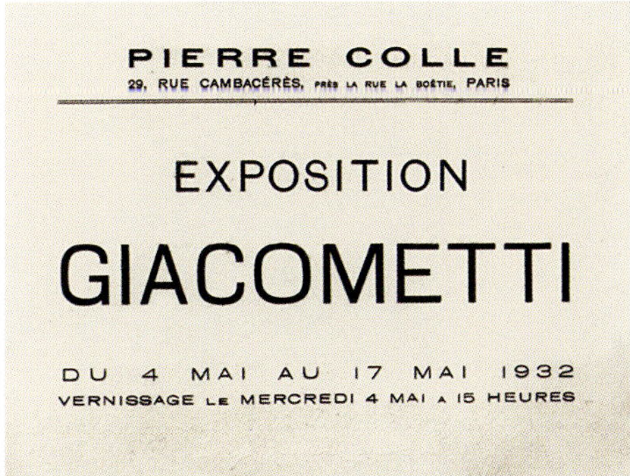

Fig. 21

Fig. 19
La Tribune de Genève
5 November 1965
Fondation Giacometti Archives,
Paris

Fig. 20
Pablo Picasso
Dedication on the 'Pablo Picasso' brochure
1941
Ink on paper, 29.5 × 19.4 cm (11 ⅝ × 7 ⅝ in.)
Fondation Giacometti, Paris

Fig. 21
Giacometti **Exhibition, Pierre Colle**
Gallery, 4–17 May 1932
Invitation card
Fondation Giacometti Archives,
Paris

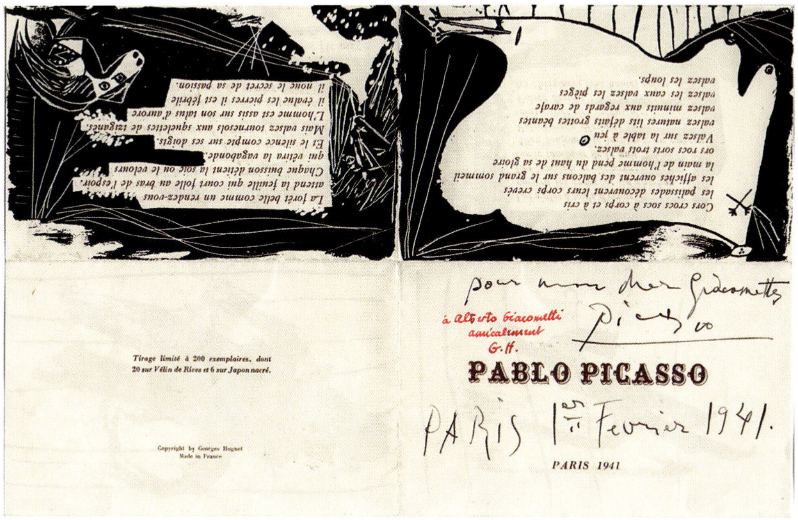

Under the Sign of the Formless: Picasso and Giacometti, 1927–1933

Agnès de La Beaumelle

❝ The history of art is the struggle between all optical experiences, invented spaces and representations. During the past twenty years the grip of mechanised reality has diminished, and hallucinatory and mythological invention has increased.

The pictorial image is a condensation, an arresting of psychological processes, a defence against fugitive time and thus against death. One could call it a distillation of dreams.**❞**

Carl Einstein, 'Aphorismes méthodiques', *Documents*, no. 1, 1929

When Carl Einstein—the astute critic of Pablo Picasso and Georges Braque's Cubist works, as well as of African sculpture—and Georges Bataille—an advocate for a critical, anti-idealist and counter-aesthetic 'gay science'—featured Picasso and Giacometti's experimental works from the late 1920s in their extraordinary review *Documents*, they shone a radically non-conformist and incredibly provocative light on the artists and brought a fresh formalist, anthropological and metapsychological perspective to the art world.[1] By including the artists in the review and placing their works alongside a variety of images submitted by ethnologists, archaeologists, art historians, poets and writers who had defected from Surrealism, such as Michel Leiris, the two contributors sought not only to break down walls between the different materials, but also to identify any subversions at play, the transgressions committed by each experiment—to provide a space for them to fraternise, establishing some kind of dialogue. In the case of Giacometti, their action would also have an enduring influence on his work, even if the sculptor joined the Surrealist group from 1931 until 1934.

Ostensibly very different from one another, Picasso and Giacometti's works during these years can be described as thoroughly progressive and radically innovative. Progressive because they rejected all formal conventions (including the conventions of Cubism, which both artists had abandoned). Their works were vested with new functions and new strengths, transformed into idols and familiar fetishes by real, human ('too human'), deeply embedded desires and fantasies. On the one hand, from 1928–1929, Giacometti, only recently discovered by André Masson and Carl Einstein and the subject of Michel Leiris' first article, produced a series of 'flat' sculptures, solid or hollowed-out frames considered as 'petrified crises' (fig. 22); these pieces were 'real fetishes we idolise (real fetishes, meaning those that resemble us and are objectivised forms of our desire), … graciously living', figures that were 'so concrete, so obvious, absolute, like the creatures we love.'[2] On the other hand, Picasso, that eminently transgressive artist, created a series of linear paintings in 1928–1929, described by Carl Einstein as the result of 'the place where psychological processes meet', fashioned from a 'tectonic hallucination'; they were 'psychically true, humanly immediate.'[3] For Michel Leiris, his large, monstrous *Heads* and deformed, 'formless' *Acrobats* from 1929–1930 were, far from being Surrealist, 'superhuman, like the most grandiose of mythological creations which are excessive but never cease to make the earth ring under their feet.' A proponent of 'base materialism', Georges Bataille cited the artist's 'decompositions of forms' in his article 'Rotten Sun'.[4]

A few preliminary remarks are needed. To unite Giacometti and Picasso under the banner of the 'formless', as raised in *Documents*, is to, once again, remove their works from the rigid framework of orthodox Surrealism, neither artist ever adhering to its idealism or the door it opens to the dreamlike realm of the marvellous, to objective chance, to the automatism promoted by André Breton.[5] Their work should not be reduced to this one critical perspective alone: while Giacometti was, until 1933, strongly marked by the spirit of the review which had adopted him, Picasso, the protean and supremely contradictory genius, was only partially influenced. Neither should the ontological autonomy of their explorations, which followed their own dynamics and procedures, be diminished. Giacometti's

1 Essentially in reference to Georges Didi-Huberman's *La Ressemblance informe ou le gai savoir visuel selon Georges Bataille*, Paris, Macula, 1995.

2 *Documents*, no. 4, 1929, p. 210.

3 *Documents*, no. 3, 1930, pp. 157–159.

4 Ibid., p. 174.

5 On the subject of Giacometti's time in the Surrealist group, refer to the monograph *Alberto Giacometti: A Biography of His Work* by Yves Bonnefoy, Paris, Flammarion, 1991; the critical article by Rosalind Krauss 'No More Play' published in *Originality of the Avant-garde and Other Modernist Myths*, Cambridge, MA, MIT Press, 1985. Regarding Picasso, refer to the catalogue *The Surrealist Picasso*, under the direction of Anne Baldassari, Fondation Beyeler/ Flammarion, 2005.

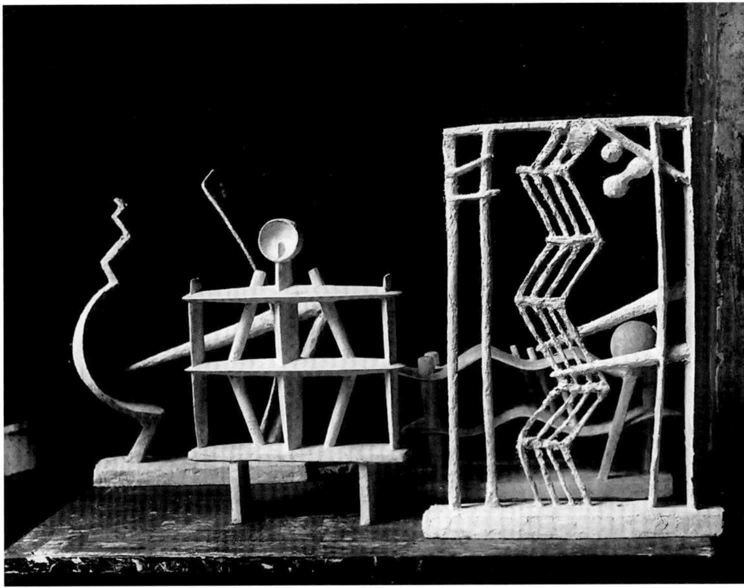

Fig. 22
Marc Vaux (1895–1971)
Group of Four Plaster Sculptures by Giacometti:
Man and Woman, Apollo, Reclining Woman Who Dreams, Three Figures Outdoors
1929
Silver print on paper,
17.2 × 22.2 cm (6 ¾ × 8 ¾ in.)
Fondation Giacometti Archives, Paris

6 Alberto Giacometti, letter to Pierre Matisse, 1947, in *Écrits*, Paris, Hermann, 1990, p. 39.

7 Refer to the exhibition catalogue for *Picasso Sculpture*, Museum of Modern Art, New York, 2015. According to Anne Umland, the revelation of Picasso's visual research was important for Giacometti, particularly for his 'transparent', grid-like constructions from 1929.

8 *Documents*, no. 4, 1929.

9 Christian Zervos, 'Sculptures des peintres d'aujourd'hui', *Cahiers d'art*, no. 7, 1928, (and notably the reproduction of the plaster model of *Sculpture [Metamorphosis]*, for the monument to Guillaume Apollinaire; 'Picasso à Dinard, été 1928', *Cahiers d'art*, no. 1, 1929 (and notably the reproduction of *Project for a Wireframe Sculpture [Figure]* and *Sculpture [Head]*; 'Les dernières oeuvres de Picasso', *Cahiers d'art*, no. 6, 1929 (paintings); 'Projets de Picasso pour un monument', *Cahiers d'art*, nos. 8–9, 1929 (drawings from notebooks from which Giacometti would make two copies in a notebook dating from 1930–1931 [Fondation Giacometti, Paris, inv. 2000-0050]); 'Exposition Picasso aux galeries Georges Petit', *Cahiers d'art*, nos. 3–5, 1932 (illustrations of which Giacometti made a dozen copies in a notebook from 1932–1933 [Fondation Giacometti, Paris, inv. 2000-0046]).

10 Christian Zervos, 'Quelques notes sur les sculptures de Giacometti', *Cahiers d'art*, nos. 8–10, 1932, photographs by Man Ray (*Despite the Hands [Caress]*, *Courrounou U-Animal [Severed Hand]*, *Tormented Woman in Her Room at Night*, *Fall of a Body onto a Diagram [Landscape/Reclining Head]*, *No More Play*, *Project for a Square*, *Disintegrating Relations [Point to the Eye]*).

11 *SASDLR*, no. 3, December 1931; no. 5, 15 May 1933; no. 6, May 1933.

12 *Minotaure*, no. 1, 1933, dedicated to Picasso: André Breton, 'Picasso dans son élément' (photographs by Brassaï: *The Sculpture Studio, Crucifixions, An Anatomy*); *Minotaure*, nos. 3–4, 1933: Giacometti, 'Je ne puis parler qu'indirectement de mes sculptures' (photographs by Brassaï: *The Palace at 4 a.m., Woman with Her Throat Cut, The Studio*).

intention was (as it remained obsessively to the end) to try to capture the reality of his vision, the *truth* of the work, an attempt which he had to continually start anew, condemned as it was to doubt and failure; since, as he observed early on, 'the form dissolved, it was little more than granules moving over a deep black void … without end, nothing to fix one's gaze upon, everything escapes.'[6] His goal could not contrast more with the approach taken by Picasso, for whom the perpetual challenge was, on the contrary, to 'invent' reality, multiply the possibilities, push the boundaries further and further: to forever transgress.

While we can make comparisons between the two artists during the period 1929–1933— and there are plenty of points of convergence— this does not establish a direct line of 'influence' of the older artist over the younger, or vice versa.[7] Both men were undoubtedly perfectly conscious of their respective artistic developments, at least those recognised and photographed in art reviews: *Documents*, of course, which gave Picasso a leading role and featured the first article on Giacometti, by Michel Leiris;[8] *Cahiers d'art*, in which Christian Zervos dedicated a large section to Picasso in 1928,[9] and, in 1932, to Giacometti with a magnificent illustration;[10] then *Le Surréalisme au service de la révolution*, to which Giacometti donated his *Moving, Mute Objects*, in 1931,[11] and lastly *Minotaure*, which featured photographs of their respective studios for the first time in 1933.[12] We know they had mutual friends— notably Einstein,[13] Leiris and Masson—so is it possible that the older painter, praised by all, and the young sculptor, still isolated in 1929, did more than just cross paths when they both exhibited at the Jeanne Bucher gallery, and later at the Pierre Loeb and Pierre Colle galleries? Giacometti, friends with Brancusi and Lipchitz, did not make Picasso's acquaintance until

1931. Yet he was familiar with his work, writing about his interest in Picasso's Cubist art as early as 1924.[14] In a letter to Pierre Matisse about *Spoon Woman* (1927), influenced just as much by African art as by Brancusi, he wrote 'the art produced by the Cubists and Picasso contained everything necessary to the birth of this sculpture.'[15]

Had he attended the major Picasso exhibition, held in June and July 1932 at the George Petit gallery (where his recent sculptures were exhibited, including both versions of *Woman in the Garden*)? Did he visit the Kunsthaus in Zurich that autumn to see its more prominent display? He produced many copies of 'convulsive' paintings in a notebook in May 1932[16] which were compiled (fig. 99) and soon reproduced in issues 3–5 of *Cahiers d'art*. As for Picasso, a voracious predator always on the hunt for new solutions, might he have been alerted by Leiris or Einstein and seen the few works exhibited by Giacometti in June 1929 at the Jeanne Bucher gallery (the first to achieve public recognition), or perhaps those shown in December by Tériade[17] at the Georges Bernheim gallery and pointed out by Zervos, a champion of Picasso, in *Cahiers d'art*?[18] It is impossible to say. Whatever the case, he was sufficiently intrigued by his friends' interest in the young Swiss sculptor—and by the aura surrounding *Suspended Ball*, which was shown in spring 1930 at the Pierre Loeb gallery and immediately aroused the enthusiasm of Breton and Salvador Dalí—to hasten to the Pierre Colle gallery in May 1932 to visit Giacometti's first solo exhibition. In fact, he was the very first visitor—and an admiring one at that, as Giacometti proudly related in a letter to his father.[19] Christian Zervos dedicated a more than favourable article to him in *Cahiers d'art*,[20] noting the 'extreme risk' taken by the young sculptor. Giacometti's first public accolade

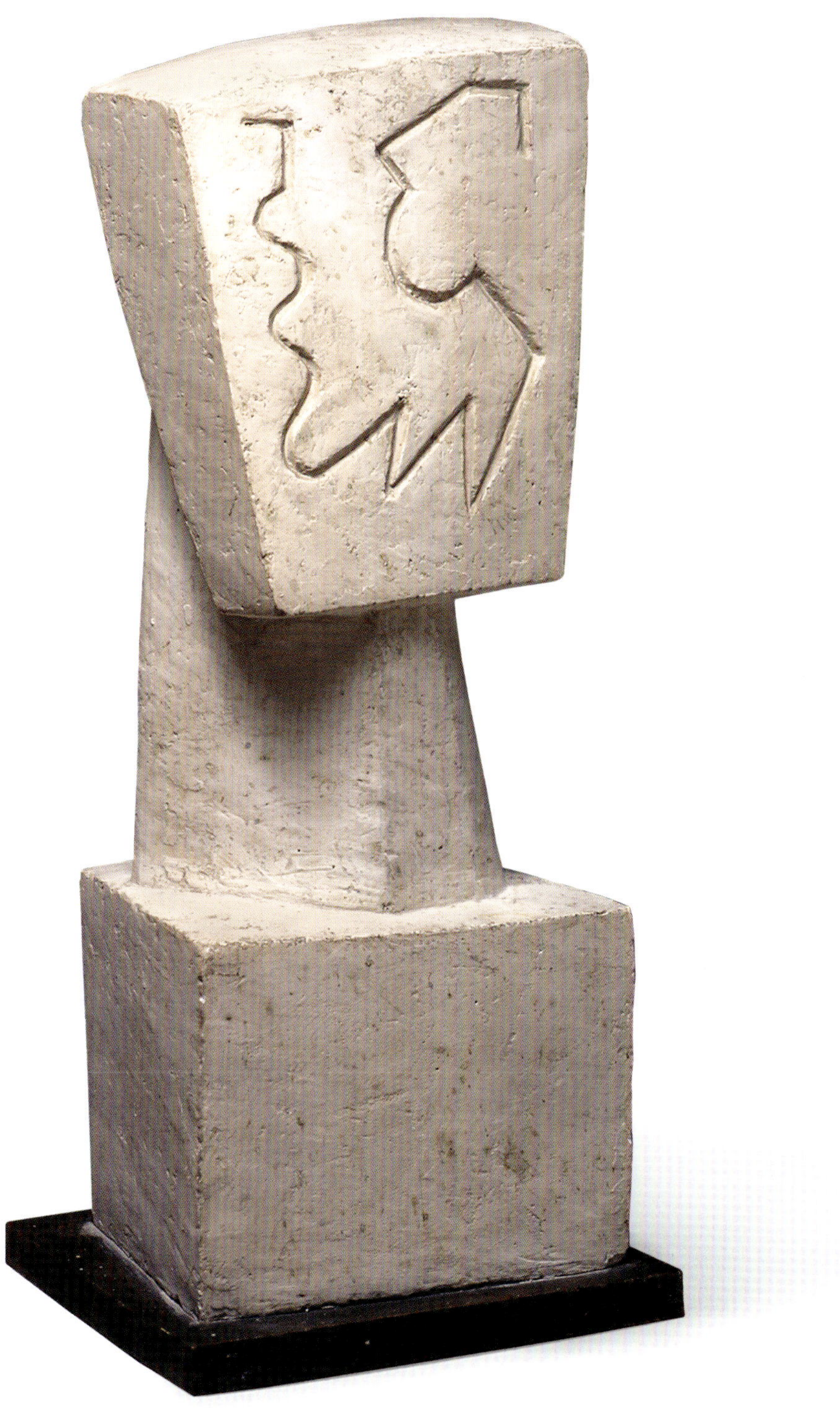

Fig. 23
Alberto Giacometti
Untitled [Head]
1926
Plaster, 43.9 × 18 × 15.2 cm (17 ¼ × 7 × 6 in.)
Private collection, former Jeanne Bucher
collection, Paris

13 From May 1929, Carl Einstein visited Giacometti's studio several times and became a regular. He took along Pierre Colle (with whom Giacometti, on his initiative, signed a contract in June) and Michel Leiris, whom he encouraged to write an article for *Documents*; in a letter from 20 November 1929 to his parents, Giacometti wrote 'Einstein, one of the people who interests me the most.' Carl Einstein had *Lame Figure Walking*, c. 1931–1932, in his possession and introduced a chapter on Giacometti in the 1931 re-edition of his *Die Kunst des 20. Jahrhunderts*, 1926.

14 In a letter to his parents from 8 April 1924 (Alberto Giacometti-Stiftung Archives, Zurich), Giacometti wrote that he had seen a Picasso exhibition, most probably *Picasso: 100 Drawings*, Paul Rosenberg Gallery, April 1924.

15 22 February 1951, Pierre Matisse Archives, Pierpont Morgan Library, New York. While he would not later deny his admiration for Picasso (*Du: Kulturelle Monatsschrift*, no. 249, October 1961), he had a closer affinity to Laurens and Braque.

16 1932–1933 notebook (Fondation Giacometti, Paris, inv. 2000-0046) in which he drew eleven copies of recent Picasso paintings.

17 Tériade owned *Point to the Eye*, 1932.

18 Christian Zervos, 'Notes sur la sculpture contemporaine, *Cahiers d'art*, no. 10, 1929.

19 Letter to Giovanni Giacometti, 6 May 1932 (Kunsthaus Zurich Archives – Alberto Giacometti-Stiftung): 'The first person to arrive was Picasso who came at half past midday! He looked and said, "*très joli*," like a child, . . . but he never commits himself, in fact he's known for it.'

20 See note 10.

21 Georges Didi-Huberman, *La Ressemblance informe ou le gai savoir selon Georges Bataille, op. cit.*, p. 9: 'Georges Bataille was no doubt the master of disrupting resemblance. The master of disrupting it and thus making it disruptive.'

22 See Michel Leiris, 'Le caput mortuum ou la femme de l'alchimiste', *Documents*, no. 8, 1930, p. 24.

came in 1933 when the two men's respective works and their sculpture studios—secret artists' laboratories—were placed practically side by side across two issues of *Minotaure*, producing a fascinating and fruitful dialogue.

'A DISRUPTIVE RESEMBLANCE'[21]: DISTORTIONS, CRUELTIES

A 'tectonic hallucination', asserted Carl Einstein, driven by desire: processes of 'alteration'—a key theme in Georges Bataille's work—are clearly manifested in the artistic explorations that Picasso and Giacometti pursued in the late 1920s and early 30s, attacking form and content, radically subverting the humanist mimesis of Western tradition from within, 'tearing up' any figural resemblance, using procedures and occupying ground common to both artists.

Flat/Hollow

Presented in *Documents*, Giacometti's 'flat' steles and plates from 1928–1929—solid surfaces or conversely, hollowed-out frames—were an abrupt departure from his earlier attempts, doomed to failure, of 'resemblance' and volumetric research (fig. 23); like Picasso's 'flat', geometrising, linear paintings, many were reproduced in the art review, a response to the criticism of anthropomorphism and the human figure led by Bataille. These residual, truncated, quasi-monstrous configurations—bodies without arms or legs, or reduced to their limbs alone—were similarly disfigured: crushed, deformed, eviscerated. 'One could speak of the cruelty of his constructive will', posited Carl Einstein about Picasso. Whether cursory masses—vaguely human effigies endowed with a few scratched or hollowed marks—or simple geometric patterns, fleshless, spindly skeletons, or linear ectoplasms, their limbs

sprawling in every direction like jellyfish or crushed spiders, these barely recognisable flattened human figures (are they heads or bodies?) are indeterminate, 'impossible'. Yet they are alive, endowed with the life of some ancient organism. Frontal figures that confront you with their endlessly blank gaze or their sexual orifices, they have the power of the masks in African and Oceanic cultures that inspired Picasso and Giacometti. The disturbing, 'fascinating' attraction they wield is not so different from the masked women photographed by Seabrook and published in *Documents*.[22] These are images of 'crises' ('petrified' crises said Leiris of Giacometti),[23] images born of an interior conflict, instinctive impulses engendered by an obsessive fear of death and a fascination with sexuality—all driving themes. A synthesis of the linear and the flat, Giacometti's sculpture *Man and Woman* (1928–1929),[24] pared down to an arrow pointing towards a concave surface, is a consummate expression of the modifying tension of desire, reduced to an impulse of cruelty; an identical tension, empty too—one example among many—is Picasso's *Head of a Woman* (1928),[25] in a dual which sets it against its 'spectator'. Other voids still, as terrifying as the open gaping mouth photographed up close by Boiffard,[26] the multiple wide mouths in figures by Picasso and Giacometti are empty, formless spaces with cannibalistic teeth, disturbing orifices emitting heart-rending screams (fig. 24).

Decompositions/Excrescences/Movements

Other distortions—superbly analysed by Georges Didi-Huberman—are crucial here. Dismemberment, dislocation, liquefaction, decomposition and, at the other extreme, excrescence and other deformities, all these 'formless' processes are intimately linked to erotic impulses—the impulses of life

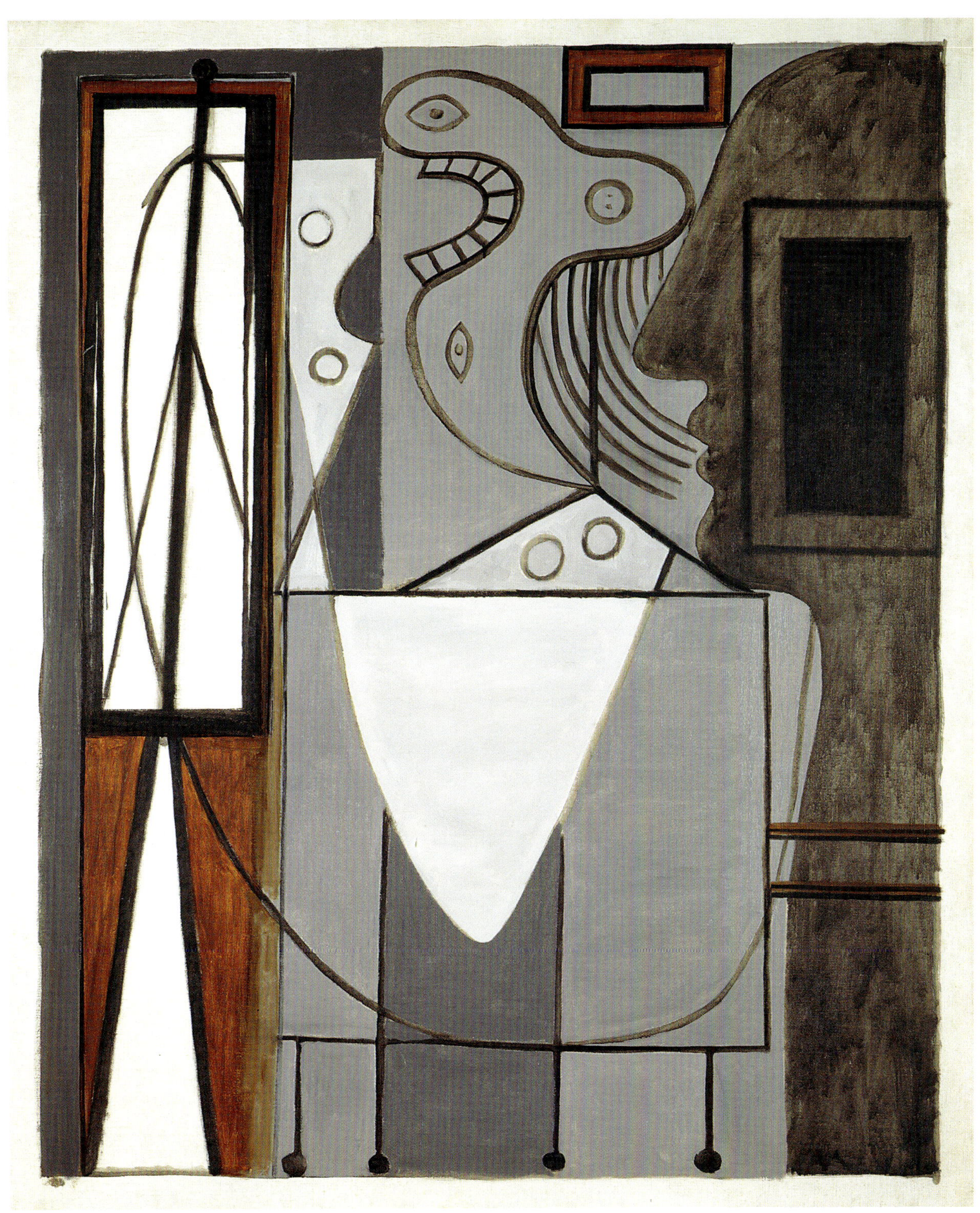

Fig. 24
Pablo Picasso
The Studio
1928–1929
Oil on canvas, 162 × 130 cm (5 ft. 3 ¾ × 4 ft. ¾ in.)
Musée National Picasso-Paris
Dation Pablo Picasso, 1979. MP111
On long-term loan to the Musée National d'Art Moderne, Centre Pompidou, Paris

23 See note 6, p. 23.

24 Centre Georges Pompidou, Paris, Musée National d'Art Moderne/Centre de Création Industrielle, inv. AM 1984-355.

25 Zervos 125.

26 *Documents*, no. 5, 1930, p. 298.

27 Carl Einstein, 'L'enfance néolithique', *Documents*, no. 8, 1930, p. 479.

28 Georges Bataille quoted from his article 'Rotten Sun'.

29 Notebooks from 1927–1928, Musée National Picasso-Paris, MP1874 and MP1990-107.

30 Musée National Picasso-Paris, MP291.

31 Zervos 98.

and death combined—and to the profound and supreme strata of sexual desire in the work of both Picasso and Giacometti. The Minotaur, that Dionysian part-man, part-beast transformed into an emblem by Picasso in 1927, permanently replaces Narcissus as the 'ecstatic' paradigm of creation. 'Evidently art-making comprises many elements of cruelty and assassination,'[27] aphorised Carl Einstein. Bataille had no scruple in using one of Picasso's drawings, *Crucifixion*, to describe liquefaction, the 'sacrilegious' decay at work in any figuration, even the most taboo.[28]

The disturbing *Bathers*, a dominant theme in Picasso's 1927–1928 notebooks,[29] where they are the subject of prolific sketches, offer a hallucinated series of organic decompositions: these are kinds of anthropomorphic creatures of indeterminate gender whose exaggerated, inflated, quasi-headless forms twist into bulbous protuberances, dislocate into tumescent limbs, into sharp, threatening elongations in all directions. Just as monstrous are the large *Figures by the Sea* painted on 12 January 1931 (fig. 102), which are poorly jointed conical excrescences; these carnivorous crabs disintegrate under the fatal force of the kiss that unites them. Monstrous too and eminently transgressive is *Head of a Woman* (1931),[30] an assembly of rough organic fragments, which take the process of dissolution to an almost scatological level. We can see the same process of distortion in many figures painted between 1930 and 1933, like the sombre and ugly *Seated Nude* (1933).[31] The 'base seduction', as theorised by Bataille, is very much at work

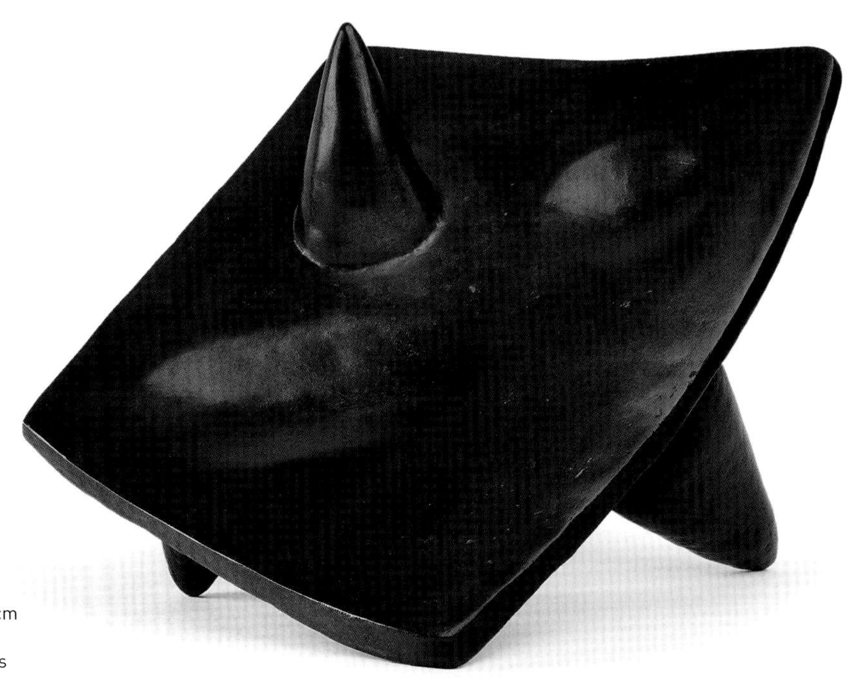

Fig. 25
Alberto Giacometti
Disagreeable Object to Be Thrown Away
1931
Bronze, 22.8 × 34.3 × 25.9 cm
(9 × 13 ½ × 10 ⅛ in.)
Fondation Giacometti, Paris

in places here. As it is likewise in most of the objects created by Giacometti in 1930 and 1931.

Like the isolated *Big Toe* photographed by Boiffard for Bataille's article[32]—fascinatingly and phallically disproportionate, and which became a 'thing in itself'—*Disagreeable Object* (1931 [fig. 108]) resembles a mutilated and swollen sexual organ; it is topped off with small menacing spikes that went on to become, in *Lame Figure Walking* (c. 1931–1932)[33] and *Disagreeable Object to Be Thrown Away* (1931 [fig. 25]), conical excrescences, members sharpened like knives. At this point, was Giacometti already familiar with Picasso's organic distortions, such as in the *Bathers* he sketched in his notebooks during the summer of 1928 in Dinard? Giacometti did indeed own a copy of the first issue of *Cahiers d'art* (January 1929), which included a dozen of the sketches. Although the analogy here is striking—and even more so when considering the blade-sharp limbs in Picasso's *Figures by the Sea* (fig. 102)—Giacometti took figurative decomposition and transgression further than Picasso; the visceral, unrestrained fragments of *Woman, Head, Tree* (1930) are disturbing, so hard are they to make out. Imprisoned within the narrow confines of *Cage* (1930–1931),[34] the mutilated members seem to devour each other and contort into hostile, withering sexual organs. The distorting cruelty of desire, a theme already seen in *Man and Woman* (1928–1929)— a duo tensed in sexual fondling—and in *Three Figures Outdoors* (1928)—a trio transpierced by one identical arrow—would be pushed to the extreme in *Hour of the Traces* (1930),[35] a veritable microcosm of decomposition. The same principle applies to *Point to the Eye* (1931) (fig. 106), where the tip of a menacing arrow/member skims a skull-like object atop a skeleton, and most notably in *Woman with Her Throat Cut* (1933) (fig. 103), a half-skeletal,

half-corporeal creature, of which Picasso produced an earlier, very similar (vertical) version in a notebook.[36] With its dislocated limbs on the ground, some decomposed, others enlarged, but all sharp and withered like those in *Figures by the Sea*, this hybrid figure captured in its final throes might be considered the paradigm of the formless. 'Love smells like death,' wrote Bataille.[37]

An all-pervasive, sadistic, devastating violence is acted out—direct and sexual with Picasso,[38] playful and mechanised for Giacometti. These works are universally exposed to 'disintegrating relations' (as Giacometti described them), fatal, attacking the integrity of the figures, posing a very immediate threat. Nonetheless, these sprawling or dismembered organisms still appear to be in motion: the limping gait in Giacometti's *Lame Figure Walking* (c. 1931–1932) and his *Disagreeable Object to Be Thrown Away*; the wild, uncontrolled gestures in Picasso's *Bathers*; oozing viscera in Giacometti's *Project for a Passageway* (c. 1930–1931)[39]; a body's final spasms in *Woman with Her Throat Cut* and *Figures by the Sea*; the crawling, swarming proliferation of liquefied limbs in several of Picasso's *Studies for a Woman Lying*,[40] and so forth.

**Ambivalence and Ambiguity:
Between Life and Death**

Giacometti and Picasso's figures are beset by the same deeply subversive, sexual ambiguity, to the point even of strangeness. Distributed randomly about the body, the eye is sex/anus/mouth/vagina all at once: oblong slit or circular hole (and invariably a rip); phallic excrescence or conical tip of the breast (always threatening). If widespread at this date in the ambit of Surrealism (in Bataille's circle) and particularly prevalent in the late 1920s–early 1930s (Bataille's own *The Solar Anus* and *Story of the*

32 Georges Bataille, 'Le gros orteil', *Documents*, no. 6, 1929.

33 Ny Carlsberg Glyptotek, Copenhagen, inv. MIN3166.

34 Moderna Museet, Stockholm, NMSK1843.

35 Tate Gallery, London, inv. T.1981.

36 Musée National Picasso-Paris, MP1874.

37 Georges Bataille, 'Le langage des fleurs', *Documents*, no. 3, 1929, p. 163.

38 For instance, the very explicit scene from *Murder*, 7 July 1934, Boisgeloup (Musée National Picasso-Paris, MP1135).

39 Alberto Giacometti-Stiftung, Zurich, inv. GS 20.

40 13 August 1931, in *Picasso Sculpture, op. cit.*, p. 176.

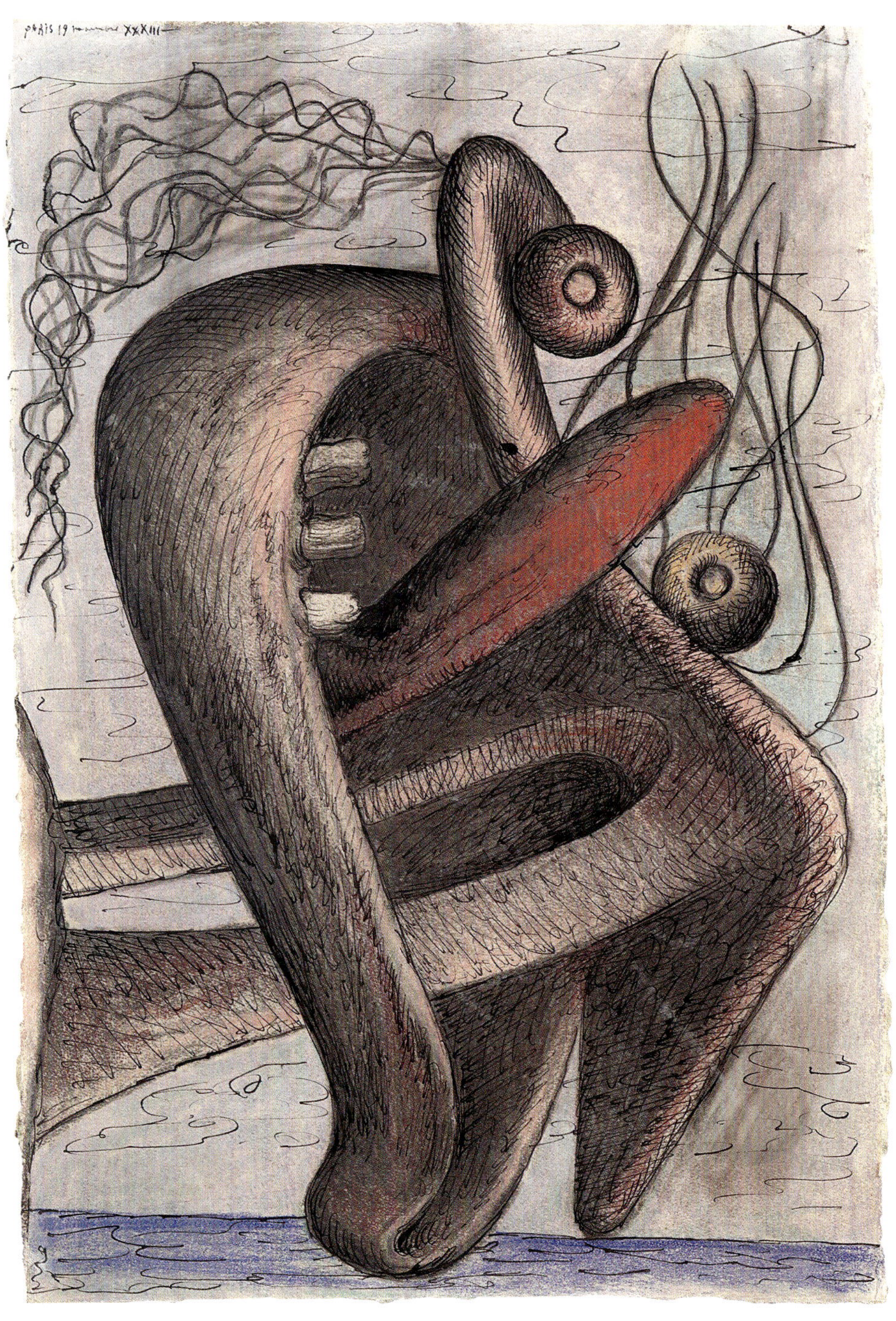

—
Fig. 26
Pablo Picasso
Figure by the Sea
Paris, 19 November 1933
Dry pastels, pen, India ink and charcoal on drawing paper,
51.1 × 35.2 cm (20 ⅛ × 13 ⅞ in.)
Musée National Picasso-Paris
Dation Pablo Picasso, 1979. MP1116
—

Eye [1928], Luis Buñuel's film *Le Chien andalou* [1929], and soon with Dalí and Masson), the sequence of alterations in semantic and formal polysemy is here omnipresent: examples, among many others, include *Point to the Eye* (1932 [fig. 106]) by Giacometti, where a sex/eye extends towards a head/vagina, and Picasso's extremely violent drawing *Figure on the Seashore* (November 19, 1933 [fig. 26]), in which a tongue/sex emerges from between two eyes/breasts. The analogy between the two constructs is striking. Elsewhere, a belly turns into a gaping mouth—solid alternating with void—as in works by Giacometti and Picasso that appear to echo one another: *Caress* (1932)[41] and *Head* (1929),[42] and also *Composition* (1933).[43]

Eye/sex, male/female: the ambivalence, the uncertainty is constant. Among the large *Heads* (1929) by Picasso, *Head, Study for a Monument*[44] displays in this respect a range of similarities with Giacometti's *Suspended Ball* (1930 [fig. 100]), whose schema Picasso studies in a drawing in the Paris 1932–1934 sketchbook (fig. 98). The assembly of those almost abstract, bisexual organic metaphors that are the ball and the horn, magnetically repelling or attracting, wounding each other or coiled around one another—it is hard to be sure—is identical. There is also the same scopic drive, erotic impulse, murderous when in action. There is the same unease with a figure/object suspended in the void, with a movement that is suggested but proscribed. These two 'desiring machines' are certainly the products of unconscious phantasms or objectified hallucinations around the inseparable, fused couple of Eros-Thanatos: symptomatic images of limit or conflictual states, which arise, as Carl Einstein wrote, from 'a contraction, a halt in the psychological process, a defence against the passage of time, and thus against death. It might be called a concentrate of dreams.' The emotional shock

sparked by these two enigmatic and disturbing works—which foist themselves on us and which, in their eminently subversive divergence, resemble us—is very much that of the archaic idol or fetish. Once again, this malaise, this chaos emerges from the formless.

Another uncertainty that is equally harrowing: most of Giacometti's and Picasso's figures are caught in that ambiguous moment between life and death, the ultimate expression of Bataillean ecstasy. In this respect, we can draw comparisons between two magnificent sculptures: Picasso's *Woman in the Garden* (1929–1930 [fig. 27]) with its distinct spirit of triumph and eroticism, and Giacometti's *Woman with Her Throat Cut* (1933 [fig. 103]), more cruel and melancholic. These figures, both assemblages—the former, vertical, the latter, horizontal—of not dissimilar fragmented and hybrid forms (plant and animal as much as human), both present a state of paroxysm, a borderline state between Eros and Thanatos, the forces of life and death. In this respect, they are examples of exceptional synthesis, visually speaking, between the hollow and solid, the linear and three-dimensional, the closed and open. Neither is the palpable morbidness in *Woman with Her Throat Cut* (1933) very different from the skeletal but smashed to smithereens *disjecta membra* in Picasso's *Crucifixion Studies* (1932) inspired by Grünewald.[45]

And the perverse and erotic power it exercises, of attraction/repulsion, is analogous to that possessed by the very somber and provocative *Woman Seated in a Red Armchair* (1932) by Picasso (fig. 91), which offers itself like an idol for fetishists. Giacometti produced an exact copy in a notebook.[46] This was just one of the copies of women he painted that same year, 1932 (fig. 99), a year in which the artist was clearly fascinated by dismembered, metamorphic and highly sexualized creatures.

41 Centre Pompidou, Paris, Musée National d'Art Moderne/Centre de Création Industrielle, inv. AM 1984-310.

42 Zervos 242, MP 1990-108 (6r), (figs. 88 and 89).

43 Zervos 148, MP 1990-108 (6r), see figs. 88 and 89.

44 Zervos 273.

45 Musée National Picasso-Paris, MP1074 and MP1075.

46 Notebook, Fondation Giacometti, Paris, inv. 2000-00046. It is not known whether these copies were executed by Giacometti looking at the works on display at the Kunsthaus in Zurich—whether he visited is not known for certain—or from illustrations published in *Cahiers d'art*, nos. 8–9, 1932.

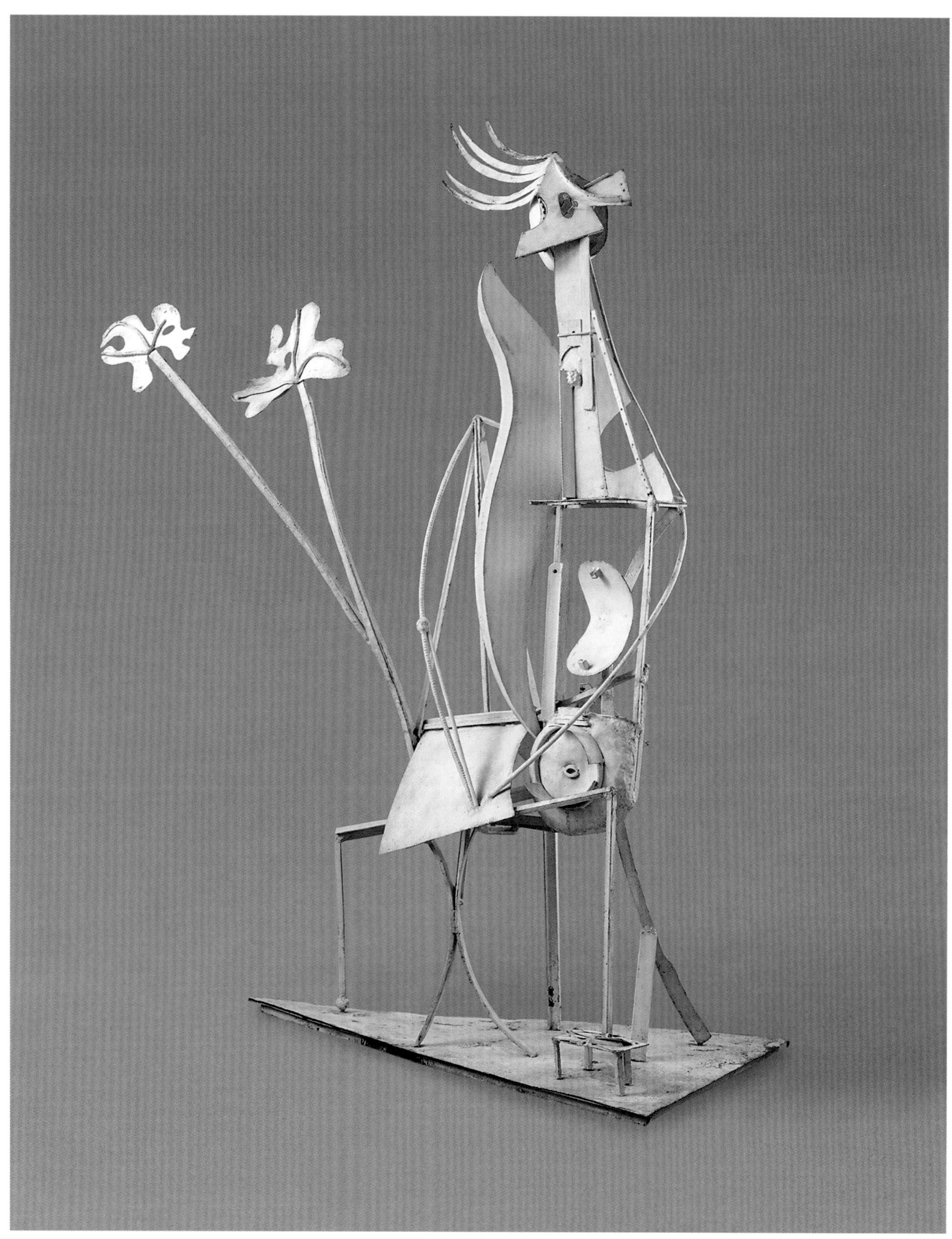

Fig. 27
Pablo Picasso
Woman in the Garden
Paris, 1929–1930
Welded and white-painted iron, 206 × 117 × 85 cm
(6 ft. 9 ⅛ in. × 3 ft. 10 in. × 2 ft. 9 ½ in.)
Musée National Picasso-Paris
Dation Pablo Picasso, 1979. MP267

Horizontal /Vertical /Unstable

It is important to point out certain differences between the artists: Picasso was unfamiliar with 'mobile and mute objects', those 'symbolic objects' made by Giacometti from 1931, in which Eros was explored in the subconscious realm of family relations. Picasso never attempted to flip sculpture on its side as Giacometti did: the fact of laying sculpture on the ground radically subverted its edifying, idealising function and provided an ultimate response to the 'base', a category of the formless appreciated by Bataille.[47] His entire 'horizontal' series from the period 1930–1933, imbued with a secret melancholy, shattered the monumental, living verticality of statuary, a verticality which Picasso had been reflecting deeply on since 1927, when contemplating the commission of *Figure*, a monument to Apollinaire (fig. 77), and large statues planned for the Croisette in Cannes.

Giacometti did not abandon verticality but pursued it in parallel in his objects: after *Spoon Woman* (1927), there was the large *Figure* (1931–1932), for the Noailles family; then *Three Figures in Maloja, Table* (c. 1930), *Walking Woman* (1932), and *The Invisible Object* and *Cube* (1933–1934). He also explored its monumental application *all'aperto*: the visual solutions that he planned (*Project for a Square* [1931] and other sketches in his notebooks)[48] show striking similarities with *Plans for a Monument* drawn by Picasso in July 1928, several pages of which were printed in issue 7–8 of *Cahiers d'art* (1929); Giacometti produced two copies in a notebook.[49] We find the same principle of assemblage of open-work monoliths, vaguely organic, composed of balls and cones and erected on the ground like funerary steles. Further similarities are the 'Surrealist' montages of objects and limbs made by Picasso in his famous *Anatomies* (1 March 1933 [fig. 93]),[50] which are not unlike those created

47 According to Rosalind Krauss, 'No More Play', *op. cit.*

48 Fondation Giacometti, Paris, inv. 2000-0042 and 2003-1075.

49 Fondation Giacometti, Paris, inv. 2000-0050.

50 Reproduced soon after in *Minotaure*, nos. 3–4, 1933.

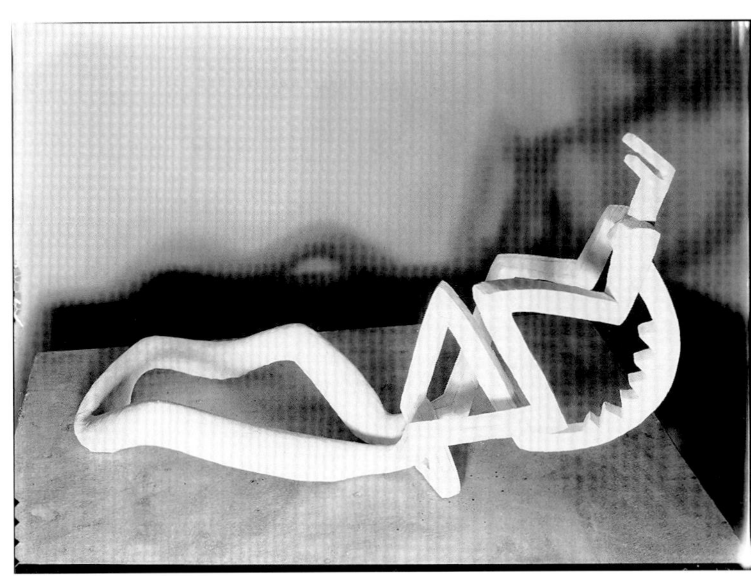

Fig. 28
Man Ray, [Emmanuel Radnitzky, known as] (1890–1976)
Tormented Woman in Her Room at Night
1931–1932
Photograph of a missing plaster sculpture, 18 × 24 cm (7 ¼ × 9 ½ in.)
Musée National d'Art Moderne/ Centre de Création Industrielle, Centre Pompidou, Paris
Inv. AM 1994-393-8519

51 Musée National Picasso-Paris, MP1875.

52 In *Die Kunst des 20. Jahrhunderts* (1926), 3rd ed. revised and corrected, 1931. Einstein introduced Giacometti's work in these terms: 'It is possibly Giacometti, that Italian Swiss, who has disconnected most significantly from all the inhibitions caused by the mass of representations handed down as a legacy.... He introduced movement into his works, so successfully that he now works on sculptures with instable formal elements.'

53 Centre Georges Pompidou, Paris, Musée National d'Art Moderne/Centre de Création Industrielle, inv. AM 1975-92.

54 See Man Ray's photo 1931–1932.

55 Zervos 275.

56 Musée National Picasso-Paris, MP1990-108 (2r).

that same year by Giacometti in *Table* (1933 [fig. 12]). The idea of an anthropomorphic piece of furniture was nothing new, as evidenced by an almost exact copy produced by Picasso in 1930.[51]

A hybrid state, neither vertical nor horizontal and just as infinitely frustrating, the unstable—a state clearly identified by Carl Einstein in Giacometti's works[52]—piqued both artists' interest. Their balance endangered, mutant organisms transforming into furniture, shapeless mollusc-like or skeleton-like figures appear on the verge of collapse: examples include seated or reclining figures in *Studies of Sculpture* (1929–1930) by Picasso, or the liquefied organism in *The Tormented Woman in Her Room at Night* (1931–1932 [fig. 28]) or in *Project for a Woman with Her Throat Cut* (c. 1932) by Giacometti.[53] Their instability in the space is only matched by their ontological instability: disturbing, as *Disagreeable Object*, which balances on the ground, threatening, like *Woman in the Form of a Spider* (1929–1930),[54] hung by Giacometti from a hook on the wall of his studio. Just as precarious are certain figures painted by Picasso, including *Figure* (13 May 1929),[55] pivoted on a ball, or *Woman Throwing a Stone* (8 March 1931 [fig. 101]), which seems to balance on top of a mound. The unstable, at the core of Giacometti's *Disagreeable Objects*, was explored by the sculptor Picasso openly in his *Project for a Head* (1928),[56] where the tripod figure is mounted on a kind of curvilinear base forming a seesaw.

'PETRIFIED CRISES': PICASSO'S *FIGURE, PROJECT FOR A MONUMENT TO GUILLAUME APOLLINAIRE* AND GIACOMETTI'S *CUBE*

Alternatives/Oscillations

The multiple distortions to which Picasso and Giacometti violently subjected the human figure reveal a state that might be described, to quote Leiris, as 'crisis'. A crisis for Giacometti following

his inability, in 1927, to produce a head based on a model or even memory: his final creations in 1927, *Head of Father II* (fig. 45) and *Head of Father III*, were 'residues', statements of failure. Giacometti would not return to 'sculpture' or painting until after the death of Giovanni Giacometti in June 1933, after the enigmatic *Cube* (1933–1934) (fig. 75) to be precise.

Picasso also experienced a state of crisis in 1927 when, creating illustrations for Balzac's *The Unknown Masterpiece* commissioned by Vollard, he had to deal with the fatal question of the painter's impasse when faced with his model. This was the same year that he was involved in a violent, personal struggle with his wife, Olga Khokhlova, the mounting conjugal tensions further exacerbated by his encounter with Marie-Thérèse Walter, the new passion of his life, in January 1927. And it was not until 1927 that he started work on the already long overdue commission (dating back to late 1920) from the Comité Apollinaire for a monument on Apollinaire's tomb. The two successive projects he presented, extremely late, contradicted one another and would never get beyond the model stage or be produced *in situ* at Père-Lachaise. It was almost as if being forced to reimagine the death of his friend and closest ally during his great Cubist years made it 'impossible' to respond to this type of commission, which could only result in a radical 'disfigurement' and would adopt formulations that were polar opposites.

The first disfigurement, *Metamorphosis I* and *II* (fig. 29)—made from plaster in 1928 and later in bronze, based on the drawings from notebook 015, and first entitled *Sculpture*— were metamorphic figures with organic volumes that were monstrous to the point of grotesque: large foot, large big toe, deformed, swollen limbs smashed to the ground, endowed with abbreviated sexual signs; deliberately

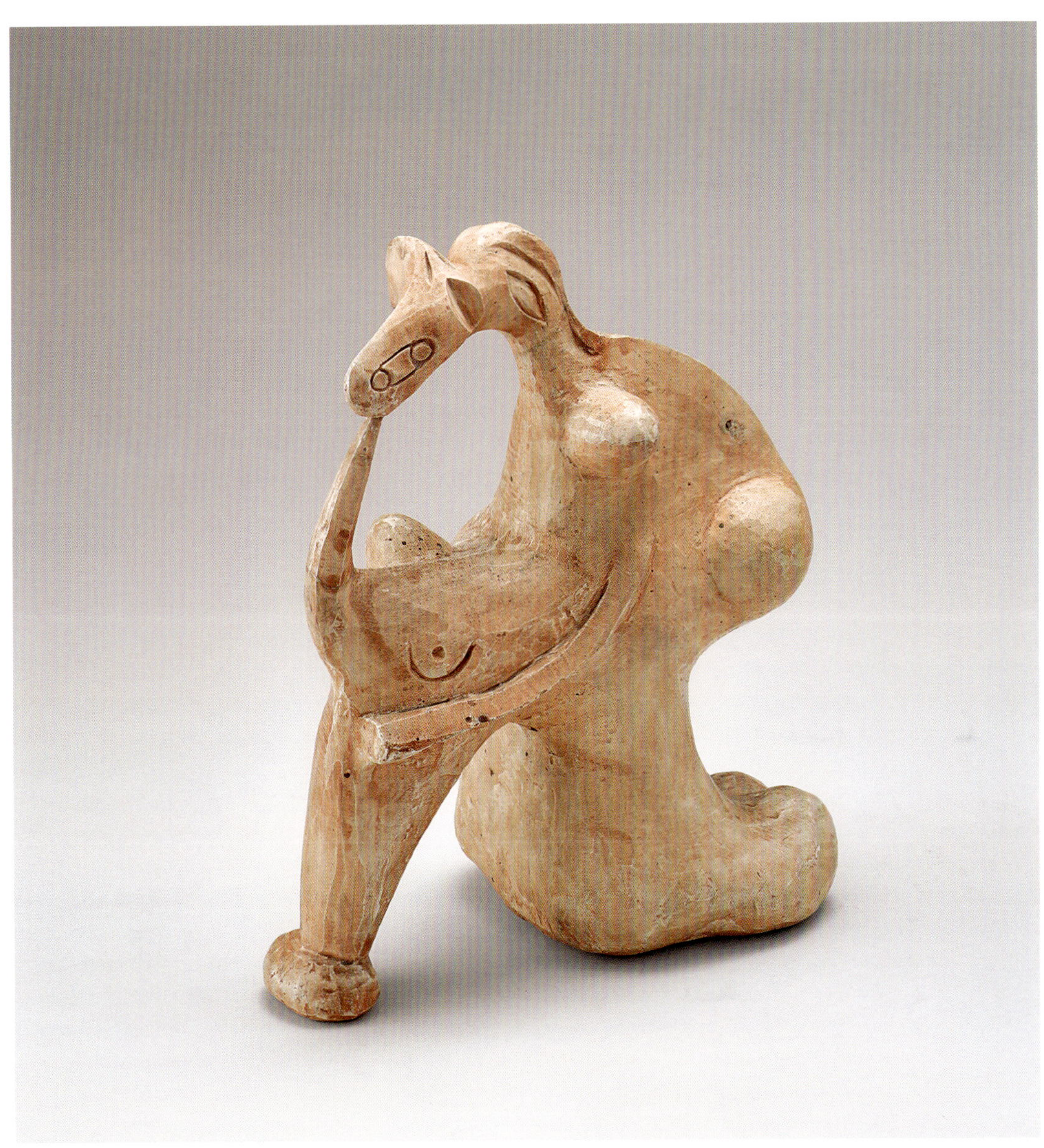

Fig. 29
Pablo Picasso
Metamorphosis II
Paris, 1928
Original plaster sculpture,
24 × 18 × 11 cm (9 ½ × 7 × 4 ⅜ in.)
Musée National Picasso-Paris
Dation Pablo Picasso, 1979. MP262

57 See Paul Léautaud, *Journal littéraire*, 14 December 1927.

58 Christian Zervos, *Cahiers d'art*, no. 7, 1928. This 'sculpture' (*Metamorphosis*) is strangely absent from the iconography in the review *Documents*.

59 Peter Read, *Picasso and Apollinaire: The Persistence of Memory*, Berkeley, University of California Press, 2010.

60 Letter from Giacometti to Pierre Matisse, 1947, in *Écrits*, *op. cit.*, pp. 41–42.

61 Cannes notebooks, summer 1927; Paris notebook, March–May 1928; Dinard notebooks, summers 1928–1929; notebook from Boisgeloup, summer 1930 (Musée National Picasso-Paris).

62 Carl Gustav Jung, for the occasion of the Picasso exhibition in Zurich in 1932, would go as far as to speak of an internal 'rift', of 'lines of fracture' in Picasso's work (*Neue Zürcher Zeitung*, 13 November 1932).

63 'Abstract anthromorphism': Georges Didi-Huberman, *Le Cube et le visage, autour d'une sculpture d'Alberto Giacometti*, Paris, Macula, 1993, pp. 143 and 214.

64 Brigitte Leal would bring up the visual analogy, more than thirty years later, with Giacometti's *Walking Man*.

transgressive, wholly aligned with the 'formless'. Following the expected rejection of this 'anti-monument', judged 'obscene' by the Comité[57] (albeit promptly acclaimed by critics),[58] Picasso presented other projects taken from his notebooks, which were made into four small models produced in iron by Julio Gonzáles, one of which was called *Figure*. This second proposal, equally subversive, was another example of disfigurement, but completely different from the first and, being three-dimensional, wholly original. These were, in effect, transparent constructions, hollowed-out schematic configurations, made of disorderly bundles of lines forming geometric patterns in the space. We are familiar with a couple of interpretations: are these 'drawings in the space' an allusion to Apollinaire's *Calligrammes*? Or a response, as suggested by Werner Spies and Peter Read,[59] to the idea of a funerary statue evoked in *The Poet Assassinated*: a 'profound statue out of nothing, like poetry and glory', suggested the Bird of Benin (Picasso), 'a statue of nothing, a void', acquiesced Tristouse? These two diametrically opposed proposals opened up a whole new, extremely fertile and original world of formal theories and fresh research for Picasso in his work as both painter and sculptor.

Hollow/solid, geometric/organic, linear/ three-dimensional, transparent/opaque, vertical/ horizontal: the work of Picasso and that of Giacometti shifted from one extreme to the other, beating to the constant rhythm of these opposing absolutes. Giacometti insisted as much to Pierre Matisse: 'But all this alternated, contradicted itself, and continued by contrast. There was also a need to find a solution between things that were rounded and calm, and sharp and violent.'[60] Beginning with his two projects in tribute to Apollinaire, Picasso played around with the same concomitant variations throughout his artistic explorations in the years 1928–1930. The proliferation of contradictory projects, their febrile, quasi-incoherent flow through the course of the notebooks from 1927 to 1930[61] (and especially in notebook 1044 from Dinard, 1928) show a deep-seated 'interior' anxiety,[62] a conflictual impulse between desire and death, an internal 'dialectic', as Carl Einstein said, that created all the tension: these elements were soon resolved, in concrete form, when Picasso opened his extraordinary sculpture studio at Boisgeloup in 1930. For Giacometti, this crisis would be transcended with the 'wall', which is how he described the final work of his 'Surrealist period', *Cube*.

Two Phantom Figures: The Possibility of Sculpture

It is important to highlight the *hapax* nature of *Figure* (fig. 77), planned for the funerary monument for Apollinaire, and *Cube* (fig. 75), which immediately echoed the father's death and was produced in stages before its completion as a monumental piece in 1933–1934: each a one-off work-as-symptom and work-as-pivot never reproduced in Picasso and Giacometti's oeuvre. Both are geometric constructions and difficult to take in owing to their multiple points of view and changing perspective. Despite being polar opposites—*Figure* is transparent, a field of fragmented forces, open; *Cube* is a compact monolith, closed in on itself, inert— they could fit together quite easily: they are both the manifestation of the same figurative 'crisis' brought on by working through the grief of a guardian.

Both are, paradoxically, abstract anthro-pomorphic figures.[63] The polyhedral threads of *Figure*, far from creating an abstract and inert form (as it can appear on first impression), actually define a body, a body that is walk-ing[64] yet made, as we have seen, of air, a 'void'.

The irregular architectonic structure of *Cube*, at first glance also abstract in form, offers the melancholic opaqueness of a reliquary entombing a body. The ontological complexity of the work, revealed by its many previous appearances, is far from being exhausted. Georges Didi-Huberman analysed all the 'anthropological breadth' therein[65]: in turn an empty trinket or cage-coffin enclosing a skeleton, a cavernous body or head-skull, a solid mass or empty crystal, before becoming, with *Cube*, a monumental monolith that seems to envelop a human silhouette[66]; one of its sides bears the engraved image of his father (plaster, Kunsthaus, Zurich).[67]

Human abstractions and/or psychic concretions? Enigmatic, *Figure* and *Cube* are figures/tombs: phantom figures enclosed in their geometric cages, figures of loss and memory, yet active figures nonetheless. The same hesitation between presence and absence, between appearance and loss, between life and death, afflicts these two 'nocturnal pavilions', to borrow the other title Giacometti gave to *Cube*.

While both works, motivated by deep psychological drives, were put on hold, spectral presences in the studio space—the four models of *Figure* were abandoned on a shelf at the studio on Rue La Boétie in Paris,[68] and *Cube* was left neglected in the corner of the studio on Rue Hippolyte-Maindron, behind other megaliths[69]—the work they sparked proved to be extraordinarily liberating and fruitful as much for Picasso as Giacometti. For Picasso, a painter but not yet 'sculptor', in the classical sense of the term, and for Giacometti, a sculptor who still did not allow himself to confront (and paint) the model, they raised conflictual questions on their creation and played the role of crucial thresholds. For Picasso, it opened the way for the 'invention' of his future sculpture—a return, after an interval of fourteen years, to plaster moulds with the extraordinary series of large, terribly concrete and sensual *Heads* modelled on Marie-Thérèse and made in Boisgeloup from 1930. And for Giacometti, it heralded a permanent return, around 1934–1935, to the sculpture and painting of human figures, which he had abandoned in 1927. Ultimately, both men learned to accept and even embrace the encounter between artist and model.

65 Georges Didi-Huberman, *Le Cube et le visage, autour d'une sculpture d'Alberto Giacometti*, *op. cit.*, p.19.

66 As indicated by an engraving, *Figure in a Polyhedron*, c. 1933–1934 (Fondation Giacometti, Paris, inv. 1994-0722). Was Giacometti inspired by Picasso for this sculpture? A page in a notebook from 1932 (Fondation Giacometti, Paris, inv. 2000-0046, p. 26) shows a copy he executed of *Woman Wearing a Shirt* (exhibited in Zurich in 1932 and reproduced in *Cahiers d'art*, nos. 3–4, 1932), whose body is enclosed in an analogue polyhedral structure.

67 Alberto Giacometti-Stiftung, Zurich, inv. GS 298.

68 Visible in photos by Brassaï reproduced in *Minotaure*, no. 1, 1933, for the article 'Picasso dans son élément' by André Breton.

69 Photograph of Giacometti in his studio, c. 1946, by Émile Savitry.

Picasso-Giacometti: 'The Challenge to the Real'[1]

Sarah Wilson

The fragile consensus of a Europe with new borders fractured into pieces during the 1930s; the collapse of the global banking system; the world economic depression; the rise of 'revolution from below'; repression in Germany; racist policies and the resulting flows of migrants from across Europe to France and Britain—all these have disturbing echoes today. The widening gap between rich and poor and the collapse of the French art market were countered, if only momentarily, by the astonishing International Exposition of Art and Technology in Modern Life of 1937—a final snapshot of the European intelligentsia at play in pavilions representing every nation, a microcosm of the real art world.[2]

Giacometti and Picasso were involved in debates about realism and both of them, in their respective works, challenged the parameters of such arguments. The year 1937 marked the apex of Picasso's career with *Guernica*, a denunciation of civilian bombings in Spain, shown at the International Exposition's Spanish pavilion. Its formal and symbolic power continues to stand the test of time; its political subtext was at the crux of its meaning, then and now. Yet in the 1940s and 1950s, Giacometti's figures were to become the emblem of Resistance and the Holocaust itself. Despite Picasso's astonishing output, longevity and fame, how was it that Giacometti's work, rather than Picasso's, came to epitomise an era of radical change?

During the 1930s, the passion of both artists for African and 'primitive' art was recontextualised by fierce criticism of colonialism. Celebrations held in Paris in 1930 to commemorate the centenary of the French conquest of Algeria segued into the Paris Colonial Exposition occupying the Bois de Vincennes in 1931. The Surrealist group embraced the *esprit du temps* with their own periodical

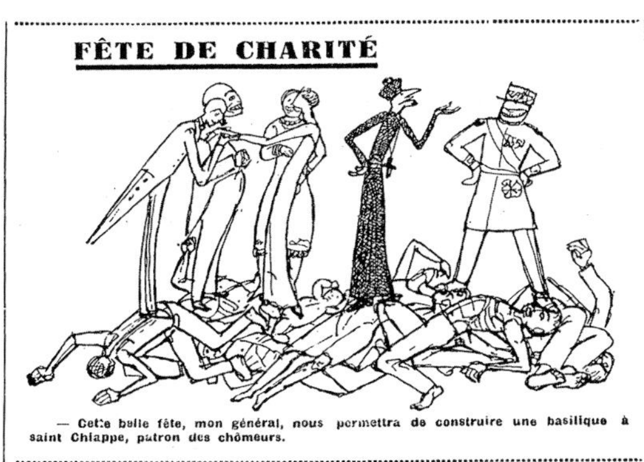

« Où va la peinture? » dit Giacometti, et il répond par un dessin :

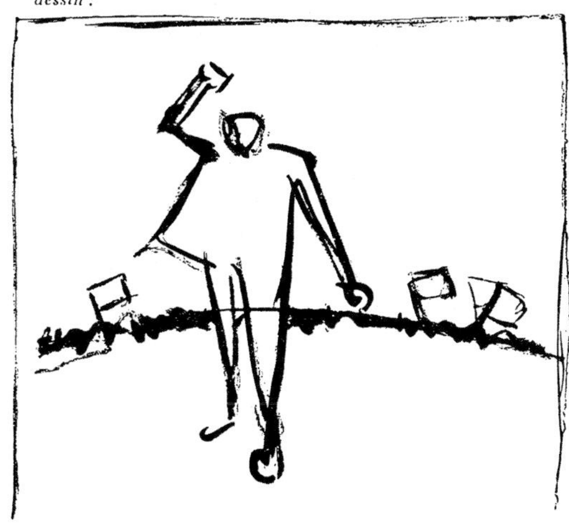

—
Fig. 30
Alberto Giacometti
Feast of Charity in *La Lutte anti-religieuse et prolétarienne*, no. 59, April 1932, 8th year
Where Is Painting Going? in *Commune*, no. 22, June 1935, 2nd year
—

Le Surréalisme au service de la révolution, while Louis Aragon spearheaded the movement for those looking to Moscow. The tract 'Ne visitez pas l'exposition coloniale!' aimed to turn visitors away from the Colonial Exposition; colonial artefacts were diverted to the counter-exhibition showing at the Comintern headquarters on Avenue Mathurin-Moreau.[3]

Under the pseudonym 'Ferrache', Giacometti published scathing political cartoons in *La Lutte anti-religieuse et prolétarienne*.[4] In *Feast of Charity*, insect-like society folk are talking while a priest is wildly gesticulating at a soldier as they all nonchalantly trample on the bodies of barefoot proletarians (fig. 30). This drawing is flanked by *Church and War* and *Voice of the USSR*, directly above Aragon's *Lament of the Jobless*.[5]

Giacometti apparently created a 'revolutionary' sculpture: 'Giacometti's social-revolutionary engagement lasted a season; he sculpted, in the naturalist style, a high-ranking figure, a proletarian with a red flag; he very quickly destroyed this piece, openly admitting that despite everything he owed his early fame to the wealthy classes.'[6] He frequented the AEAR (Association of Revolutionary Writers and Artists), formed in December 1932, but soon left: 'To my mind, the AEAR is like a rotten staircase coming out of a pond.'[7] Aragon continued to publish his early drawings: *Massacres of Workers* set against a schematic Communards' Wall in the Père Lachaise cemetery would appear in *Commune*, in June 1935. To the question 'Where is painting going?' Giacometti's response was a sketch of a man with a raised fist (fig. 30).[8]

This wide-ranging survey anticipated Aragon's lectures and publication of *Pour un réalisme socialiste*.[9] In May 1936, after the triumph of the Popular Front, 'The Quarrel over Realism' restaged—and reversed—the quarrel of the Ancients and the Moderns: now realism and not 'old' abstraction had become the 'art of

1 This essay's title is a reference to Louis Aragon's text 'The Challenge to Painting' in *Les Collages*, Paris, Hermann, 1965, pp. 35–71.

2 Here I am paraphrasing Walter Benjamin, 'Surrealism: The Last Snapshot of the European Intelligentsia' (published in German in *Die literarische Welt*, February 1929).

3 See Catherine Hodeir and Michel Pierre, *L'Exposition coloniale de 1931*, Paris, André Versailles Éditeur, 2011; Charlotte Billard, 'Aragon et le colonialisme', SIELEC website, 2011.

4 See Louis Aragon, 'Grandeur nature', *Les Lettres françaises*, 1, 115, 20 January 1966, pp. 16–17; *Alberto Giacometti, retour à la figuration, 1933–1947*, Christian Derouet (dir.), Paris, Centre Georges Pompidou, Musée National d'Art Moderne/Centre de Création Industrielle, 1986; Leslie Rubin, *The Lost Years: Alberto Giacometti's Return to Figuration, 1932–1937*, MA, The Courtauld Institute of Art, University of London, 1990 (under my direction).

5 Leslie Rubin, plate 2, front cover, *La Lutte anti-religieuse et prolétarienne, organe de l'Union fédérale des libres-penseurs révolutionnaires de France*, no. 59, April 1932.

6 Reinhold Hohl, *Alberto Giacometti*, Lausanne, Clairefontaine, 1971, p. 250.

7 Giacometti, *Écrits*, Paris, Hermann, 2007, p. 167, dated 'c. 1933–1934'.

8 The clumsier versions of the latter two drawings left in Aragon's personal collection (today at Jean Ristat) suggest that the sharpest drawings were given to the printers—and that the publications in *Commune* were AEAR-period cartoons remaining in his friend's possession.

9 Louis Aragon, *Pour un réalisme socialiste*, Paris, Denoël et Steele, 1935.

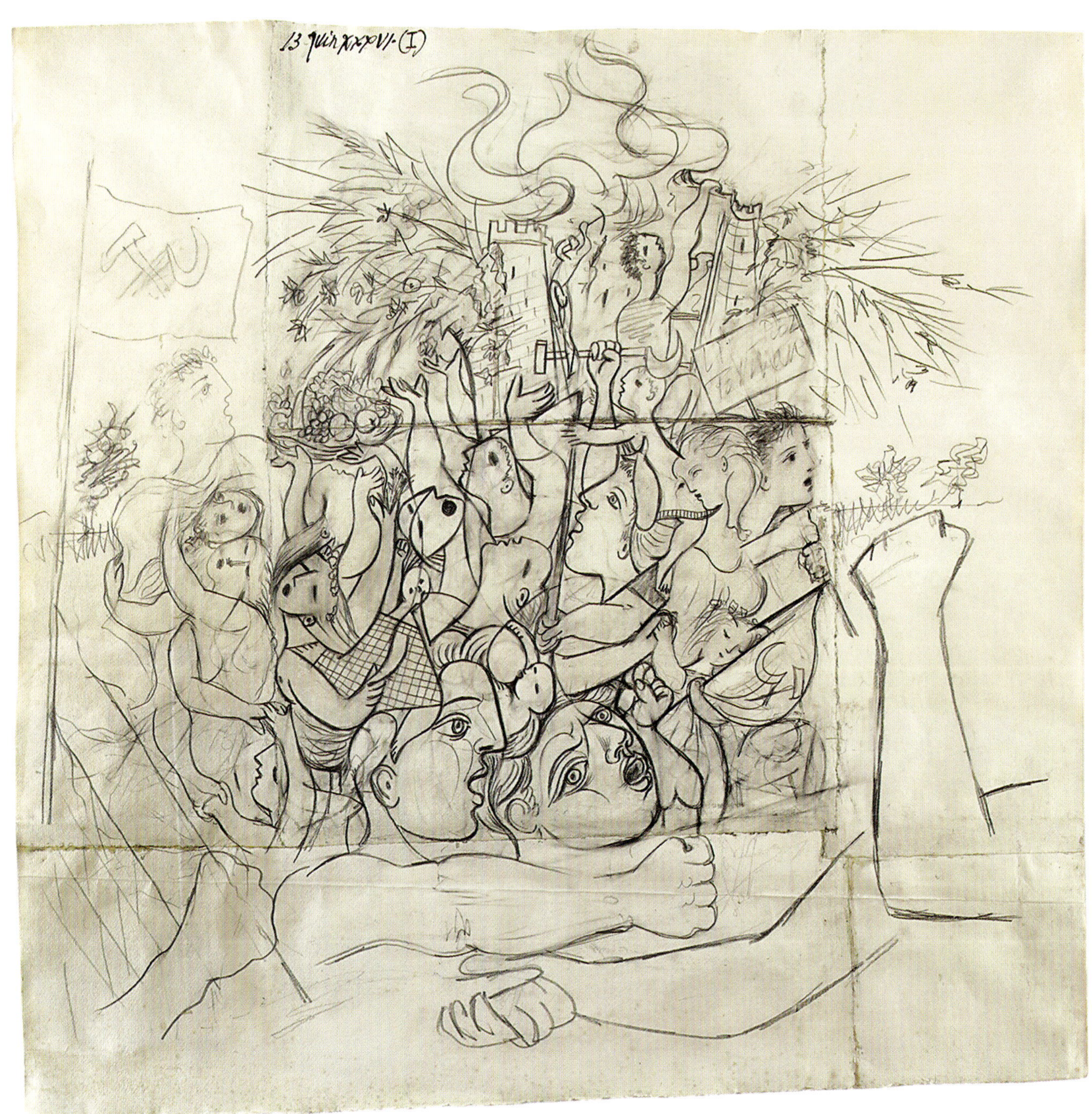

—
Fig. 31
Pablo Picasso
The Fourteenth of July
Graphite pencil on six assembled pieces of wove graph paper,
68 × 67 cm (26 ¾ × 26 ⅜ in.)
Musée National Picasso-Paris
Dation Pablo Picasso, 1979. MP1167
—

the left'.[10] The Soviet directives, proponents of an anti-Modernist 'revolutionary realism', were hurtling towards a head-on collision with the legacy of Picasso's 'Ingrism', the international call to order, oneiric Surrealism and younger movements such as the *Forces Nouvelles*, who advocated a new form of realism.

If Picasso stepped away from the 1935–36 debates, his *maison-atelier* on Rue La Boétie was near the Billiet-Worms gallery, a key conduit for most art exchanges with Moscow, sponsored by the VOKS (All-Union Society for Cultural Relations with Foreign Countries). He met with the younger generation of Communist painters in 1936 at the old Alhambra, now the Théâtre Populaire, who exhibited their works with some of their elder peers, such as Fernand Léger, in the theatre's foyer: a taster for Picasso's allegorical *The Fourteenth of July* stage curtain created for Romain Rolland's eponymous play, which depicted an eagle-headed monster carrying a dead Minotaur dressed in a Harlequin costume opposite a beautiful youth on the shoulders of a bearded man, covered in the skin of a corrida horse.[11] This allegory replaced an earlier more 'realist' drawing, where the flaming Bastille is the backdrop to an anti-fascist demonstration: amidst a crowd of maenad heads and raised fists we see a hammer, a sickle and a protest placard which reads 'Libérez Thaelmann' (Free Thaelmann) (fig. 31) .

At this time, Giacometti played with the relationship between constructive drawing and the diagram.[12] His *Mobile and Mute Objects* (1931), diagrams of sculptures in the round, are close to what Picasso produced, more prolifically, for *An Anatomy* (*Minotaure* 1, 1933). His sketching of sculptures like *The Palace at 4 a.m.* (fig. 35) sets up a dialogue between the cage and the perspective box. The two explanatory studio drawings from 1932 showing the position of his sculptures may be compared with *Studio with the Turntable* (1931), a drawing in close-up with conventional shading.[13] His schematic drawings of 1932 contrast, in this period of intense reflection, with the return to realism seen in certain portraits drawn and sculpted by Giacometti: angles and lines crisscross over faces in his portraits; streaked and flattened faces from earlier drawings give way to a deliberate intention to capture likeness in the heads of Diego, Rita and Isabel Nicholas. The Cubist sculptor Jacques Lipchitz produced a head of Géricault, which was later the subject of a painting by his former student at the Maison de la Culture, Boris Taslitzky.[14] Unlike Picasso, Giacometti befriended the young generation of Communist artists at the time including Francis Gruber, Francis Tailleux and Pierre Tal-Coat.[15] Indeed, Tal-Coat's self-portrait of 1936, acknowledging everything he owed to Giacometti, features an apparently Picassoesque drawing of a head pinned (satirically?) on the wall.

Giacometti's new paintings of 1937 returned to the simplest encounter with the otherness of an object: an apple on a table. Giacometti's anxiety and presence are etched on its surface, marked by an uncertain perspective, perilous equilibrium, and the interface of the purely optical and memory: like that of Cézanne.[16] Jean-Paul Sartre's *Nausea* (originally *Melancholia*), published in 1938, mirrored this development whereby anguished perception and matter became entwined, as in Roquentin's reaction to the root of the chestnut tree: 'Knotty, inert, nameless, it fascinated me, filled my eyes, brought me back unceasingly to its own existence.' An absorbing yet chiastic experience: 'I *was* the root of the chestnut tree … lost in it, nothing but it.'[17]

After the outbreak of war, in 1941 Giacometti and Sartre had their first period

10   Aragon *et al.*, 'The Quarrel over Realism', 1936, reprinted in Christopher Phillips, *Photography in the Modern Era*, New York, Metropolitan Museum of Art, 1990.

11   See Sarah Wilson, '14 July: A Stage Curtain for the Popular Front', in *Picasso/Marx and Socialist Realism in France*, Liverpool, Liverpool University Press, 2013, pp. 46–65.

12   Here I draw inspiration from Christopher D. Johnson, 'Warburg's *Zwischenraum*: Between Hieroglyph and Diagram', *Aby Warburg 150: Work, Legacy and Promise*, London, Warburg Institute, June 2016.

13   See plates 54–56, *Alberto Giacometti*, Paris, Musée d'Art Moderne de la Ville de Paris, 1991–1992, pp. 144–145.

14   Headed by Aragon, the Maison de la Culture left the Rue d'Anjou and moved to 12 Rue de Navarin. Boris Taslitzky was editorial manager of the *Journal des peintres et sculpteurs de la Maison de la culture* and Aragon its publishing manager.

15   His friendships with older realist painters, such as André Derain and Balthus, were also important. James Lord, *Giacometti: A Biography*, London, Thames and Hudson, pp. 167–172.

16   I defend the idea that Giacometti anticipates here 'Cézanne's Doubt' by Maurice Merleau-Ponty, *Fontaine*, no. 47, December 1945.

17   Jean-Paul Sartre, *Nausea*, New York, New Directions Publishing Corp., 1964.

18 See Reinhold Hohl, 'Documentary Biography', in *Alberto Giacometti, op. cit.*, pp. 276–277.

19 Alberto Giacometti, 'À propos de Jacques Callot', *Labyrinthe*, no. 7, 15 April 1945, p. 3; 'The Dream, the Sphinx and the Death of T.', *Labyrinthe*, no. 22–23, 15 December 1946, pp. 12–13.

20 See Sarah Wilson, 'Francis Gruber: espace politique, espace eschatologique', in *Francis Gruber, l'oeil à vif*, Nancy, Musée des Beaux-Arts, 2009, pp. 65–76.

21 *Picasso, 50 Years of His Art*, Alfred H. Barr (dir.), New York, Museum of Modern Art, 1946, p. 250.

22 Francis Gruber, *Arts de France*, no. 5, 1946, p. 28.

23 This undated letter by Giacometti is available as a photocopy, Boris Taslitzky archives.

24 Roger Garaudy, 'Artists without Uniform', *Arts de France*, no. 9, 1946, *The Charnel House* compared to *Buchenwald*, oil by Taslitzky, 3 × 5 m (10 × 16 ½ ft.).

25 See Jean-Paul Sartre, 'La recherche de l'absolu', *Les Temps modernes*, no. 28, January 1948; 'The Search for the Absolute', *Alberto Giacometti*, Pierre Matisse Gallery, 1948, pp. 2–22.

of intense discussion, during which they questioned 'existence' versus 'essence' and the ambiguities of perception.[18] Unlike Picasso who endured the darkness, the violence of Paris under occupation, the stench of persecution, expressed in skull-like women's heads, the frozen *Aubade* and the kicked-around bronze *Skull,* Giacometti found himself marooned in Geneva. He published his vision of occupation, atrocity and pillage in 1945 in his commentary to Jacques Callot's engravings *The Miseries and the Misfortunes of War* (1633), whose minute details contrasted hugely with Giacometti's bizarre timespace diagrams illustrating 'The Dream, the Sphinx and the Death of T.' (published in *Labyrinthe*): 'There is nothing but scenes of massacre and destruction, torture and rape, fire and shipwreck … the sexual or erotic element in Callot's works is only presented by rape and martyrs, and by obscene allusions made by buffoons. The only permanent and positive element in Callot is the space, the large gaping space in which his figures gesticulate, annihilate and do away with themselves.'[19] Francis Gruber's *Hommage à Jacques Callot* had used the rape of the female body as an allegory of Occupied Paris in 1942. Following his melancholy *Job,* he persisted with masculine pathos in *Les Cadavres* for the exhibition *Art et Résistance* held in February 1946[20] and at which Taslitzky, now a returned deportee, also exhibited.

The show was dominated, however, by Picasso's *The Charnel House,* a composition in black and white grisaille—the colours of mourning, of emptiness (fig. 32). 'The fury and shrieking violence which make the agonies of *Guernica* tolerable are here reduced to silence. For the man, the woman, and the child, this picture is a *pietà* without grief, an entombment without mourners, a requiem without pomp.'[21] Alfred Barr grasped the *unheimlich* (uncanny)

character of these cadaverous hieroglyphs, of this still life of contorted corpses. Gruber would subsequently refer to the concentration camp as the very measure of contemporary art: 'If in Cézanne's time painting an apple demonstrated a very advanced intellectual position, producing history paintings in the time of Guernica and extermination camps is also a progressive intellectual and moral position … Giacometti's magnificent studies for the portrait of Colonel Rol-Tanguy and the many drawings produced by Boris Taslitzky in Buchenwald are practically the only eye-witness accounts of quality of the years we have just lived through'[22] (fig. 33).

Here Gruber was reporting on the French art exhibition held at the Musée du Luxembourg in September 1946. Giacometti attended the show and protested vehemently when Taslitzky's *La Pesée*—an indictment on the starvation of political prisoners in Vichy France—was relegated to the back of the show: 'I find it scandalous and wicked to see it banished to the last room when it merits being in one of the first, and in the number one spot as far as I'm concerned … I regret not having taken along a sculpture so that I could immediately take it back in protest against the prime position given to Stasliski [*sic*]'.[23]

By November, the debate around style, 'Picasso or Taslitzky', and 'Modernism' versus 'Realist' expression, had pitched the stakes of the battle for Socialist Realism.[24] It intensified the anti-Modernist diktats from Moscow. Picasso's work would be replaced by his dove and the promotion of 'the man of the dove', the 'genius' of the arts.

In January 1948, Sartre's 'The Search for the Absolute' appeared in *Les Temps modernes* and was used as the preface to Giacometti's first New York exhibition.[25] The artist's 'Letter to Pierre Matisse' in the catalogue summarised his sculptural career with tiny

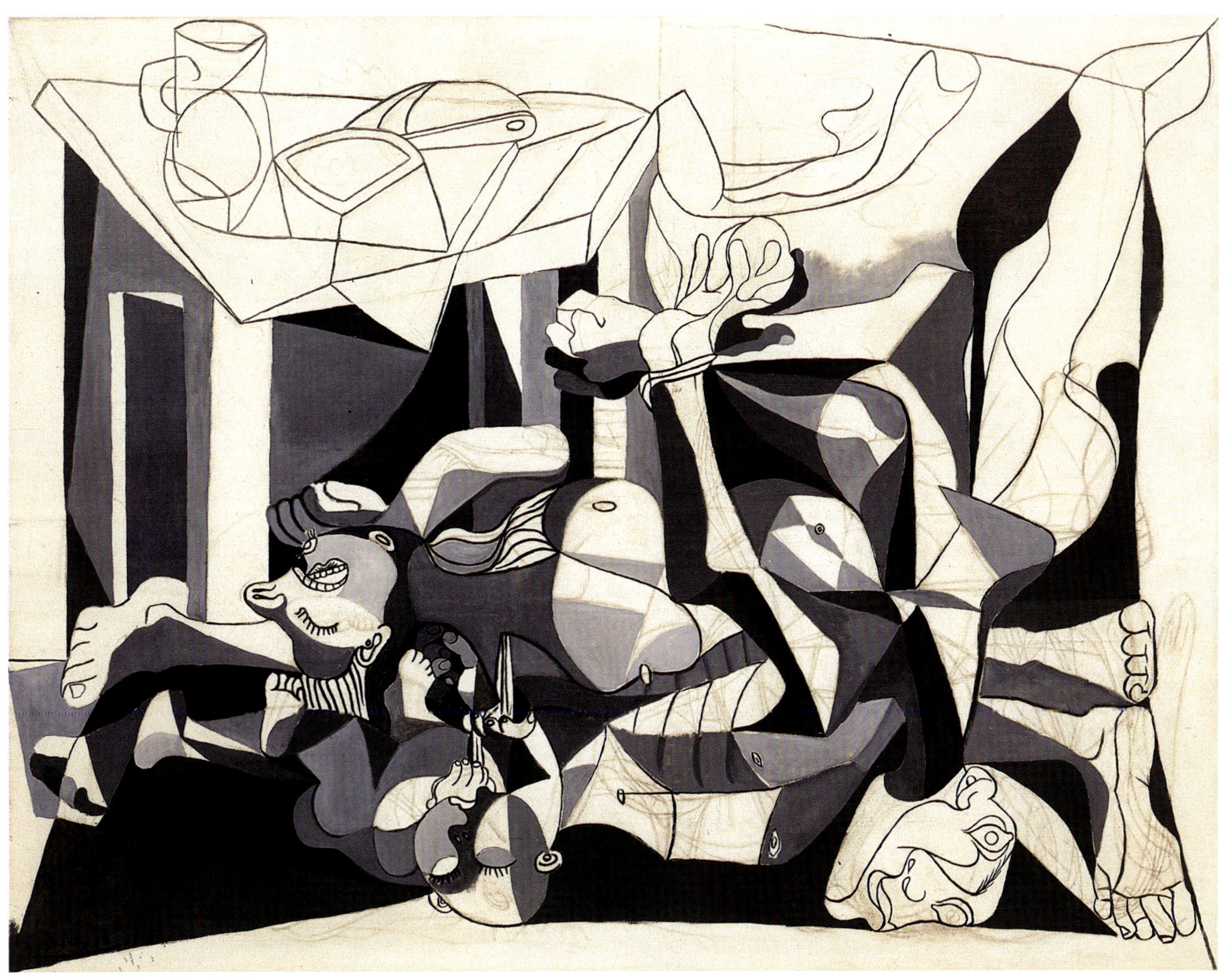

—
Fig. 32
Pablo Picasso
The Charnel House
Paris, 1944–1945
Oil on canvas and charcoal,
199.8 × 250.1 cm (6 ft. 6 ¾ in. × 8 ft. 2 ½ in.)
Museum of Modern Art (MoMA), New York
Inv. 93.1971
—

26   Both forewords by Sartre (see 'Les peintures de Giacometti', *Derrière le miroir*, no. 65, May 1954) and the one by Genet, ('L'atelier d'Alberto Giacometti', *Derrière le miroir*, no. 98, June 1957, pp. 3–26); Jean Genet, *The Studio of Giacometti*, London, Grey Tiger Books, 2013) are analysed in Sarah Wilson, 'Paris Post War: In Search of the Absolute', in *Paris Post War: Art and Existentialism, 1945–1955*, London, Tate Gallery, 1993, pp. 25–52.

27   *Picasso, sculptures, dessins : Maison de la pensée française … Paris … 1950-1951*, with a foreword by Louis Aragon, Paris, Mourlot, 1952, was a major work.

diagrams. Far from his sexualised Surrealist compositions, his new, tremulous figures with their worked-to-nothing surfaces were like beings transfixed to the spot yet endowed with a historical transversality; the man of Eyzies and the man of Altamira confronting the 'fleshless martyrs of Buchenwald', as Sartre suggested: the beginning and the end of human history. Signs of unspeakable, spectral presences, Giacometti's solitary sculptures express the imminence of their near extinction. Sartre's narrative paradigms in *Being and Nothingness* continued to achieve form in bronze: the implied gulf in *Falling Man;* alienation and disconnection in *City Square;* absurdity in *Head on a Rod* (fig. 113) or *The Nose*. The intrusion of sexual desire in Sartre's 1948 text is further elaborated in his more Heideggerian preface of 1954, in which the chiastic relationship between subject and object shifts to a focus on origin and disclosure (*aletheia* [truth] as a frozen strip-tease: the *Four Figures on a Pedestal*, their plinth the receding dance floor). In Jean Genet's preface from 1957, the sexuality stems more from the phallic stiffness of these figures. Giacometti's sculptures, shrouded in his studio, also evoke the fear of death, echoing the sentiment one might feel standing before a mummy or the Egyptian statue of the priestess of Osiris at the Louvre.[26]

A sense of fear, of dark memory-spaces framing or enclosing his subjects, pervades Giacometti's paintings and sculptures. In contrast, Picasso (who visited Auschwitz in 1948) remained gnomic, as he had been with *The Charnel House*: diagrammatic in his bright Mediterranean gambols (the Antibes frescoes); frustratingly obscure with the collision of Poussin, Goya, Manet and Degas in a no-man's land (*Massacre in Korea*, 1951); characteristically violent using the contrasts of contour and bright colour (*Women of Algiers*);

caricatural and aggressive in his *War and Peace* murals at the Temple de la Paix, Vallauris, though his later bronzes show a return to joy in their celebration of female fullness and the magic of assemblage in *Little Girl Jumping Rope, She-Goat* (figs. 140 and 141) and *Baboon and Young* made from two toy cars.[27]

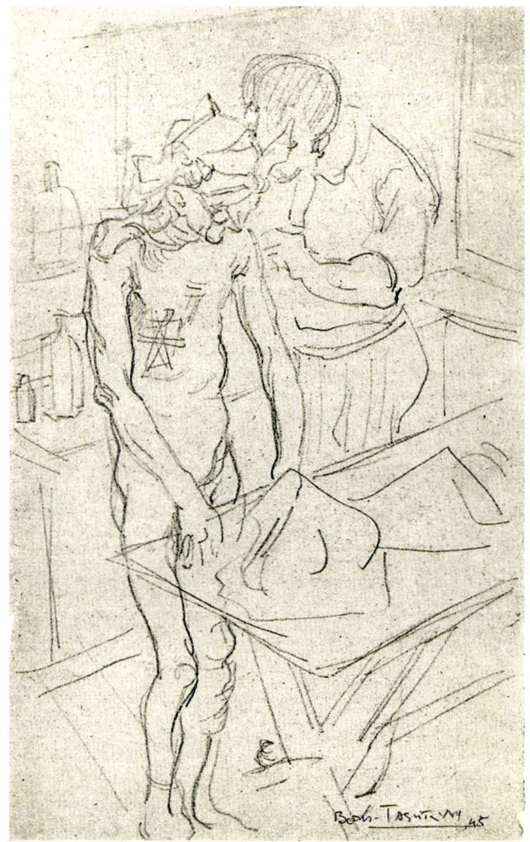

—
Fig. 33
Boris Taslitzky (1911–2005)
Professor Halbwachs Enduring Medical Care a Few Days Before His Death
Buchenwald camp, 1945
Pencil on paper
Private collection
—

Even after Paris regained its colour and *joie de vivre*, Giacometti and his work remained tragic. His gesturing sculptures and intense portraits, stripped down to the bare minimum (*dépouilllés*), where the active looking and empathic identification permeate the notion of mortal remains (*dépouille*) and create a vast *vanitas*: a monument to an era and—etymologically—a warning. Compare Ernst Scheidegger's stark immortalisation of Giacometti in black and white, tropes of struggle, failure and persistence, with Picasso playing the clown in the south of France, for the amusement of the photographer David Douglas Duncan.[28]

To relate the personalities of these great masters, the development of their respective ideas and oeuvres in a few pages is impossibly reductive. It is significant, however, that Picasso did not feature in *New Images of Man* at the Museum of Modern Art in New York, in 1959, the last great museum exhibition of the twentieth century in the United States to show European artists alongside American artists. Giacometti dominated his international rivals: *Tall Figure* (1949) was the show's emblem and catalogue cover.[29] In the catalogue's foreword, the theologian Paul Tillich spoke of 'the dehumanising structure of the totalitarian systems in one half of the world, and the dehumanising consequences of technical mass civilisation in the other half.'

Picasso's output during the Cold War contrasts strongly with the immemorial sculptural presences of Giacometti: the *locus classicus* for a postwar humanism and the encounter between art and phenomenology. Could one argue that Picasso's *The Charnel House* is fatally anti-humanist in its recognition of corpses not trampled 'in the name of God and the Fatherland' (as in Giacometti's 1931 drawing), but by the capitalist machinery of industrialised death?[30] It was ultimately bought by Walter P. Chrysler and entered the New York MoMA's collection in 1971 (its title remains incomprehensible for most of its contemporary public). Both artists were leaders, both became 'too dominant'—Picasso notoriously, but also Giacometti before his earlier death in 1966. Daniel Buren said of him: 'I saw Giacometti as an image, "the artist" in all his splendour, the bohemian, Romantic artist, carrying something of a curse … an image that I was absolutely determined to avoid.'[31]

The ubiquity of both great masters was ultimately countered by their 'anxiety of influence'.[32]

28 Ernst Scheidegger, *Alberto Giacometti: Spuren einer Freundschaft, Schirn Kunsthalle Frankfurt*, Zurich, Verlag Scheidegger & Spiess AG, 1998; David Douglas Duncan, *The Private World of Pablo Picasso*, New York, Harper, 1958.

29 *New Images of Man*, Peter Selz (dir.), prefaced by Paul Tillich, New York, Museum of Modern Art, 1959. See Sarah Wilson, 'New Images of Man: Postwar Humanism and its Challenges in the West', in *Postwar: Between the Pacific and the Atlantic*, Okwui Enwezor (dir.), Munich, Haus der Kunst, 2016.

30 As compared with Walter Benjamin on the 'insurgent technique' (*The Work of Art in the Age of Mechanical Reproduction*), *Zeitschrift für Sozialforschung*, vol. V, 1936, p. 66, and Zygmunt Bauman, *Modernity and the Holocaust*, Cornell, Cornell University Press, 1989. 'Charnel house' means 'ossuary' before the twentieth century; it therefore does not refer to the Holocaust as does the French word *charnier*.

31 *Daniel Buren & Alberto Giacometti, Contemporary Works, 1964–1966*, Paris, Kamel Mennour Gallery, 2010, n. p.

32 See Harold Bloom, *The Anxiety of Influence*, New York, Oxford University Press, 1973.

Picasso and Giacometti: Sculptures or 'the Poetics of Space'[1]

Virginie Perdrisot

"Space! It can only be captured by feeling, or by transgression, by testing its limits, by drawing on flat geometry: midpoints, axes, diagonals, circles, and so forth, or indeed by making use of lines in the space, lines which share it, divide it. Only then can it be captured and understood. Then the space arranged as lines can expand until it forms surfaces and these surfaces can crystallise into bodies, which constitute variations around the essence of the space and its totality."

Oskar Schlemmer, *Journal*, 1928, quoted in Thierry Dufrêne, *Giacometti: Les dimensions de la réalité*, Geneva, Skira, 1994, p. 158.

THE EXPERIENCE OF PRESENCE

'I think that Giacometti, conscious of everything that needs to be kept alive within, day after day, in order to retain the memory of the real, was always afraid that inside him there might be a latent Picasso.... And Picasso was useful in allowing him to remember who he was.'[2] Even though Yves Bonnefoy sees a 'latent Picasso' in Alberto Giacometti, the formal and ideological differences that separate the two artists are what really stand out. Giacometti, an artist who reduced his creative vocabulary to an expression of the essence of being, appears to contrast strongly with Picasso, the prolific demiurge who saw art as a laboratory of forms, an infinite terrain for experimenting. They thus each assigned a very different role to sculpture. While Giacometti sought to tackle the impossible task of restoring the ontological dimension to art, to 'reveal the presence in the model',[3] Picasso did not consider the experience of presence to be 'a forbidden dimension'; neither did he see it as 'the obsessive task that Giacometti tried to accomplish while believing that he would not be able to succeed'.[4] Sculpture, with its protean dimension, becomes the tool for finding an artistic equivalent to reality. Hence, according to Michel Leiris, 'Picasso spent his life trying out all sorts of ways of artistically transcribing reality and making figures present.'[5]

Within this perspective, the techniques the two artists used sometimes travelled in opposite directions: Picasso often preferred to apply the assemblage technique to his sculpted work, a method based on the act of adding, while the sculptor gives the material and the found object new life by including them in the sphere of art. Giacometti's work is characterised by the paring down of the material to its bare essence, convinced as he was that 'art is not the measure of reality but its decantation', the only thing capable of expressing 'a certain feeling for forms which lies inside'.[6] As sculptors, Picasso and Giacometti were both faced with the question of how to incorporate the work of art into its environment, how to position it in space. The act of establishing a space specific to the work quickly became central to Giacometti's artistic explorations, while in Picasso's work sculpture also created its own space on several occasions. The result is the phenomenon of 'poetics[7] of space', in the sense that the sculpted work invents its own space and sets the boundaries of that space.

SPACE AND ITS DRAMATISATION

Sculpture's relationship to its environment takes on a profoundly innovative dimension in Picasso and Giacometti's work. As Michel Leiris points out in *Pierres pour un Alberto Giacometti*, 'while a sculpture is usually … an object with space around it, Giacometti is now concerned with creating space containing one or more objects.'[8] What then surfaces is an aesthetic of appearance born of the dramatisation of space. Picasso's dramatisation of space is initially expressed in his Cubist constructions and relief paintings, where the sculpture emerges

1 Title borrowed from Gaston Bachelard, *The Poetics of Space*, Boston, Beacon Press, 1969.

2 Yves Bonnefoy, *Remarques sur le regard, Picasso, Giacometti, Morandi*, Paris, Calmann-Lévy, 2002, p. 118.

3 Ibid., p. 24.

4 Ibid., p. 120.

5 Michel Leiris, *Écrits sur l'art*, Paris, 1973; new edition, Paris, CNRS Éditions, 2011, p. 363.

6 Thierry Dufrêne, *Giacometti, les dimensions de la réalité, op. cit.*, p. 13.

7 Or 'poietic', from the Greek *poiein*, 'to create', 'to invent', 'to make'.

8 Michel Leiris, 'Pierres pour un Alberto Giacometti', *Derrière le miroir*, nos. 39–40, June–July 1951, reprint, 1991, Paris, L'Échoppe, p. 243.

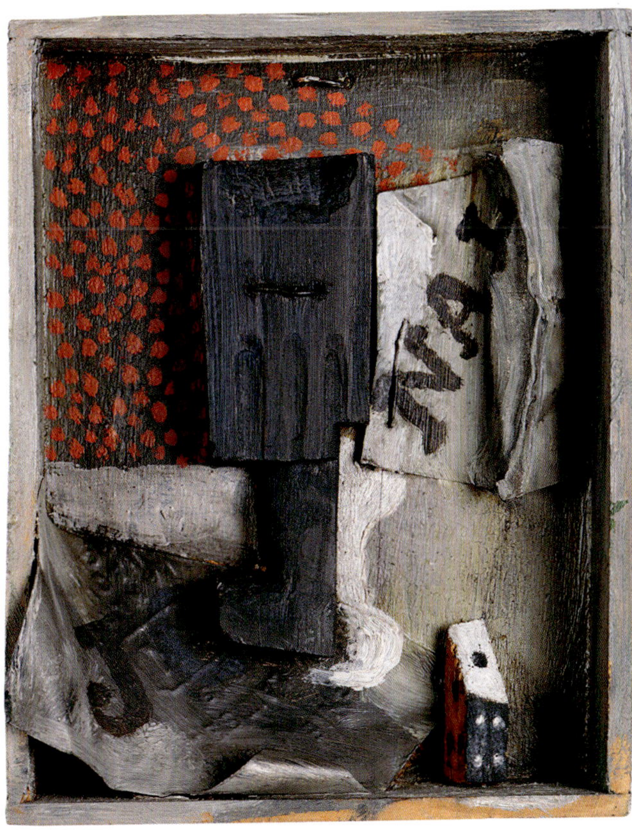

Fig. 34
Pablo Picasso
Glass, Dice and Newspaper
Avignon, summer 1914
Cut-out and painted wood
and tin elements, iron wire
on oil-painted wood panel,
17.4 × 13.5 × 3 cm (6 ⅞ × 5 ¼ × 1 ⅛ in.)
Musée National Picasso-Paris
Dation Pablo Picasso, 1979. MP45

9 Pablo Picasso, *Mandolin and Clarinet*, Paris, autumn 1913, elements in pine wood with paint and pencil marks, 58 × 36 × 23 cm (22 ⅞ × 14 ⅛ × 9 in.), Musée National Picasso-Paris, MP247. Spies 54.

10 See in particular Pablo Picasso, *Glass, Dice and Newspaper*, Avignon, summer 1914, cut-out and painted wood and tin elements, wire on a background of wood painted in oil, 17.4 × 13.5 × 3 cm (6 ⅞ × 5 ¼ × 1 ⅛ in.), Musée National Picasso-Paris, MP45. Spies 42.

11 Werner Spies, *Picasso, the Sculptures*, catalogue raisonné compiled with Christine Piot, Paris, Centre Georges Pompidou, Musée National d'Art Moderne/Centre de Création Industrielle, 2000.

12 Christian Zervos, *Pablo Picasso, catalogue raisonné des œuvres (1895–1972)*, Paris, *Cahiers d'Art*, 1932–1978, vol. 7, introduction, n. p.

13 Pablo Picasso, *Figure*, Paris, autumn 1928, wire and sheet metal, Musée National Picasso-Paris, MP264, MP265 and MP266. Spies 68, 69 and 71.

14 Werner Spies, *Picasso, the Sculptures, op. cit.*

15 Alberto Giacometti, *Man (Apollo)*, 1929, bronze, 39.4 × 30.9 × 8.2 cm (15 ½ × 12 ⅛ × 3 ¼ in.), Fondation Giacometti, Paris, inv. 2015-0001.

16 Alberto Giacometti, *The Palace at 4 a.m.*, 1932, wood, wire, glass and string, 63.5 × 71.8 × 40 cm (25 × 28 ¼ × 15 ¾ in.), Museum of Modern Art, New York.

17 Werner Spies, *Picasso, the Sculptures, op. cit.*

18 Alberto Giacometti, *Écrits*, presented by Michel Leiris and Jacques Dupin, Paris, Hermann, 2001, letter to Pierre Matisse, December 1950, reproduced p. 3.

19 Werner Spies, *Picasso, the Sculptures, op. cit.*

20 Michael Brenson, *The Early Work of Alberto Giacometti: 1922–35*, The Johns Hopkins University, PhD, 1974, unpublished, cited in Catherine Grenier, 'Giacometti ou la perspective dépravée,' in *Alberto Giacometti*, Saint-Thonan, Cloître Imprimeur, 2015, p. 16.

from the painting's surface. By creating an autonomous and dramatised space, the relief painting is a hybrid creation, half-painting and half-sculpture, which offers an alternative place where the experience of observing is highly intense for the observer. Thus, *Mandolin and Clarinet*[9] (fig. 61) from October 1913 is a work that invites the observer inside, where a new type of three-dimensional space is defined, demarcated on the vertical plane by the shape of a frame and a wooden board while the mandolin's neck projects forward. The work's space thus encompasses the viewer in a *mise en abyme* where the viewer's gaze increases the intensity of the work's experience. The 'box' as a principle for construction features in a whole series of relief paintings where Picasso uses the inside of a cigar box[10] (fig. 34) to create a virtual space containing a variation on the theme of a still life of a glass that draws its strength from the constraints of the space. These box-shaped sculptures introduce a new relationship between the inside and outside of the artwork, which brings to mind the structure of Giacometti's space of frames and cages, where a new virtual space takes form, seeking to dramatise how the work is seen in order to intensify its presence.

The years 1927 and 1928 saw the advent of Picasso's sculptural period when, to use Werner Spies' description, 'thought is deployed in three dimensions'.[11] As Christian Zervos writes in the introduction to the seventh volume of the *catalogue raisonné*: 'It could be said that there is not one painting from that period untouched by the spirit of sculpture.'[12] In the 'drawings in space' formed by the welded wire sculptures that Picasso created as plans for the monument in homage to Guillaume Apollinaire[13] (fig. 77), the material is replaced by force lines. The 'figure' is contained in a graphic structure where a veritable 'equation between the body and the line'[14] is established within a landscape of constellations, welding knots and points punctuating a space crisscrossed by the sculpture's metal shafts. These open-work sculptures created by Picasso inevitably bring to mind Giacometti's sculptures from the 1930s. According to Werner Spies, this graphic incorporation of the figure in a restricted and structuring space was a source of inspiration for Giacometti: 'At that time, [Picasso] seemed to leave a strong impression on Giacometti in particular. Behind the physical stretching and dematerialisation that Giacometti began to adopt, lies a fascination for this new artistic conception. With *Man* (1929),[15] he offers an absolute version of the whole series of anthropomorphic wire constructions, and in *The Palace at 4 a.m.* (1932–1933)[16] (fig. 35), he uses the spatial background, the basis for Picasso's construction of his characters, to create the space in which he dramatizes surrealist objects.'[17] In the same way as in Picasso's welded wire *Figures* (fig. 77), the perception of Giacometti's *Man* (fig. 76) is structured by a very powerful graphic arrangement, a clearly drawn block that forms, in Giacometti's own words, a 'skeleton within the space': 'For me, this provided a certain part of the vision of reality; but what was missing was my feeling for the whole thing, a structure, an intense aspect that I also saw in it, a sort of skeleton within the space.'[18]

Manifestly, in both Picasso's wire pieces and Giacometti's metal skeletons, the 'notion of space is at play'.[19] In contrast to the box sculptures of the Cubist period, Giacometti and Picasso's open-work sculptures have a transparency that enables a 'multiplication of the principle of perspective',[20] where sculpture is arrayed according to a *continuum* of viewpoints. The void thus becomes an essential component of the space. We know to what extent the notion of the void and nothingness is prevalent in the monument to Guillaume Apollinaire, inspired, according to Peter Read,[21] by these words of the Bird of Benin character in Guillaume Apollinaire's *The Poet Assassinated*: 'I must model a profound statue out of nothing, like poetry and glory.'[22] Sculpting the void thus offers an opportunity to take control over a space with artistic means, to define the nothingness enclosed in a visual architecture, operating as 'a clear and orthogonal system of coordinates with very distinct lines'.[23] As Giacometti himself wrote: 'I never considered the figures to be a compact mass, but as a transparent construction.... There was a third element that affected me within reality: movement.... I could only make this movement real and effective, and I wanted to create the impression that I was producing it.'[24]

Despite a certain formal complicity, Picasso and Giacometti's open-work sculptures differ radically when it comes to their intrinsic meaning. As Werner Spies underlines, 'Giacometti's cage is not so much a formal message as a psychological message of oppression. It is like a portion of space where objects and people

21   Peter Read, *Picasso and Apollinaire: The Persistence of Memory*, Berkeley, University of California Press, 2010.

22   Guillaume Apollinaire, *The Poet Assassinated*, London, Turnaround, 2000.

23   Werner Spies, *Picasso, the Sculptures, op. cit.*

24   Alberto Giacometti, *Écrits, op. cit.*, letter to Pierre Matisse, p. 4.

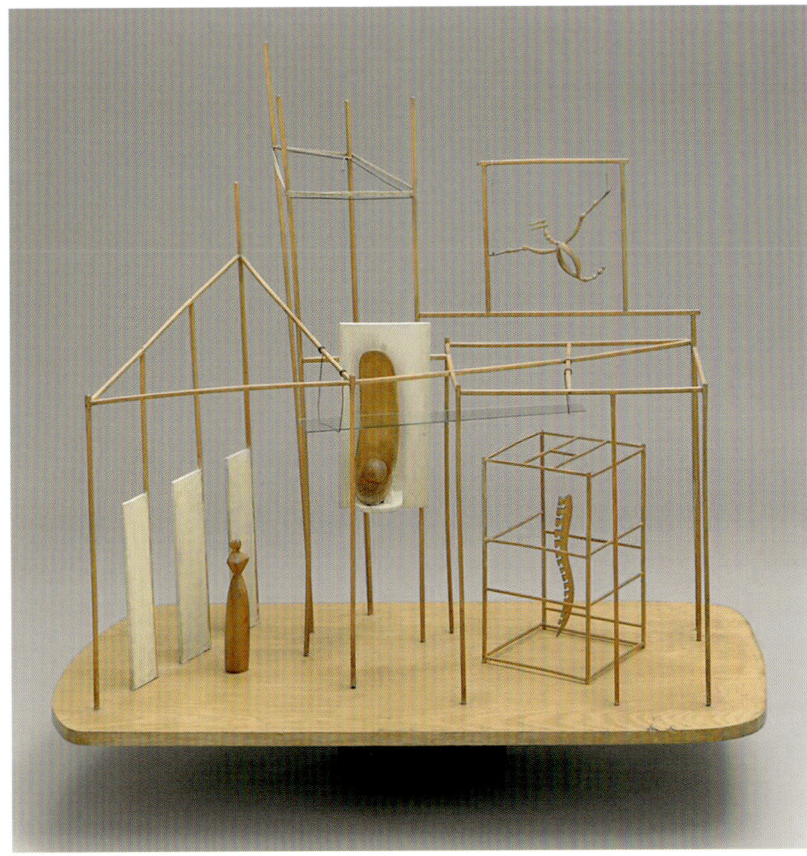

Fig. 35
Alberto Giacometti
The Palace at 4 a.m.
1932
Wood, iron wire,
glass and string,
63.5 × 71.8 × 40 cm
(25 × 28 ¼ × 15 ¾ in.)
Museum of Modern Art
(MoMA), New York
Inv. 90.1936

25 Werner Spies, *Picasso,
the Sculptures, op. cit.*

26 Alberto Giacometti, *Head on a
Rod*, 1947, painted plaster, Fondation
Giacometti, Paris, inv. 1994-0440.

27 Alberto Giacometti, *Suspended
Ball*, 1930–1931, 1965 version,
plaster, painted metal, string,
60.6 × 35.6 × 36.1 cm
(23 ⅞ × 14 × 14 ¼ in.), Fondation
Giacometti, Paris, inv. 1994-0250.

28 Alberto Giacometti, *Point to
the Eye*, 1931, original plaster,
11.5 × 45.2 × 2.8 cm
(4 ½ × 17 ⅞ × 1 ⅛ in.), Musée
National d'Art Moderne, Paris.

29 Jean Clair, *Le Nez de Giacometti,
faces de carême, figures de carnaval*,
Paris, Gallimard, 1992, p. 275.

30 Alberto Giacometti, *The Invisible
Object (Hands Holding the Void)*,
1934, plaster, 156.2 × 33 × 30.5 cm
(5 ft. 1 ½ in. × 1 ft. 1 in. × 1 ft.), Yale
University Art Gallery, New Haven.

31 Yves Bonnefoy, *Remarques
sur le regard, Picasso, Giacometti,
Morandi, op. cit.*, p. 110.

are confined.'[25] In Giacometti's work, the formal void becomes 'the invisible', imbued with the existential angst caused by the unpredictability of life. Surrounded by the void, *Head on a Rod* (fig. 113)[26] stands as the 'emergence of human beings into the solitude of the world', while *Suspended Ball* (fig. 100)[27] and *Point to the Eye* (fig. 106)[28] invite the void into the artwork as part of a fragile balance between form and nothingness, presence and absence. Where Picasso's transparent wire sculptures present the figure

as the humanisation of space, in Giacometti's work the void becomes ontologically invisible, space as a negative. In Jean Clair's words, 'this form of the invisible is reality itself, with which Giacometti always grappled: space, time, the earth, the shifting distance which separates us from it.'[29] In 1934's *Invisible Object* (fig. 7),[30] the figure of a woman embodies both presence and absence, her hands close together, holding 'the still to be discovered work that he yet had to learn to execute'.[31]

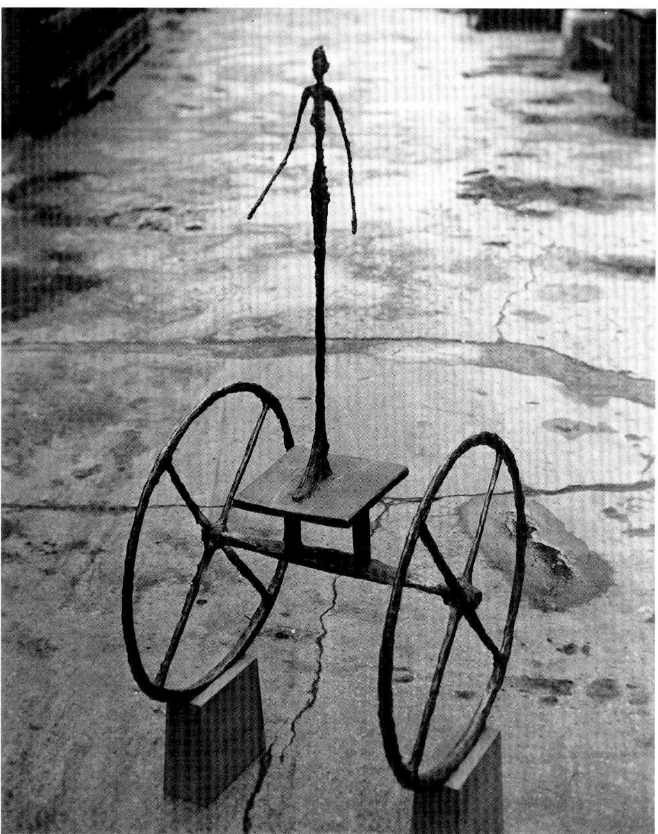

—
Fig. 36
Ernst Scheidegger
The Chariot in Bronze
c. 1951
Silver print on paper,
23.8 × 18.6 cm (9 ⅜ × 7 ⅜ in.)
Fondation Giacometti Archives, Paris
—

POSITIONING SCULPTURES IN SPACE

Added to the question of space as the environment of the work, one of its components, is the question of the distancing of the work, of its dimensions and its positioning. To use Jean-Paul Sartre's[32] description, Giacometti's sculptures appear to us at an 'absolute distance'. The sculptures do not occupy the space but offer themselves up with the space, simultaneously delineating and defining it. Within this perspective, the sculpture's distance from the ground is crucial to fully appreciating it. To take the example of *The Chariot*[33] (fig. 36), in a letter to Pierre Matisse in December 1950 during the second exhibition at the Pierre Matisse Gallery, Giacometti stresses the importance of 'the need to once again have the figure in the void so it can better be seen and be situated at a specific distance from the floor.'[34] The work is distanced from the floor by the plinth, which displays the sculpture, 'dramatises' it and endows it with a presence that is almost magical, sacred. In *The Studio of Giacometti*, Jean Genet describes all that the plinth or pedestal adds to the work's presence: 'I feel that here Giacometti … is performing a private ritual whereby he will give the statute an authoritative, earthy, feudal base. The effect of this base on us is magical.'[35] The plinth operates as a vector for presence, playing a role in expressing the figure's mystery. Thierry Dufrêne, placing as he does the question of dimensions at the heart of Giacometti's analysis of his work, points out the enhanced presence the base offers to these 'tiny figures of women, barely three centimetres tall, above the plinths that are enormous in comparison … which endowed the figures with a very strong presence, the mystery of a goddess appearing on the boundary between the visible and the invisible.'[36]

Although instances of the presence of a plinth designed by the artist amplifying the work's power are rare in Picasso's oeuvre, we can nevertheless observe in his sculptures a certain taste for staging. To borrow Werner Spies' definition, Picasso's sculptures operate like elements of a 'small theatre',[37] moved around like wooden figures on a stage by the artist as director. Photographs taken in Picasso's studio illustrate this art of dramatisation as sculptures are given a role to play, such as the small bronze figure photographed by Dora Maar around 1941 in the Grands-Augustins studio in Paris. Isolated in a corner of the space, it resembles a timeless effigy (fig. 1). The photographs of the sculptures displayed in the studio are so powerfully evocative that J. Wood even uses the term 'white magic'[38] when describing the intensely creative place that the Boisgeloup studio in Normandy proved to be for Picasso (fig. 6). The sculpted portraits of Marie-Thérèse Walter, magnified by the white of the plaster, establish a dialogue on their turntables, some of them close together, others presented at different heights. This dramatisation, intensified by the central light shed by an oil lamp placed at the heart of the studio, confers the majesty and eternity of the ancient world on the 'population of sculptures'.[39]

This art of composition, common to both artists, has at times led to an analogy with the theatre; the absence of a link between figures 'placed there, with no apparent role' gives Giacometti's sculptures the resonance of a Greek tragedy: 'We can compare these figures created by Giacometti with those to be found in the new theatre (Beckett, Genet, R. Wilson, etc.). Space is made conscious by the repetition of figures placed there, with no apparent role. They all tend towards an identification with the chorus in a Greek tragedy. The characters in the chorus were there to help the tragic

32 Jean-Paul Sartre, 'The Search for the Absolute', *Les Temps modernes*, no. 28, January 1948.

33 Alberto Giacometti, *The Chariot*, 1950, bronze, 167 × 69 × 69 cm (5 ft. ⅝ in. × 2 ft. ⅜ in. × 2 ft. ⅜ in.), Alberto Giacometti-Stiftung collection, Zurich, inv. GS 44.

34 Alberto Giacometti, *Écrits*, op. cit., p. 14.

35 Jean Genet, *The Studio of Giacometti*, London, Grey Tiger Books, 2013.

36 Thierry Dufrêne, *Giacometti, les dimensions de la réalité*, op. cit., p. 110.

37 'Interview with Werner Spies', in *Picasso. Sculptures*, Paris, Somogy, 2016, p. 30.

38 Jonathan Wood, 'Magie blanche. Boisgeloup et la présentation des sculptures de Picasso vers 1930-1935', *Revue de l'art*, no. 154, 2006, pp. 49–56.

39 Brassaï (pseudonym of Gyula Halász), *Conversations with Picasso*, Chicago, University of Chicago Press, 1999.

40 Thierry Dufrêne, *Giacometti, les dimensions de la réalité, op. cit.*, p. 168.

41 Auguste Rodin, *The Burghers of Calais*, 1895, bronze, Musée Rodin, Paris.

42 Thierry Dufrêne, *Giacometti, les dimensions de la réalité, op. cit.*, p. 157.

43 Alberto Giacometti, *Nine Figures (The Glade)*, 1950, patinated bronze, 58.7 × 65.3 × 52.5 cm (23 × 25 ¾ × 20 ⅝ in.), Fondation Giacometti, Paris, inv. 2007-0223.

44 Alberto Giacometti, *Écrits, op. cit.*, pp. 157–158.

45 Pablo Picasso, *The Bathers*, Cannes, summer 1956, bronze, Musée National Picasso-Paris, MP352 to 357. Spies 503 II to 508 II.

46 Particularly Pablo Picasso, *On the Beach (Bathers)*, 16 September 1956, private collection.

47 Pablo Picasso, *The Bathers: The Child*, Cannes, summer 1956, bronze, 136 × 67 × 46 cm (4 ft. 5 ½ in. × 2 ft. 2 ½ in. × 1 ft. 6 in.), Musée National Picasso-Paris, MP355. Spies 506 II.

48 Pablo Picasso, *The Bathers: Woman Diver*, Cannes, summer 1956, bronze, 264 × 83.5 × 83.5 cm (8 ft. ⅞ in. × 2 ft. 10 ½ in. × 2 ft. 8 ⅞ in.), Musée National Picasso-Paris, MP352. Spies 503 II.

hero achieve awareness: are Giacometti's characters not there to provide awareness of our perception?'[40]

COMPOSITIONS AND SCULPTED GROUPS

The sculpted group is the form that most insistently demands the incorporation and structuring of figures in space. Giacometti adopted Rodin's 'sited' compositions,[41] but radically changed the approach by creating a multi-dimensional world, a network of tensions where the positioning of the figures in relation to each other constantly revitalises the work's creative power: 'The artist confirms the creative possibility of permanent accommodation and the shift from one scale to another, one dimension to another. The variation in size thus becomes a stage in the process of giving form…. A creative variable.'[42]

The question of scale is thus essential in that it gives life to the constantly evolving composition. Giacometti's *Nine Figures*, better known as *The Glade*, has a similar composition technique to *The Forest*[43] (fig. 165). The artist wrote a letter to Pierre Matisse in 1950 about the work: 'excess becomes the very foundation of the composition', since 'the variation in scale triggers the feeling of a huge space swallowed up by a restricted space.'[44] The question of placing the composition in space is at the heart of *The Bathers*[45] (fig. 164), the only sculpted group of Picasso's, produced in Cannes in the summer of 1956. A whole series of drawings and studies[46] (fig. 37) produced by the artist in autumn 1956, a few weeks after creating his wooden assemblages, attest to Picasso's deliberations on the positioning of his sculptures, devised as a presentation on several levels in the open-air setting of a beach

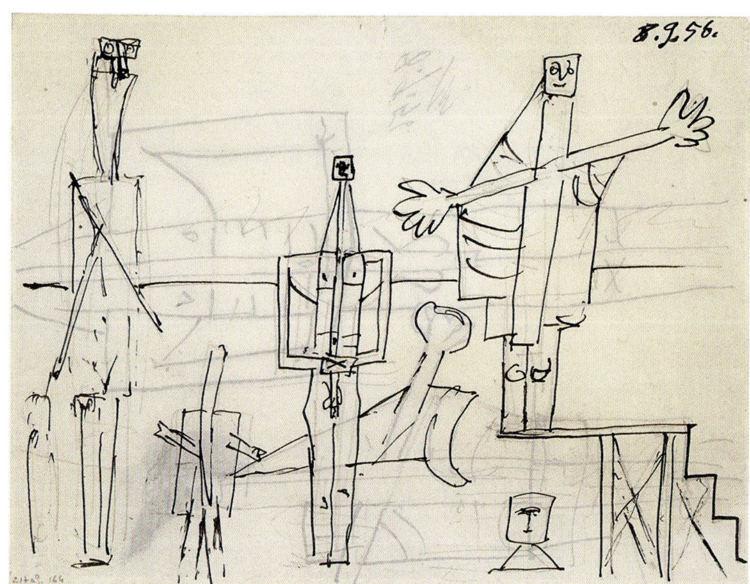

Fig. 37
Pablo Picasso
Study for The Bathers: The Diving Board
Cannes, 8 September 1956
Pen and India ink on graphite pencil marks on fine-textured wove paper, 20.8 × 26.8 cm (8 ¼ × 10 ½ in.)
Musée National Picasso-Paris
Dation Pablo Picasso, 1979.
MP1513

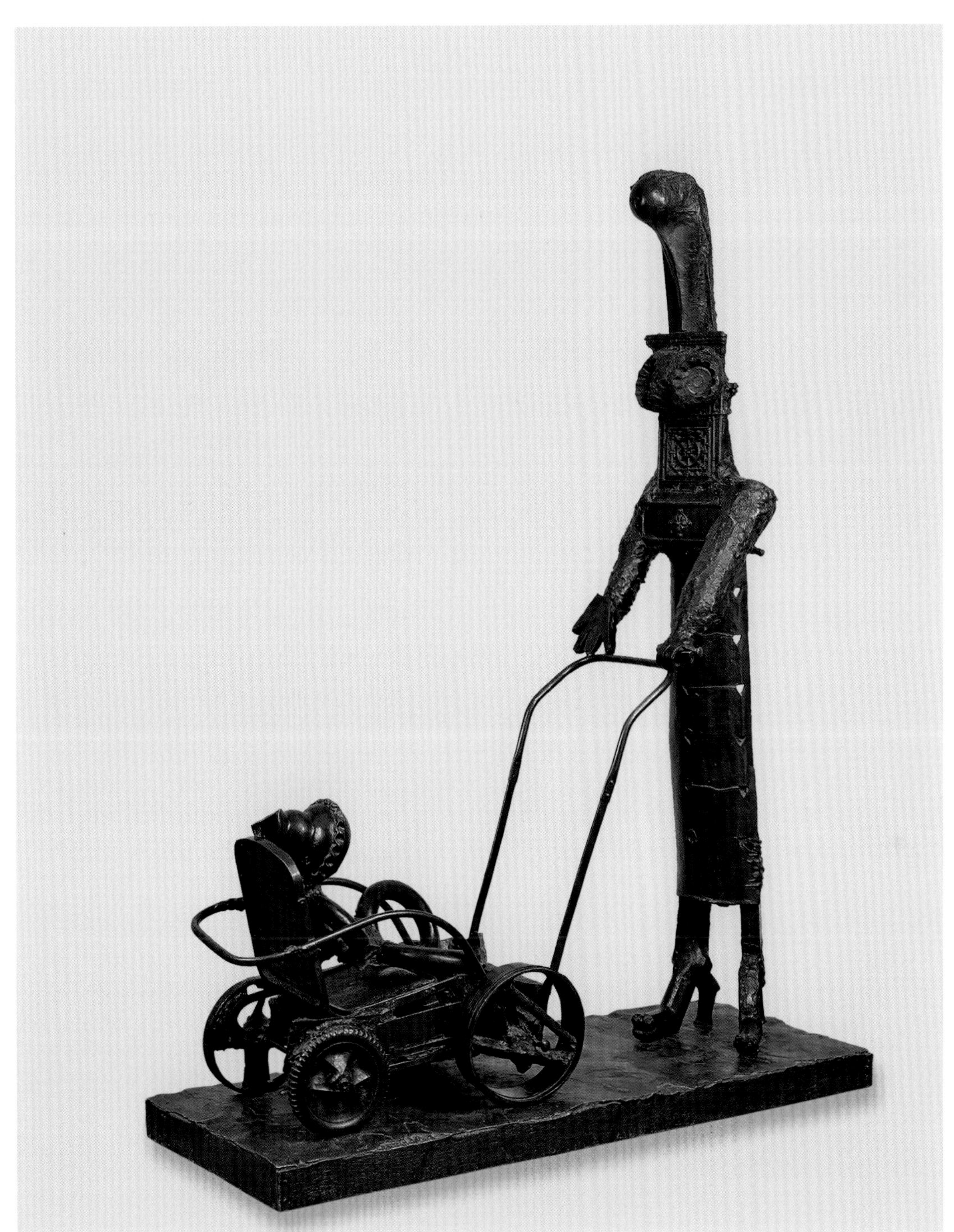

Fig. 38
Pablo Picasso
Woman with Stroller
Vallauris, 1950
Bronze, 203 × 145 × 61 cm (6 ft. 8 in. × 4 ft. 9 ⅛ in. × 2 ft.)
Musée National Picasso-Paris
Dation Pablo Picasso, 1979. MP337

49 Pablo Picasso, *The Bathers: Fountain Man*, Cannes, summer 1956, bronze, 228 × 88 × 77.5 cm (7 ft. 5 ¾ in. × 2 ft. 10 ¾ in. × 1 ft. 2 ⅛ in.), Musée National Picasso-Paris, MP354. Spies 505 II.

50 Pablo Picasso, *The Bathers: Man with Clasped Hands*, Cannes, summer 1956, bronze, 213.5 × 73 × 36 cm (7 ft. × 2 ft. 4 ½ in. × 1 ft. 2 ⅛ in.), Musée National Picasso-Paris, MP353. Spies 504 II.

51 Pablo Picasso, *The Bathers: Woman with Outstretched Arms*, Cannes, summer 1956, bronze, 198 × 174 × 46 cm (6 ft. 6 in × 5 ft. 8 ½ in. × 1 ft. 6 in.), Musée National Picasso-Paris, MP356. Spies 507 II.

52 Pablo Picasso, *The Bathers: The Young Man*, Cannes, summer 1956, bronze, 76 × 65 × 46 cm (30 × 25 ⅝ × 18 in.), Musée National Picasso-Paris, MP357. Spies 508 II.

53 David Douglas Duncan, *Picasso Working on* The Bathers *at La Garoupe*, gelatin silver print, David Douglas Duncan archives.

54 Jean Genet, *The Studio of Giacometti, op. cit.*

55 Giacometti had underlined the fact that his work came prior to Picasso's: 'In 1947, I saw the completed sculpture in front of me.' 'In 1950, it was already in the past.' Yves Bonnefoy, *Remarques sur le regard, Picasso, Giacometti, Morandi, op. cit.*, p. 118.

56 See note 33.

57 Pablo Picasso, *Woman with Stroller*, Vallauris, 1950, bronze, 203 × 145 × 61 cm (6 ft. 7 ⅞ in. × 4 ft. 9 ⅛ in. × 2 ft.), Musée National Picasso-Paris, MP337. Spies 407 II.

58 Alberto Giacometti, *Walking Man*, 1960, plaster, 180.5 × 27 × 97 cm (5 ft. 11 in × 10 ⅝ in. × 3 ft. 2 ⅛ in.), Fondation Giacometti, Paris.

59 Werner Spies, *Picasso, the Sculptures, op. cit.*

60 See in particular Spies 629 to 635.

61 Werner Spies, *Picasso, the Sculptures, op. cit.*

62 Ibid., p. 290.

63 Jean Genet, *The Studio of Giacometti, op. cit.*

scene. Despite the flat shape and frontality from the viewer's perspective, each figure belongs to a space that determines its position and form: cut off at the waist, *The Child*[47] is immersed in a pool, while *Woman Diver*,[48] *Fountain Man*[49] and *Man with Clasped Hands*[50] are on a jetty, and *Woman with Outstretched Arms*[51] and *The Young Man*[52] are positioned higher up on a diving board (fig. 164). In a composition that shifts with different drawings and paintings, pointing to a playfulness in Picasso rather than a quest for the 'exact place', the artist even seems to make use of his sculptures as templates for the bathers in his paintings, as illustrated by a photograph taken by David Douglas Duncan at the La Californie studio in Cannes.[53] The image shows Picasso applying the *Woman with Outstretched Arms* to the canvas where the painting follows the outline of the sculpture.

THE MOVEMENT OF PERCEPTION

In 1956, as Picasso was creating *The Bathers*, Giacometti was presenting his large figures of women at the Venice Biennale. Jean Genet rightly highlighted the 'immobile movement' of these sculptures which, set in motion by the gaze of the viewer, shift forwards and backwards without moving: 'They [the sculptures] arouse a curious feeling in me: they are familiar, they are walking in the street. And yet, they are at the beginning of time, at the origin of the world, constantly approaching then drawing back in sovereign immobility.'[54] While Picasso and Giacometti[55] had both virtually endowed sculpture with the power to move in works like *The Chariot*[56] (fig. 36) and *Woman with Stroller*[57] (fig. 38), movement here is introduced by the viewer's gaze. The piece *Walking Man*[58] thus marks a real revolution where the mobility of perception embeds the work in a dynamic space.

In the early 1960s, Picasso created sculptures in folded and painted sheet metal that, to use Werner Spies' expression, are veritable 'optical experiences'. It is certainly true that these 'optical works … introduce vision and the disappearance of vision as subjects of the piece'.[59] Thanks to its folded surface, the sculpture is perceived discontinuously, the viewer's gaze discovering the heads sculpted in the metal in fits and starts[60] (fig. 39), creating a surprise effect as the sculpture comes to life: 'What we have before us remains a flat image and, in contrast to a modelled figure, we cannot base our perception on an anticipated continuous unfolding…. Our vision is confronted with an irrational situation. The subject is out of sync, inaugurating something dramatic, a new conception of time.'[61] Under the influence of the movement of perception and 'dramatisation of the light' which 'encounters the surfaces in different ways,'[62] the sculpture vibrates and seems to come alive.

Jean Genet referred to Giacometti's large figures of women when describing Picasso's sheet metal sculptures, and his words are apposite here: 'The space around them vibrates. There is no longer anything that remains still. It is possibly because each angle … or curve, or bump, or ridge, or torn tip of the metal are themselves no longer still. Each of them continues to emit the sensibility that created them. No tip, ridge or edge that cuts up or tears space is dead.'[63]

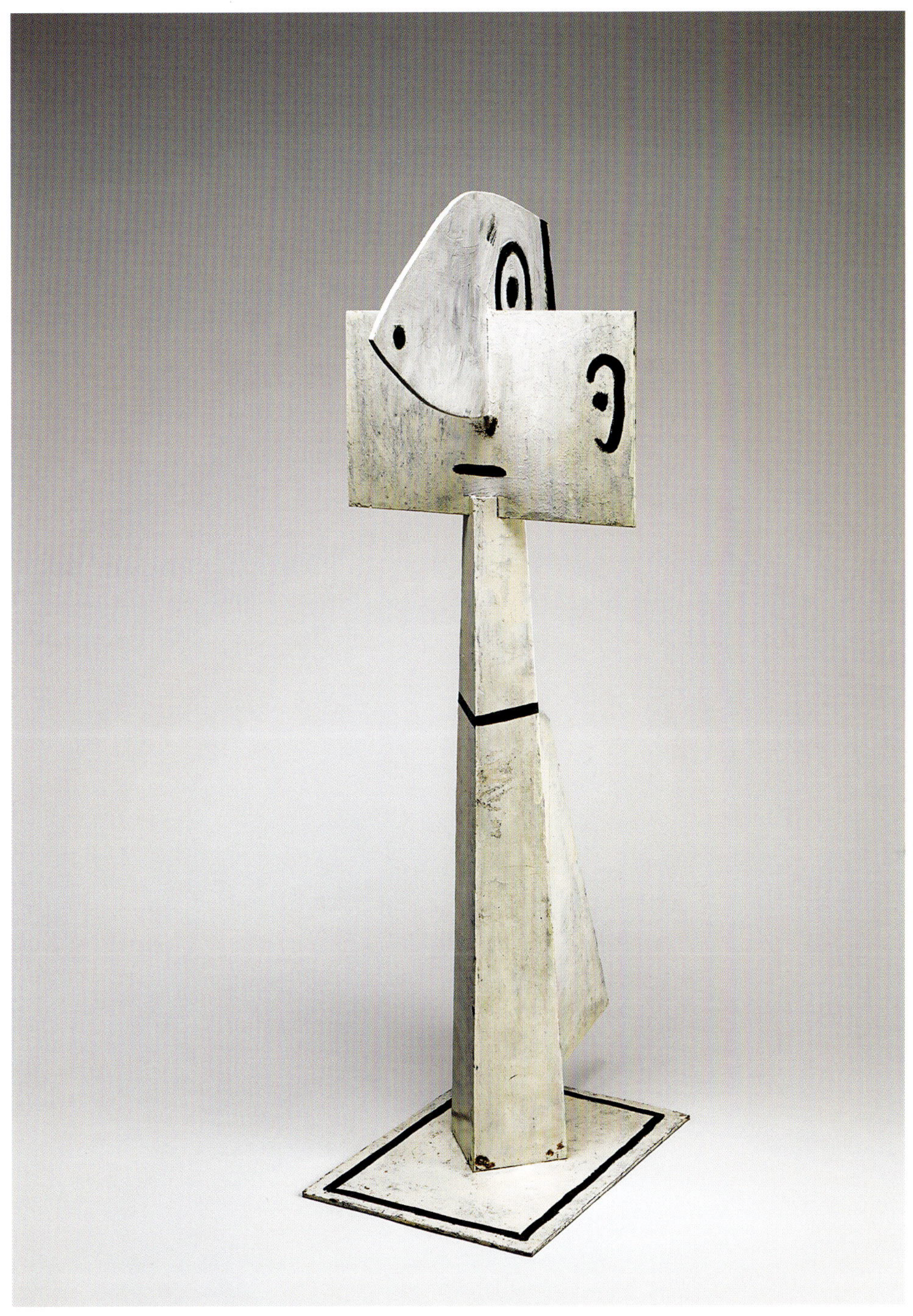

Pablo Picasso
Head of a Woman
Cannes, 1957
Cut-out and painted sheet metal, 87 × 28 × 42 cm (34 ¼ × 11 × 16 ½ in.)
Musée National Picasso-Paris
Dation Pablo Picasso, 1979. MP351
—

Works

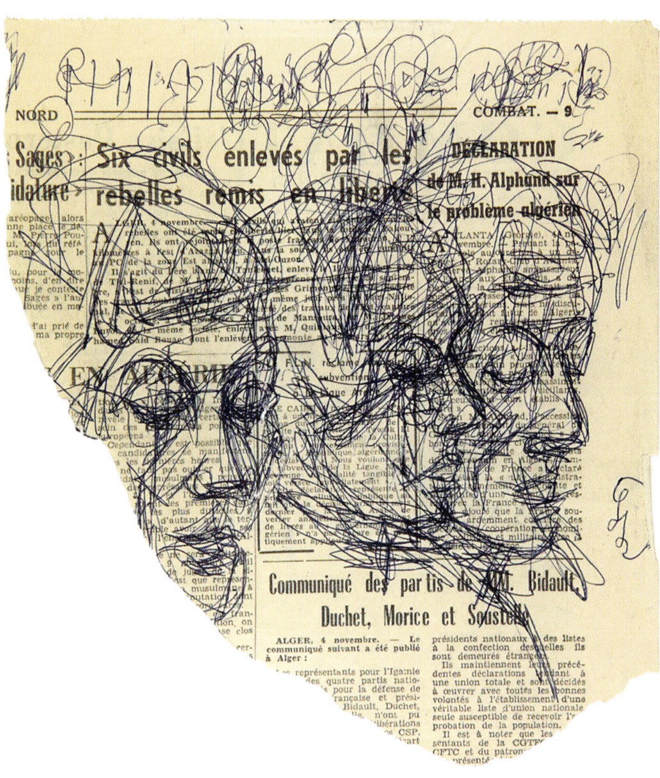

Fig. 40
Alberto Giacometti
Three Heads
n. d.
Blue ballpoint pen on newsprint from *Combat*,
22.2 × 19.5 cm (8 ¾ × 7 ⅝ in)
Fondation Giacometti, Paris

—

Fig. 41
Pablo Picasso
Three-Quarter View of the Back of a Man's Head
Paris, winter 1906–1907
Reconstituted black chalk or Conté crayon on a scrap
of the newspaper *Le Matin*, 30 December 1906,
12.4 × 8 cm (4 ⅞ × 3 ⅛ in.)
Musée National Picasso-Paris
Dation Pablo Picasso, 1979. MP525

—

Signs of Genius

Pablo Picasso and Alberto Giacometti began to paint and sculpt very early on. The sons of artists, they each grew up in their father's studio, where they worked on their first pieces under a watchful paternal eye. They trained by creating portraits of family members, in which they strived for a faithful representation of the model. At the tender age of fourteen Picasso created *The Barefoot Girl* (early 1895) and Giacometti *Still Life with Apples* (c. 1915), both of which attest to a paternal influence through the attention paid to rendering reality. After a short spell training at art school, the two young artists decided to leave their countries of origin and settle in Paris, the then capital of the arts.

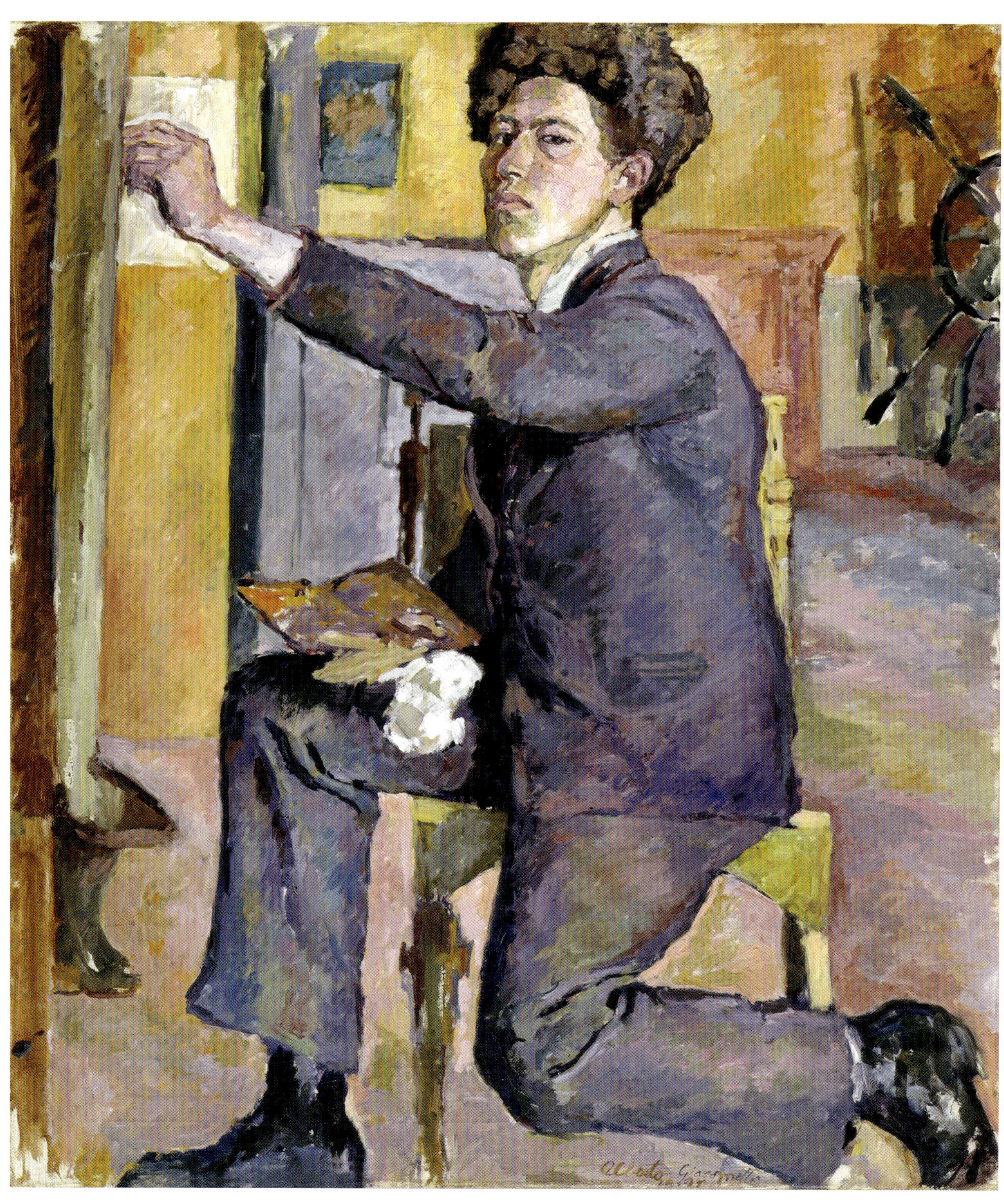

Fig. 42
Alberto Giacometti
Self-Portrait
1921
Oil on canvas, 82.5 × 72 cm (32 ½ × 28 ⅜ in.)
Kunsthaus Zürich – Alberto Giacometti Stiftung
Inv. GS 62

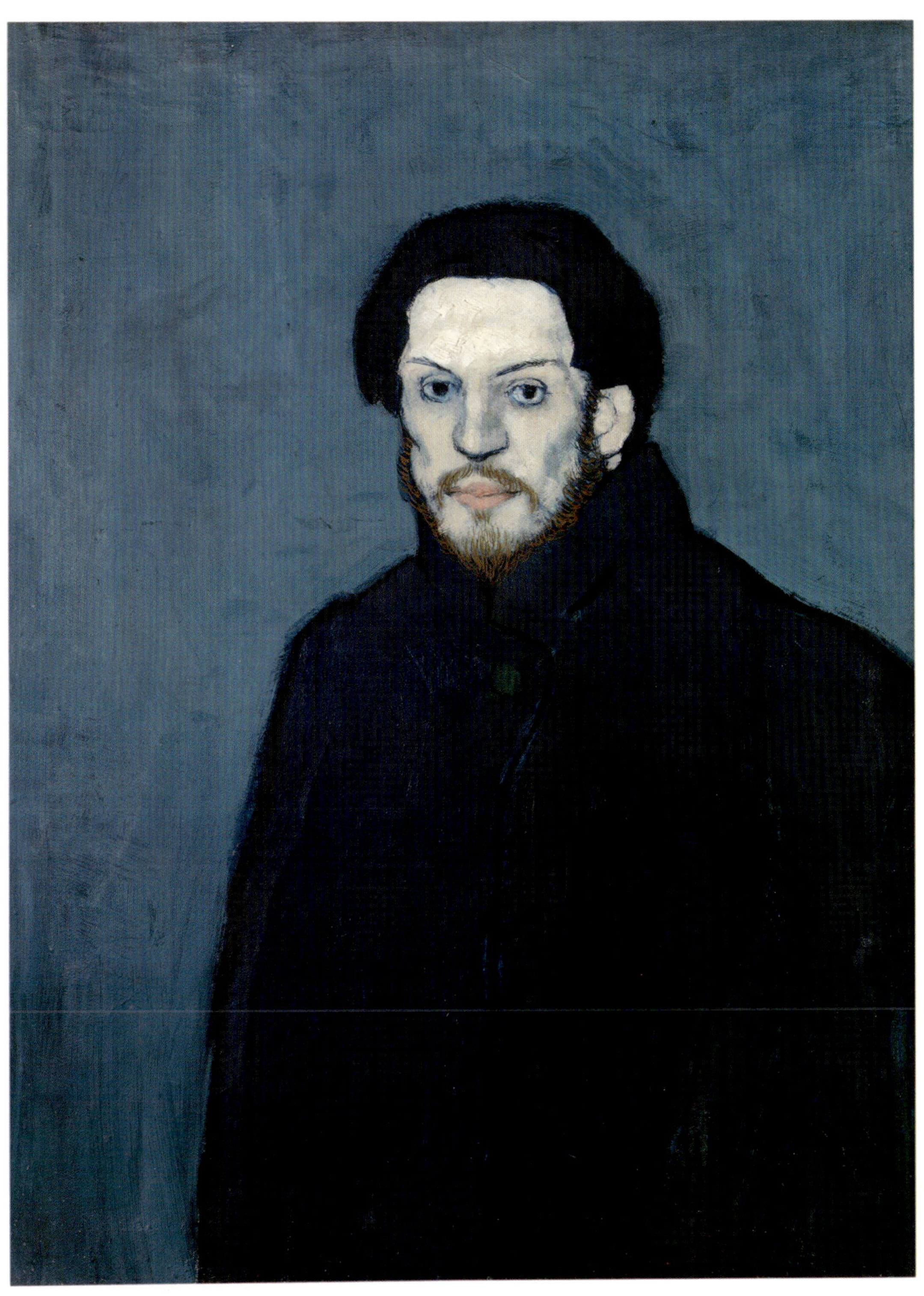

—
Fig. 43
Pablo Picasso
Self-Portrait
Paris, late 1901
Oil on canvas, 81 × 60 cm (32 ⁷⁄₈ × 23 ⁵⁄₈ in.)
Musée National Picasso-Paris
Dation Pablo Picasso, 1979. MP4
—

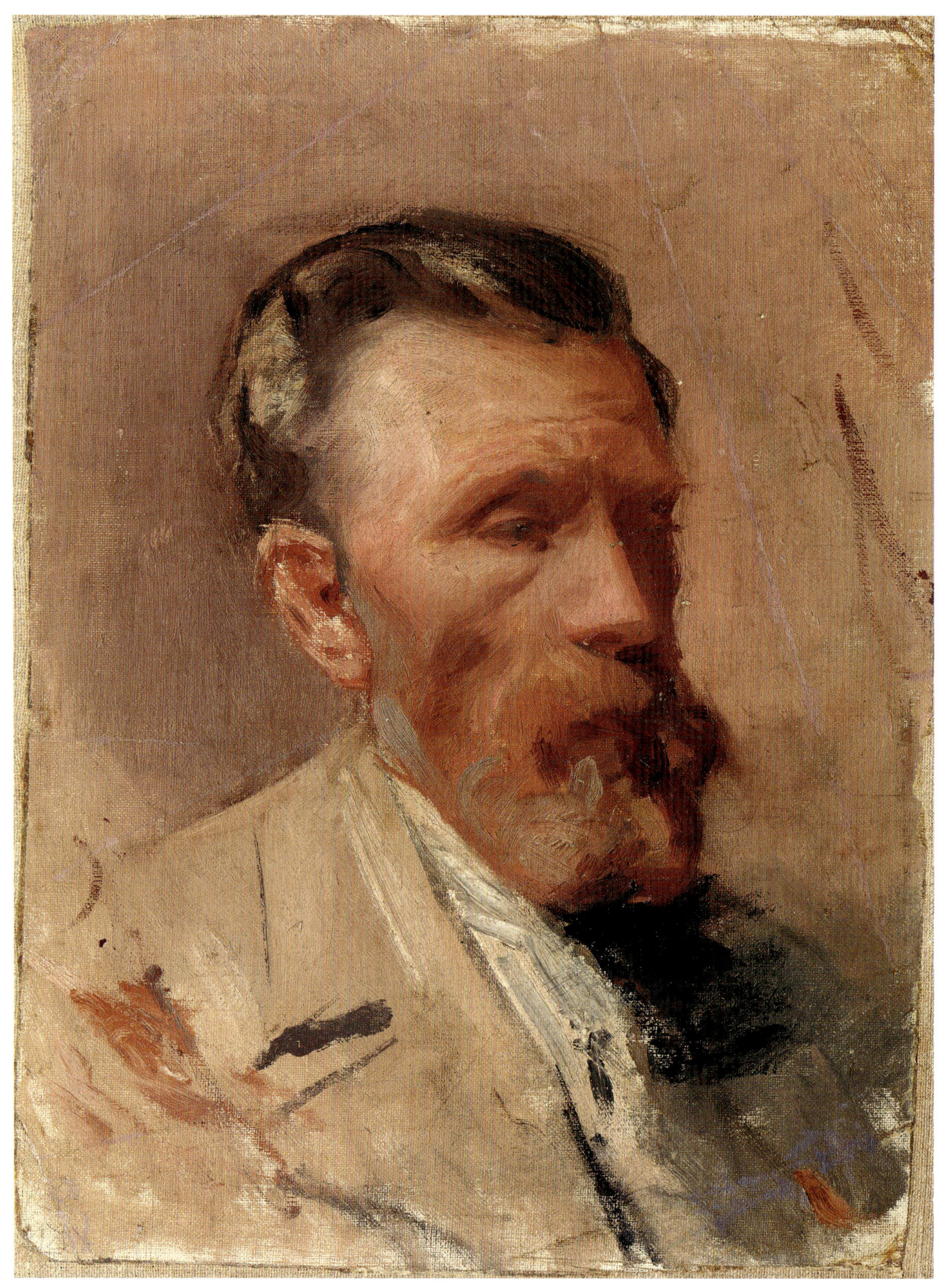

Pablo Picasso
The Artist's Father
Barcelona, c. 1896
Oil and graphite pencil on canvas, 42.3 × 30.8 cm (16 ⅝ × 12 ⅛ in.)
Museu Picasso, Barcelona
Donation Pablo Picasso, 1970. MPB 110.027

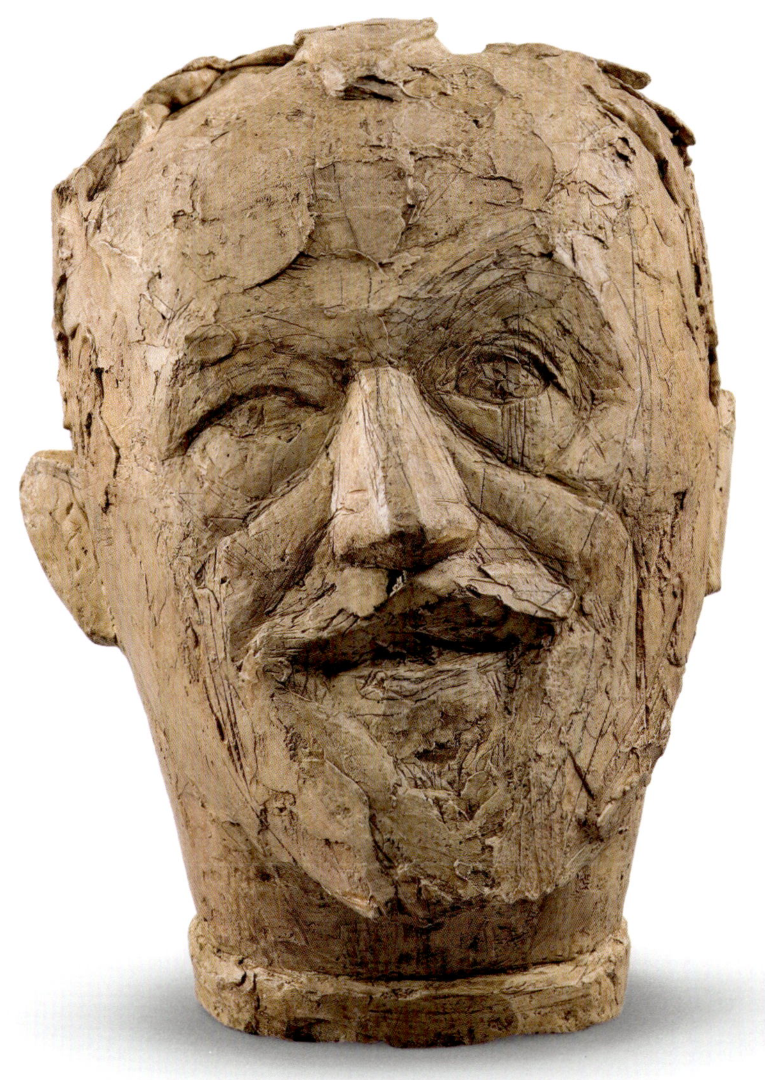

—
Fig. 45
Alberto Giacometti
Father's Head, Round II
c. 1927–1930
Plaster, 28.9 × 21.2 × 23 cm (11 ⅜ × 8 ⅜ × 9 in.)
Fondation Giacometti, Paris
—

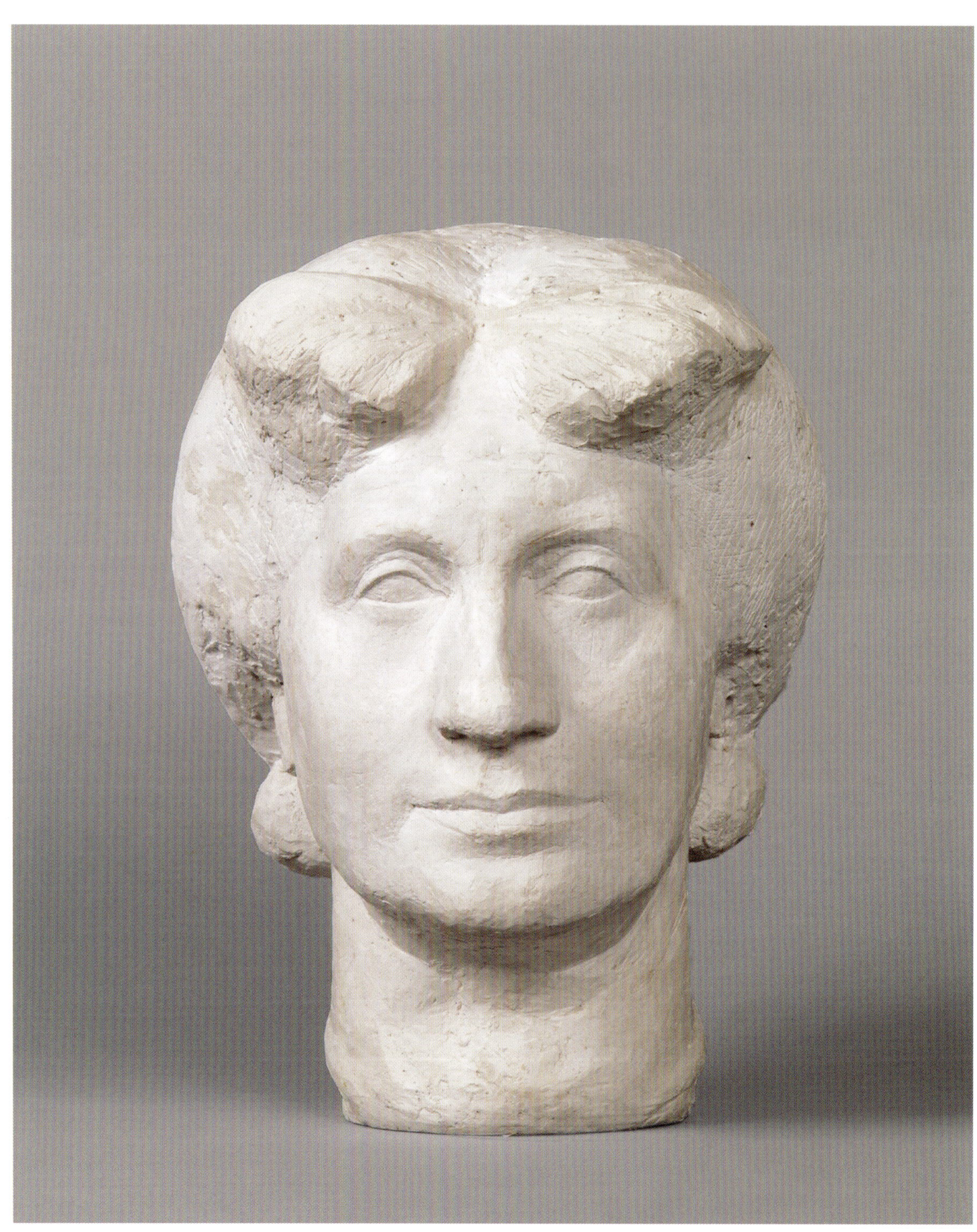

Fig. 46
Alberto Giacometti
Head (Large Head of the Mother)
c. 1925
Plaster, 31 × 22.8 × 27.5 cm (12 × 9 × 10 ⅞ in.)
Fondation Giacometti, Paris

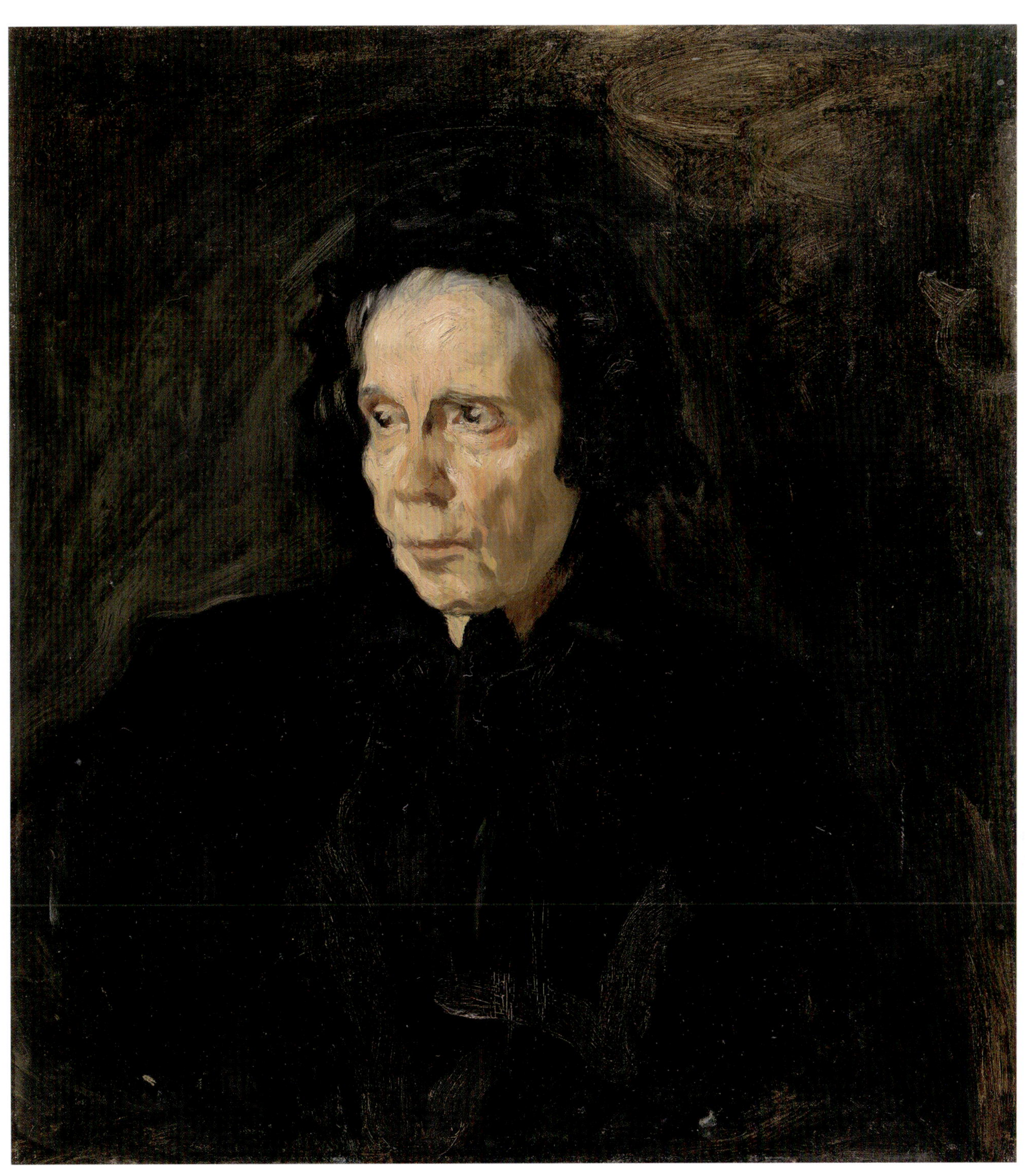

—
Fig. 47
Pablo Picasso
Aunt Pepa
Málaga, June–July 1896
Oil on canvas, 57.5 × 50.5 cm (22 ⅝ × 28 ⅜ in.)
Museu Picasso, Barcelona
Donation Pablo Picasso, 1970. MPB 110.010
—

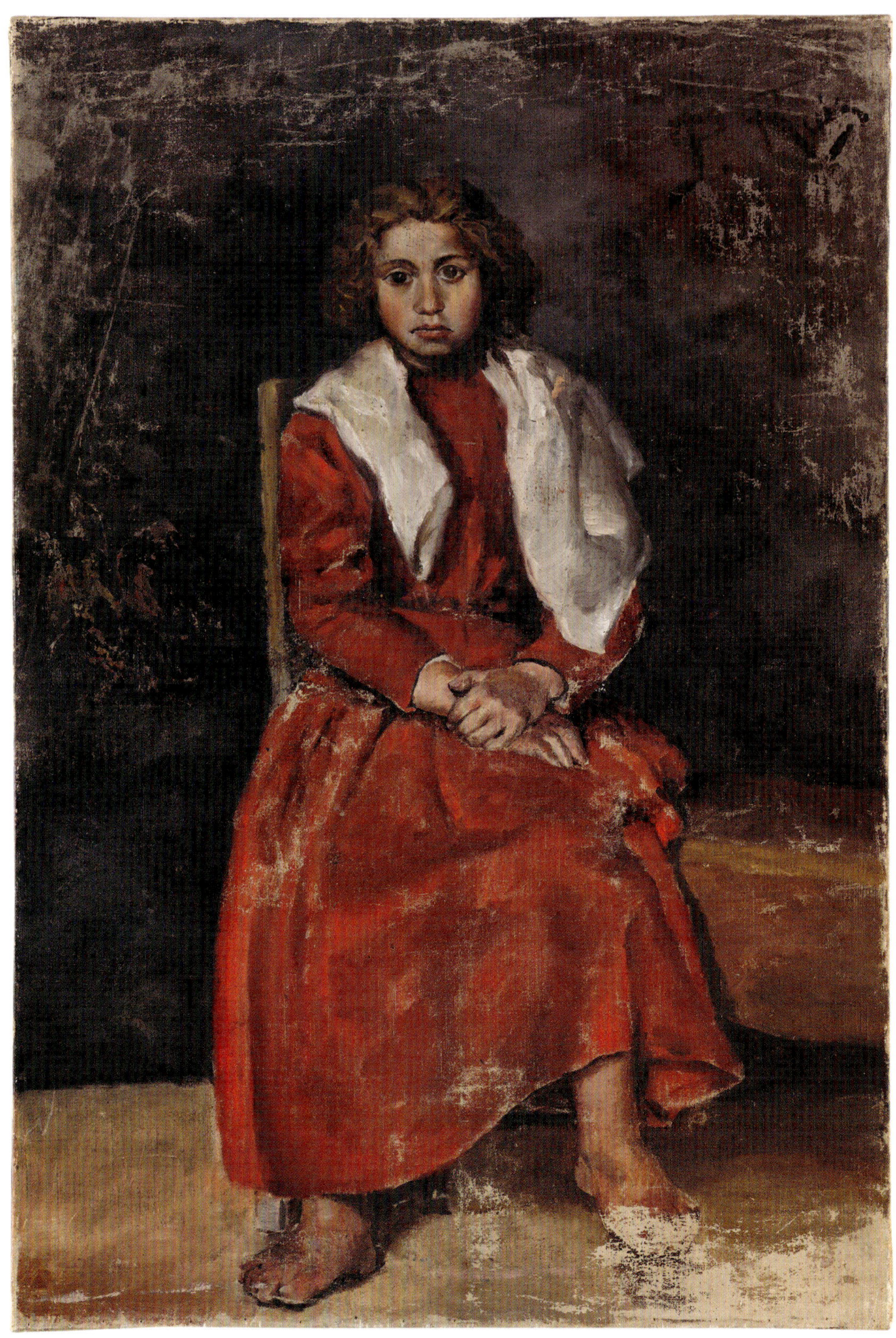

—
Fig. 48
Pablo Picasso
The Barefoot Girl
Corunna, early 1895
Oil on canvas, 75 × 50 cm (29 ½ × 19 ⅝ in.)
Musée National Picasso-Paris
Dation Pablo Picasso, 1979. MP2
—

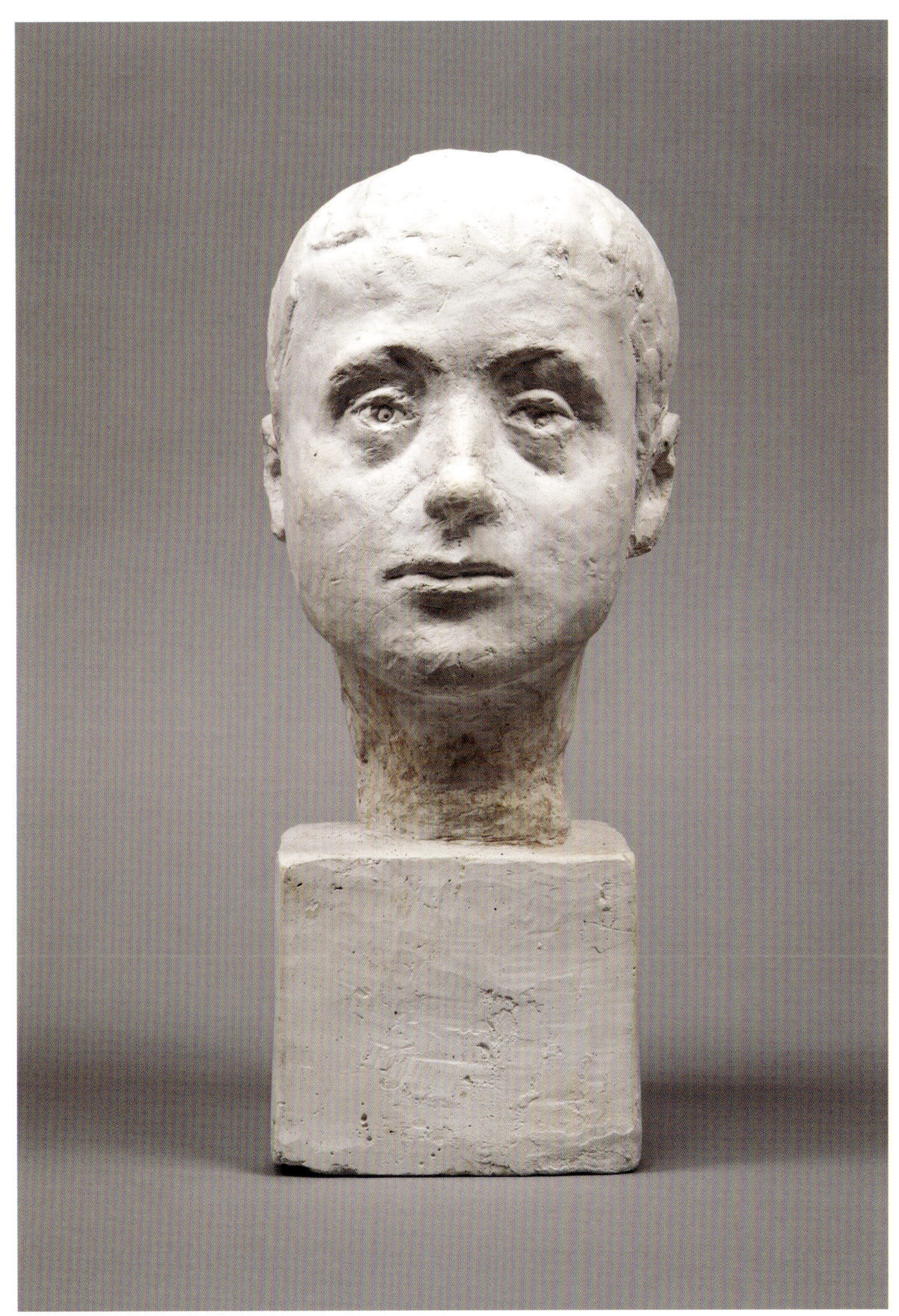

Fig. 49
Alberto Giacometti
Head of Diego as a Child
c. 1914–1915
Plaster, 27 × 11.1 × 13.8 cm (10 ⅝ × 4 ⅜ × 5 ⅜ in.)
Fondation Giacometti, Paris

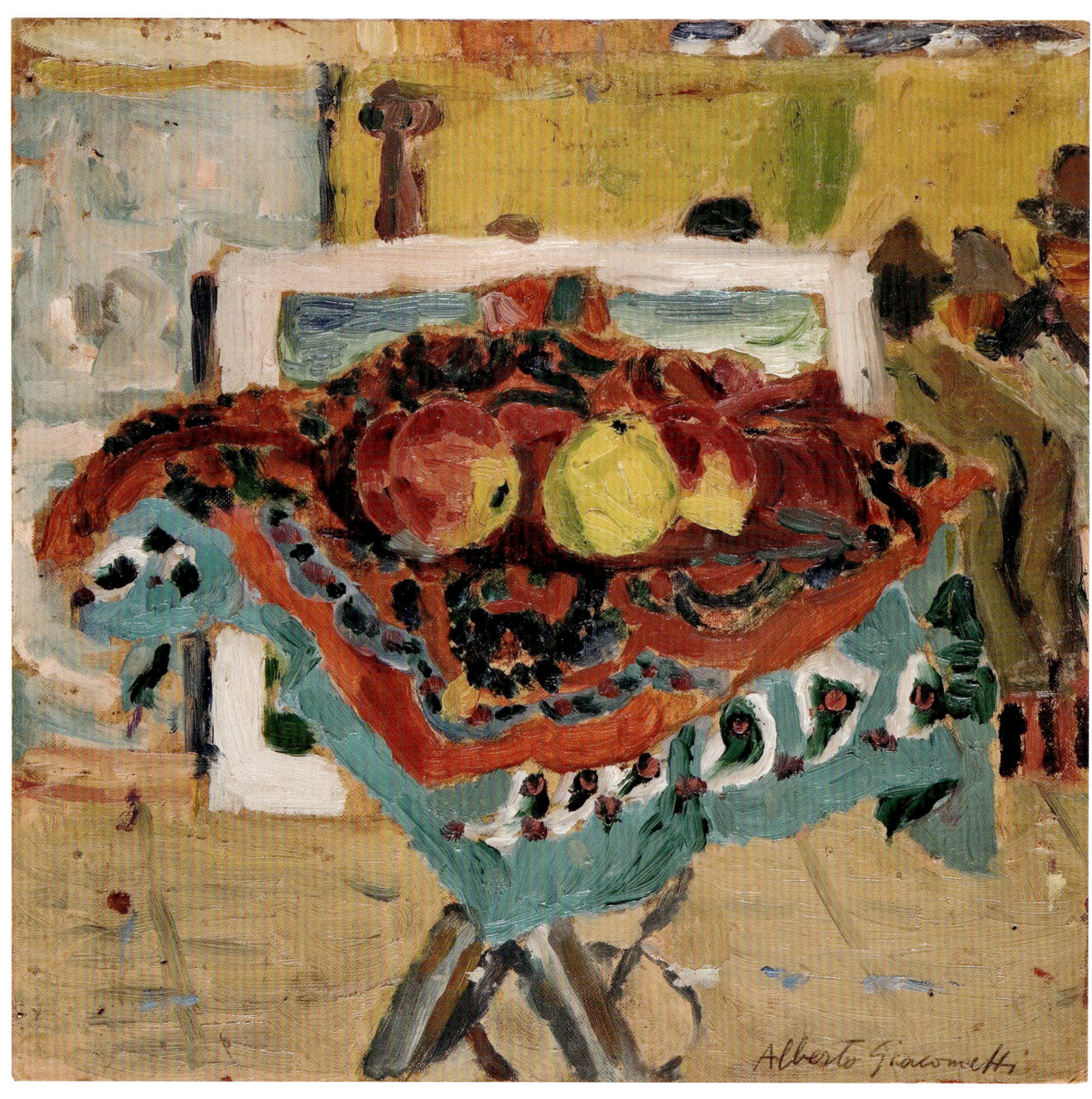

Fig. 50
Alberto Giacometti
Still Life with Apples
c. 1915
Oil on cardboard, 36.2 × 36.6 cm (14 ¼ × 14 ⅜ in.)
Fondation Giacometti, Paris

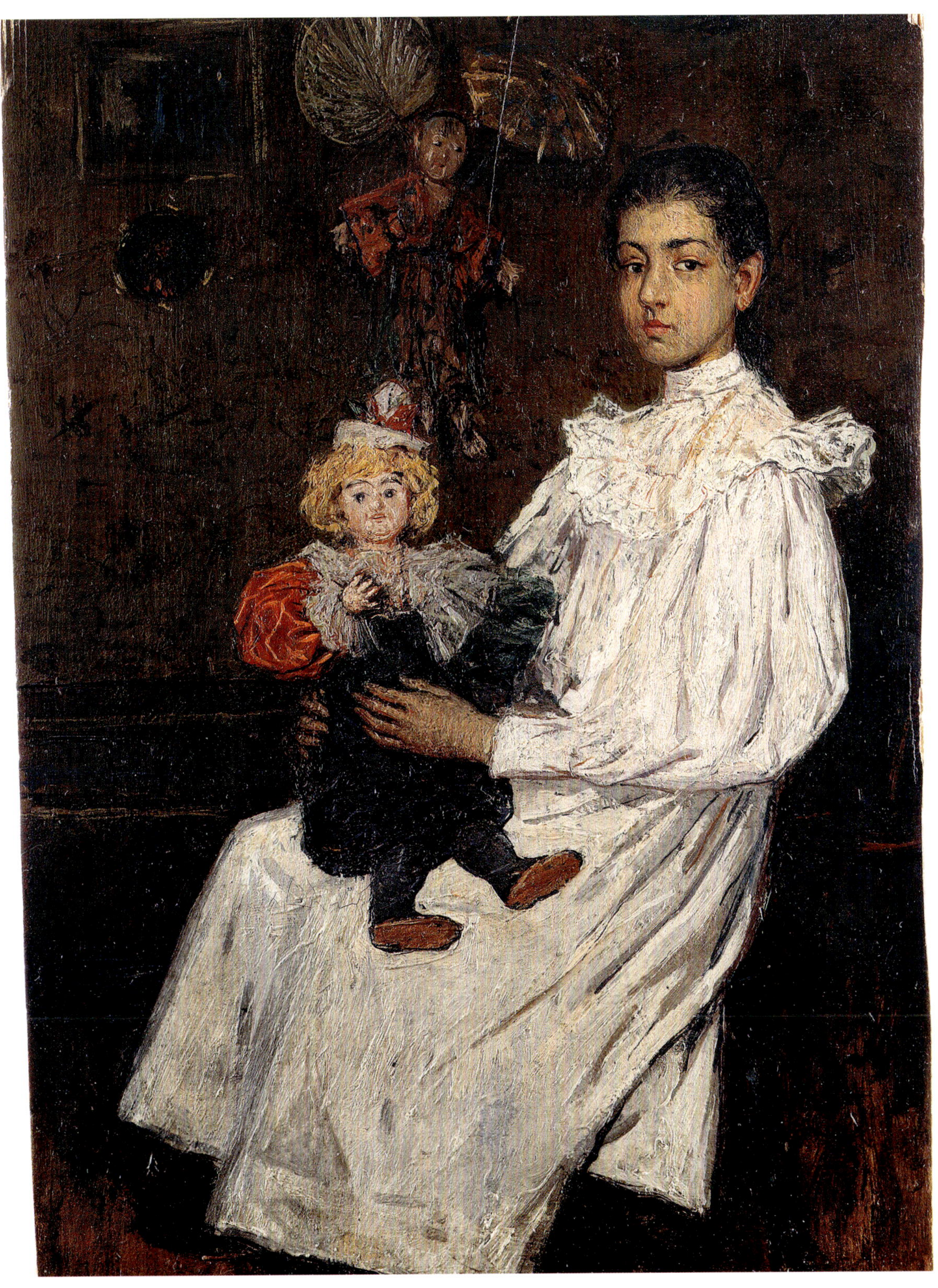

Fig. 51
Pablo Picasso
The Child and the Doll
Barcelona, 1896–1897
Oil on canvas, 35.5 × 22.5 cm (14 × 8 ⅞ in.)
Private collection. Courtesy Fundación Almine y Bernard Ruiz-Picasso
para el Arte, on loan to the Museo Picasso, Málaga

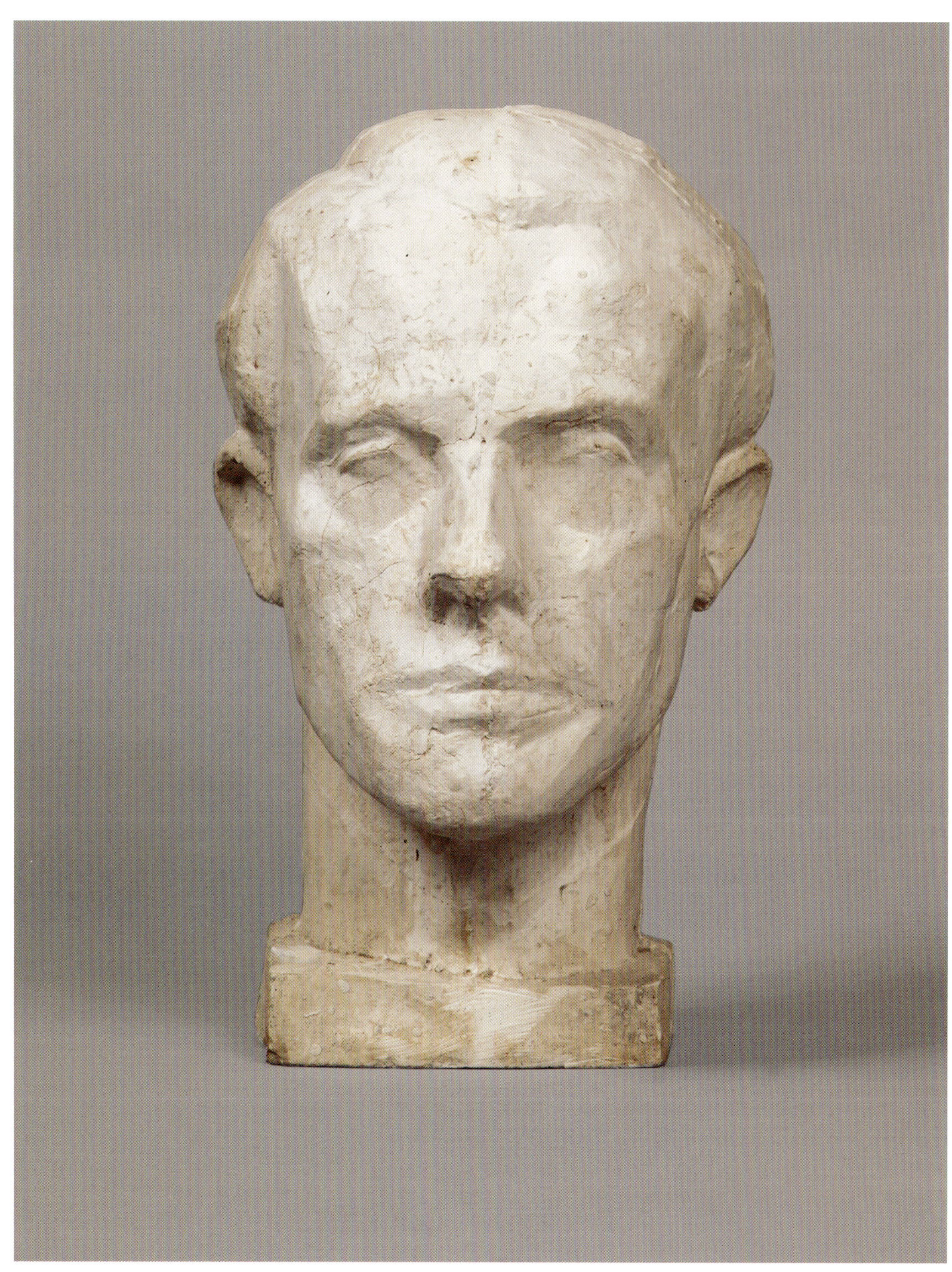

—
Fig. 52
Alberto Giacometti
Head of Diego
c. 1934
Plaster, 31 × 18.2 × 23.9 cm (12 × 7 ⅛ × 9 ⅜ in.)
Fondation Giacometti, Paris
—

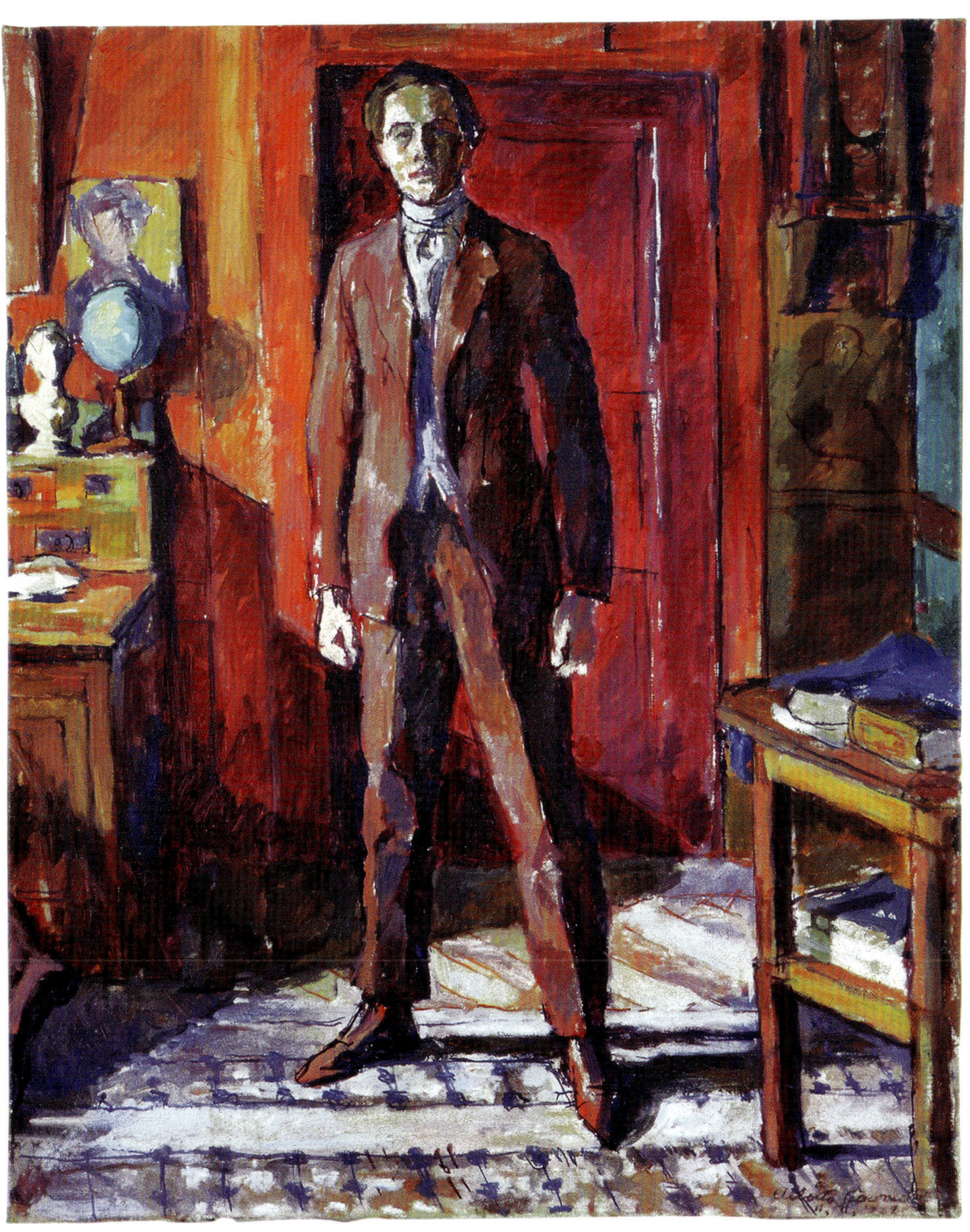

Fig. 53
Alberto Giacometti
Diego Standing in the Living Room at Stampa
1922
Oil on canvas, 63.6 × 50.2 (25 × 19 ¾ in.)
Fondation Giacometti, Paris

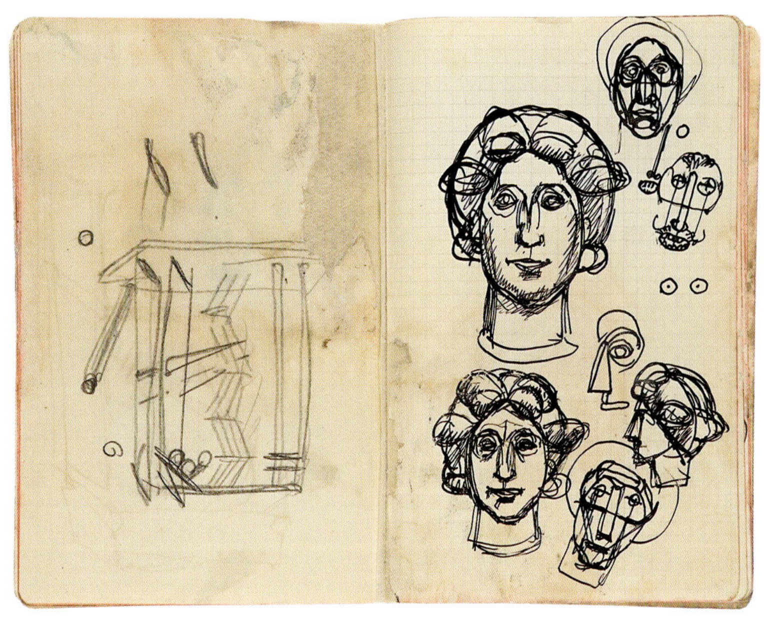

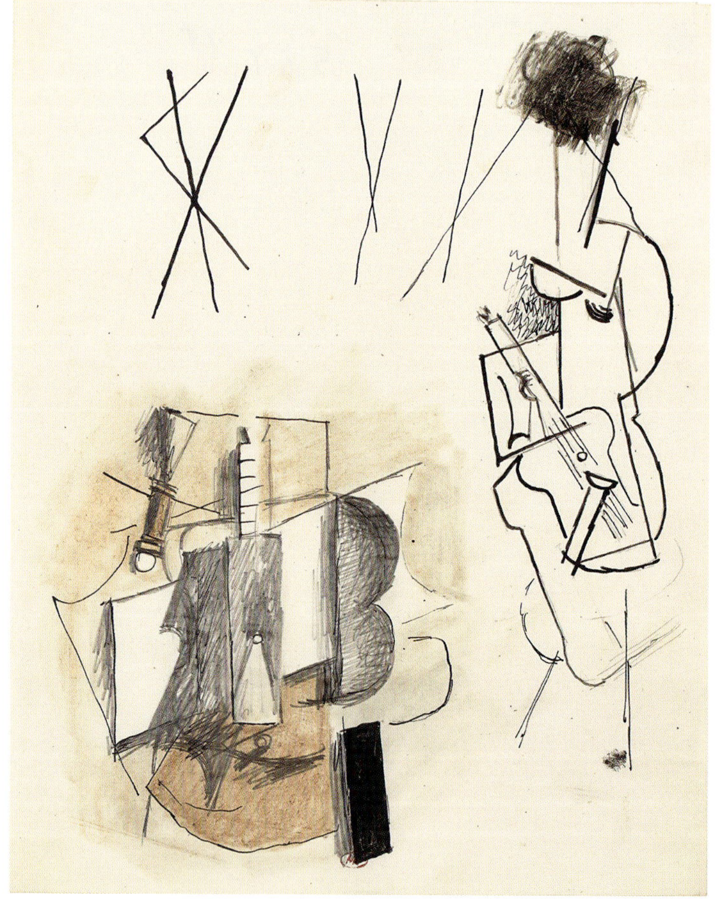

—
Fig. 54
Alberto Giacometti
Sketches for **Three Figures Outdoors**
and **Head of Mother**
c. 1929–1930
Graphite pencil and black ink on notebook page,
17.3 × 10.8 cm (6 ⁷⁄₈ × 4 ¼ in.)
Fondation Giacometti, Paris
—
Fig. 55
Pablo Picasso
Studies for **Guitar and Bottle of Bass**
1913
Pen, India ink, graphite pencil, brown pencil
and frottage on fine-textured wove paper,
27.5 × 21.4 cm (10 ⁷⁄₈ × 8 ½ in.)
Musée National Picasso-Paris
Dation Pablo Picasso, 1979. MP709
—

From Traditional to Modern Sculpture

Early sculptures by both Picasso and Giacometti followed the visual conventions established by Auguste Rodin. While Giacometti studied under Antoine Bourdelle at the Grande Chaumière art academy in Paris, Picasso never trained as a sculptor. Yet when the two artists realised the impossibility of 'truthfully' creating a portrait sculpture in the realist style, the solutions they developed took parallel trajectories. Giacometti followed in the footsteps of the older artist, whose work he discovered upon his arrival in Paris in 1922. He abandoned the classical style as seen in the head of his sister Ottilia (c. 1925) for the stylised lines and multifaceted Cubist planes used by Picasso in the 1909 portrait sculpture of his companion, Fernande Olivier.

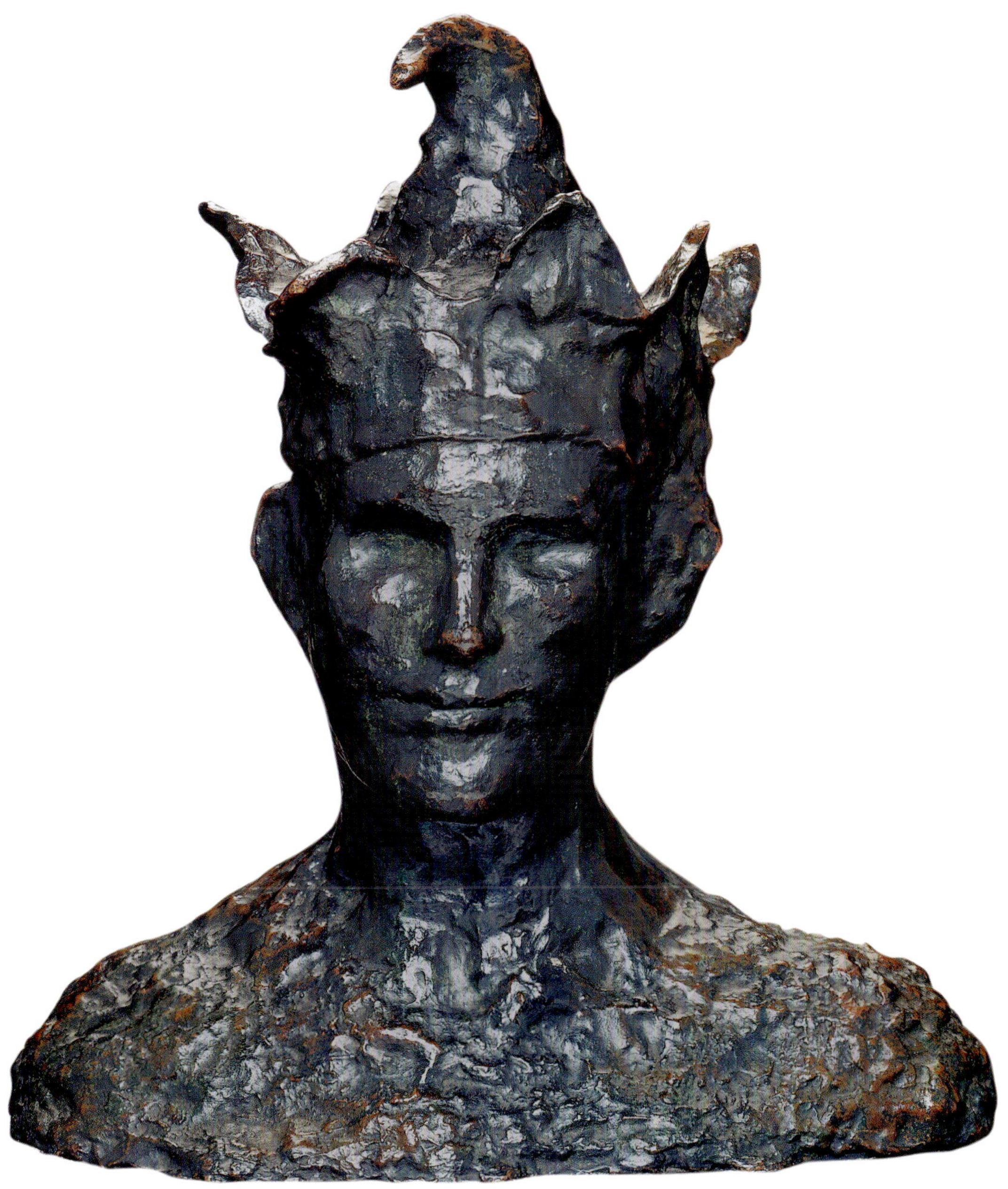

Fig. 56
Pablo Picasso
The Jester
Paris, 1905
Bronze, 41.5 × 37 × 22 cm (16 ⅜ × 14 ½ × 8 ⅝ in.)
Fondation Pierre Gianadda collection, Martigny (Switzerland)

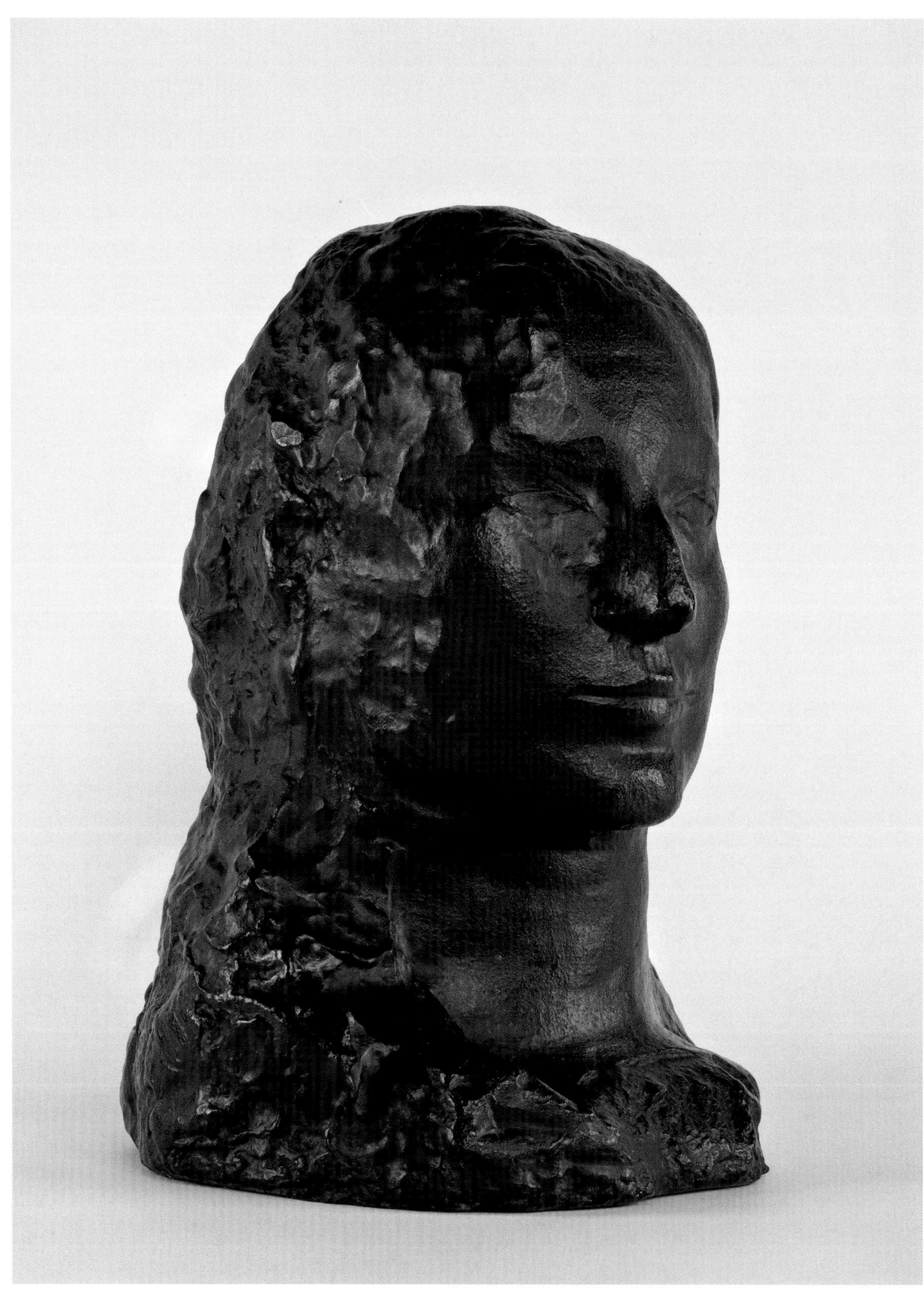

—
Fig. 57
Pablo Picasso
Head of a Woman (Fernande)
Paris, 1906
Bronze, 35 × 24 × 25 cm (13 ¾ × 9 ½ × 9 ⅞ in.)
Musée National Picasso-Paris
Dation Pablo Picasso, 1979. MP234
—

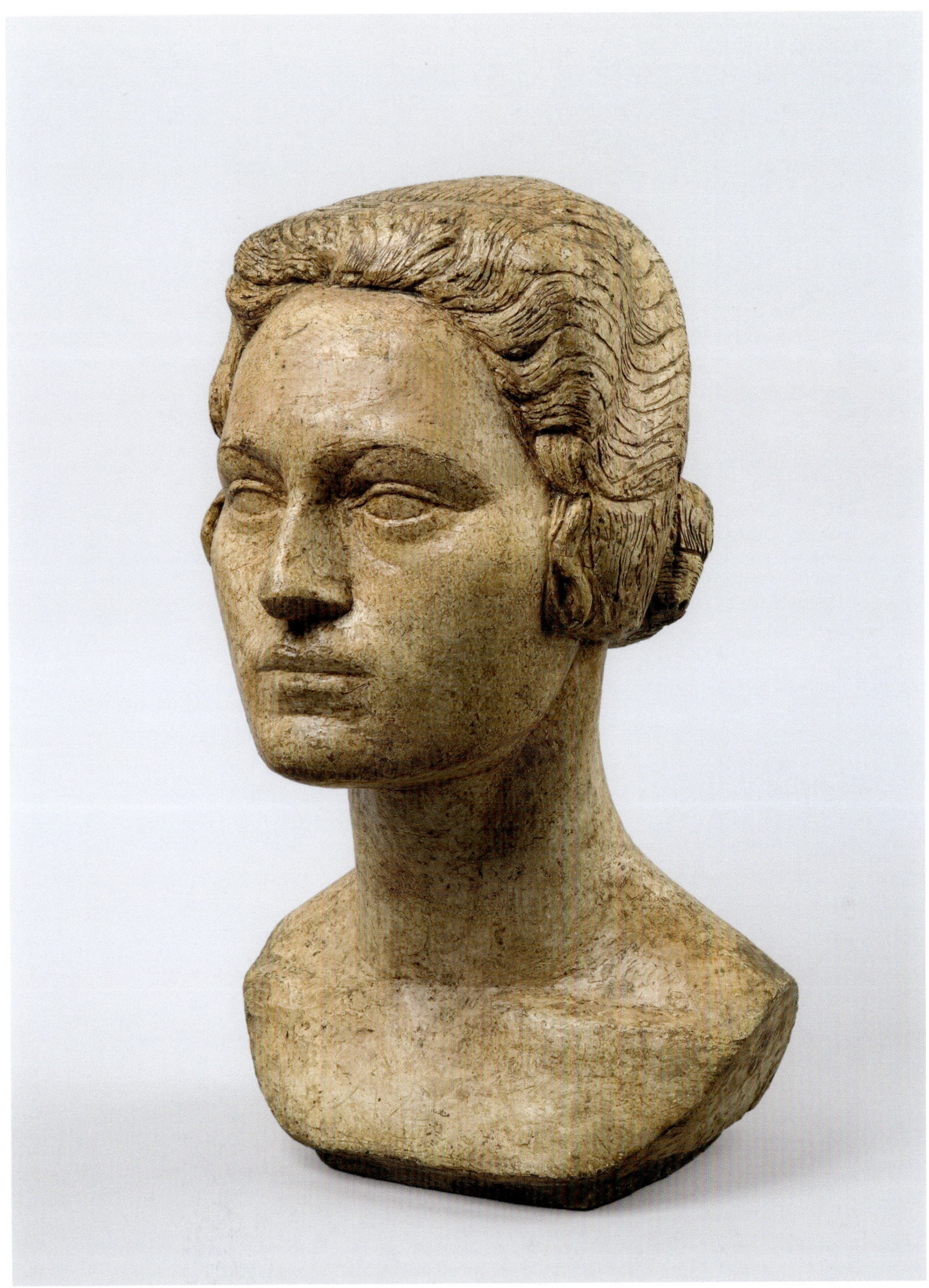

—
Fig. 58
Alberto Giacometti
Head of Ottilia
c. 1925
Plaster, 38 × 21.5 × 16.6 cm (15 × 8 ⅛ × 6 ½ in.)
Fondation Giacometti, Paris
—

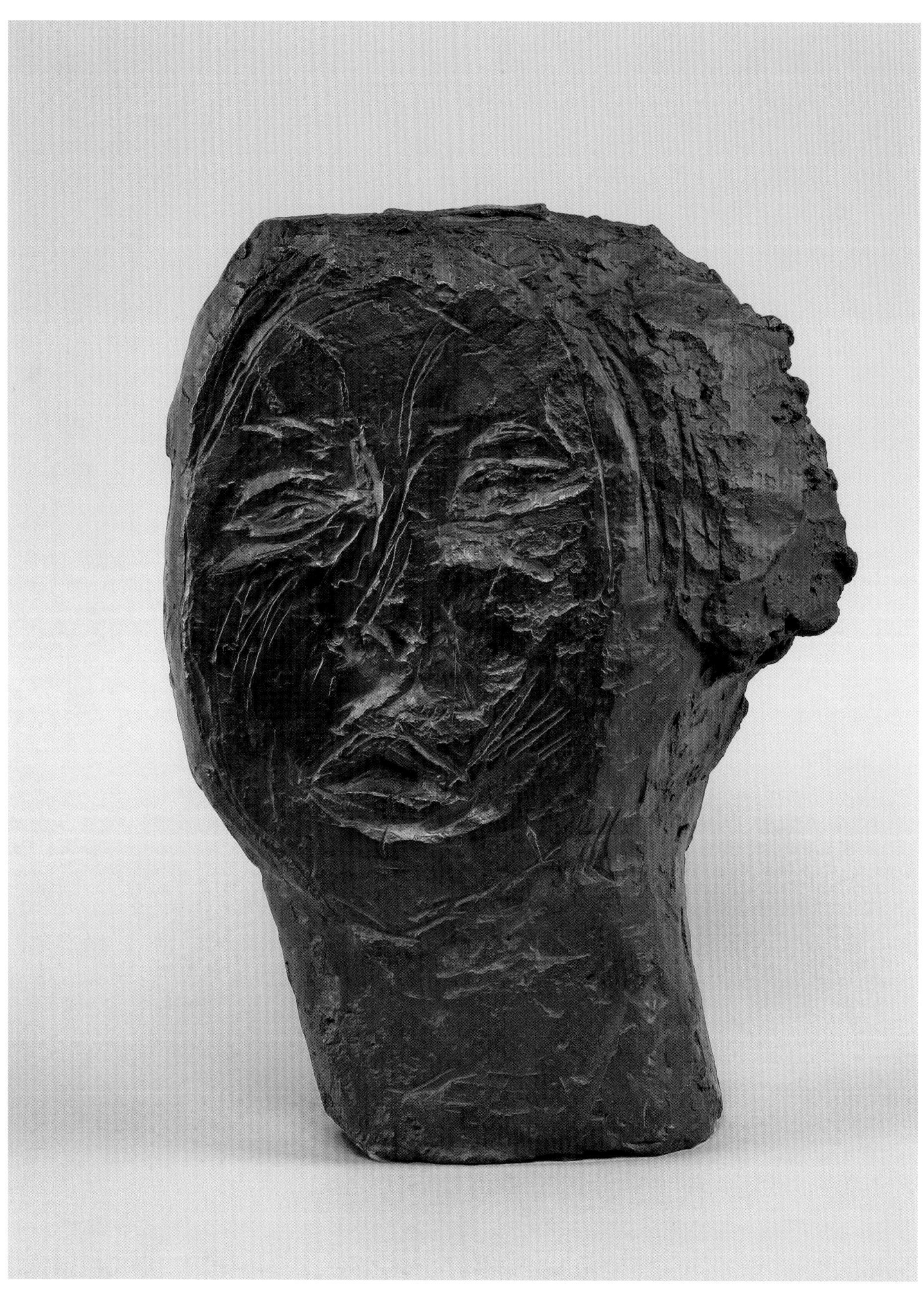

Fig. 59
Alberto Giacometti
Head of a Woman (Flora Mayo)
1926
Bronze, 30.3 × 23.1 × 8.6 cm (12 × 9 × 3 ⅜ in.)
Fondation Giacometti, Paris

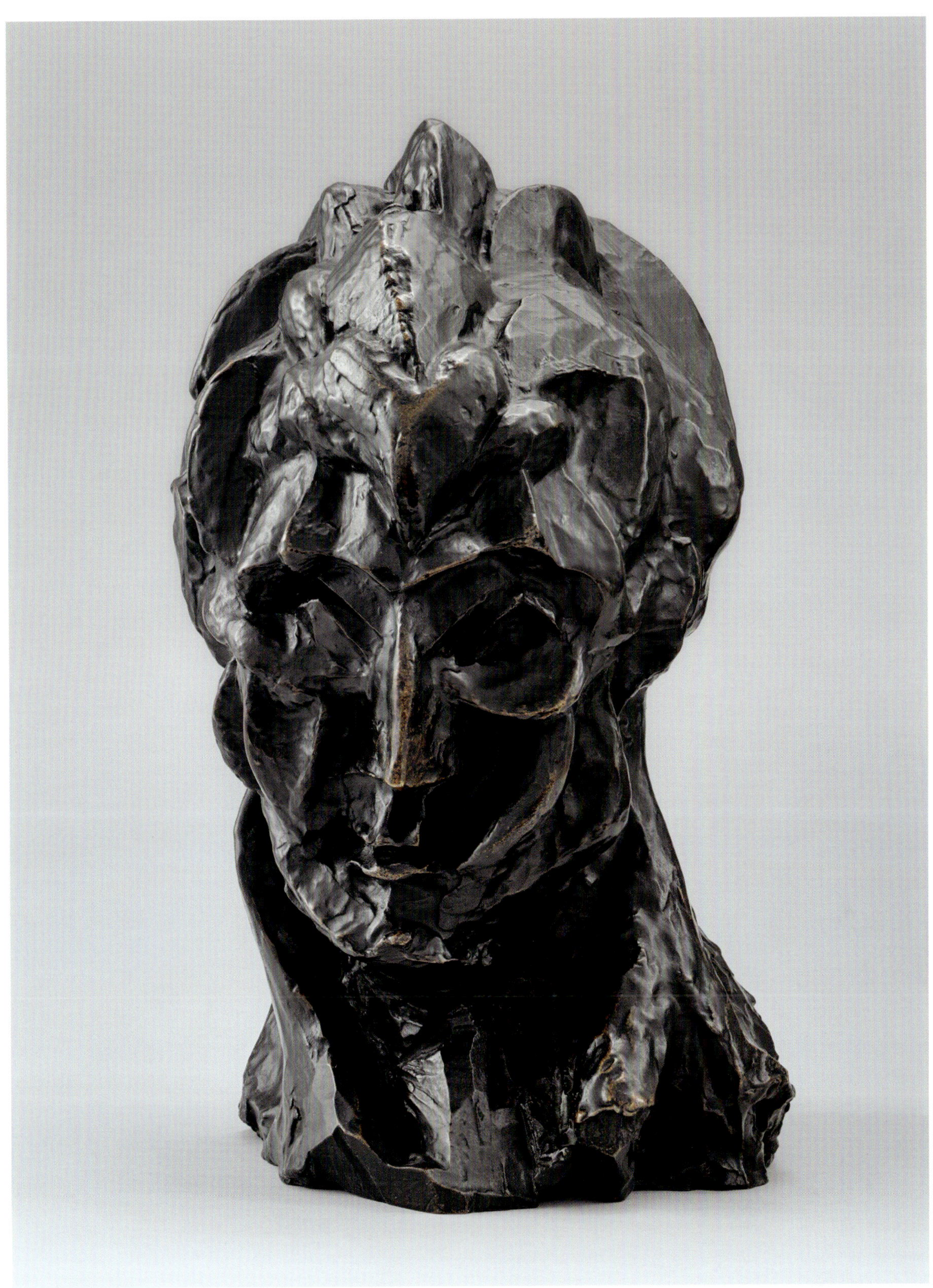

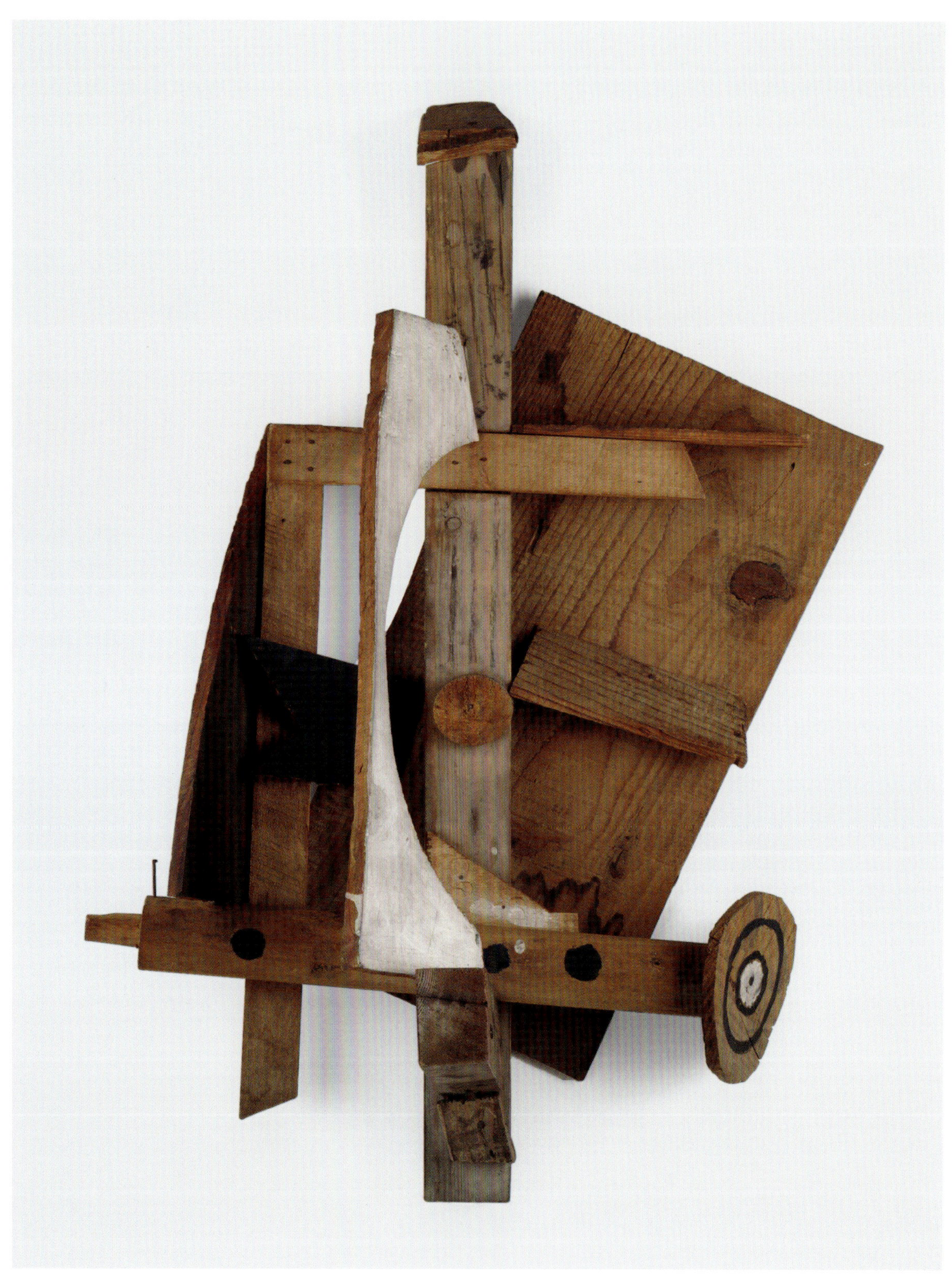

Pablo Picasso
Mandolin and Clarinet
Paris, autumn 1913
Fir wood, paint and pencil, 58 × 36 × 23 cm (22 ⅞ × 14 ⅛ × 9 in.)
Musée National Picasso-Paris
Dation Pablo Picasso, 1979. MP247

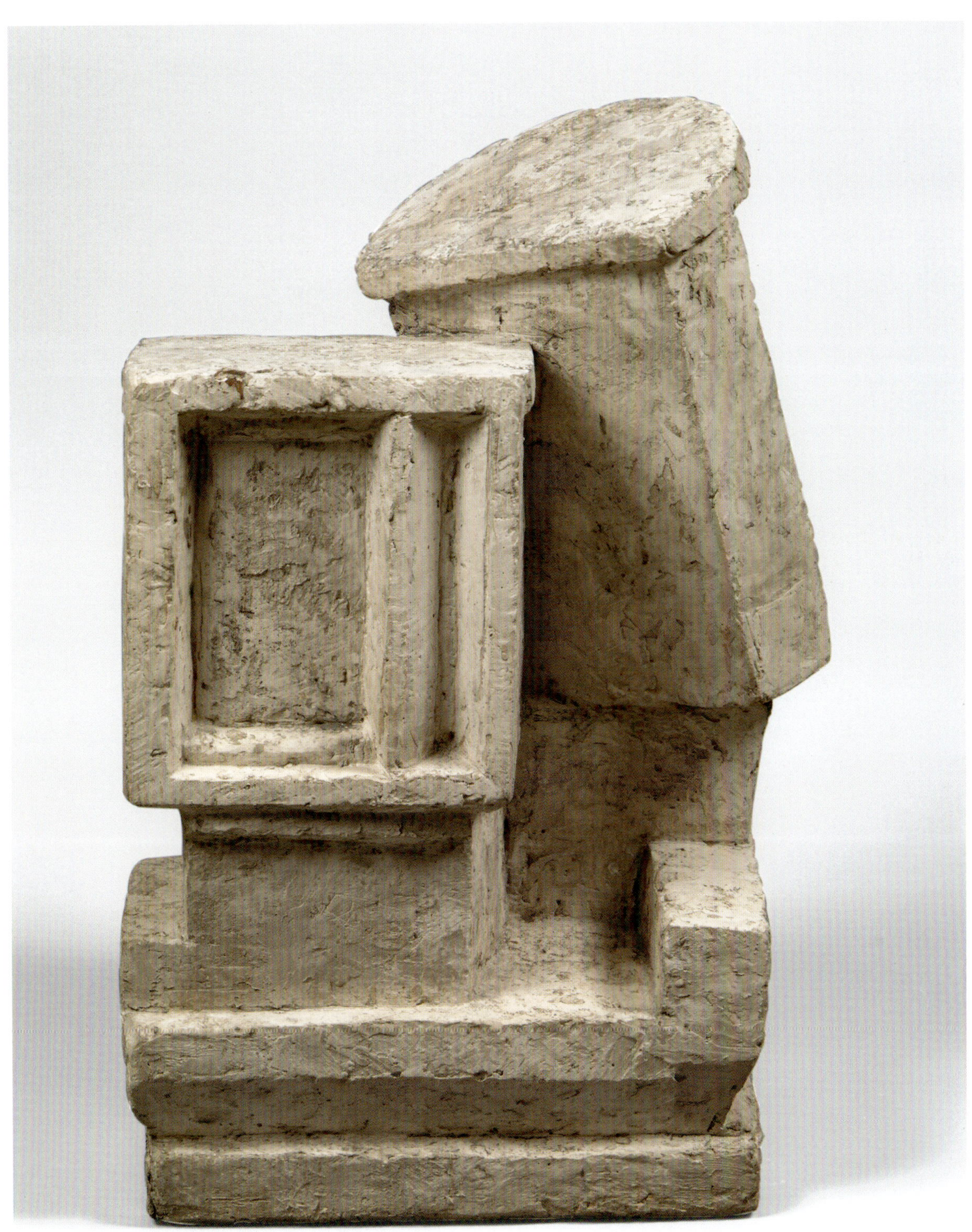

—
Fig. 62
Alberto Giacometti
Composition (Cubist I, Couple)
c. 1926–1927
Plaster, 68.2 × 45 × 38.6 cm (26 ⅞ × 14 ⅛ × 9 in.)
Fondation Giacometti, Paris
—

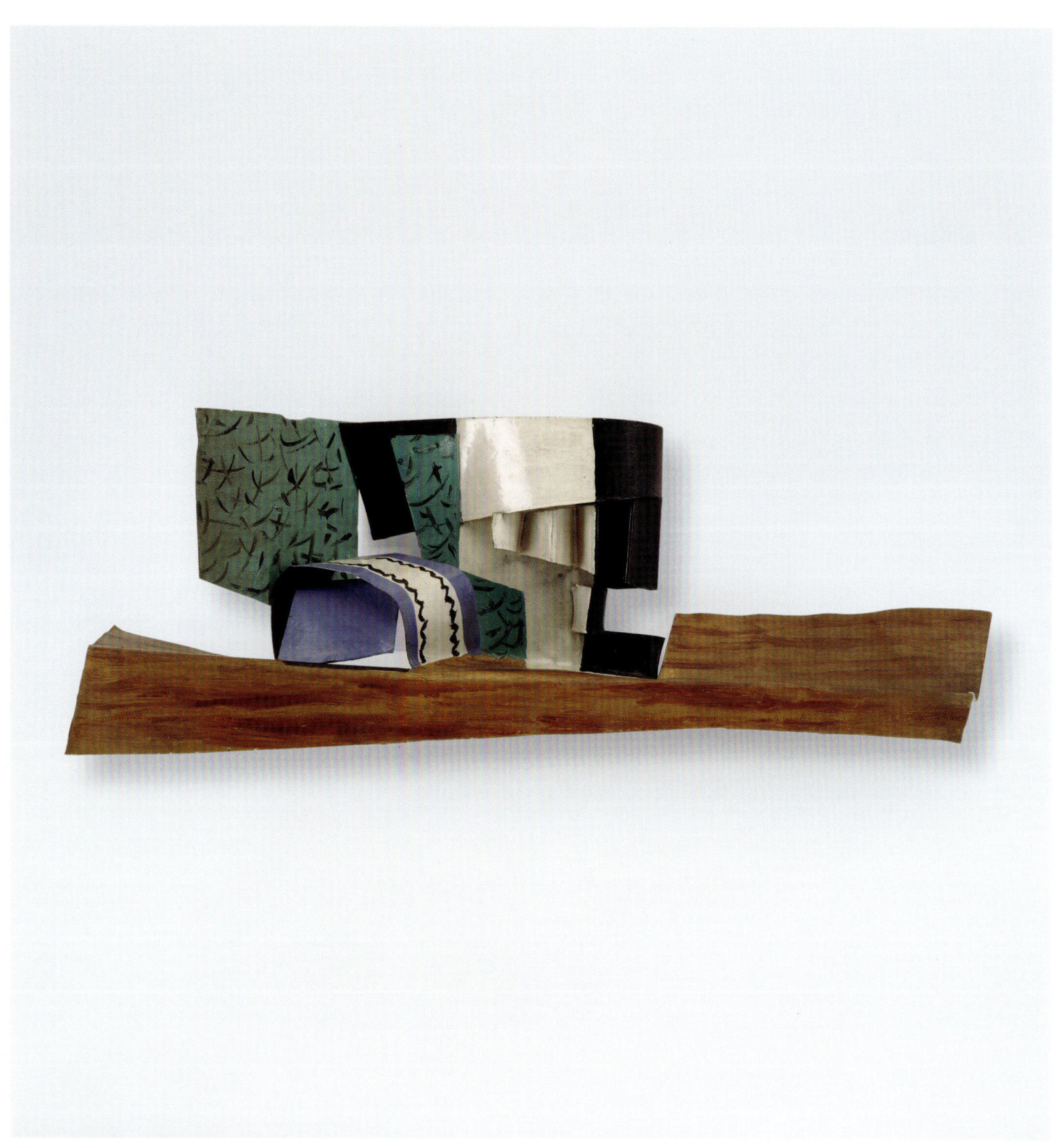

—
Fig. 63
Pablo Picasso
Glass and Packet of Tobacco
Paris, 1921
Cut-out, folded and painted sheet-iron, and wire,
14.7 × 48.5 × 17.5 cm (5 ⅞ × 19 × 6 ⅞ in.)
Musée National Picasso-Paris
Dation Pablo Picasso, 1979. MP259
—

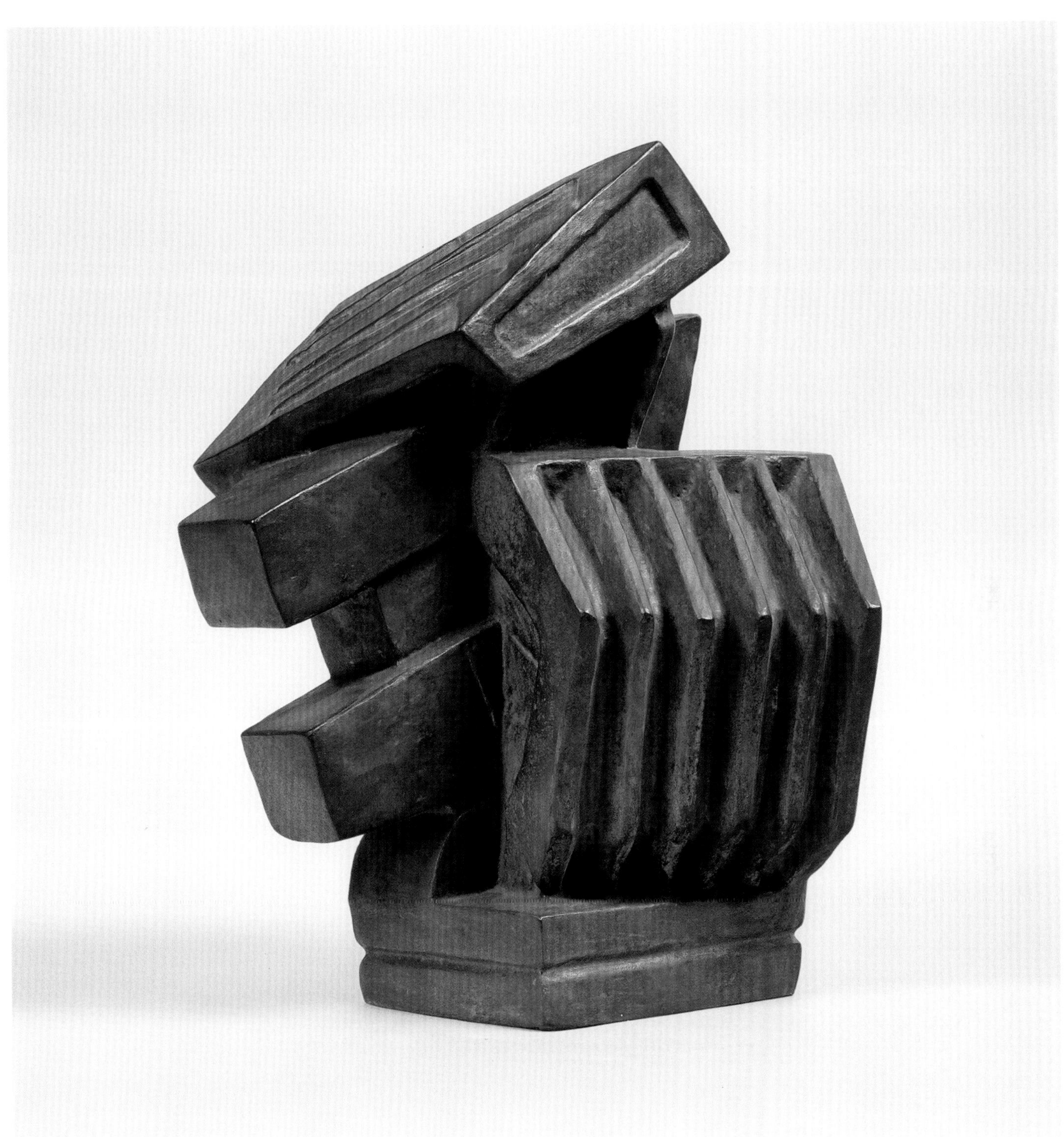

—
Fig. 64
Alberto Giacometti
Composition (Cubist II)
c. 1927
Bronze, 38.2 × 28.4 × 27.1 cm
(15 × 11 ¼ × 10 ⅝ in.)
Fondation Giacometti, Paris
—

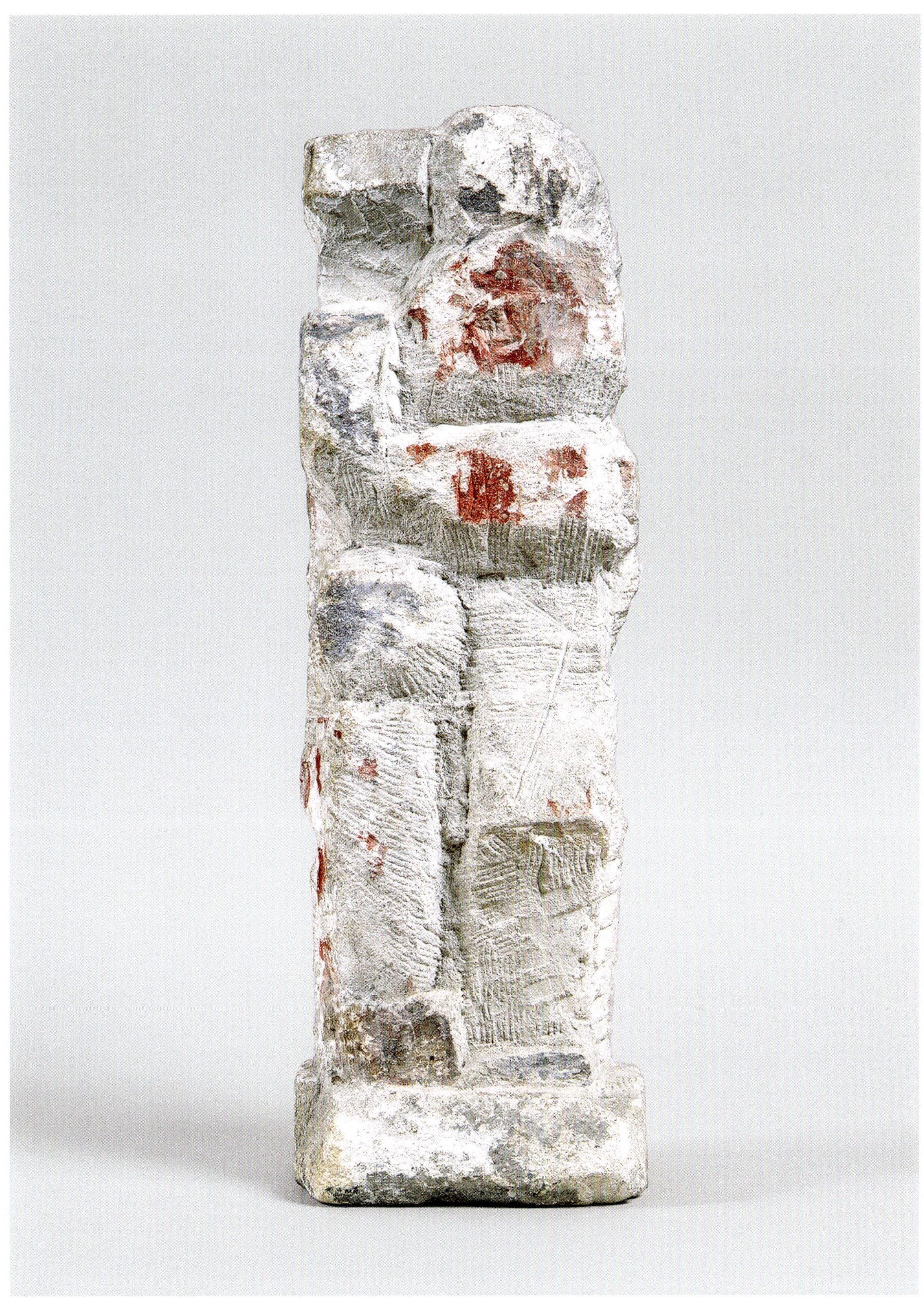

—
Fig. 65
Alberto Giacometti
Couple
c. 1925–1927
Painted stone, 49.5 × 16.4 × 15.1 cm
(19 ½ × 6 ½ × 6 in.)
Fondation Giacometti, Paris
—

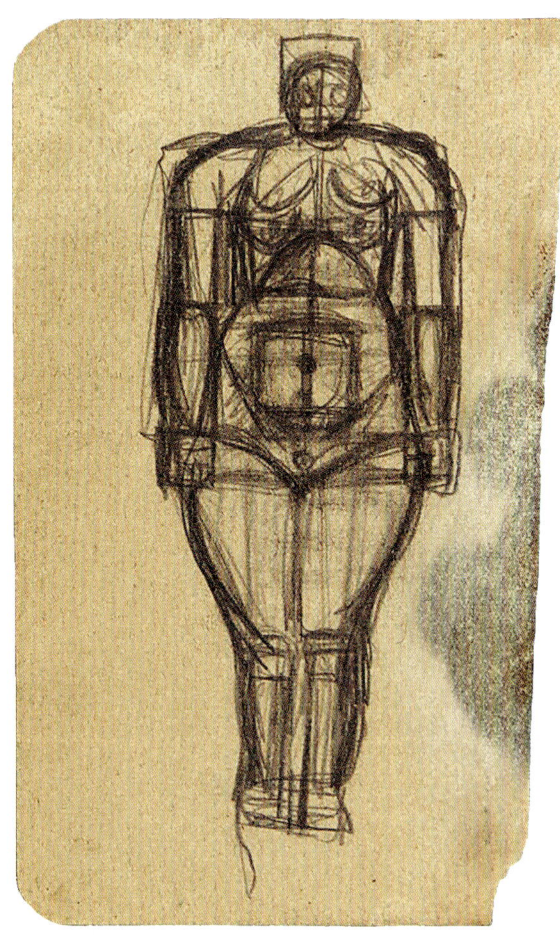

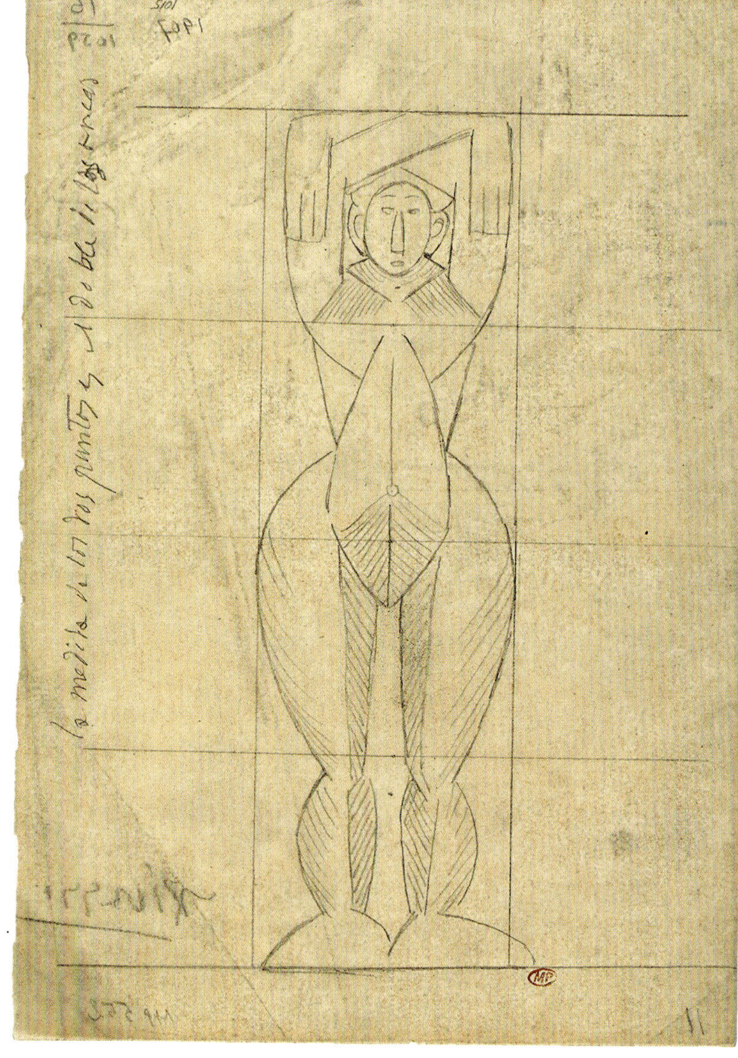

—
Fig. 66
Alberto Giacometti
Standing Woman
n. d.
Graphite pencil on a sheet from a sketchbook,
14.6 × 9 cm (5 ¾ × 3 ½ in.)
Fondation Giacometti, Paris

—
Fig. 67
Pablo Picasso
*Study of a Nude with Hieratic Face, Arms Crossed
above the Head with Handwritten Notes Showing
the Proportions*
Paris, La-Rue-des-Bois, 1908
Graphite pencil on squared-up tracing paper,
31 × 21 cm (12 ¼ × 8 ¼ in.)
Musée National Picasso-Paris
Dation Pablo Picasso, 1979. MP552
—

Other Influences

Picasso and Giacometti were keen observers of non-Western art and archaeological objects. They drew inspiration from art reviews and the collections of the Louvre and the Musée d'Ethnographie du Trocadéro, taking details of masks, shields and statuettes, and re-imagining them in their own way. Picasso's totems and Giacometti's steles display the same stylised forms and evoke the same magical quality as artworks from the Cyclades, Asian antiquities and sculptures from Africa and Oceania.

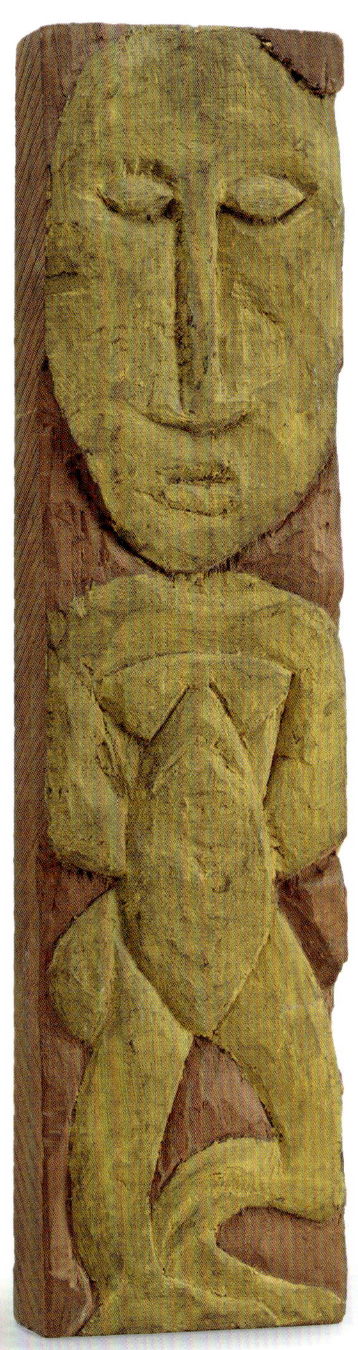

Fig. 68
Pablo Picasso
Standing Nude
Paris, 1907
Fruit-tree wood, carved with a chisel and painted,
31.8 × 8 × 2.7 cm (12 ½ × 3 ⅛ × 1 in.)
Musée National Picasso-Paris
Dation Pablo Picasso, 1979. MP236(r)

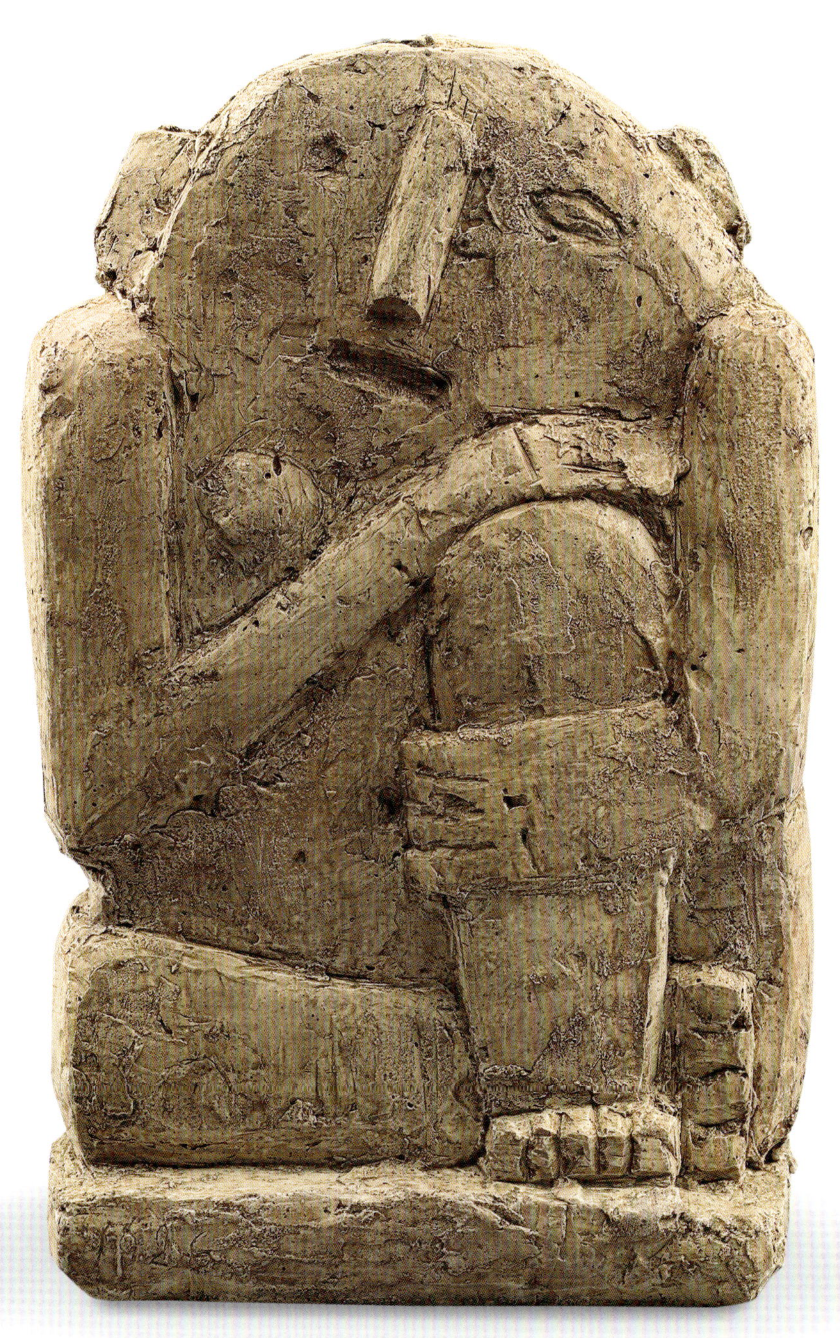

Fig. 69
Alberto Giacometti
Squatting Figure
c. 1926
Plaster, 29 × 18 × 10 cm (11 ½ × 7 × 4 in.)
Fondation Giacometti, Paris

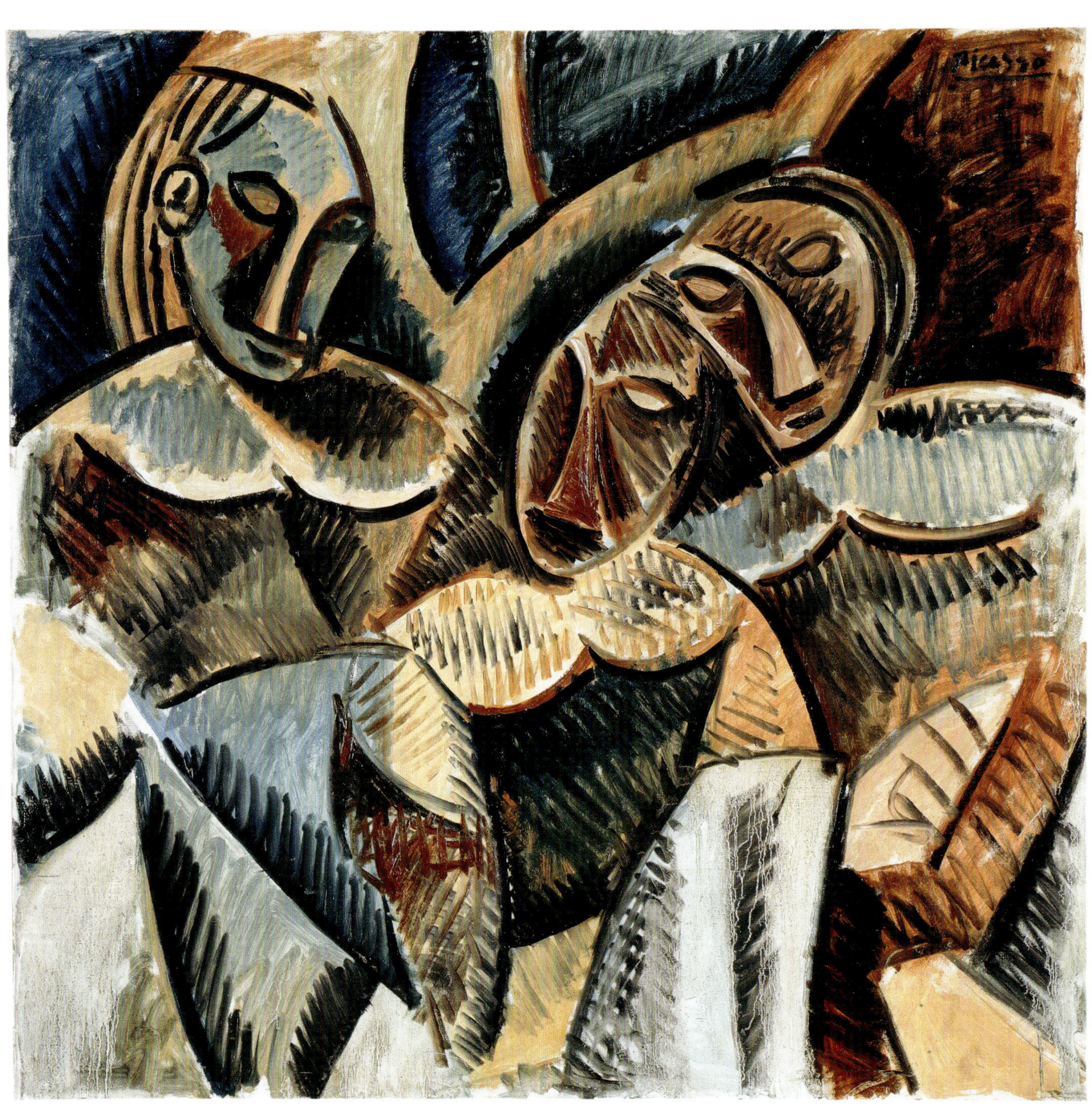

—
Fig. 70
Pablo Picasso
Three Figures under a Tree
Paris, winter 1907–1908
Oil on canvas, 99 × 99 cm (3 ft. 3 in. × 3 ft. 3 in.)
Musée National Picasso-Paris
Gift of William A. McCarty Cooper, 1986. MP1986-2
—

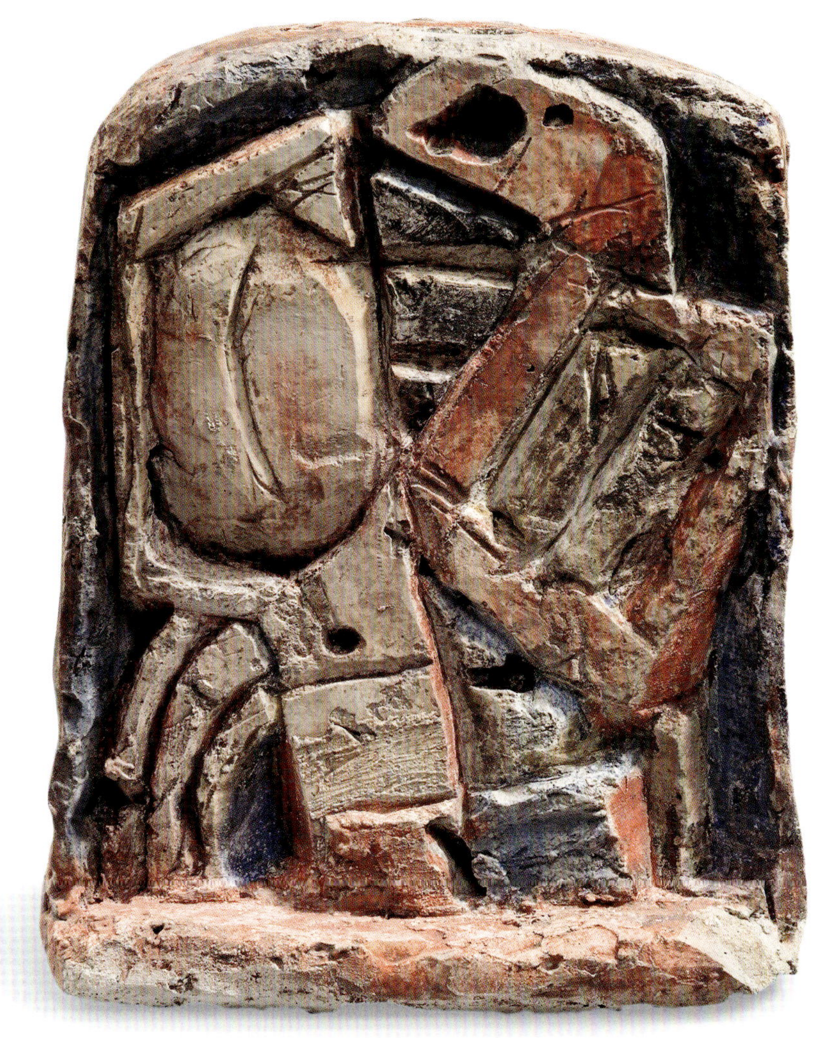

Fig. 71
Alberto Giacometti
Stele
c. 1925–1927
Painted plaster, 24.4 × 19.4 × 8 cm (9 ⅝ × 7 ⅝ × 3 ⅛ in.)
Fondation Giacometti, Paris

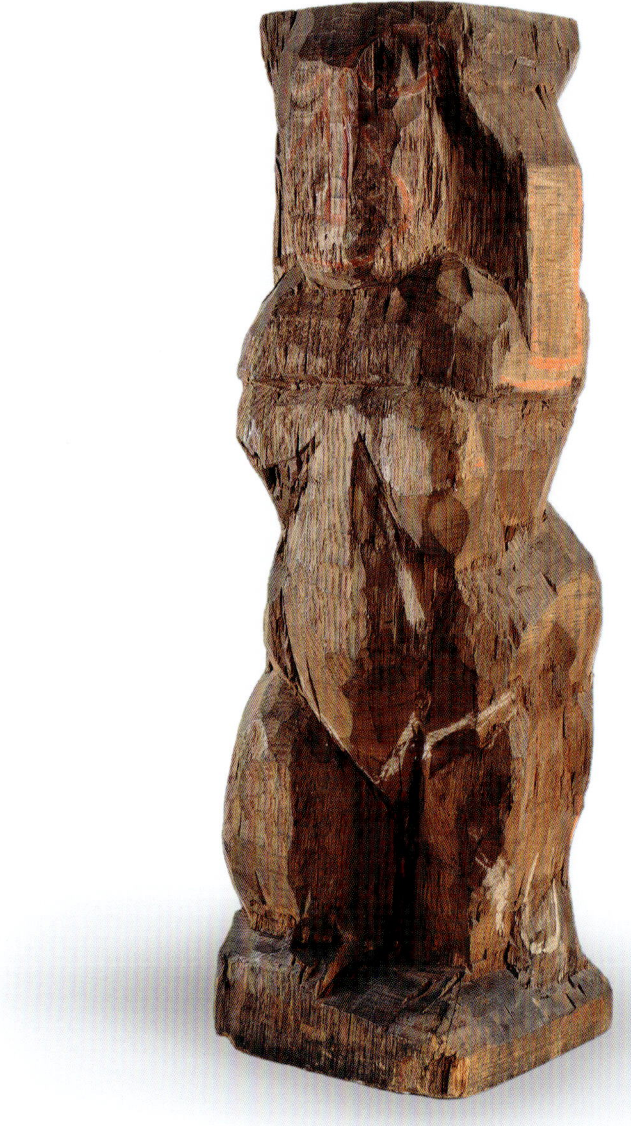

—
Fig. 72
Pablo Picasso
Figure
Paris, 1908
Carved oak with paint highlights, 80.5 × 24 × 20.8 cm (31 ¾ × 9 ½ × 8 ⅛ in.)
Musée National Picasso-Paris
Dation Pablo Picasso, 1979. MP238
—

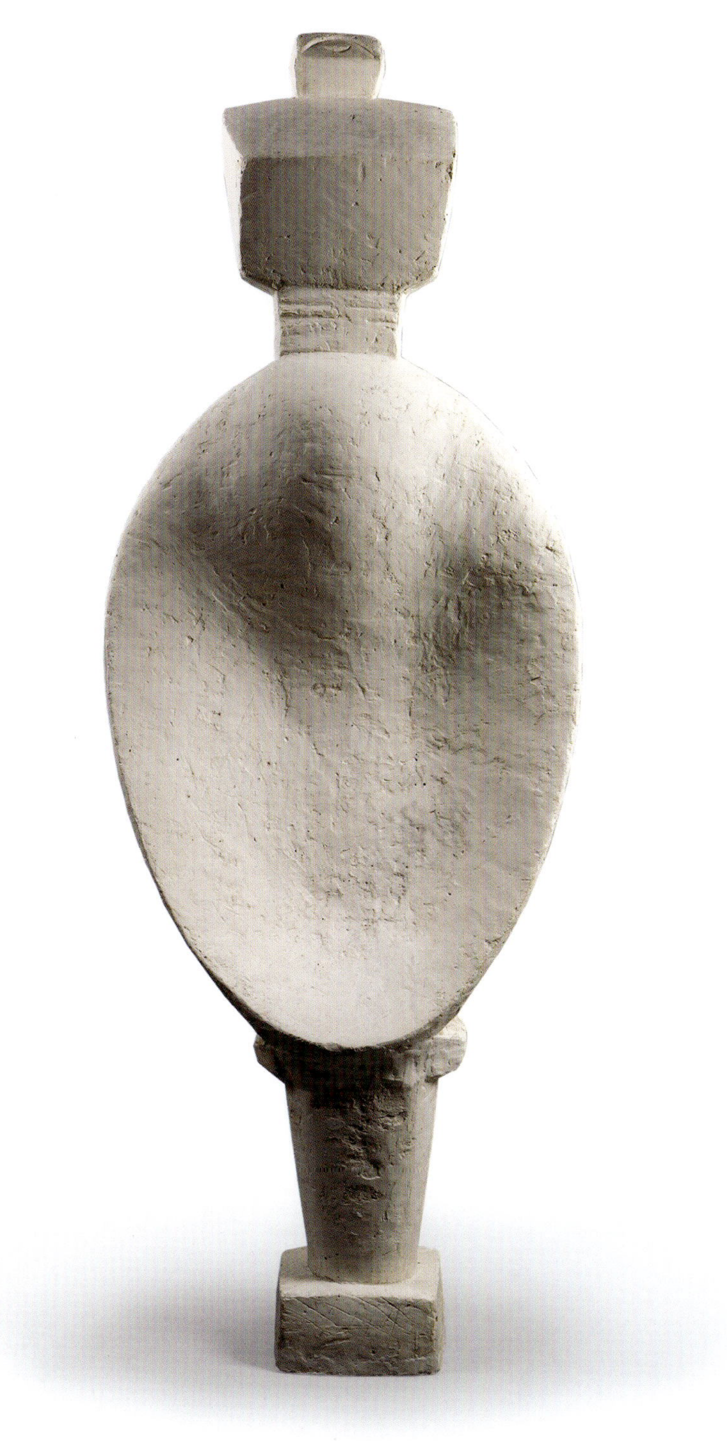

Fig. 73
Alberto Giacometti
Spoon Woman
1927
Plaster, 146.5 × 51.6 × 21.5 cm (4 ft. 9 ¾ in. × 1 ft. 8 ⅜ in. × 8 ½ in.)
Fondation Giacometti, Paris

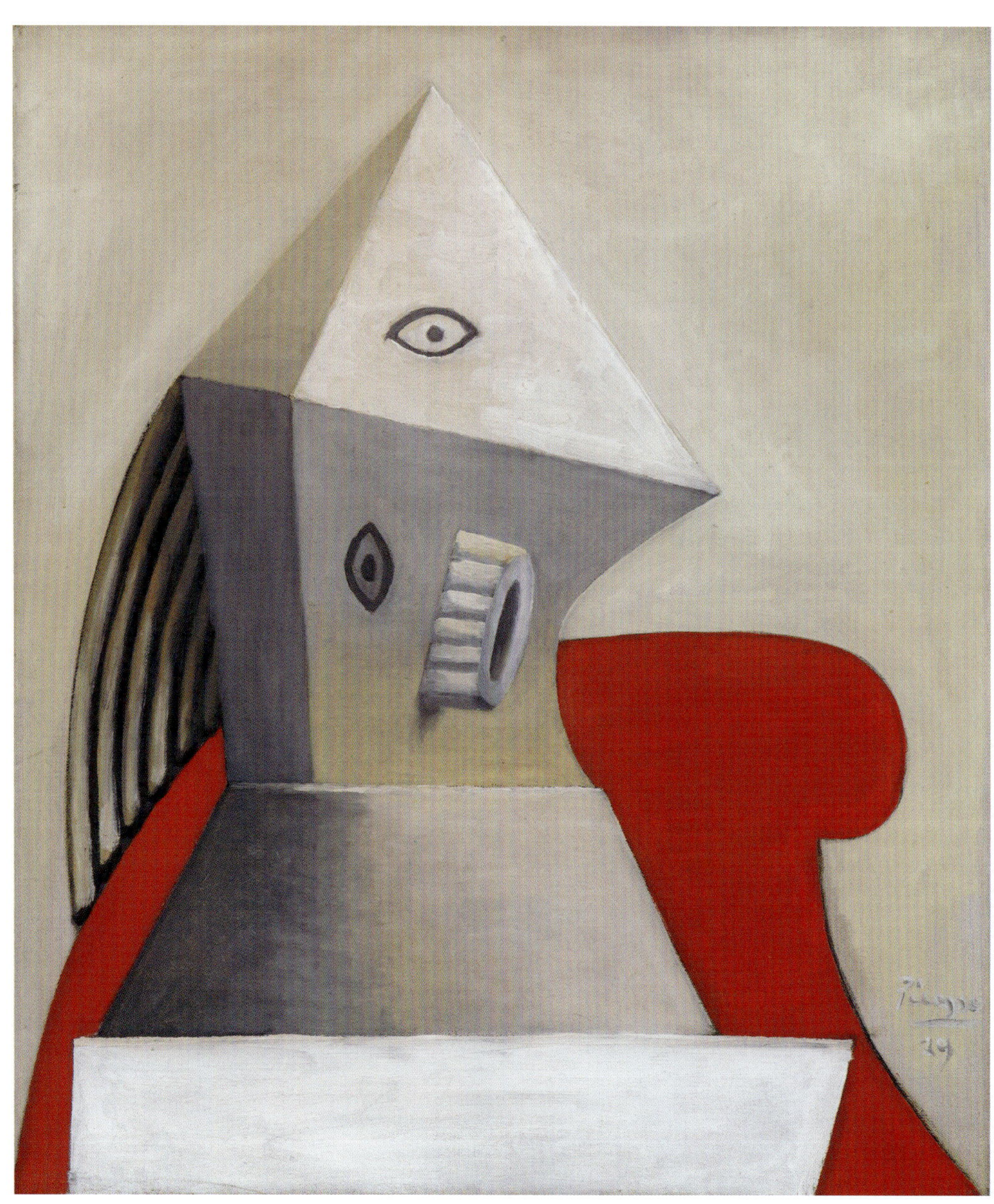

—
Fig. 74
Pablo Picasso
Woman in a Red Armchair
Paris, 1929
Oil on canvas, 64.5 × 54 cm (25 ⅜ × 21 ¼ in.)
Musée National Picasso-Paris
Dation Pablo Picasso, 1979. MP112
—

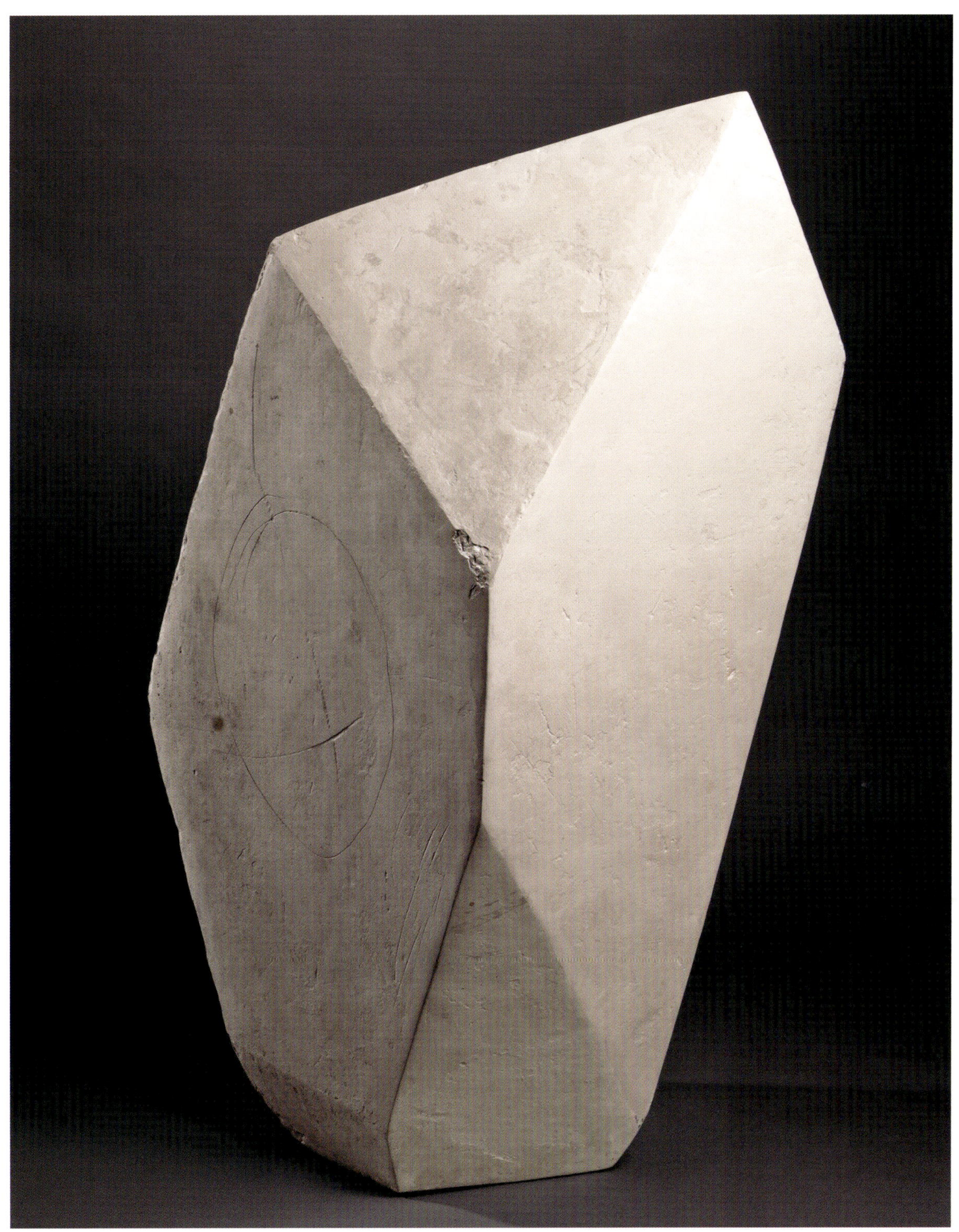

Fig. 75
Alberto Giacometti
Cube
1933–1934
Plaster, 94 × 60 × 60 cm (3 ft. 1 in. × 1 ft. 11 ⅝ in.)
Musée National d'Art Moderne/Centre de Création Industrielle,
Centre Pompidou, Paris
Inv. AM 1986-1155

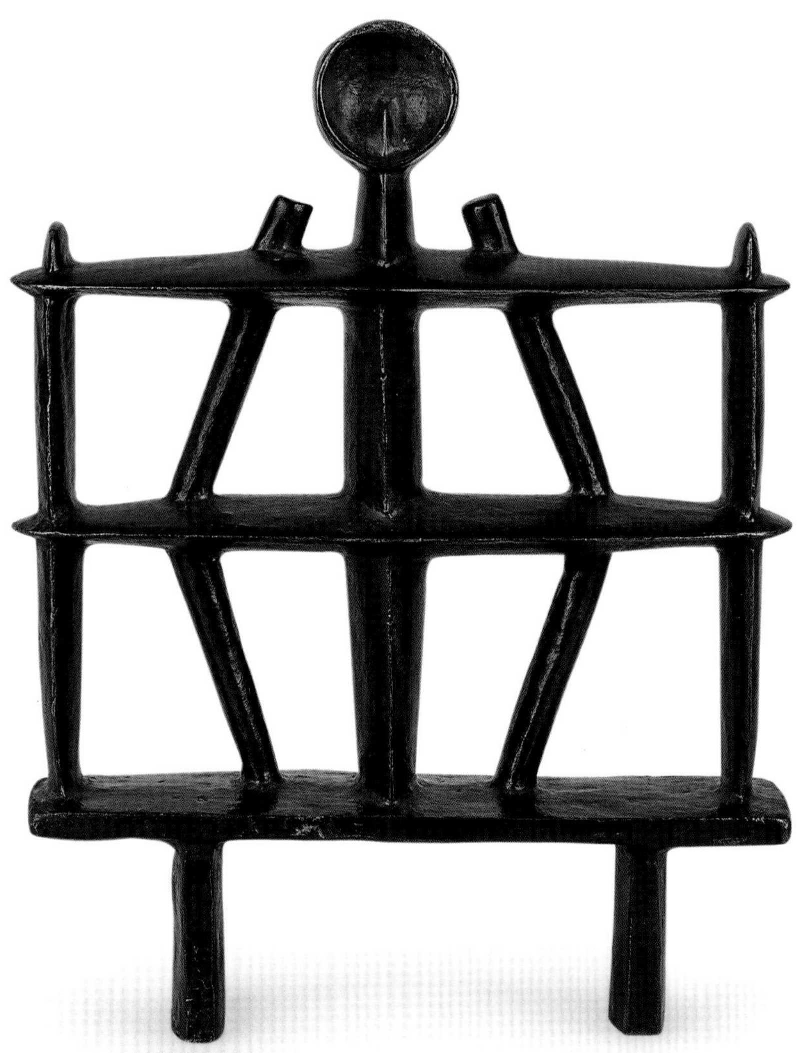

—
Fig. 76
Alberto Giacometti
Man (Apollo)
1929
Bronze, 39.4 × 30.9 × 8.2 cm (15 ½ × 12 ⅛ × 3 ¼ in.)
Fondation Giacometti, Paris
—

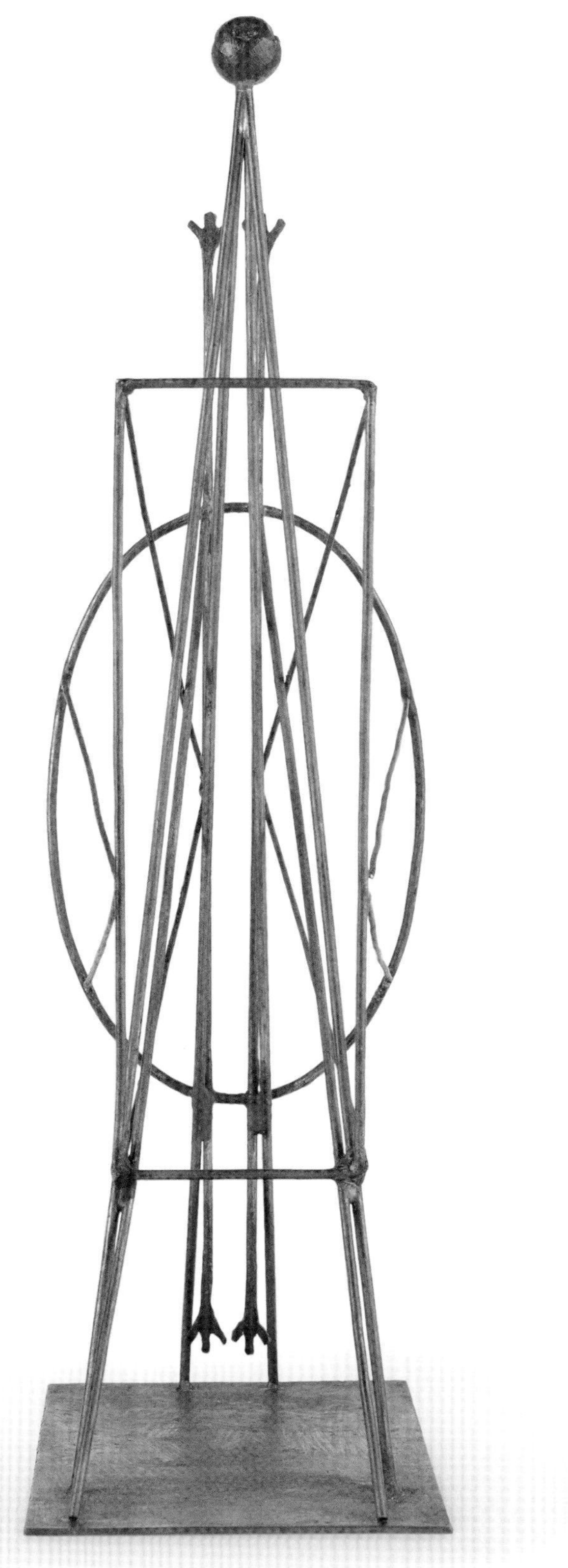

—
Fig. 77
Pablo Picasso
Figure
Paris, autumn 1928
Wire and sheet metal, 37.5 × 10 × 19.6 cm (4 ft. 9 ⅛ in. × 3 ft. 11 ¼ in. × 7 ft. 8 ⅝ in.)
Musée National Picasso-Paris. On long-term loan to the Musée National d'Art
Moderne/Centre de Création Industrielle, Centre Pompidou, Paris
Dation Pablo Picasso, 1979. MP266
—

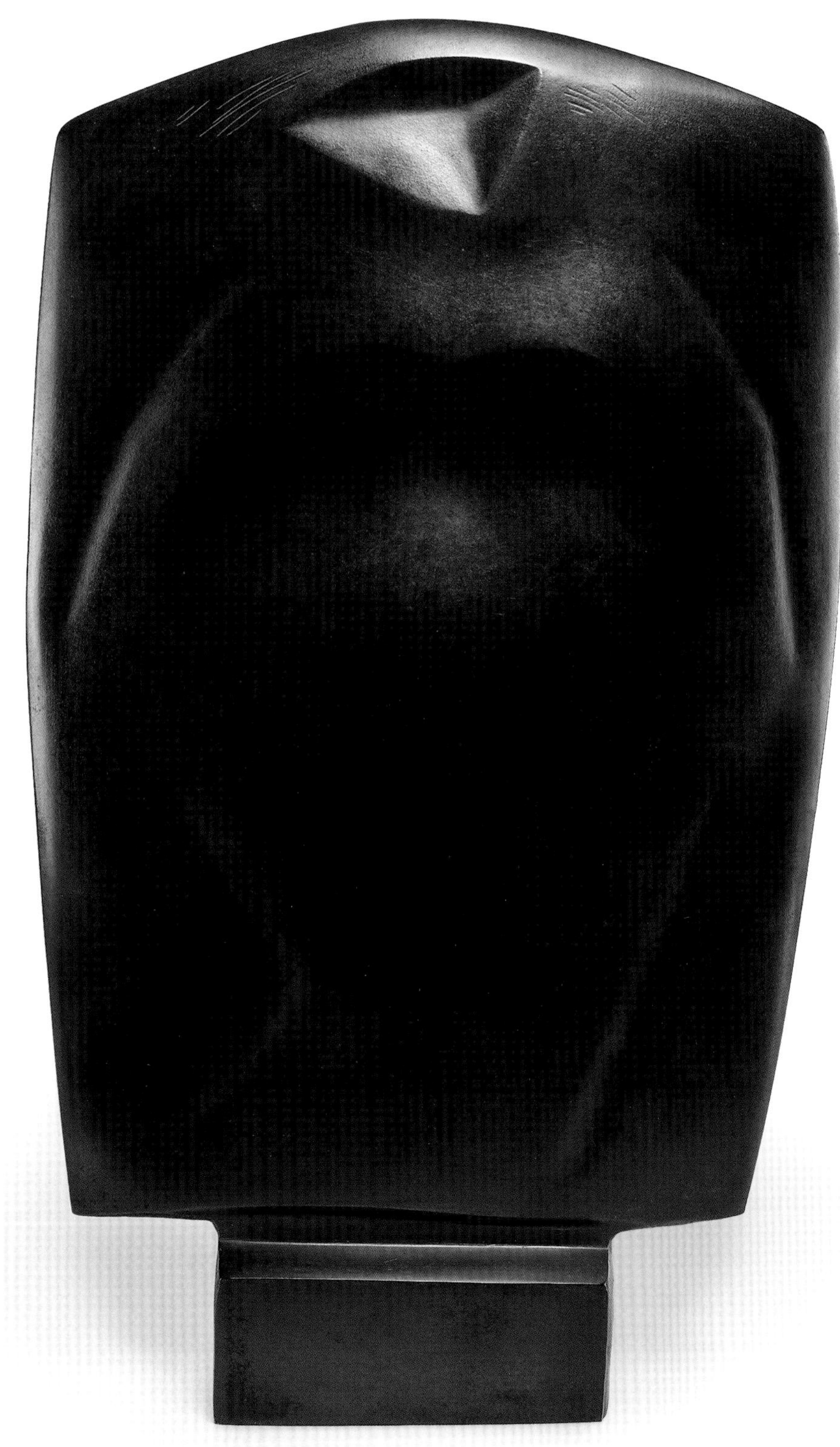

—
Fig. 78
Alberto Giacometti
Woman (Flat V)
c. 1929
Bronze, 55.5 × 33.6 × 7.7 cm (21 ⅞ × 13 ¼ × 3 in.)
Fondation Giacometti, Paris
—

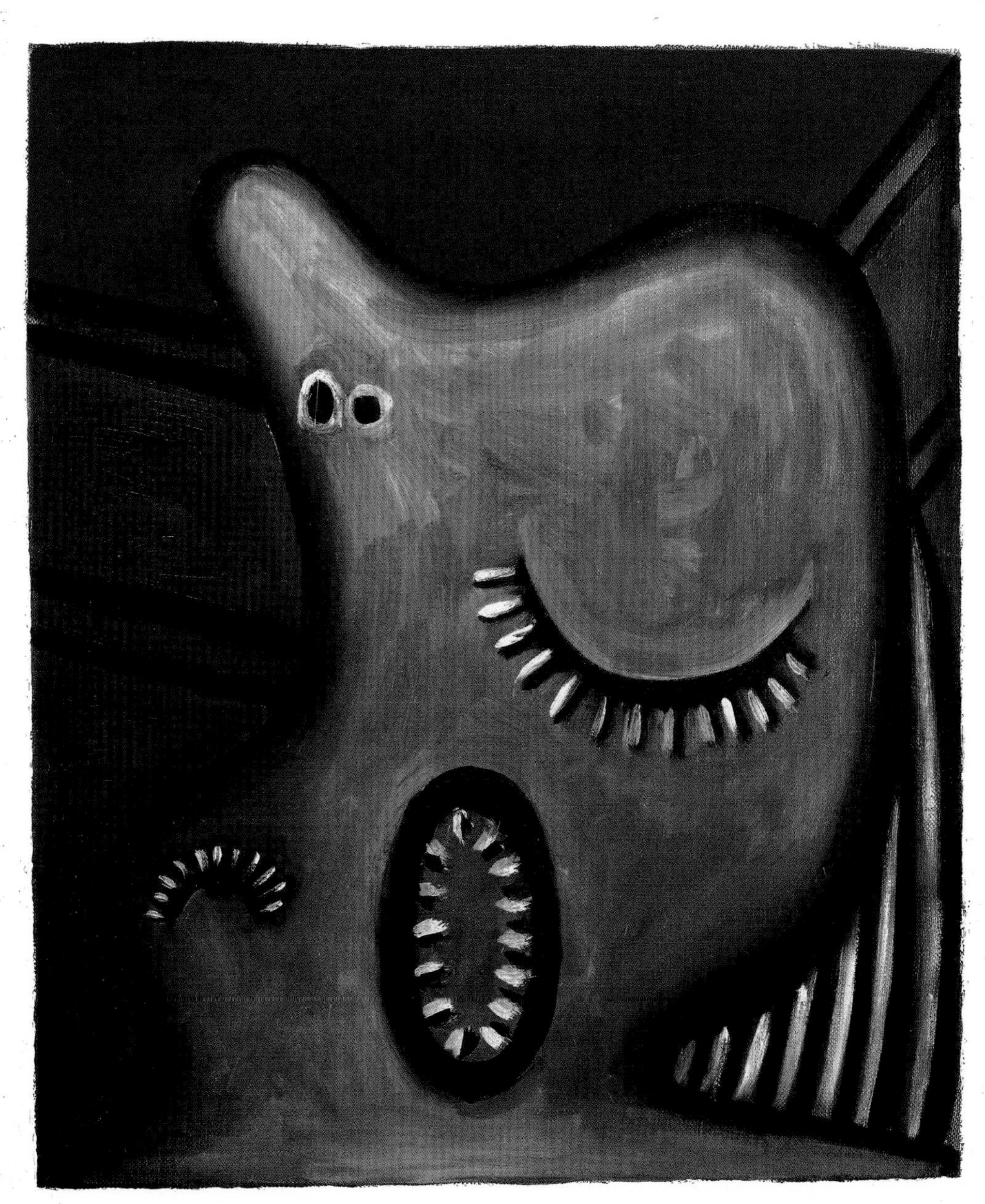

—
Fig. 79
Pablo Picasso
Sleeping Woman
Paris, 1927
Oil on canvas, 46 × 38 cm (18 × 15 in.)
Musée National Picasso-Paris
Dation Pablo Picasso, 1979. MP98
—

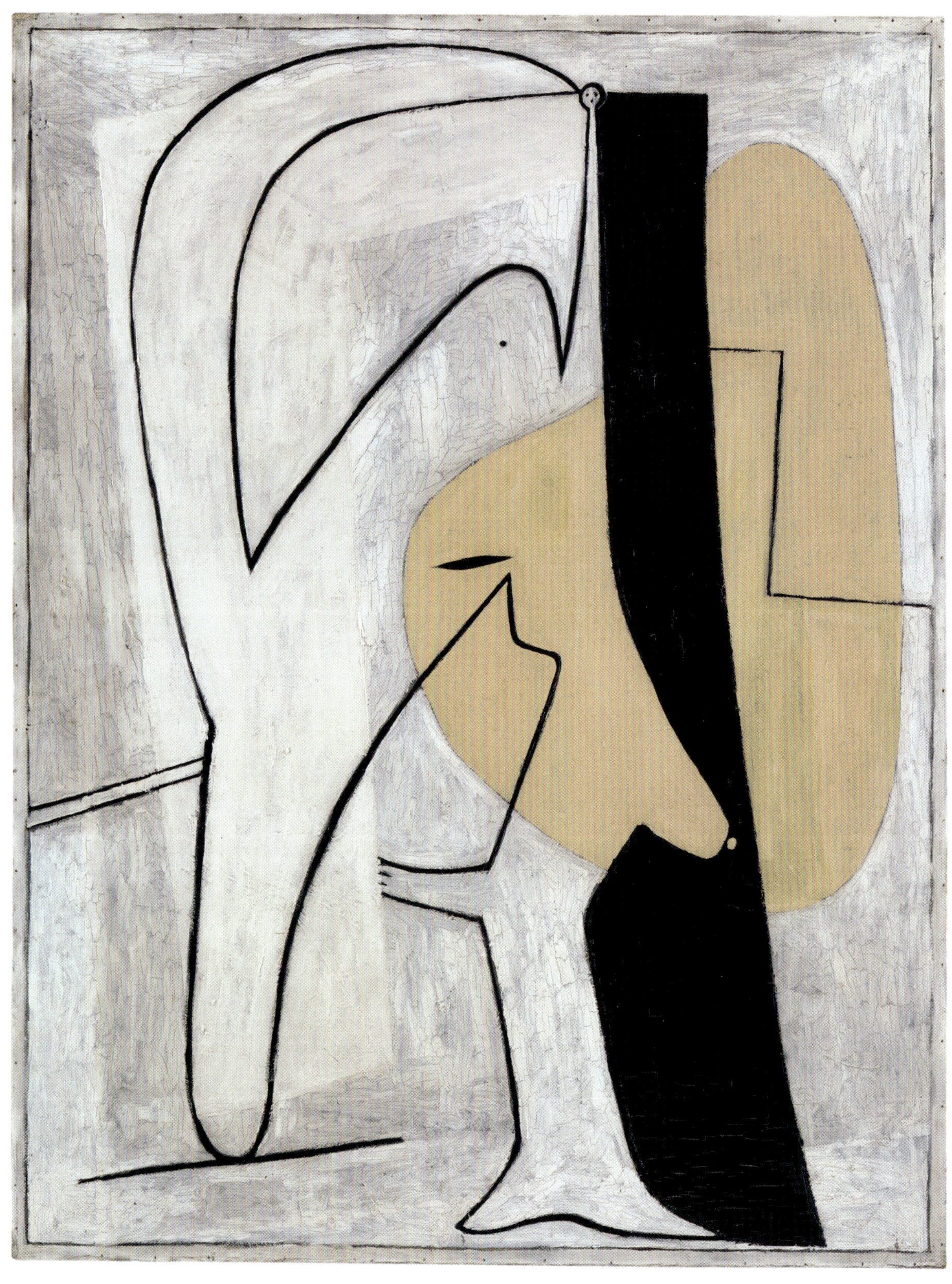

—
Fig. 80
Pablo Picasso
Figure
1927
Oil on plywood, 129 × 96 cm (4 ft. 2 ¾ in. × 3 ft. 1 ⅞ in.)
Musée National Picasso-Paris
Dation Pablo Picasso, 1979. MP101
—

Fig. 81
Alberto Giacometti
Woman (Flat III)
c. 1928–1929
Plaster, 36.6 × 17.7 × 8.8 cm (14 ⅜ × 7 × 3 ½ in.)
Fondation Giacometti, Paris

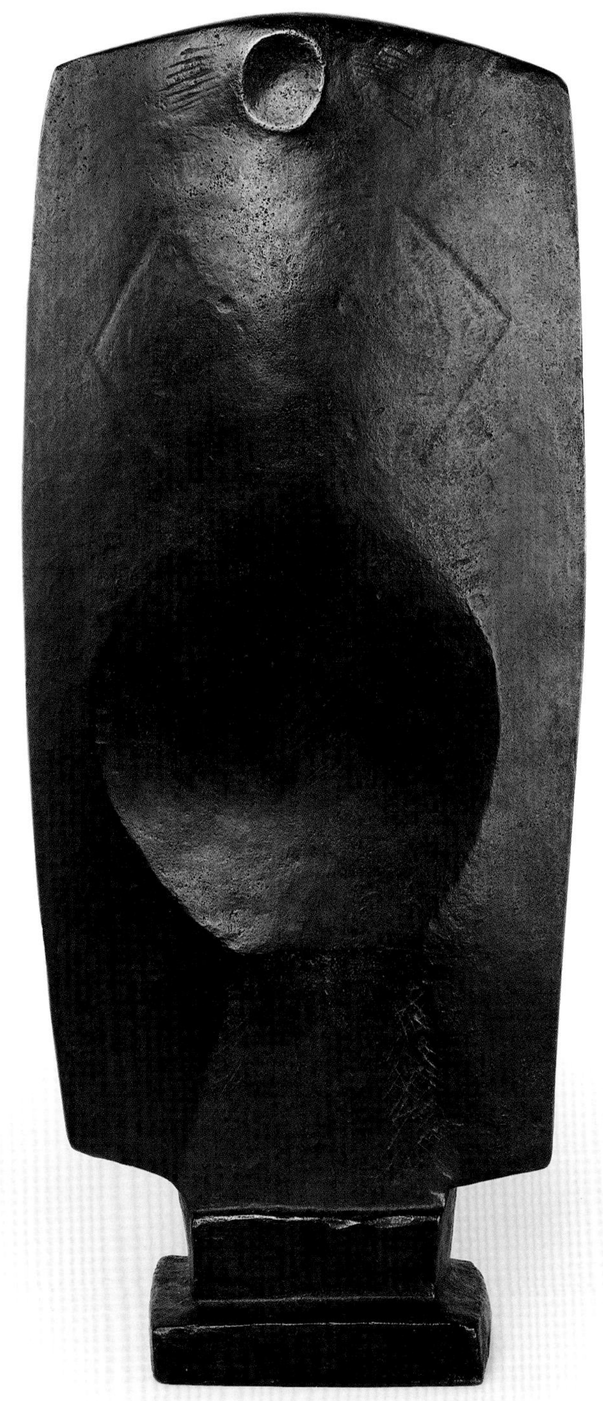

Fig. 82
Alberto Giacometti
Woman (Flat II)
c. 1928–1929
Bronze, 39.4 × 17 × 7.8 cm (15 ½ × 6 ⅝ × 3 in.)
Fondation Giacometti, Paris

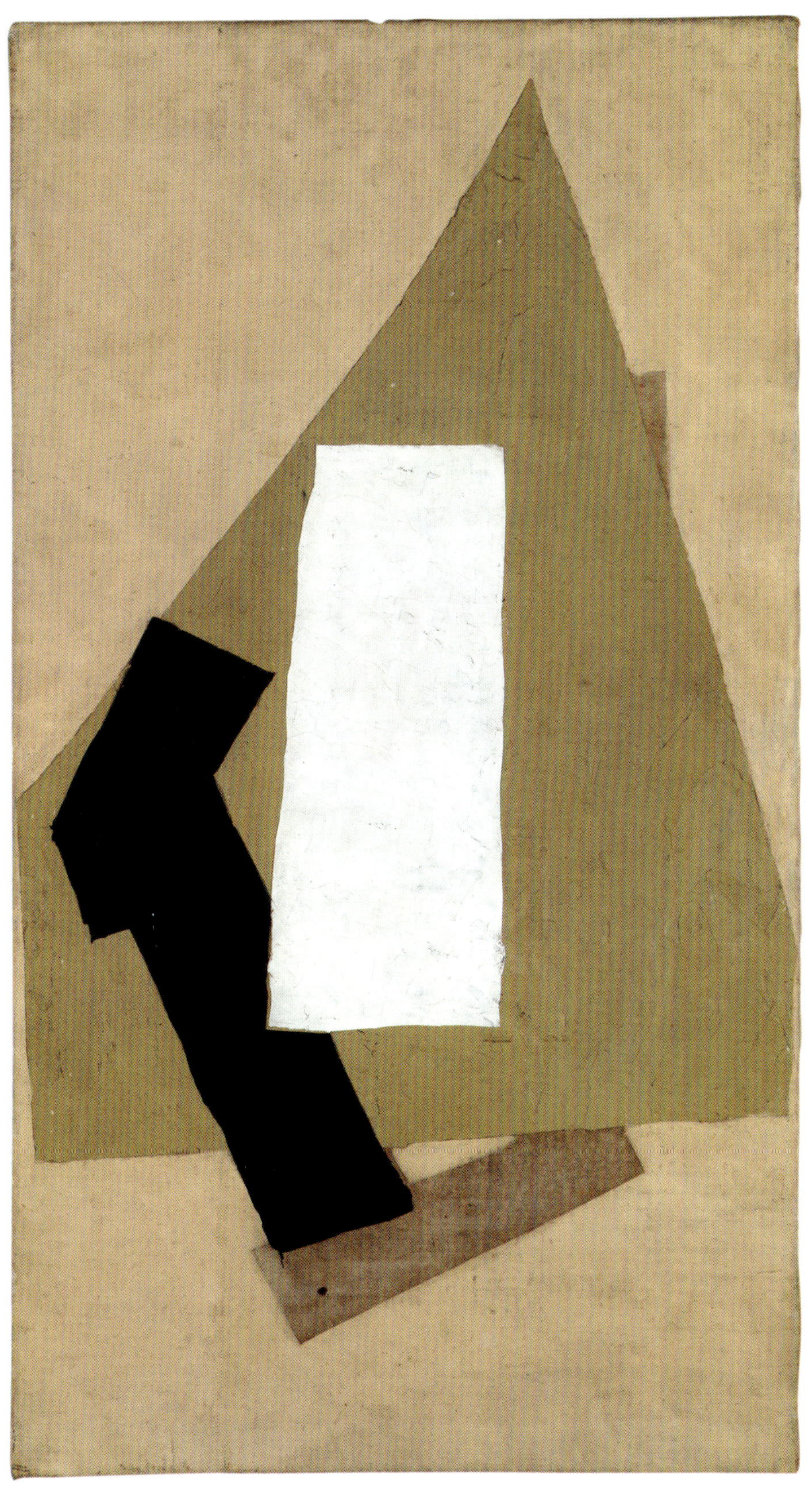

Fig. 83
Pablo Picasso
Guitar
Céret, spring 1913
Oil on canvas glued on wood, 87 × 47.5 cm (34 ½ × 18 ¾ in.)
Musée National Picasso-Paris
Dation Pablo Picasso, 1979. MP38

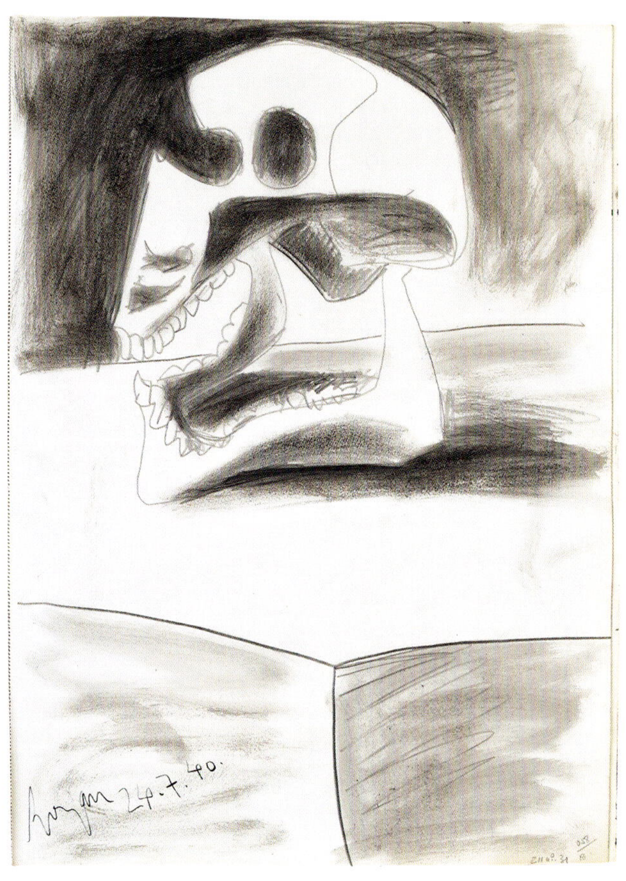

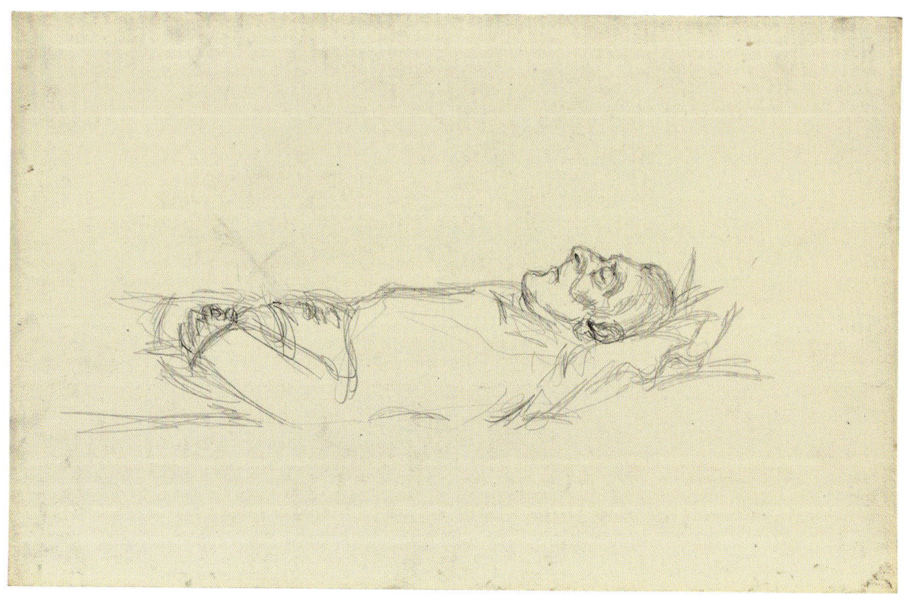

—
Fig. 84
Pablo Picasso
Skull
Royan and Paris, 30 May 1940–19 February 1942
Graphite pencil and India ink wash on paper,
30.5 × 41.3 cm (12 × 16 ¼ in.)
Sketchbook 46, 34 sheets
Musée National Picasso-Paris
Dation Pablo Picasso, 1979. MP1880 (19r)
—
Fig. 85
Alberto Giacometti
Braque on His Deathbed
1963
Pencil on paper, 32.5 × 50.1 cm
(12 ¾ in. × 19 ¾ in.)
Fondation Giacometti, Paris
—

Eros and Thanatos

The trivialisation of the body after death and its objectification are two themes common to both Picasso and Giacometti's works, which frequently feature recumbent effigies—often a loved one—and skulls. In representations of love, where all forms of shapelessness are explored, images of Eros (love) are subjected to just as much dismemberment of the human body as those of Thanatos (death). The living urges of sexual desire rub shoulders with the instincts of death. The distortions of the human body recomposed into an architectonic montage culminate in organic metaphors whose strength of synthesis expresses, in the words of Carl Einstein, a 'concentrate of dreams'.

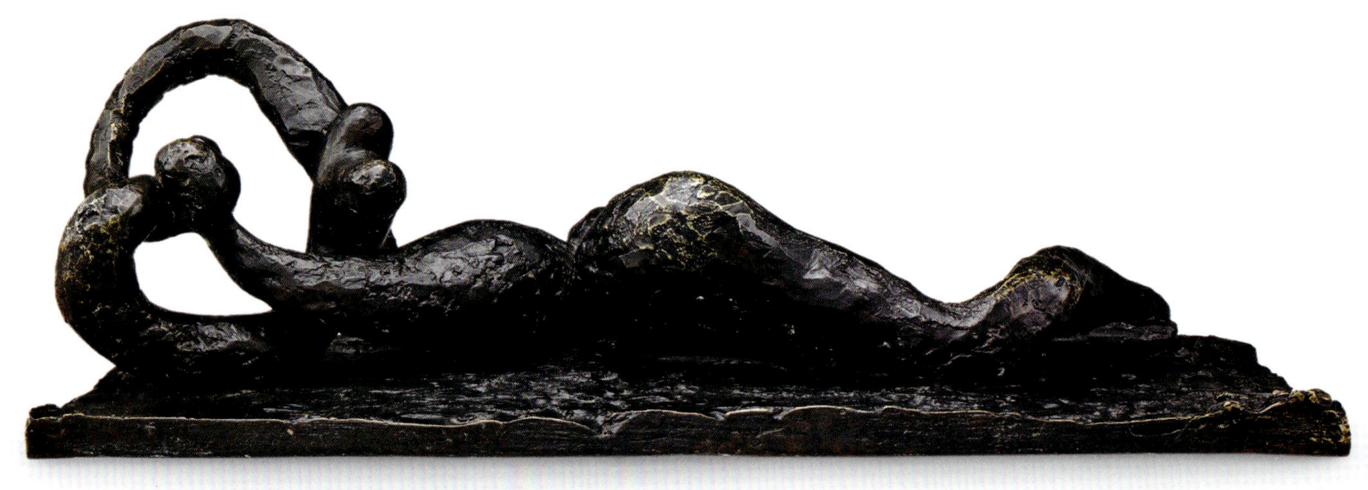

—
Fig. 86
Pablo Picasso
Reclining Bather
Boisgeloup, 1931
Bronze, 23 × 72 × 31 cm (9 × 28 ⅜ × 12 ¼ in.)
Musée National Picasso-Paris
Dation Pablo Picasso, 1979. MP290
—

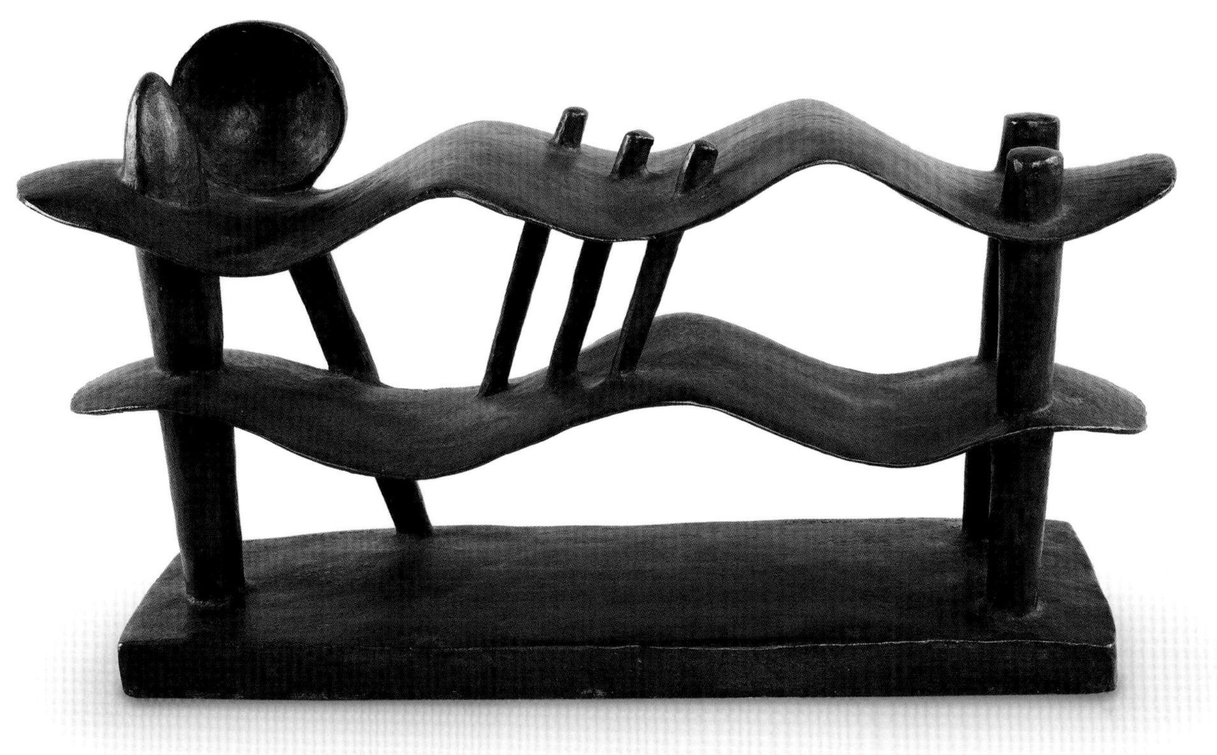

Fig. 87
Alberto Giacometti
Reclining Woman Who Dreams
1929
Bronze, 23.7 × 42.6 × 13.6 cm (9 ⅜ × 16 ¾ × 5 ⅜ in.)
Fondation Giacometti, Paris

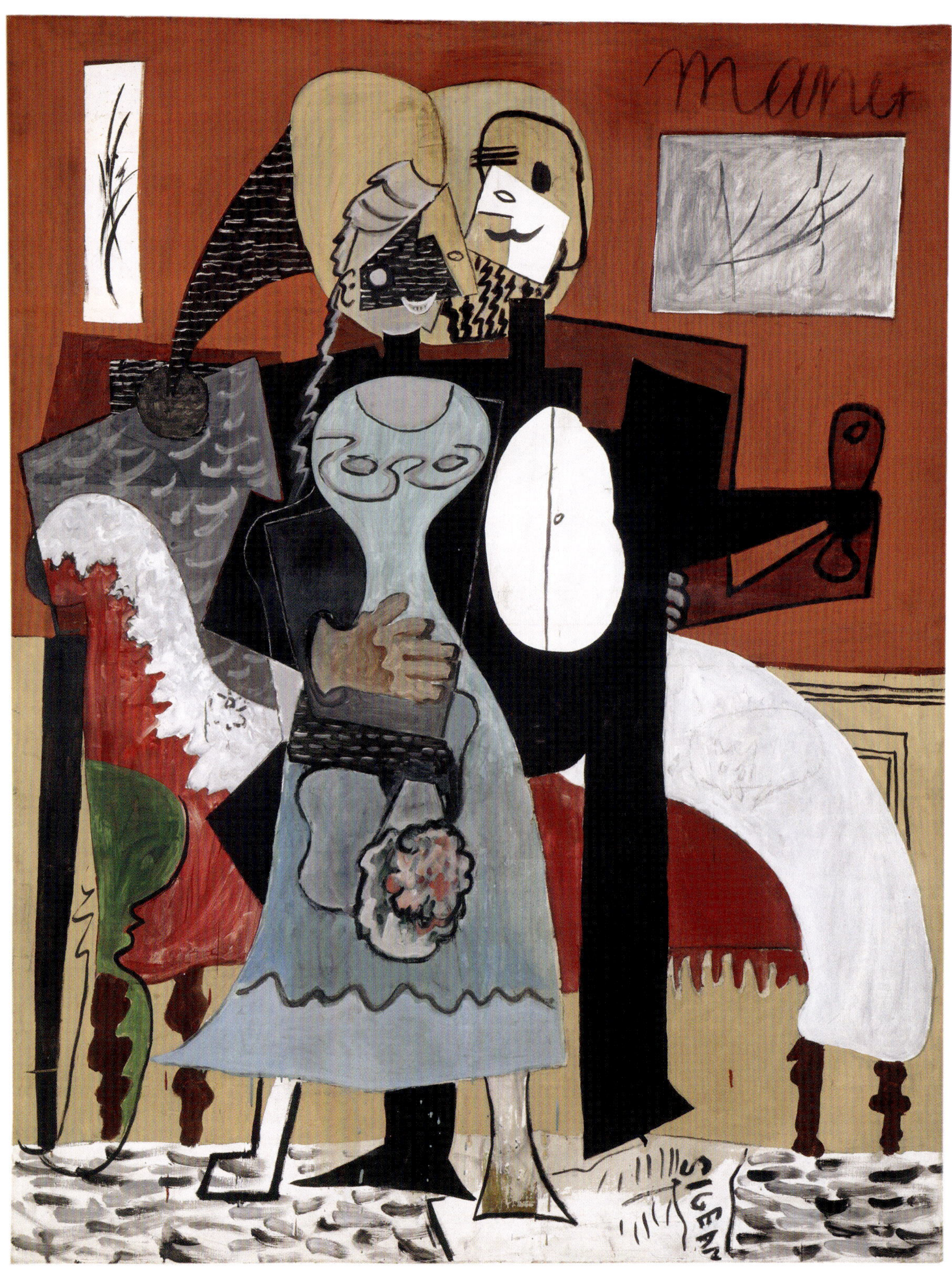

Fig. 88
Pablo Picasso
The Lovers
Paris, 1919
Oil on canvas, 185 × 140 cm (6 ft. 1 in. × 4 ft. 7 ¼ in.)
Musée National Picasso-Paris
Dation Pablo Picasso, 1979. MP62

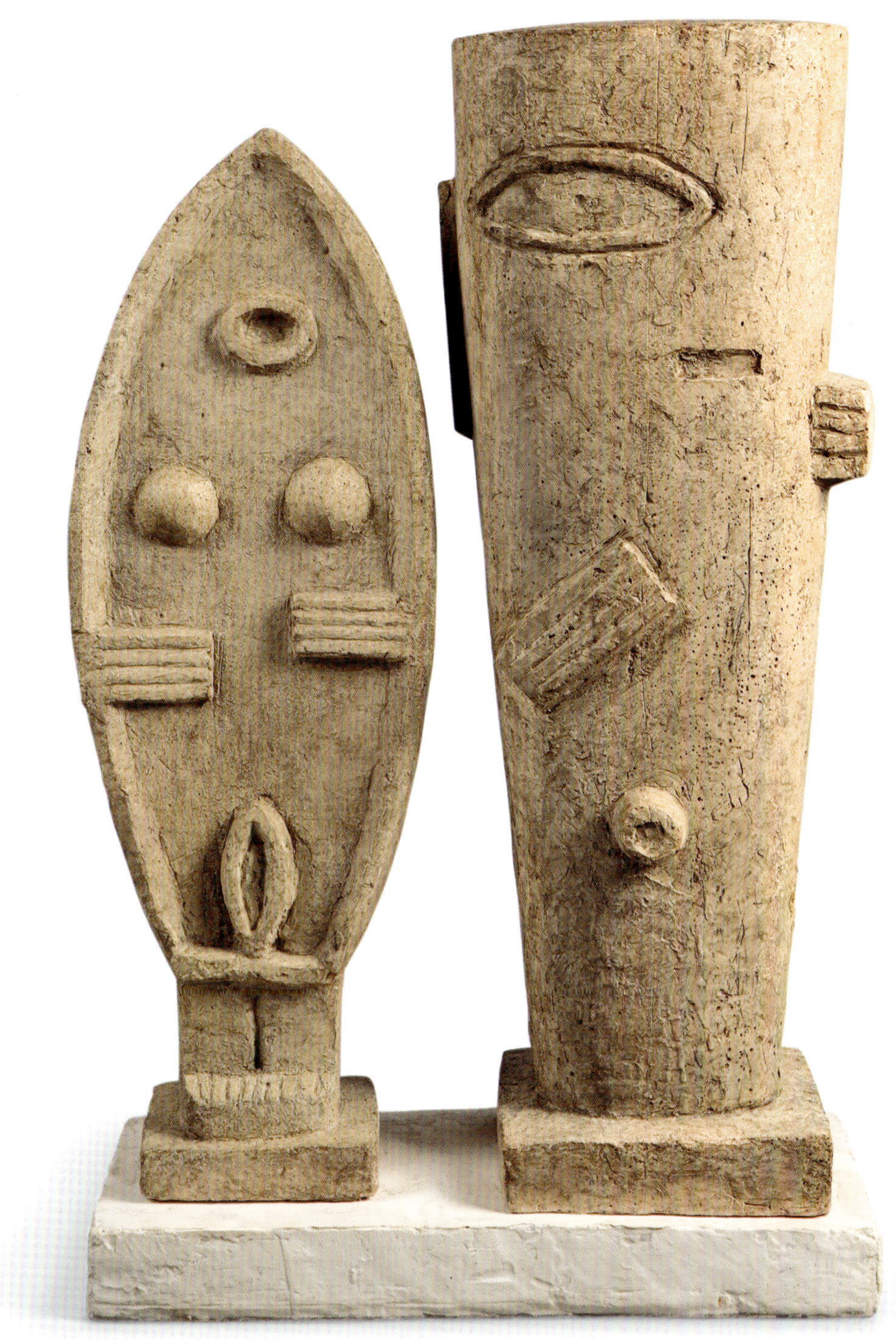

—
Fig. 89
Alberto Giacometti
The Couple
1927
Plaster, 60.4 × 37.7 × 18 cm (23 ¾ × 14 ⅞ × 7 ⅛ in.)
Fondation Giacometti, Paris
—

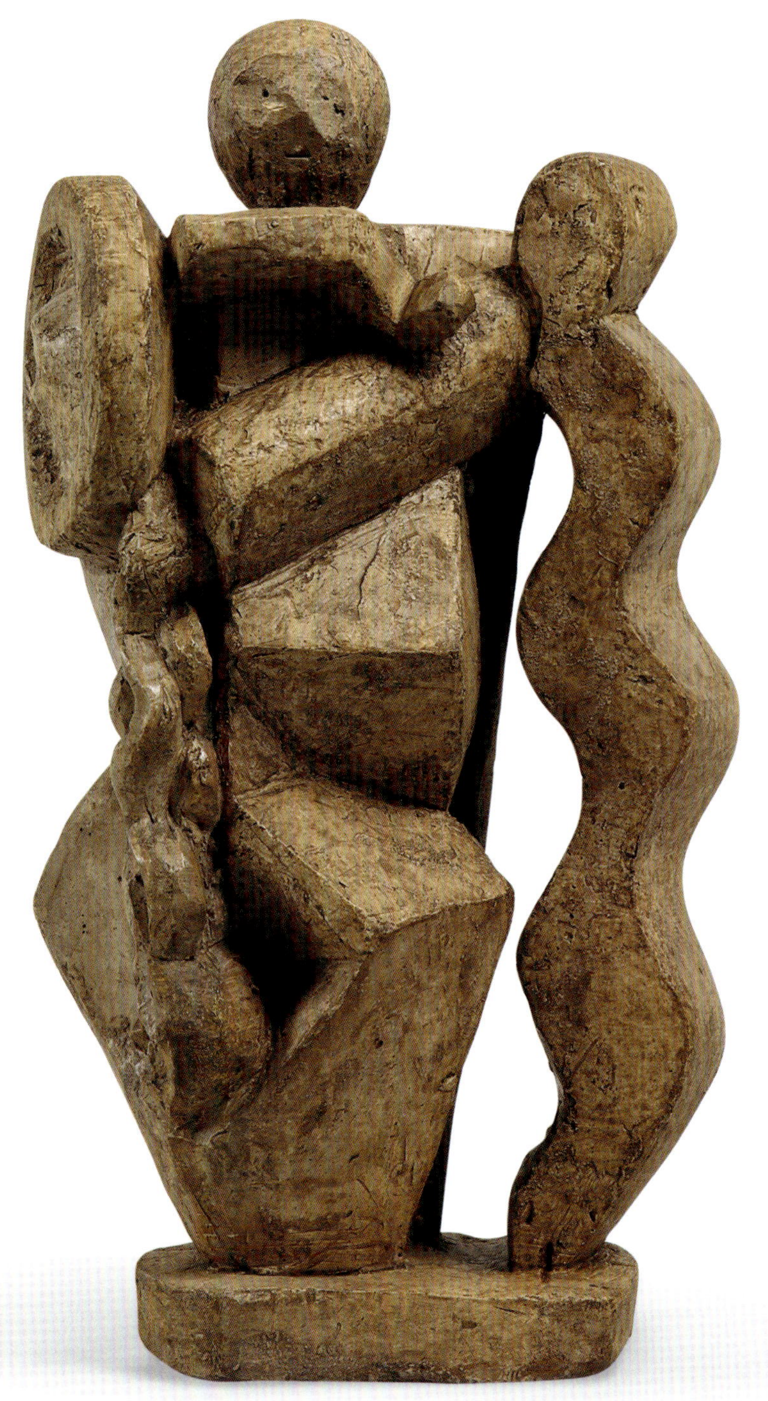

Fig. 90
Alberto Giacometti
Composition
c. 1927–1928
Plaster, 32.8 × 16 × 14.1 cm (13 × 6 ¼ × 5 ½ in.)
Fondation Giacometti, Paris

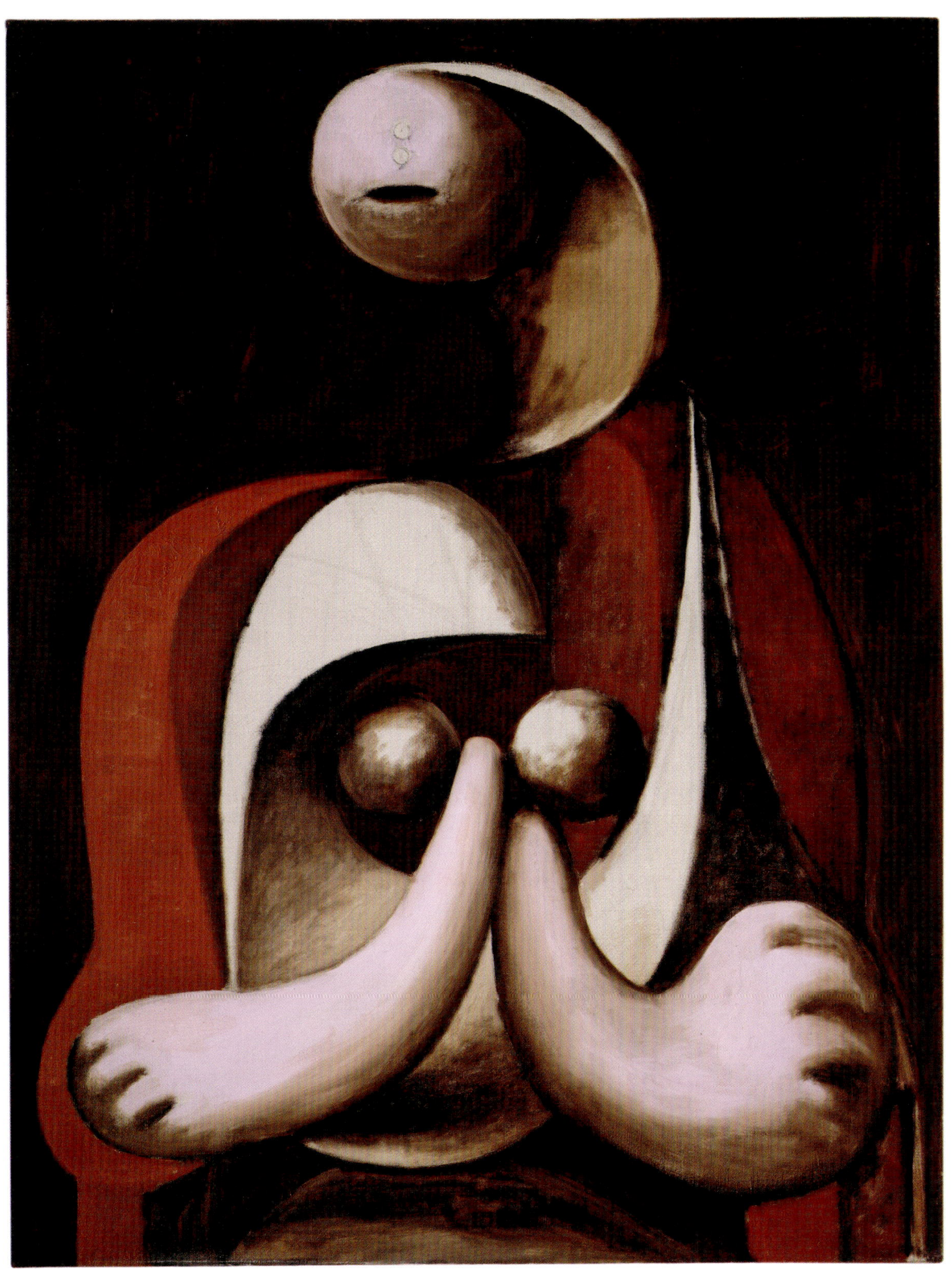

Fig. 91
Pablo Picasso
Woman Seated in a Red Armchair
Boisgeloup, 1932
Oil on canvas, 130 × 97.5 cm (4 ft. 3 ¼ in. × 3 ft. 2 ⅜ in.)
Musée National Picasso-Paris
Dation Pablo Picasso, 1979. MP139

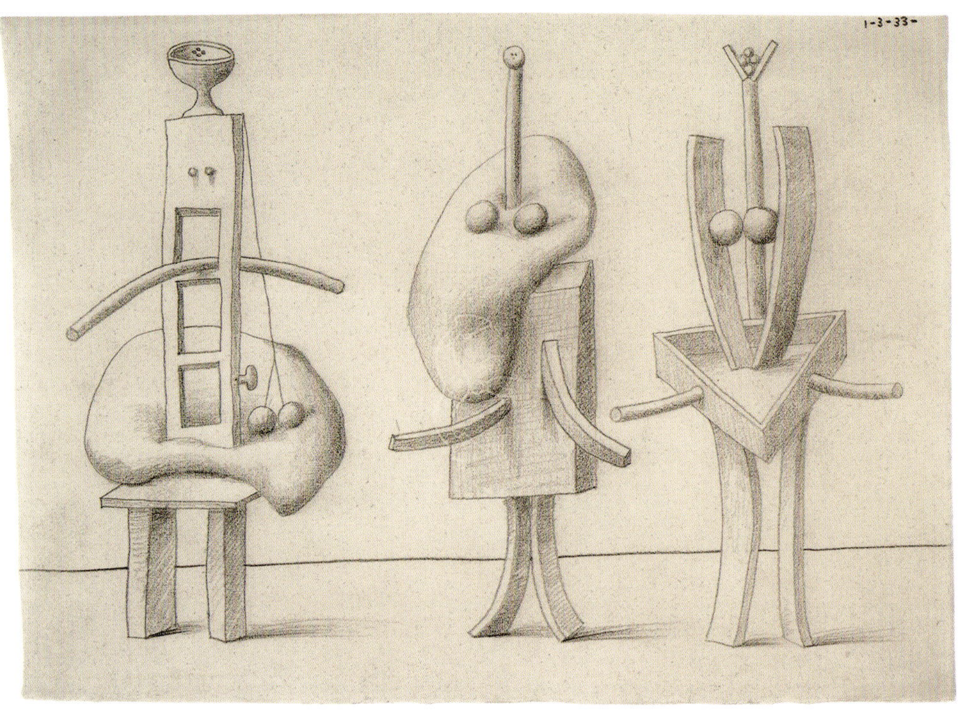

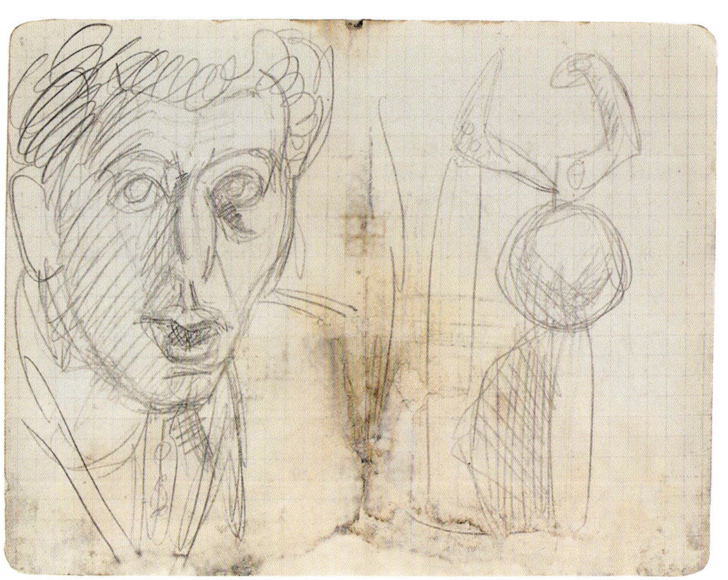

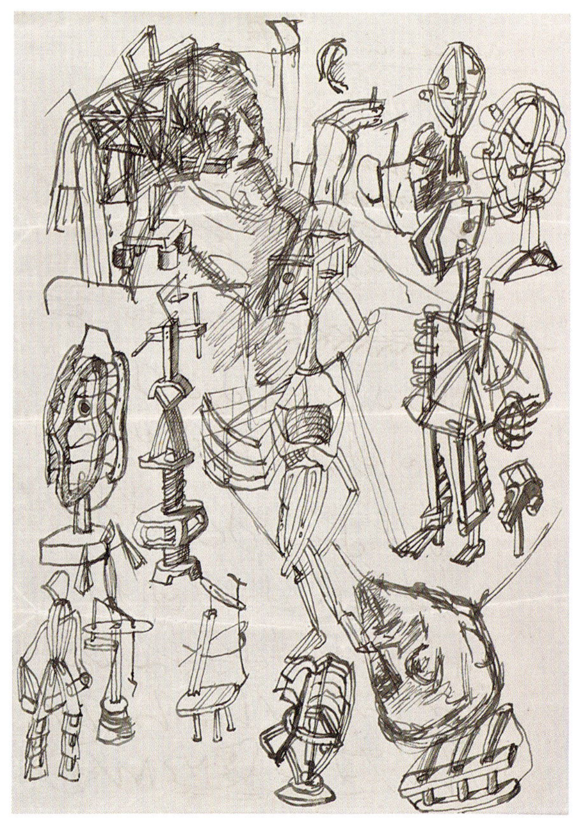

Alberto Giacometti
Self-Portrait and Copies after Picasso's
Project for a Sculpture
c. 1929–1930
Graphite pencil on sheets from a notebook
with squared-up pages, 14.5 × 19.6 cm (5 ¾ × 7 ¾ in.)
Fondation Giacometti, Paris

Pablo Picasso
An Anatomy: Three Women
Paris, 1 March 1933
Pencil on wove paper with a fine linen finish,
20 × 27.1 cm (7 ⅞ × 10 ⅝ in.)
Musée National Picasso-Paris
Dation Pablo Picasso, 1979. MP1098

Alberto Giacometti
Heads of Father and Sculpture Projects
c. 1930
Pen and black ink on paper,
27.7 × 19 cm (11 × 7 ½ in.)
Fondation Giacometti, Paris

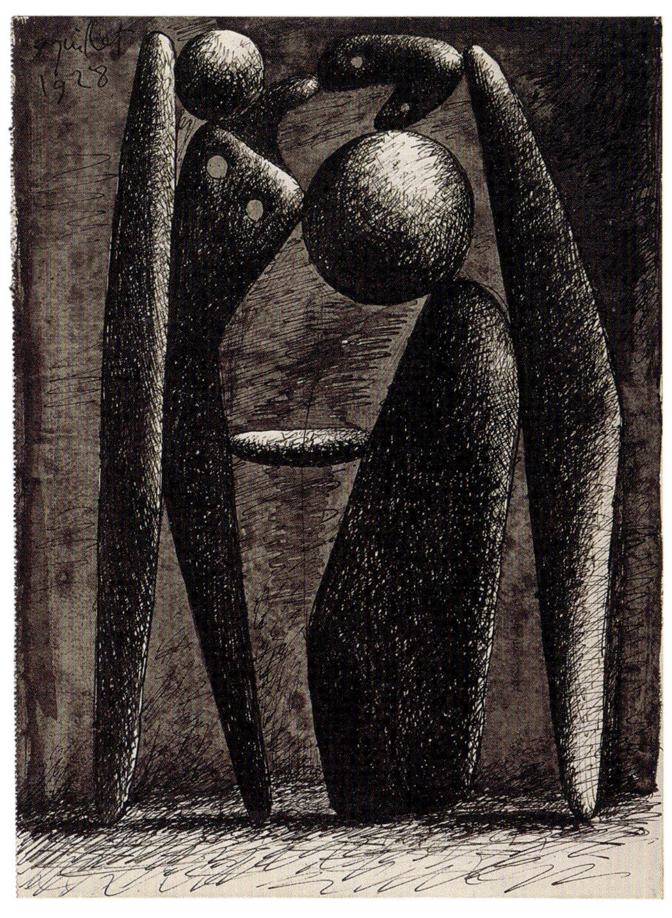

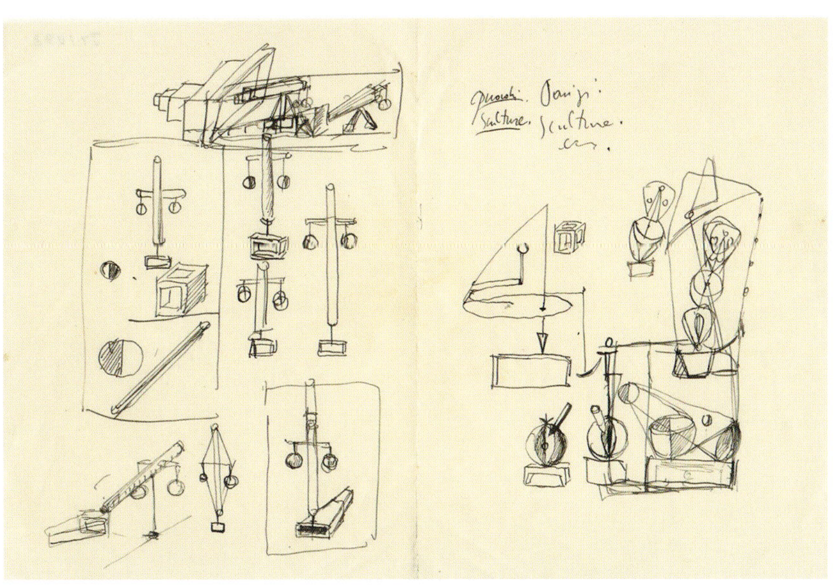

Fig. 95
Pablo Picasso
Bathers
Dinard, 8 July 1928
Pen, India ink and wash on a sheet of cylinder-mould laid
paper from a sketchbook, 30.2 × 22.1 cm (12 × 8 ¾ in.)
Musée National Picasso-Paris
Dation Pablo Picasso, 1979. MP1030

Fig. 96
Alberto Giacometti
Projects for Sculptures
n. d.
Pen and black ink on watermarked paper,
19 × 27.7 cm (7 ½ × 11 in.)
Fondation Giacometti, Paris

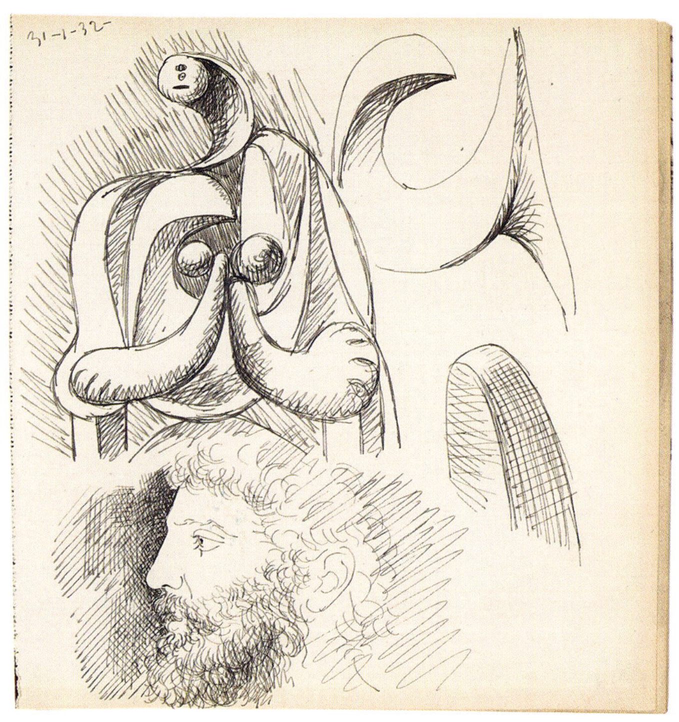

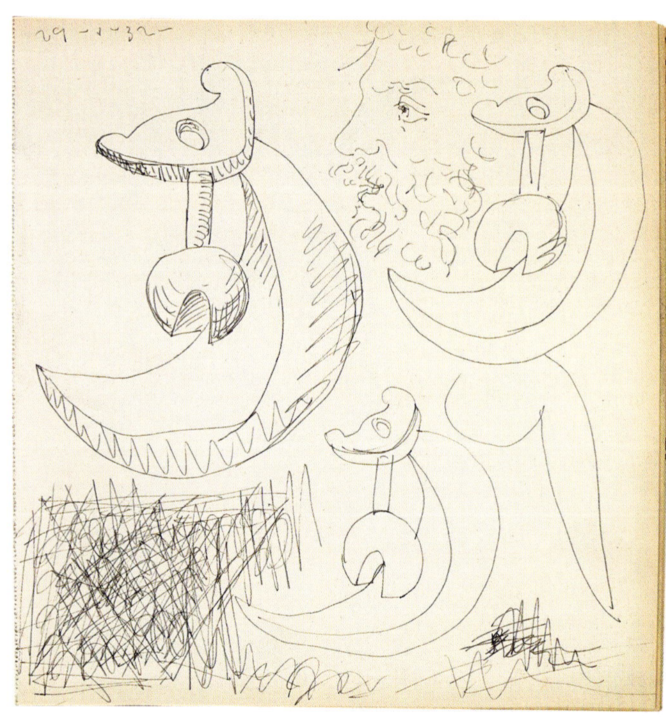

Fig. 97
Pablo Picasso
The Sculptor: Studies after **Woman Seated in a Red Armchair**
Paris, 31 January 1932
Pen and India ink on beige laid paper,
28 × 26.5 cm (11 × 10 ⅜ in.)
Musée National Picasso-Paris
Dation Jacqueline Picasso, 1990. MP1990-110 (12r)

Fig. 98
Pablo Picasso
The Sculptor: Studies after **Woman Seated in a Red Armchair**
Paris, 29 January 1932
Pen and India ink on beige laid paper,
28 × 26.5 cm (11 × 10 ⅜ in.)
Musée National Picasso-Paris
Dation Jacqueline Picasso, 1990. MP1990-110 (11r)

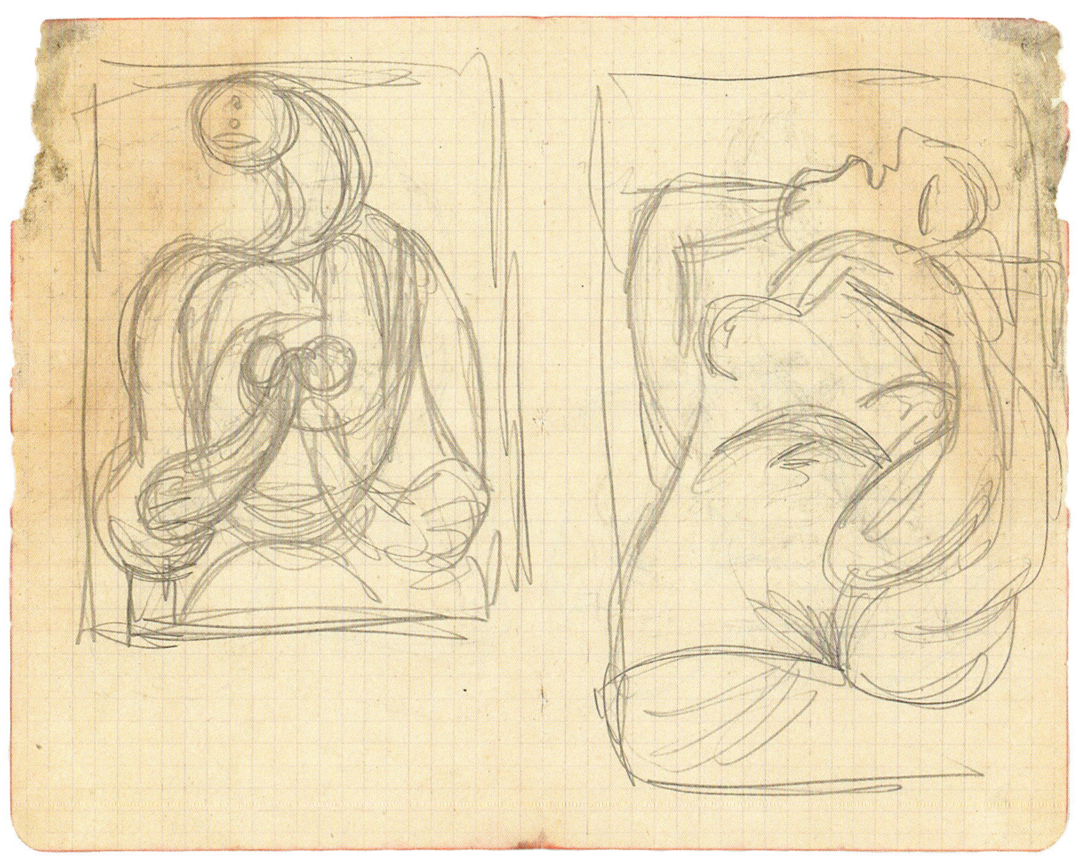

—
Fig. 99
Alberto Giacometti
Copies after Picasso's **Woman Seated
in a Red Armchair** *and* **Sleep**
1932
Graphite pencil on pages of a notebook,
15 × 19.2 cm (6 × 7 ½ in.)
Fondation Giacometti, Paris
—

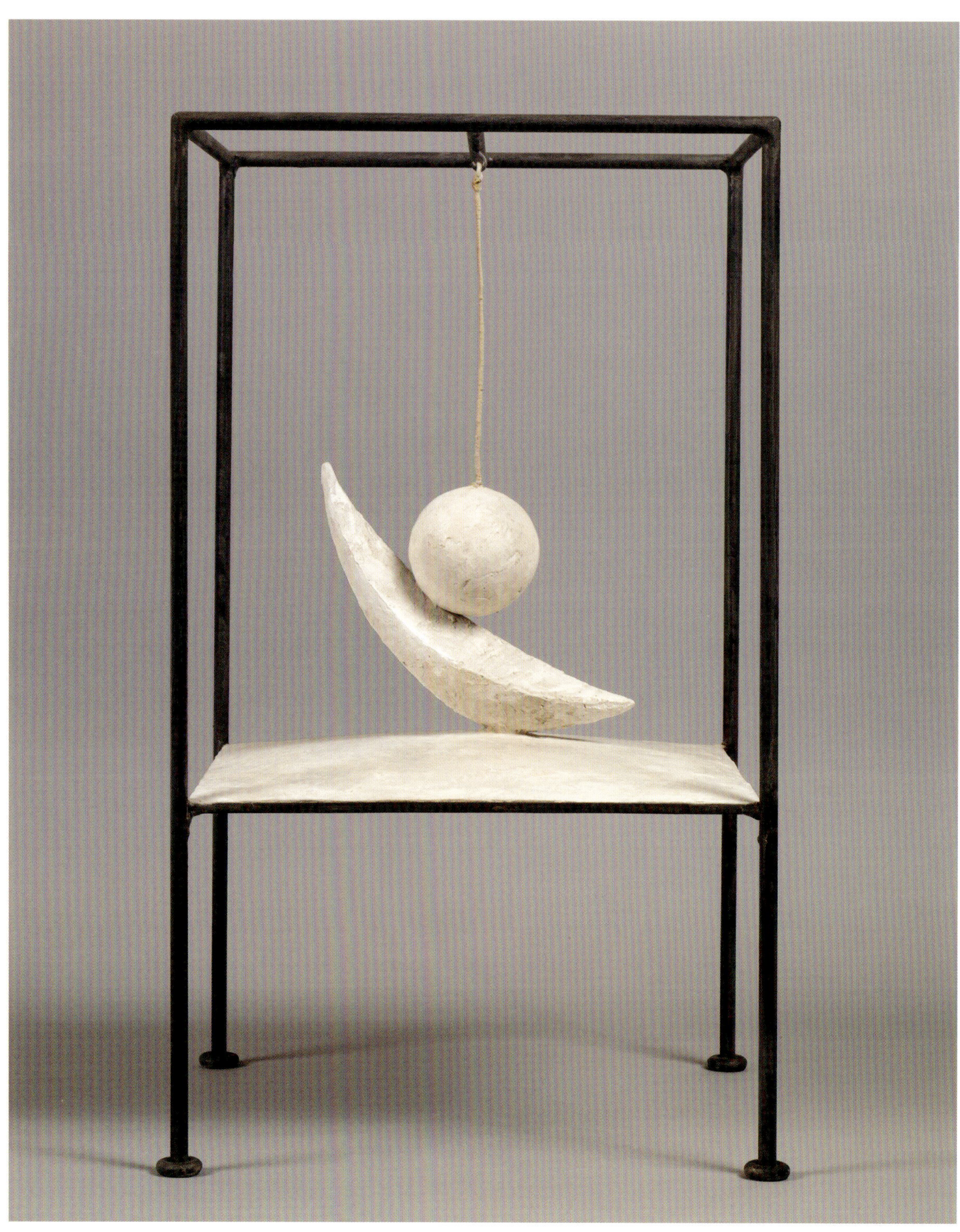

—
Fig. 100
Alberto Giacometti
Suspended Ball
1930–1931
Plaster, painted metal and string,
60.6 × 35.6 × 36.1 cm (23 ⅞ × 14 × 14 ¼ in.)
Fondation Giacometti, Paris
—

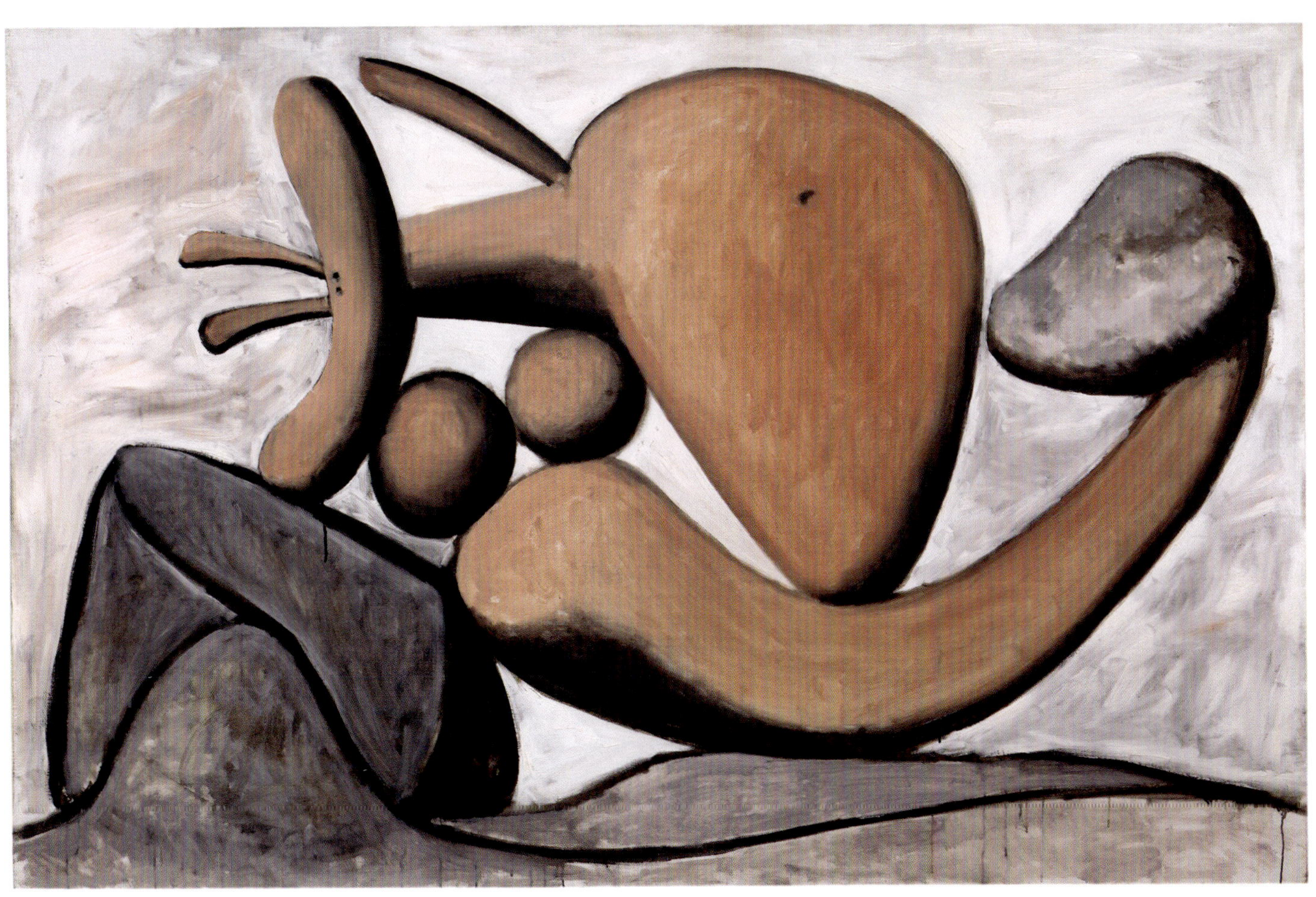

Fig. 101
Pablo Picasso
Woman Throwing a Stone
Paris, 8 March 1931
Oil on canvas, 130.5 × 195.5 cm (4 ft. 3 ⅜ in. × 6 ft. 5 in.)
Musée National Picasso-Paris
Dation Pablo Picasso, 1979. MP133

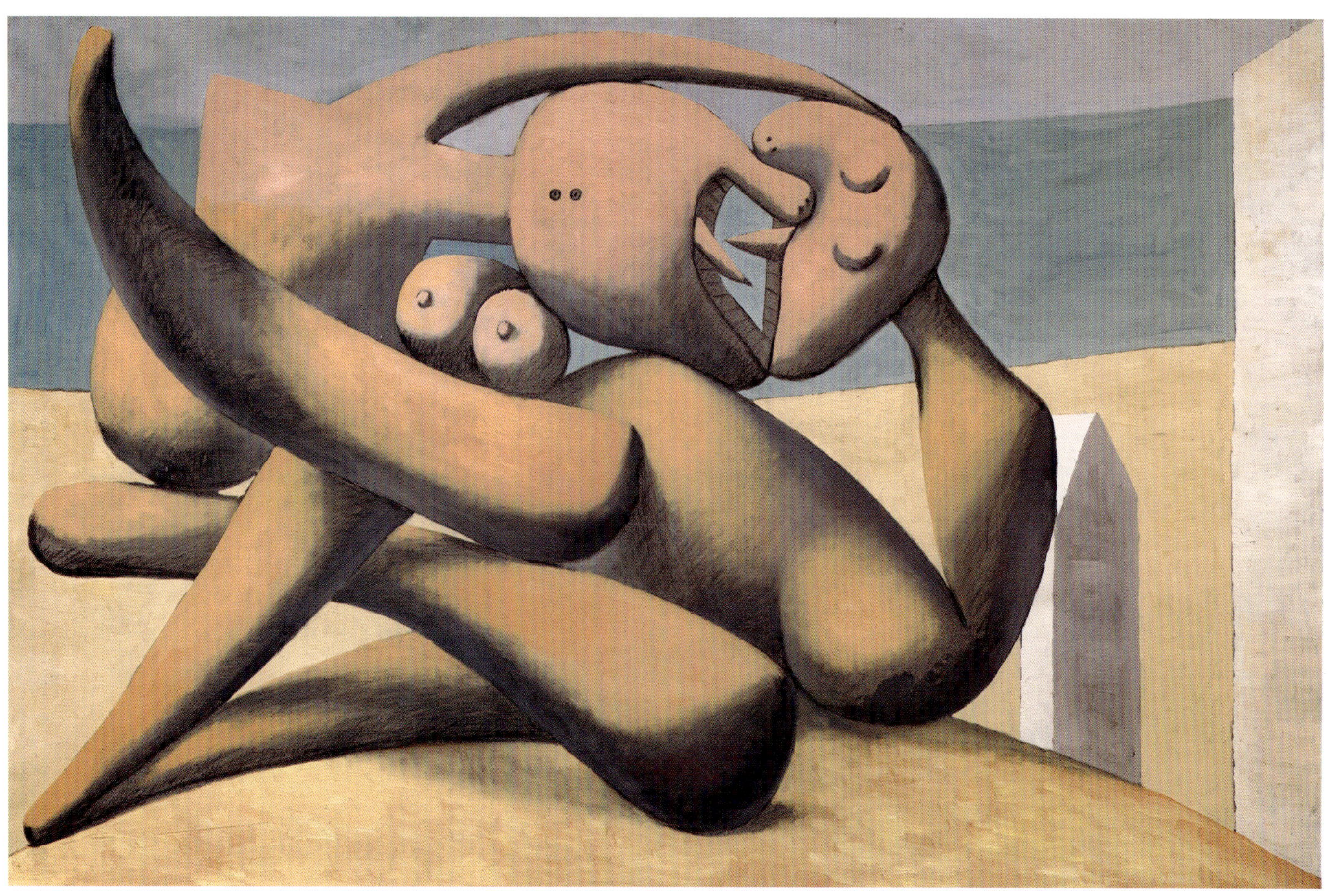

—

Fig. 102
Pablo Picasso
Figures on the Seashore
Paris, 12 January 1931
Oil on canvas, 130 × 195 cm (4 ft. 3 ¼ in. × 6 ft. 4 ⅞ in.)
Musée National Picasso-Paris
Dation Pablo Picasso, 1979. MP131

—

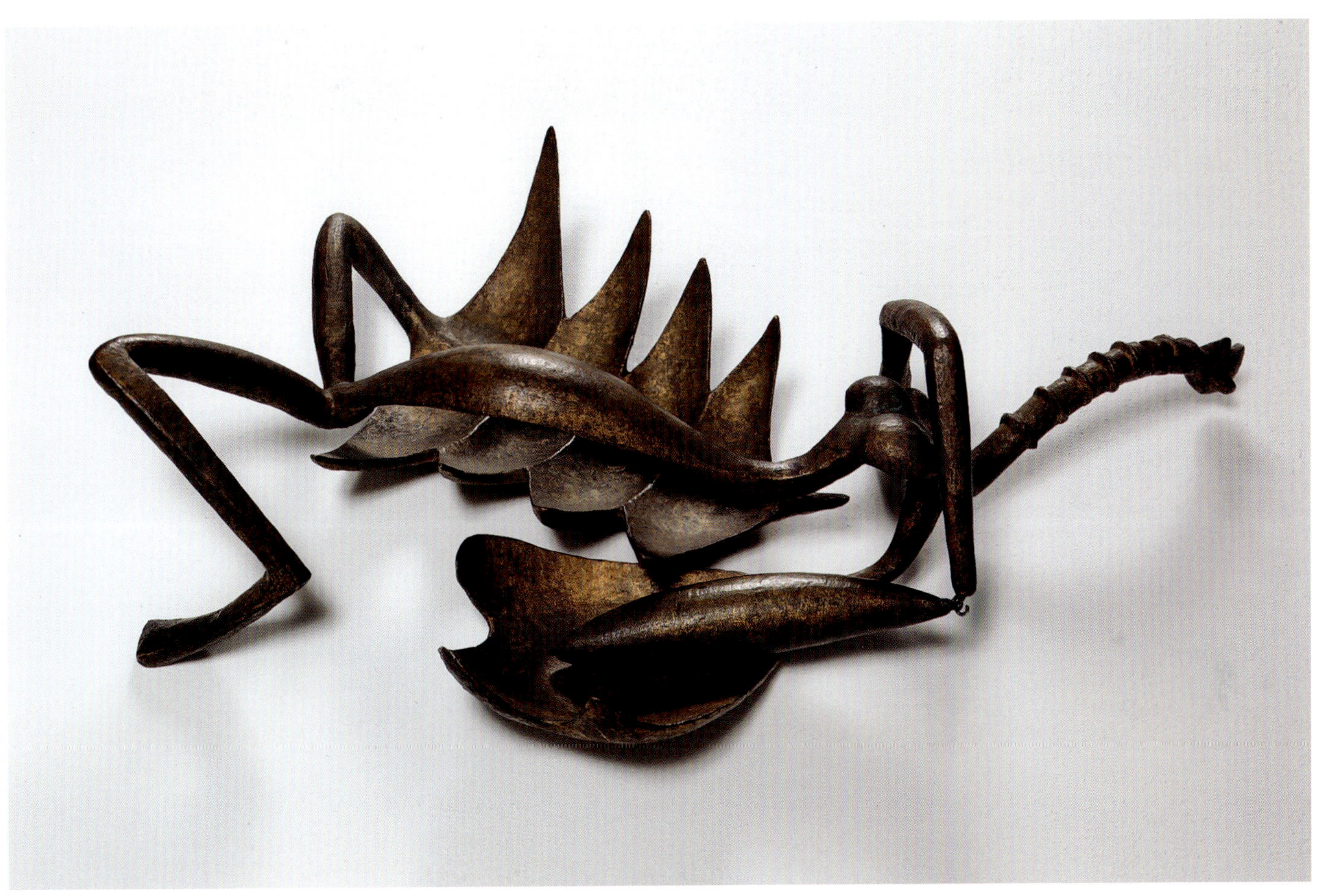

—

Fig. 103
Alberto Giacometti
Woman with Her Throat Cut
1933
Bronze, 21.5 × 82.2 × 55 cm (8 ½ × 32 ⅜ × 21 ⅝ in.)
Musée National d'Art Moderne/Centre de Création Industrielle,
Centre Pompidou, Paris
AM 1992-359

—

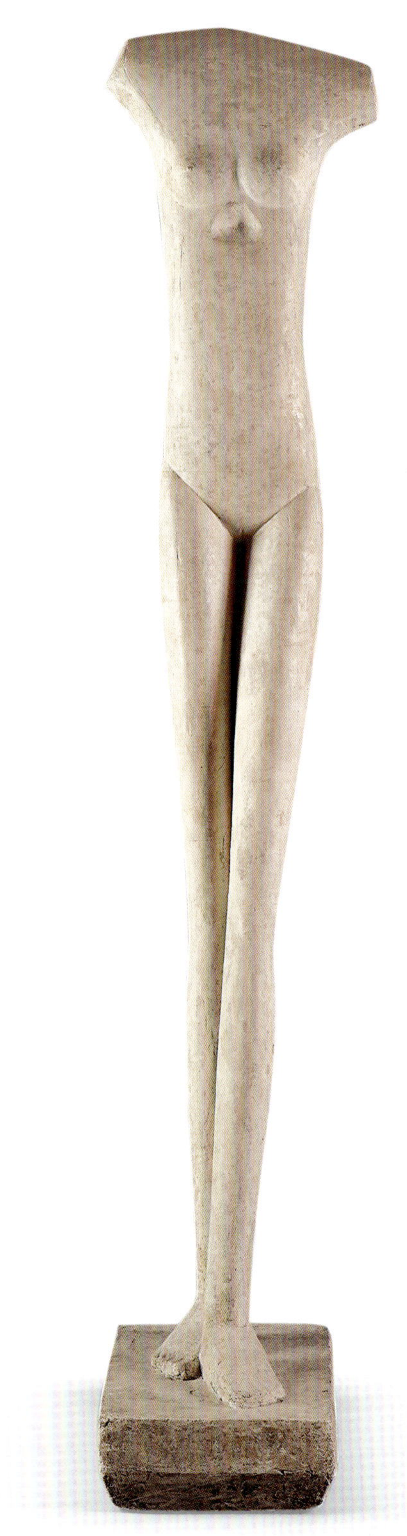

Fig. 104
Alberto Giacometti
Walking Woman (I)
1932
Plaster, 152.1 × 28.2 × 39 cm (5 ft. × 11 ⅛ in. × 15 ⅜ in.)
Fondation Giacometti, Paris

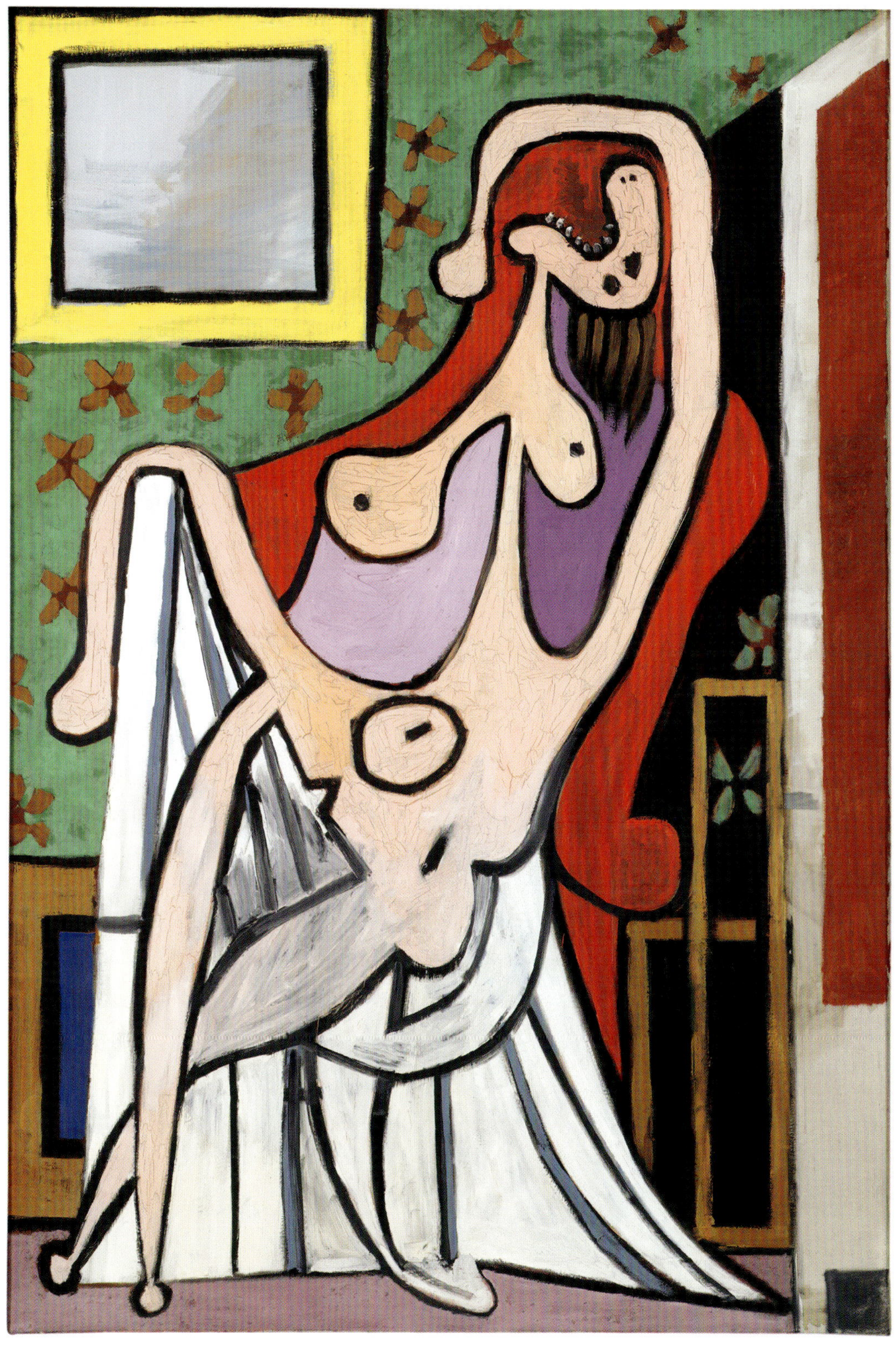

Fig. 105
Pablo Picasso
Large Nude in a Red Armchair
Paris, 5 May 1929
Oil on canvas, 195 × 129 cm (6 ft. 4 ⅞ in. × 4 ft. 2 ¾ in.)
Musée National Picasso-Paris
Dation Pablo Picasso, 1979. MP113

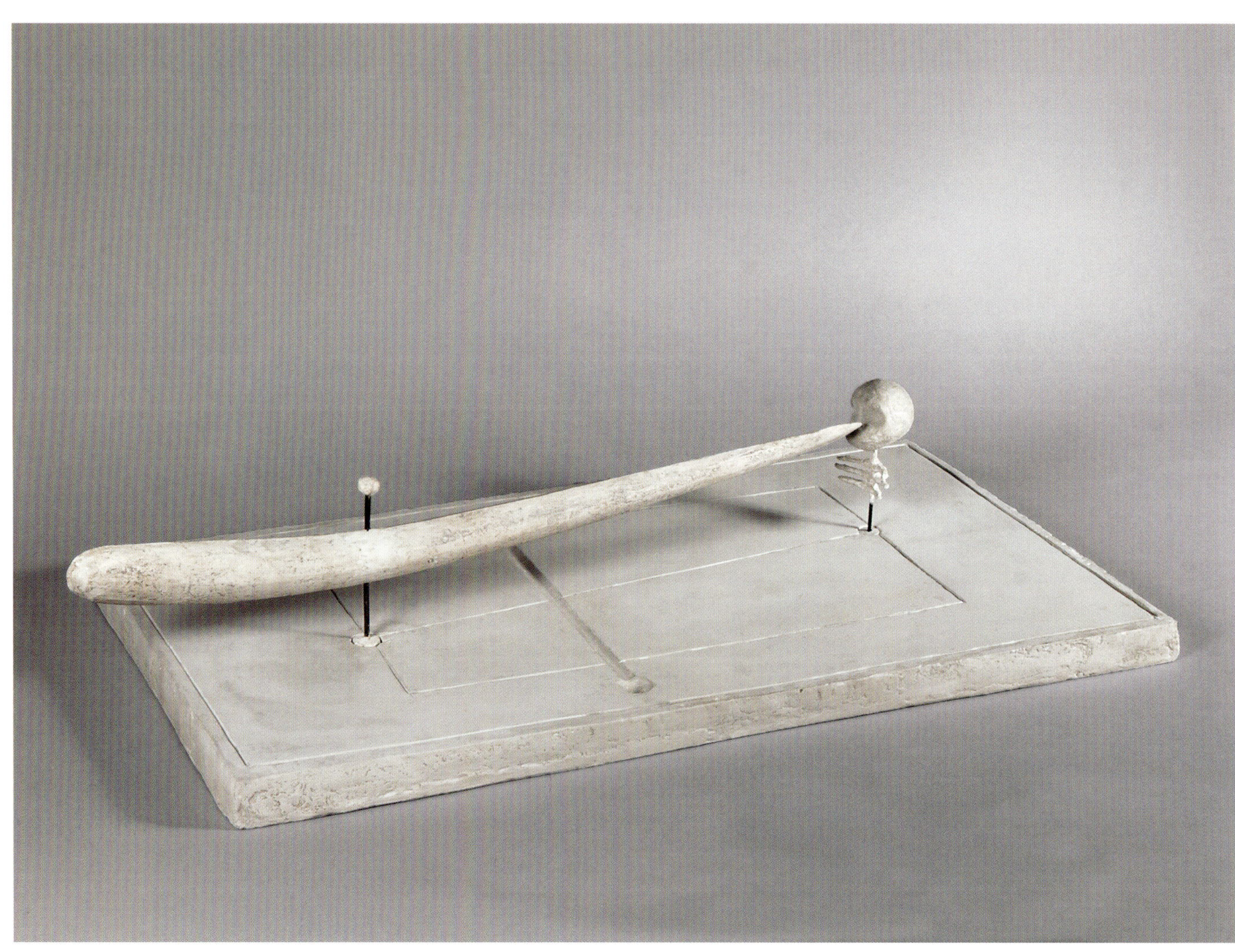

—
Fig. 106
Alberto Giacometti
Point to the Eye
1931–1932
Plaster and metal, 13.5 × 59.5 × 31 cm (5 ⅜ × 23 ⅜ × 12 ¼ in.)
Partial reconstitution realized in collaboration with the
Kunsthaus Zürich, Alberto Giacometti-Stiftung
Fondation Giacometti, Paris
—

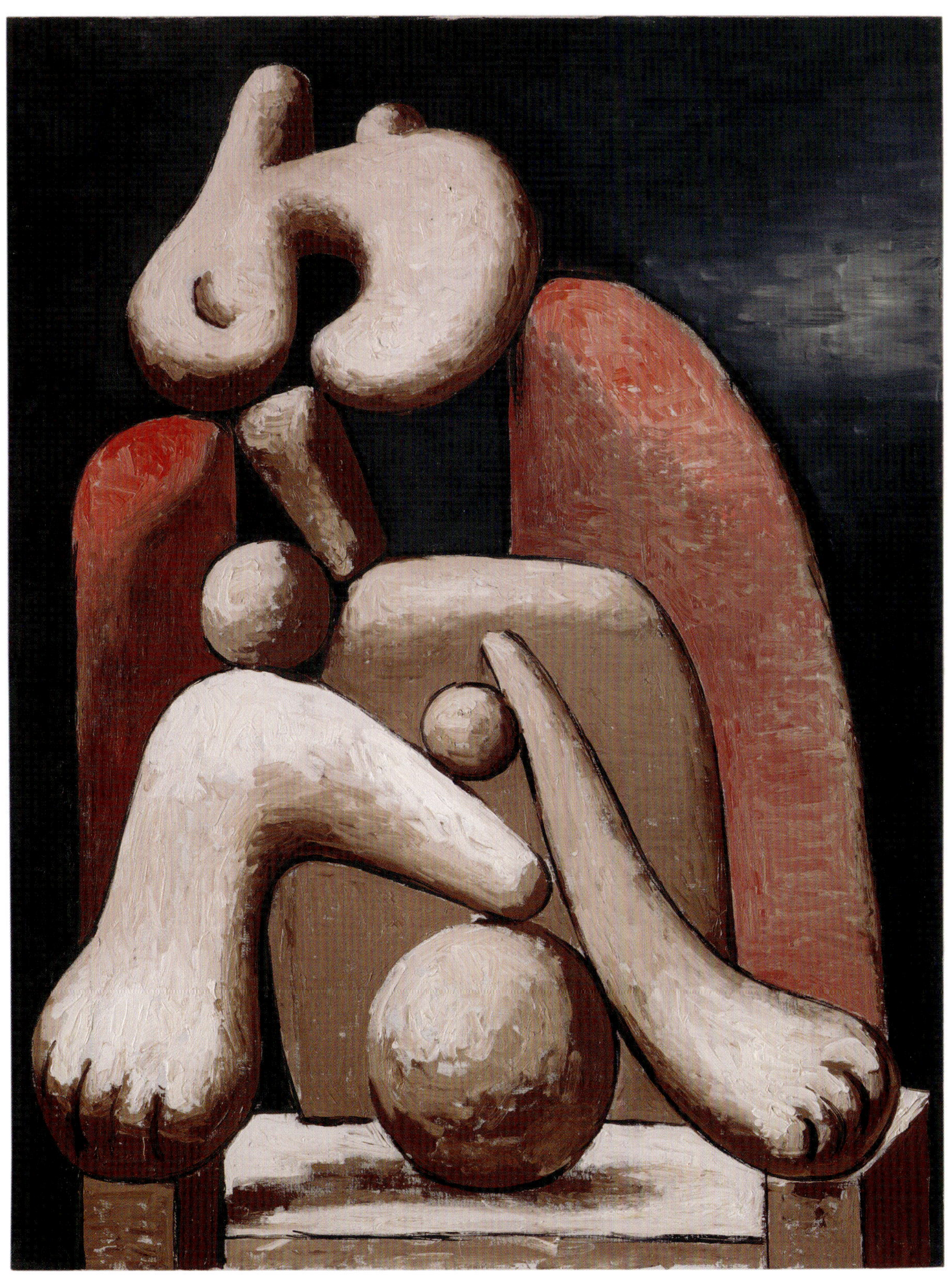

—
Fig. 107
Pablo Picasso
Woman in a Red Armchair
Boisgeloup, 27 January 1932
Oil on canvas, 130.2 × 97 cm (4 ft. 3 ¼ in. × 3 ft. 2 ⅛ in.)
Musée National Picasso-Paris
Dation Pablo Picasso, 1979. MP138
—

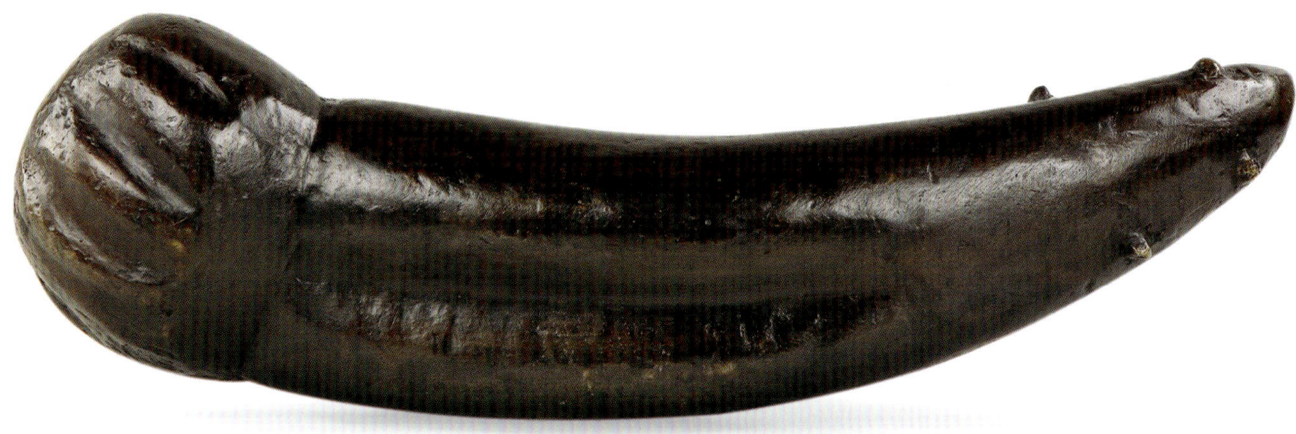

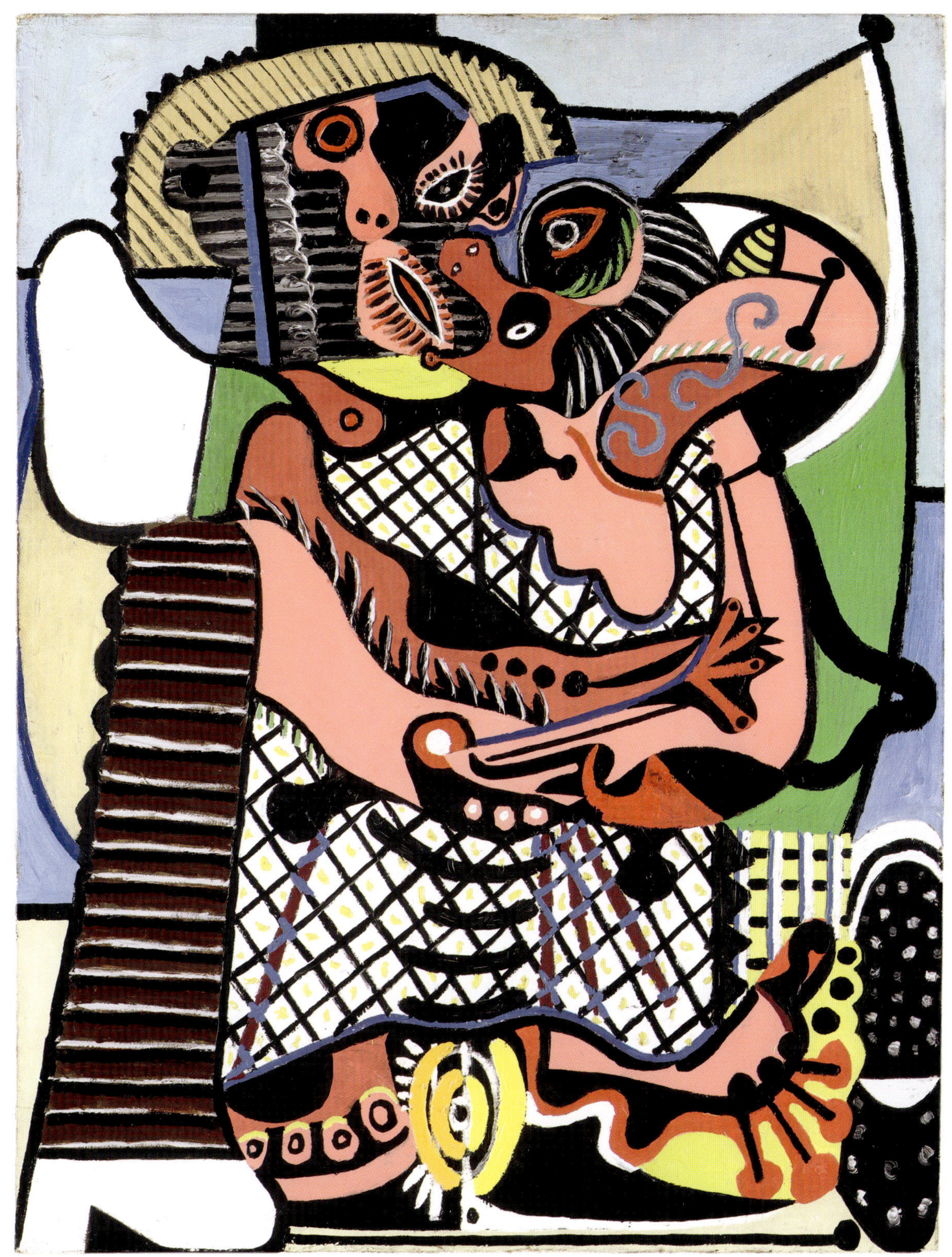

Fig. 109
Pablo Picasso
The Kiss
Juan-les-Pins, summer 1925
Oil on canvas, 130.5 × 97.7 cm (4 ft. 3 ⅜ in. × 3 ft. 2 ⅜ in.)
Musée National Picasso-Paris
Dation Pablo Picasso, 1979. MP85

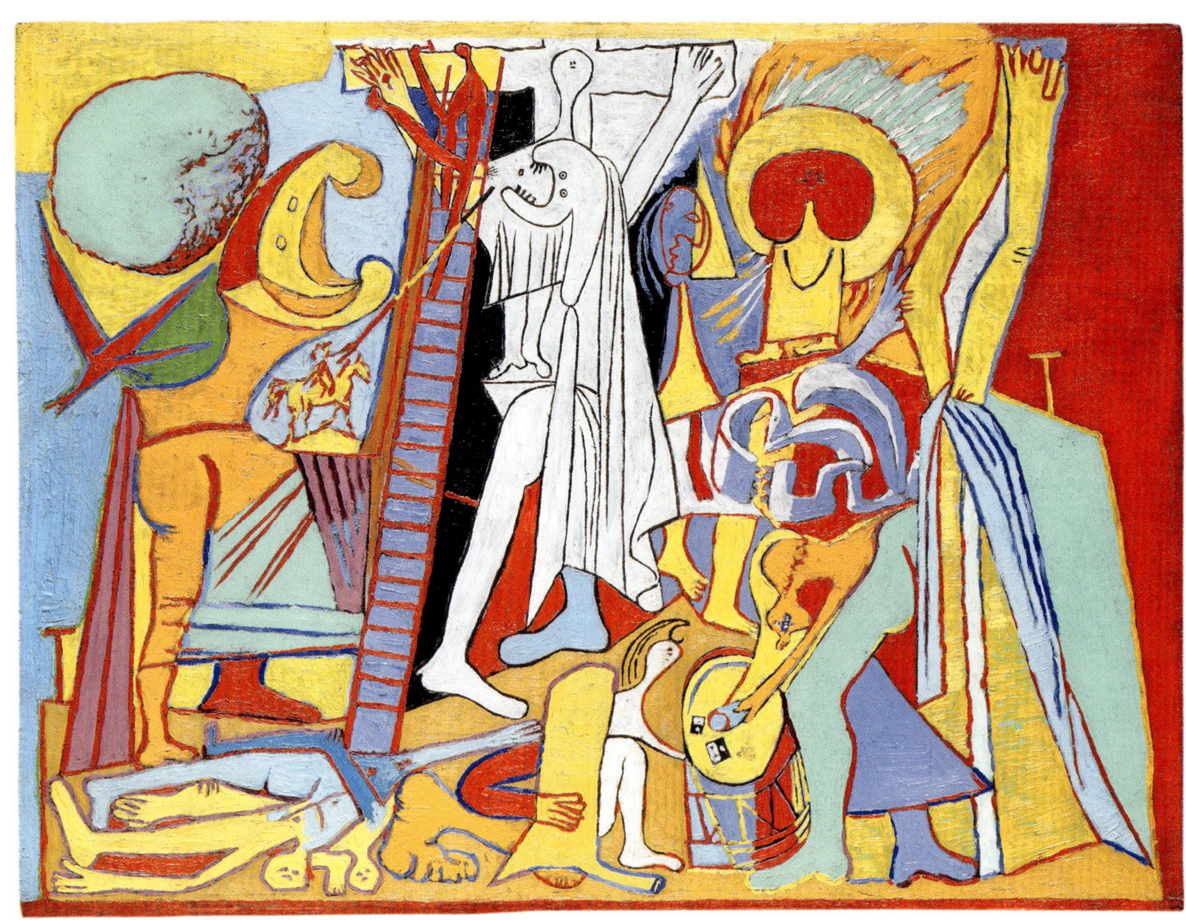

Fig. 110
Pablo Picasso
The Crucifixion
Paris, 7 February 1930
Oil on plywood, 51.5 × 66.5 cm (20 ¼ × 26 ⅛ in.)
Musée National Picasso-Paris
Dation Pablo Picasso, 1979. MP122

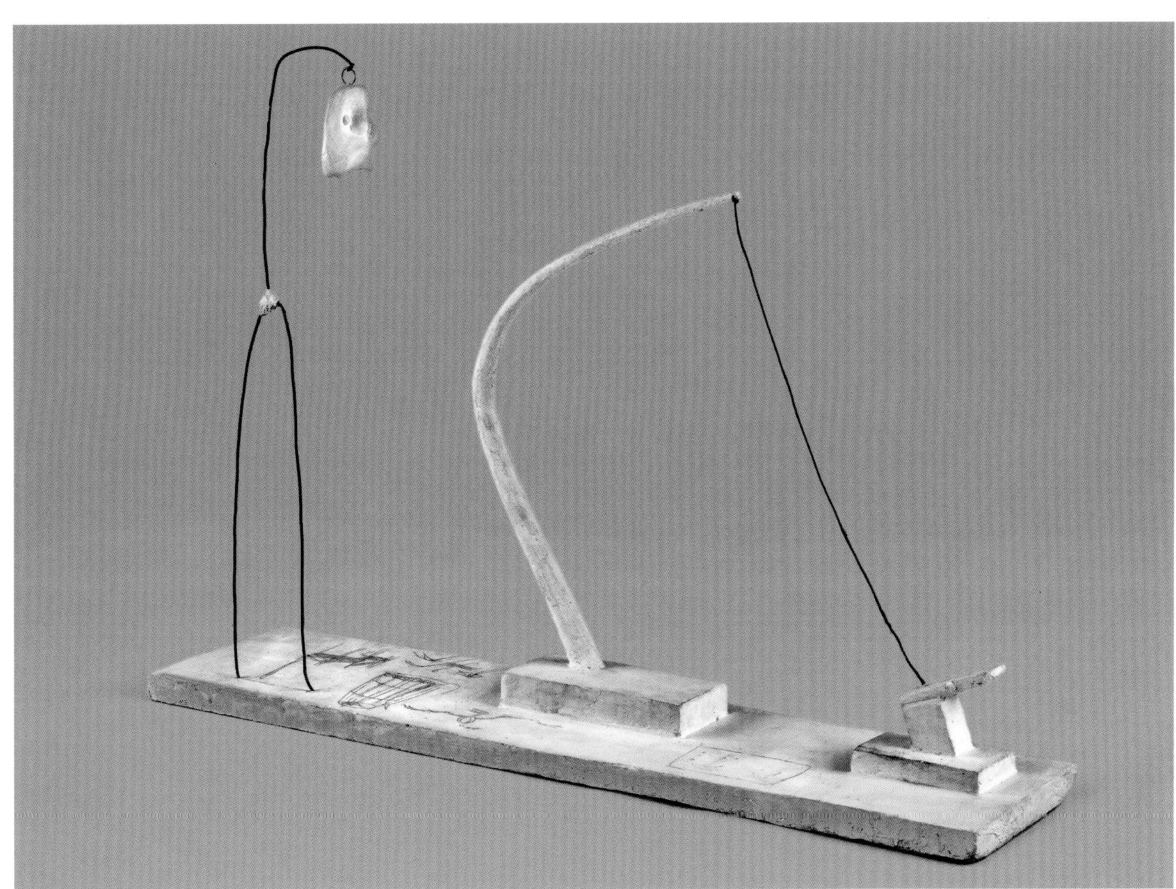

Fig. 111
Alberto Giacometti
Taut Thread (Flower in Danger)
1932
Plaster, metal and pencil,
52.2 × 78 × 18.5 cm (20 ½ × 30 ¾ × 7 ¼ in.)
Model for the final version in wood
(Flower reconstructed in 2015 with the
collaboration of the Kunsthaus Zurich,
Alberto Giacometti-Stiftung)
Fondation Giacometti, Paris

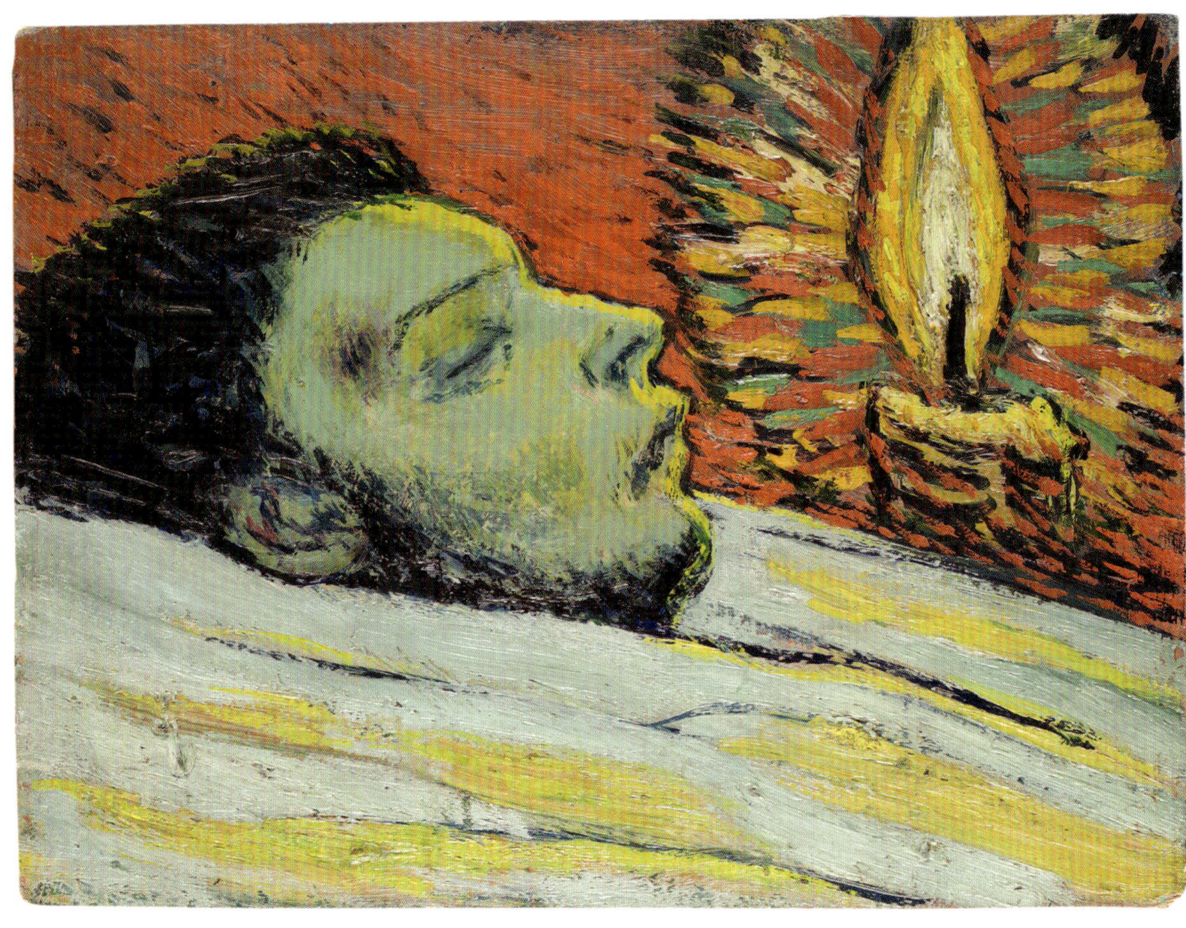

Fig. 112
Pablo Picasso
The Death of Casagemas
Paris, summer 1901
Oil on wood panel, 27 × 35 cm (10 ⅝ × 13 ¾ in.)
Musée National Picasso-Paris
Dation Pablo Picasso, 1979. MP3

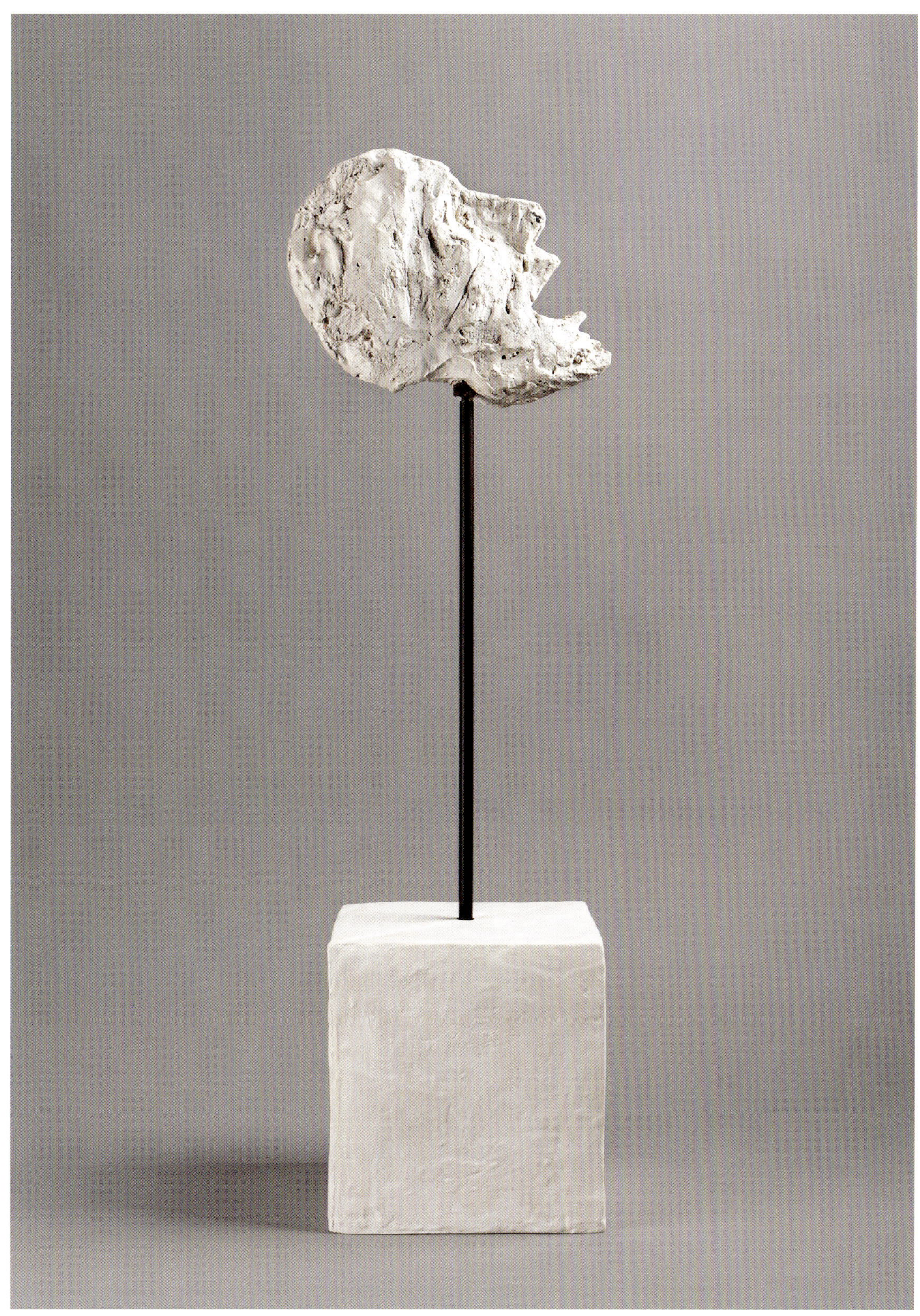

—
Fig. 113
Alberto Giacometti
Head on a Rod
1947
Painted plaster, 54 × 19 × 15 cm (21 ¼ × 7 ½ × 6 in.)
Fondation Giacometti, Paris
—

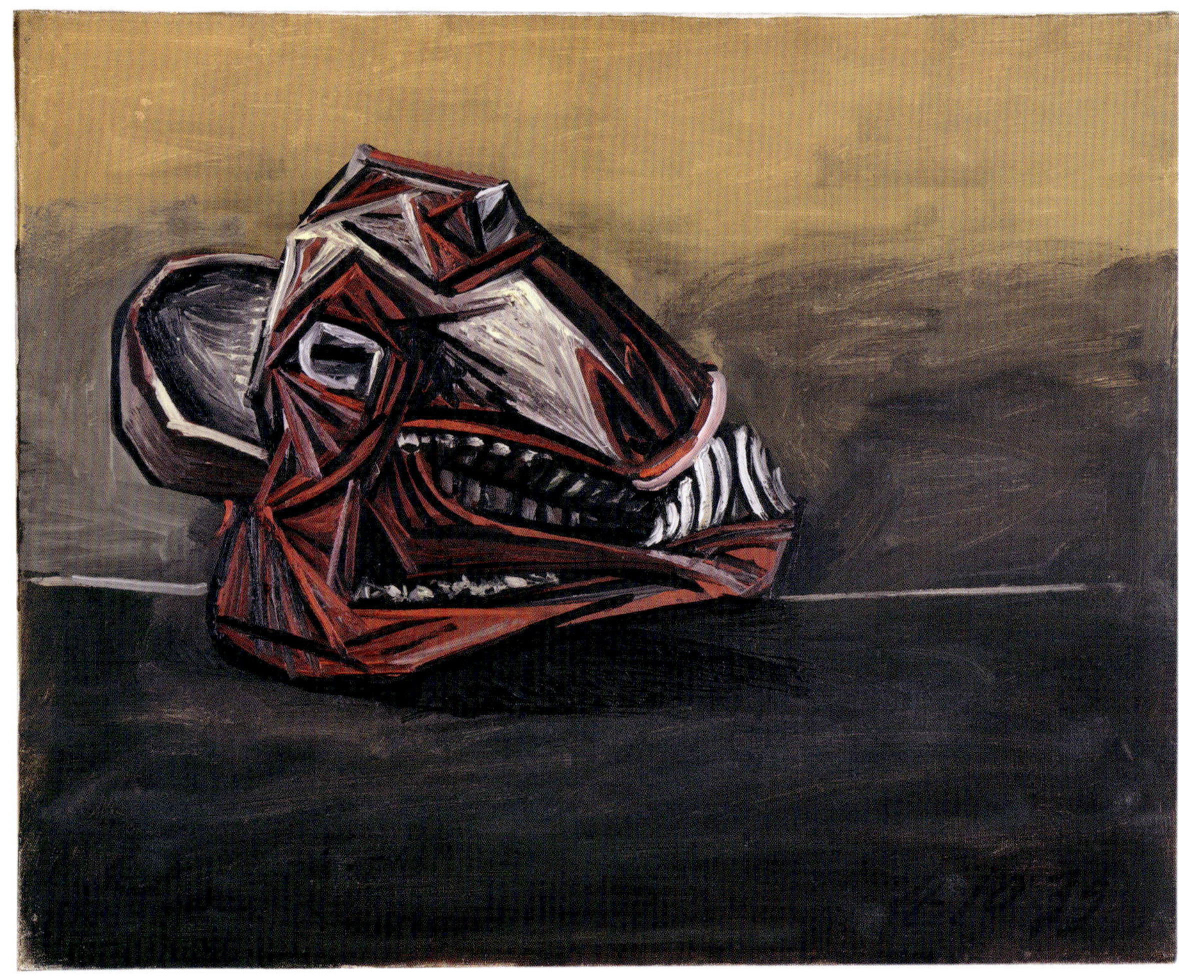

Fig. 114
Pablo Picasso
Flayed Head of a Sheep
Royan, 4 October 1939
Oil on canvas, 50 × 61 cm (19 ⅝ × 24 in.)
Musée National Picasso-Paris
Dation Jacqueline Picasso, 1990. MP1990-20

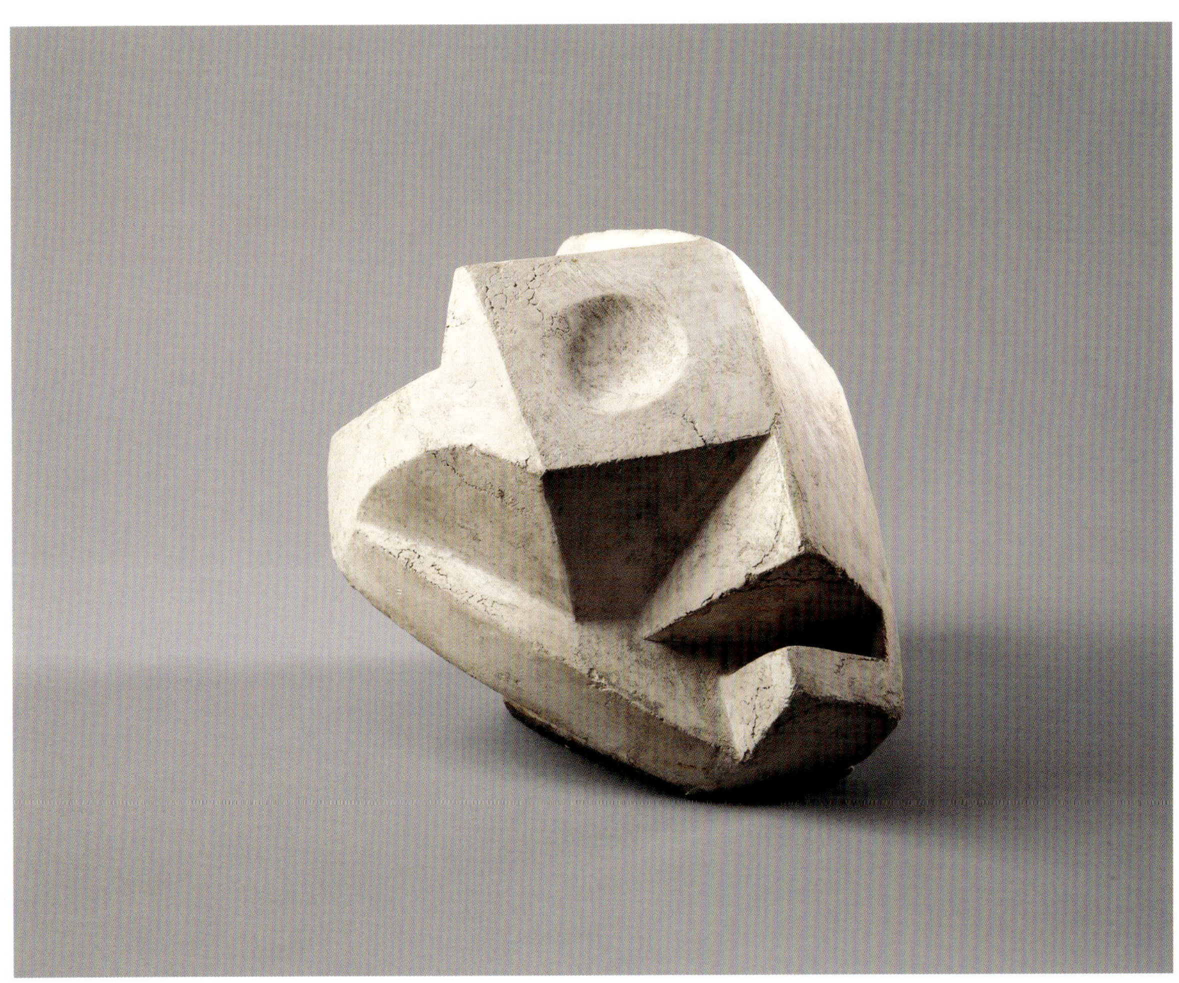

—
Fig. 115
Alberto Giacometti
Head-Skull
1934
Plaster, 18.3 × 19.9 × 22.1 cm (7 ¼ × 7 ⅞ × 8 ⅝ in.)
Fondation Giacometti, Paris
—

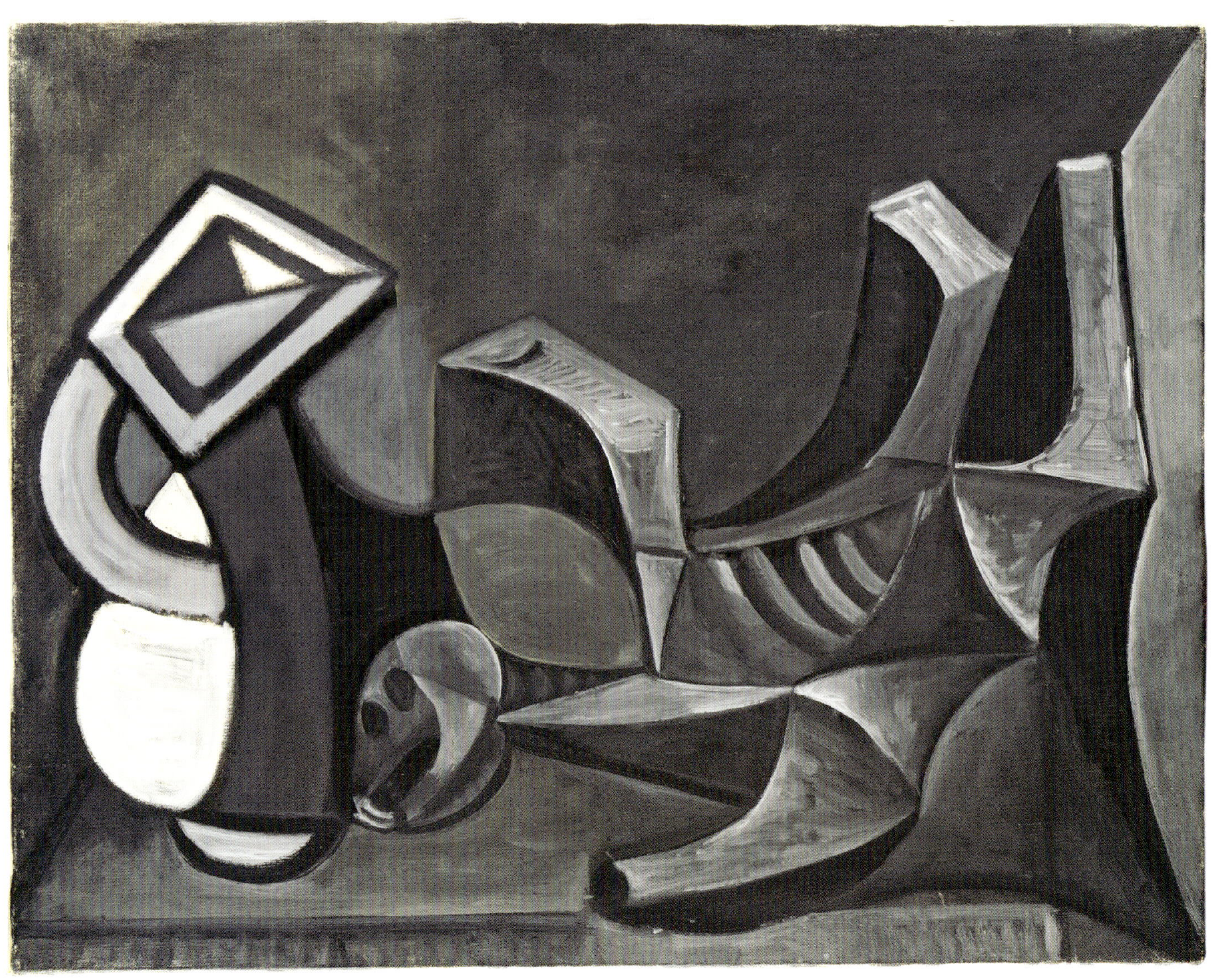

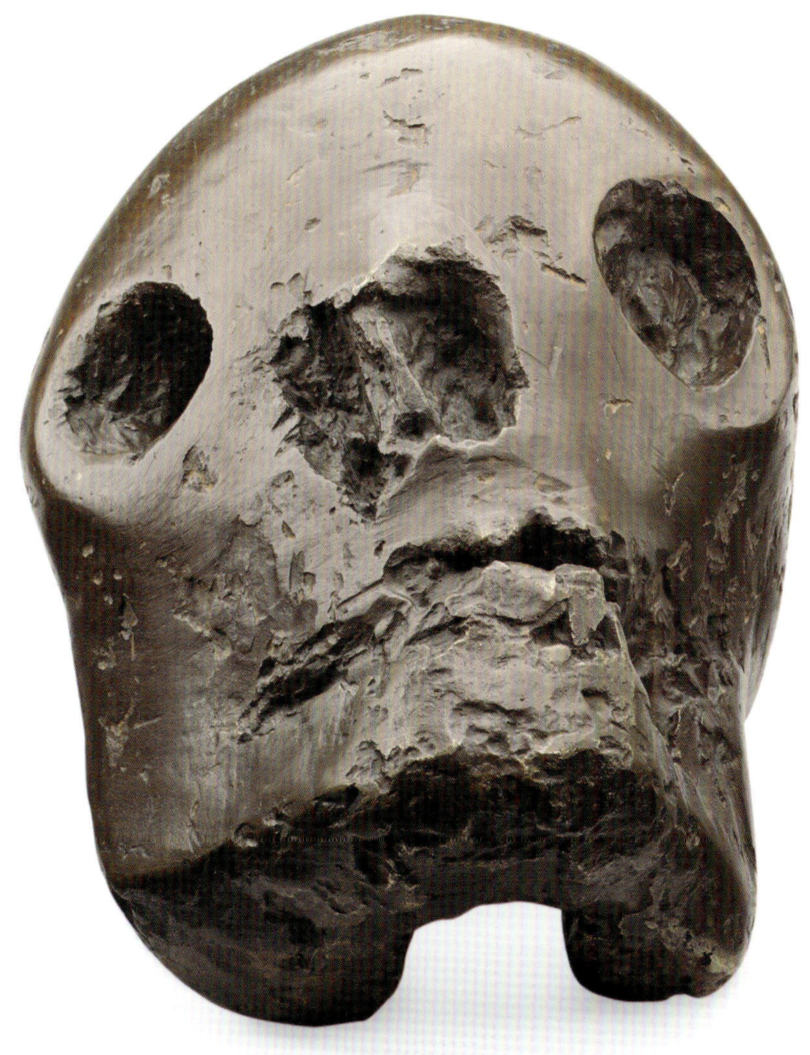

—
Fig. 117
Pablo Picasso
Death's Head
Paris, 1943
Bronze and copper, 25 × 21 × 31 cm (9 ⅞ × 8 ¼ × 12 ¼ in.)
Musée National Picasso-Paris
Dation Pablo Picasso, 1979. MP326
—

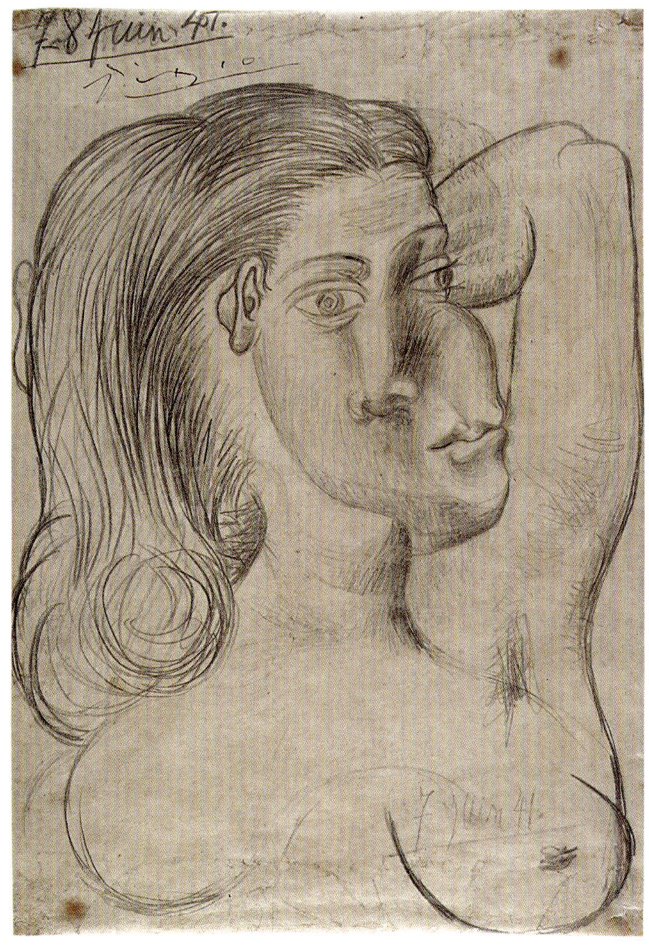

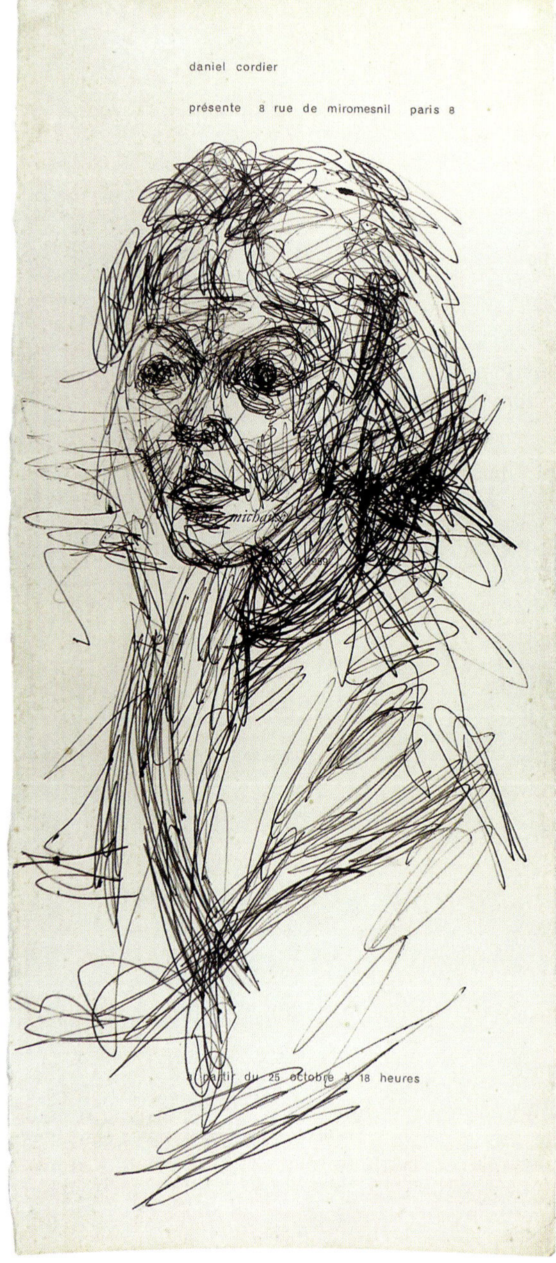

Fig. 118
Pablo Picasso
Dora Maar
7–8 June 1941
Graphite pencil on paper,
32.4 × 21.9 cm (12 ¾ × 8 ⅝ in.)
Musée National Picasso-Paris
Purchase, 1997. MP1997-2
—
Fig. 119
Alberto Giacometti
Annette
After 1959
Ballpoint pen on invitation card,
29.7 × 12.7 cm (11 ⅝ × 5 in.)
Fondation Giacometti, Paris
—

The Lover and the Model

A series of painted and sculpted portraits of the beloved woman develops the inexhaustible dialectic of the lover and his model. Though Picasso and Giacometti sought to capture the truth and reality of a muse, their works also convey the psychological intensity of their relationship with the model. Thus, the face of Dora Maar, Picasso's lover and principal model from 1935 to 1943, saturates the canvas with her tortured presence. Annette, Giacometti's future wife whom he met in 1943, offered to sit for him for long periods at a time. Her face is subjected to the scrutiny of an artist struggling with the impossible 'search for the absolute' (J-P Sartre) in order to recreate the aura of a being.

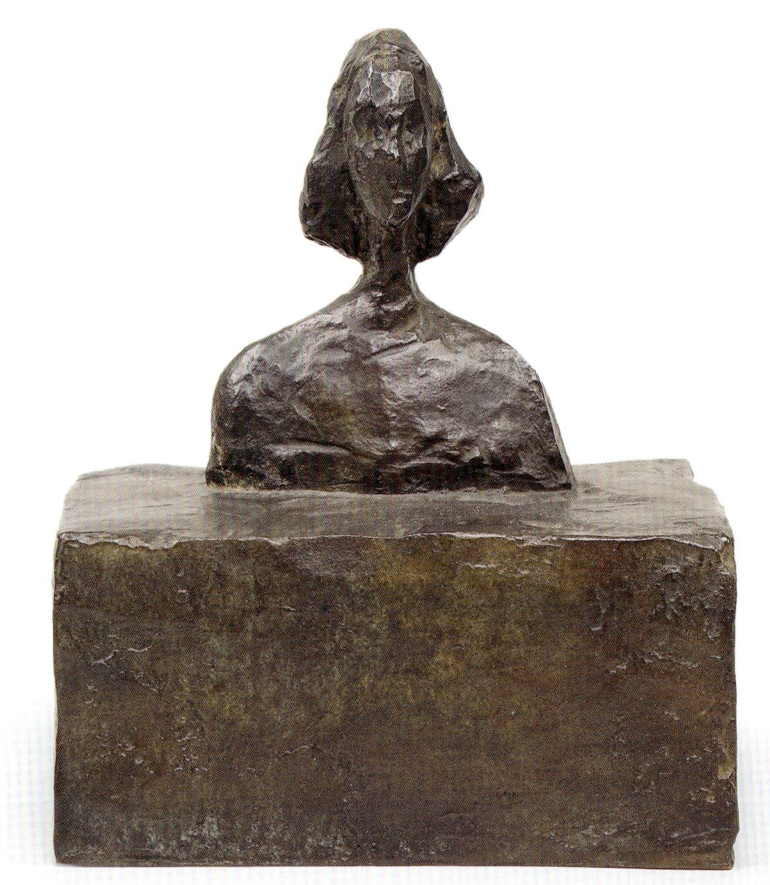

Fig. 120
Alberto Giacometti
Small Bust of Annette
c. 1946
Bronze, 16 × 13.6 × 8.5 cm (6 ¼ × 5 ⅜ × 3 ⅜ in.)
Fondation Giacometti, Paris

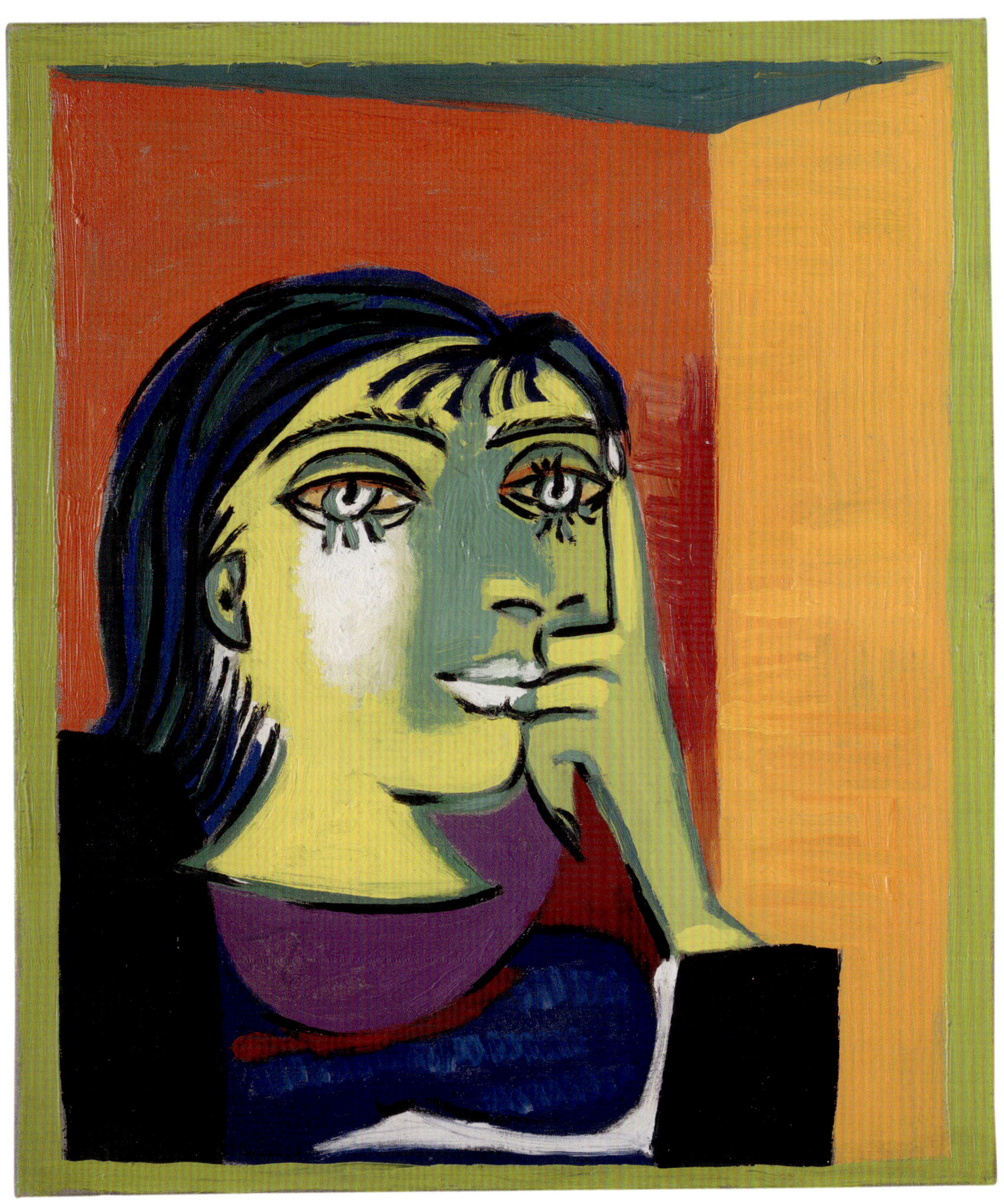

Fig. 121
Pablo Picasso
Portrait of Dora Maar
Paris, 23 November 1937
Oil on canvas, 55.3 × 46.3 cm (21 ¾ × 18 ¼ in.)
Musée National Picasso-Paris
Dation Pablo Picasso, 1979. MP166

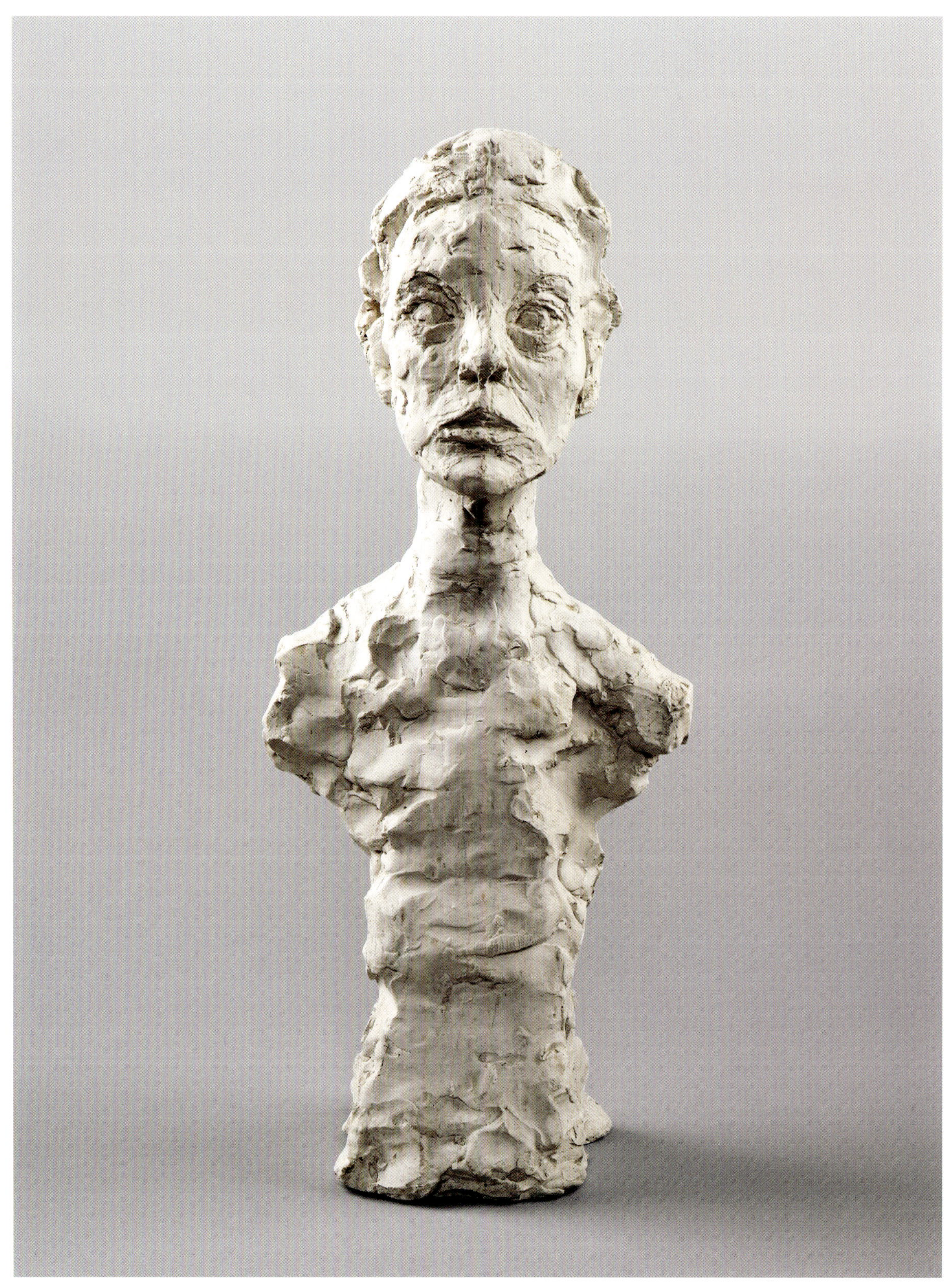

—
Fig. 122
Alberto Giacometti
Bust of Annette X
1965
Plaster, 45 × 18.5 × 13.4 cm (17 ¾ × 7 ¼ × 5 ¼ in.)
Fondation Giacometti, Paris
—

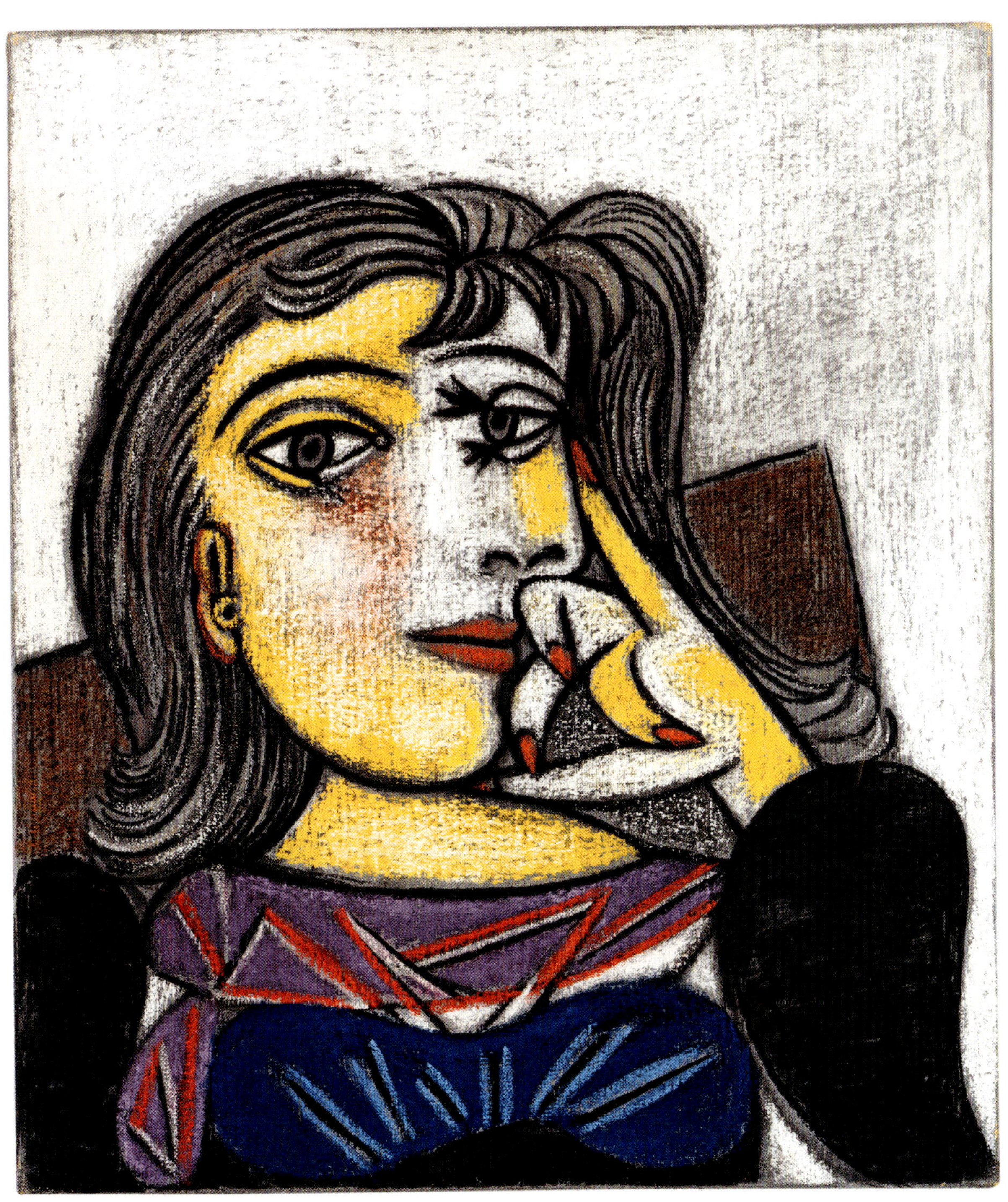

Fig. 123
Pablo Picasso
Portrait of Dora Maar
Paris, 1 October 1937
Oil and pastel on canvas,
55 × 45.5 cm (21 ⅝ × 18 in.)
Musée National Picasso-Paris
Dation Pablo Picasso, 1979. MP164

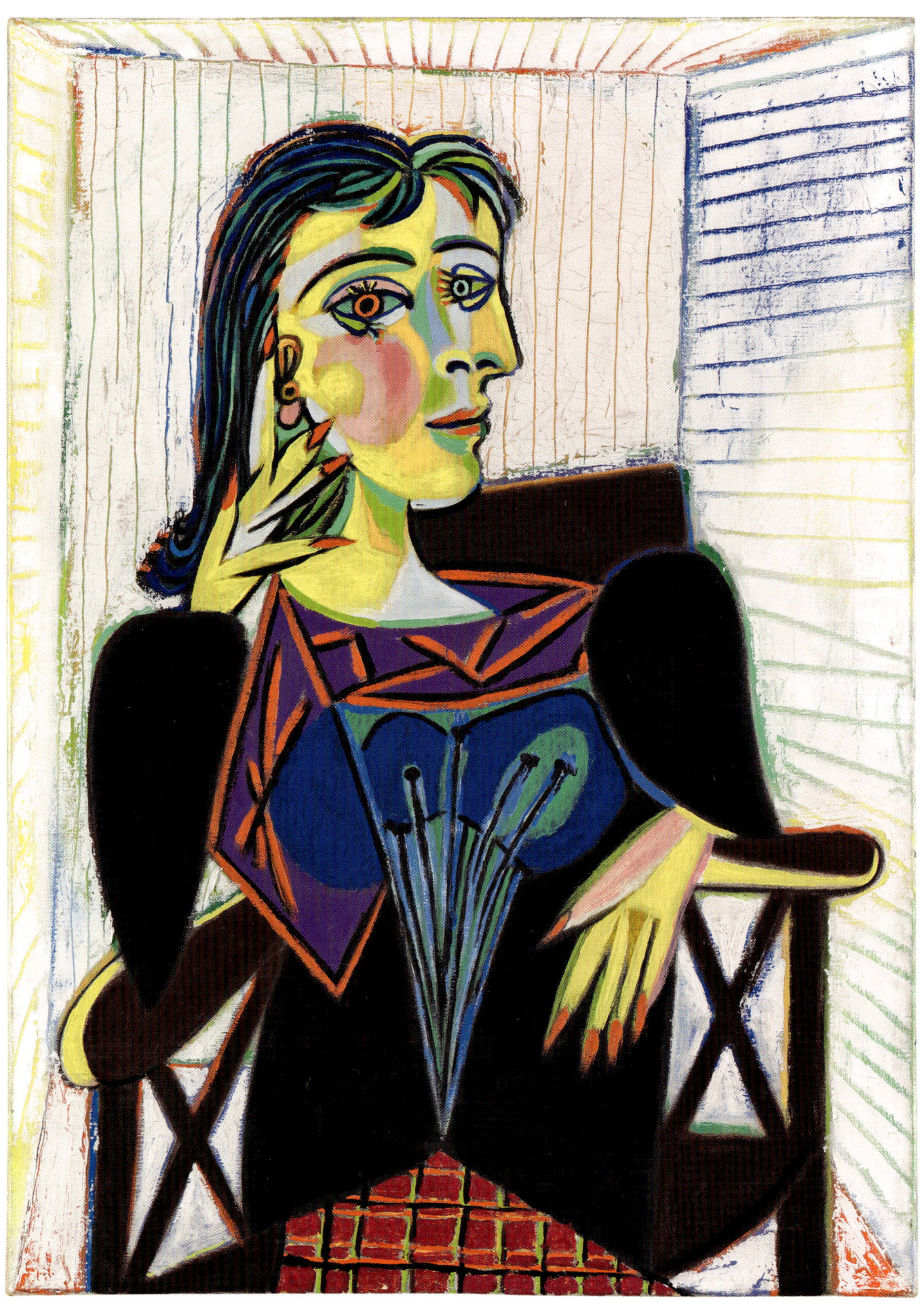

—
Fig. 124
Pablo Picasso
Portrait of Dora Maar
Paris, 1937
Oil on canvas, 92 × 65 cm (3 ft. ¼ in. × 2 ft. ½ in.)
Musée National Picasso-Paris
Dation Pablo Picasso, 1979. MP158
—

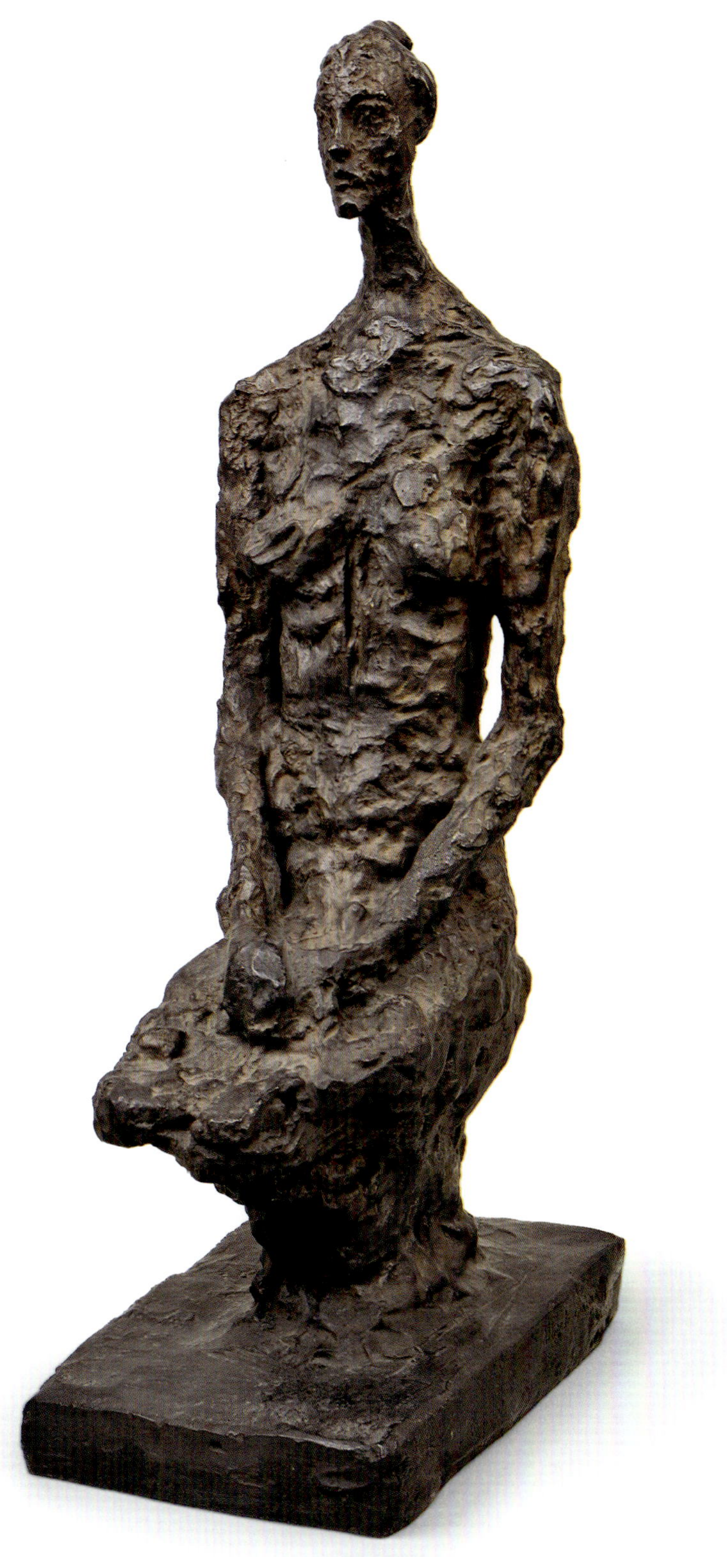

Fig. 125
Alberto Giacometti
Seated Woman
1956
Bronze, 51.3 × 15.6 × 23.9 cm (20 ¼ × 6 ⅛ × 9 ⅜ in.)
Fondation Giacometti, Paris

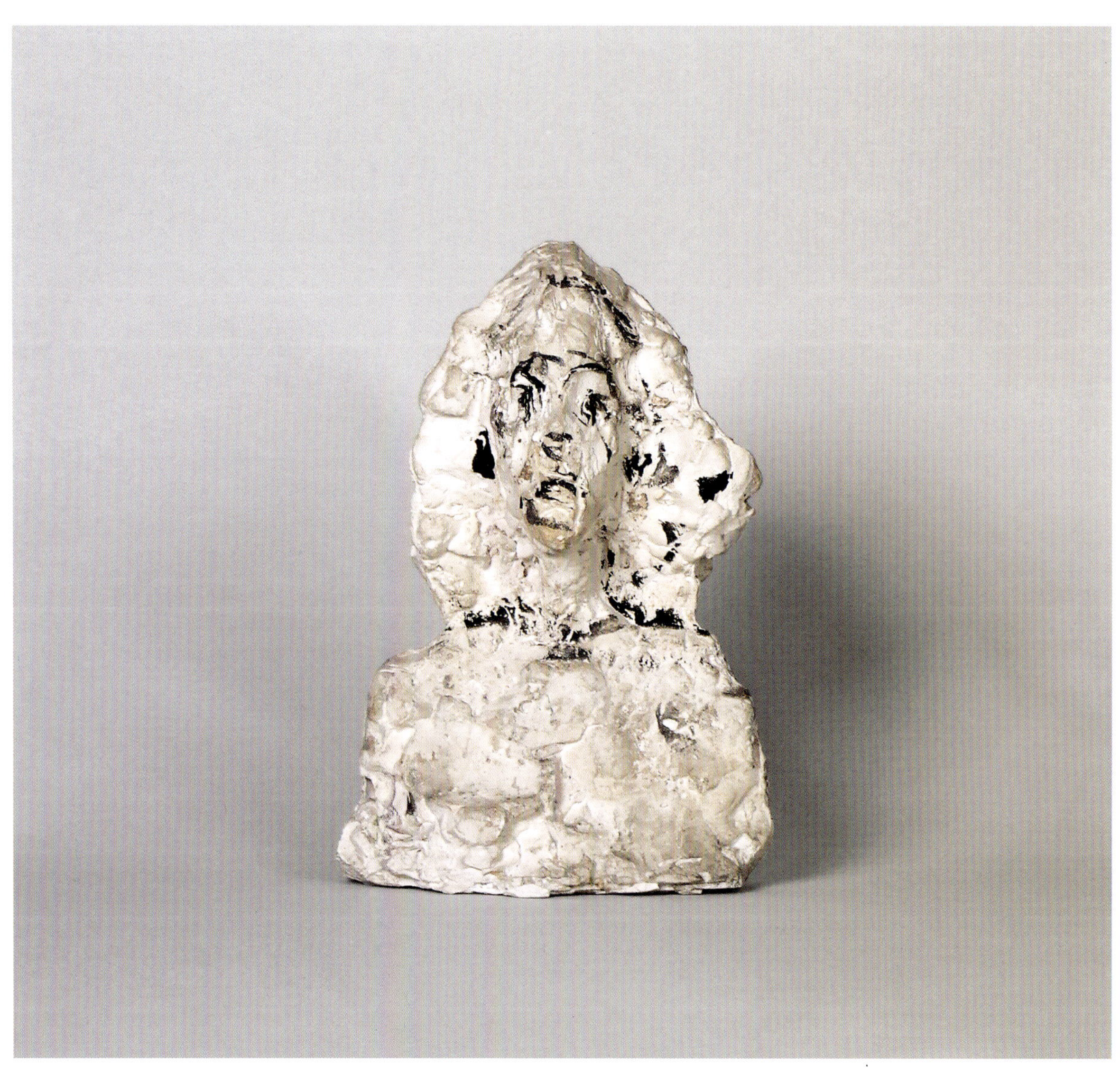

—
Fig. 126
Alberto Giacometti
Small Bust of Annette
c. 1951
Painted plaster, 21.5 × 14.5 × 9.4 cm (8 ½ × 5 ¾ × 3 ¾ in.)
Fondation Giacometti, Paris
—

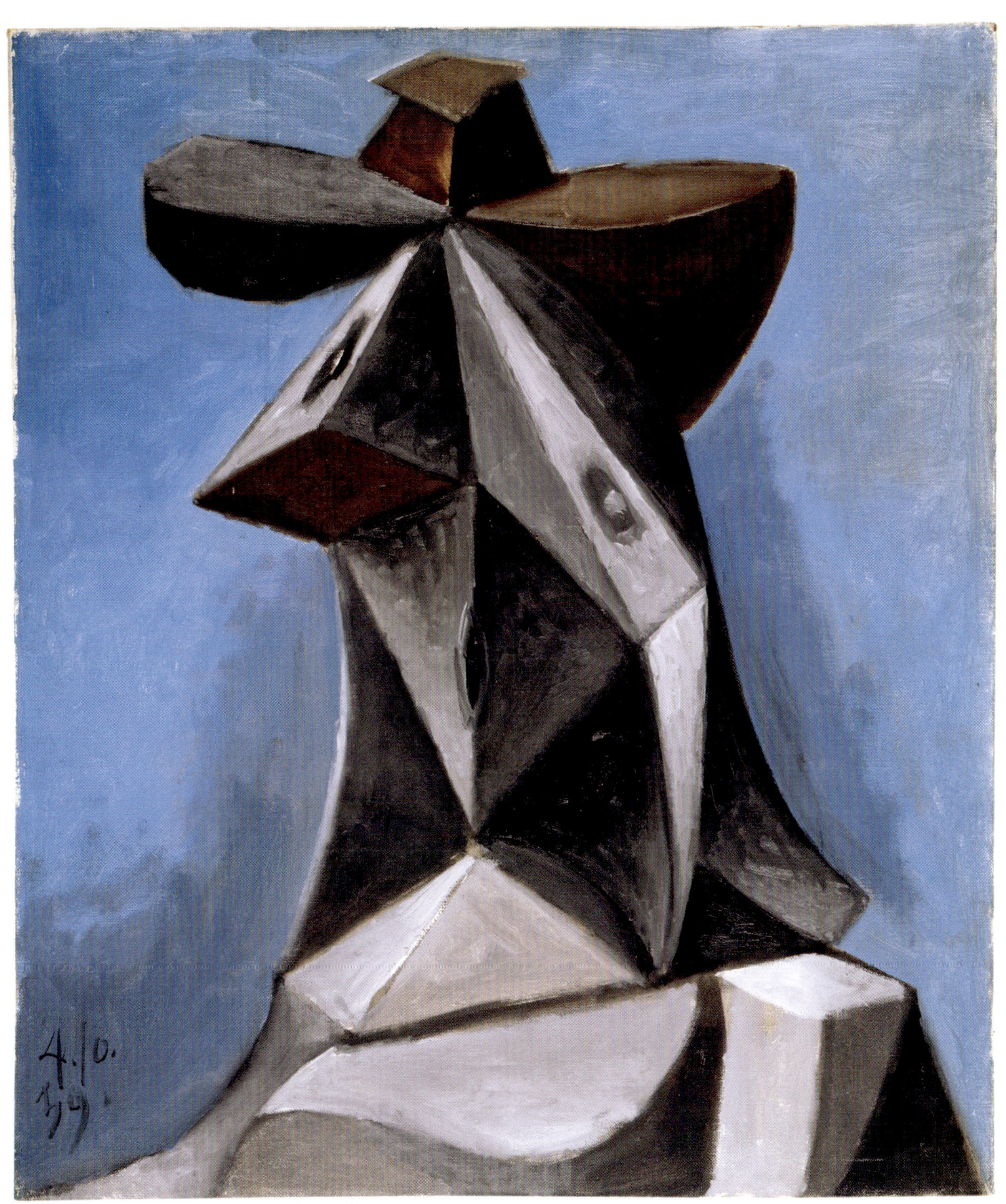

Fig. 127
Pablo Picasso
Head of a Woman
Royan, 4 October 1939
Oil on canvas, 65.5 × 54.5 cm (25 ¼ × 21 ½ in.)
Musée National Picasso-Paris
Dation Pablo Picasso, 1979. MP182

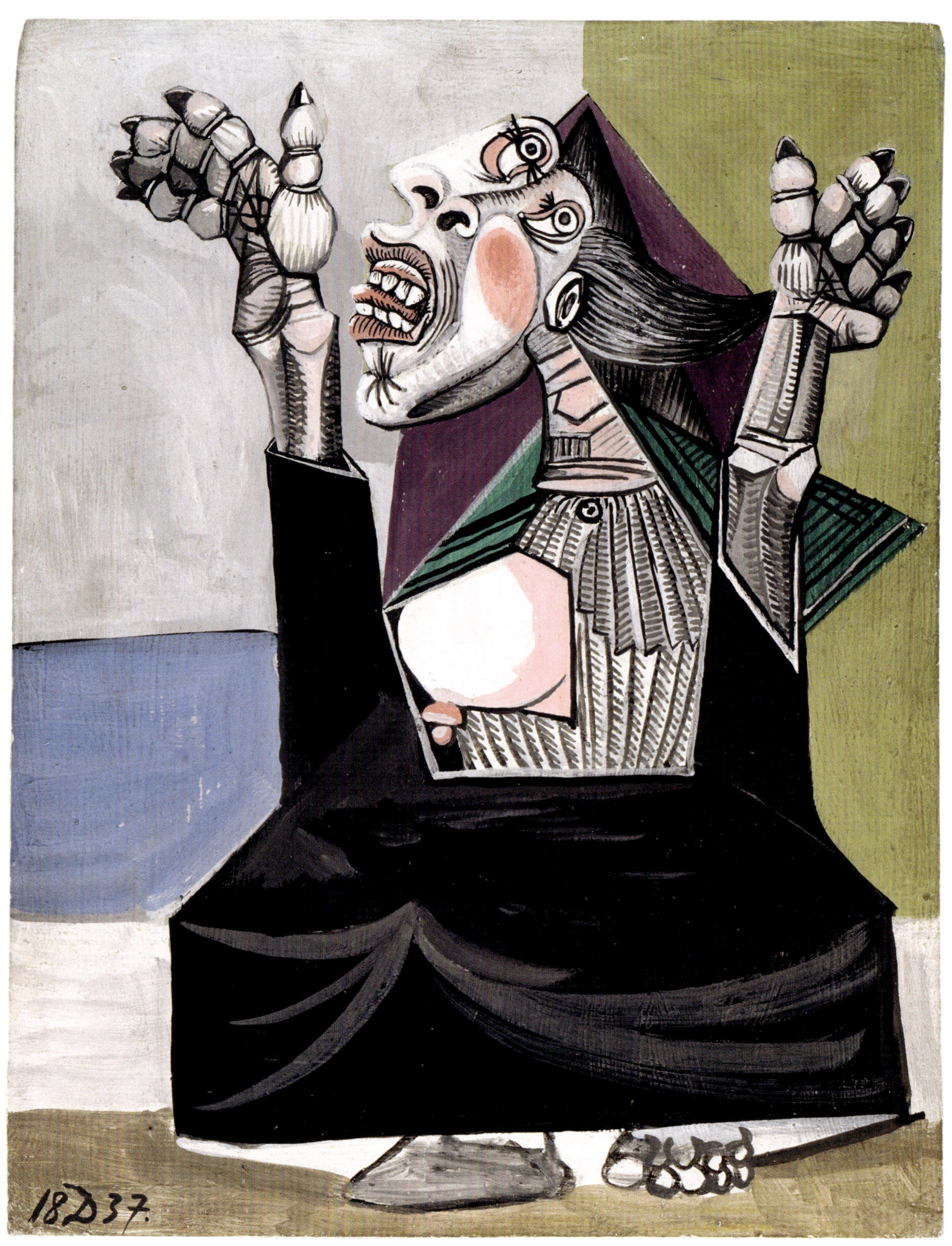

—
Fig. 128
Pablo Picasso
The Suppliant
Paris, 18 December 1937
Gouache on wood panel, 24 × 18.5 cm (9 ½ × 7 ¼ in.)
Musée National Picasso-Paris
Dation Pablo Picasso, 1979. MP168
—

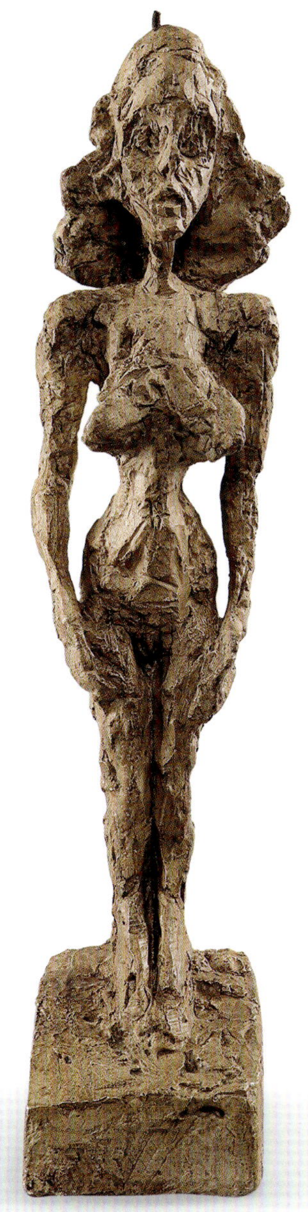

Fig. 129
Alberto Giacometti
Standing Nude II
1953
Plaster, 51.6 × 11.1 × 17 cm (20 ⅜ × 4 ⅜ × 6 ⅝ in.)
Fondation Giacometti, Paris

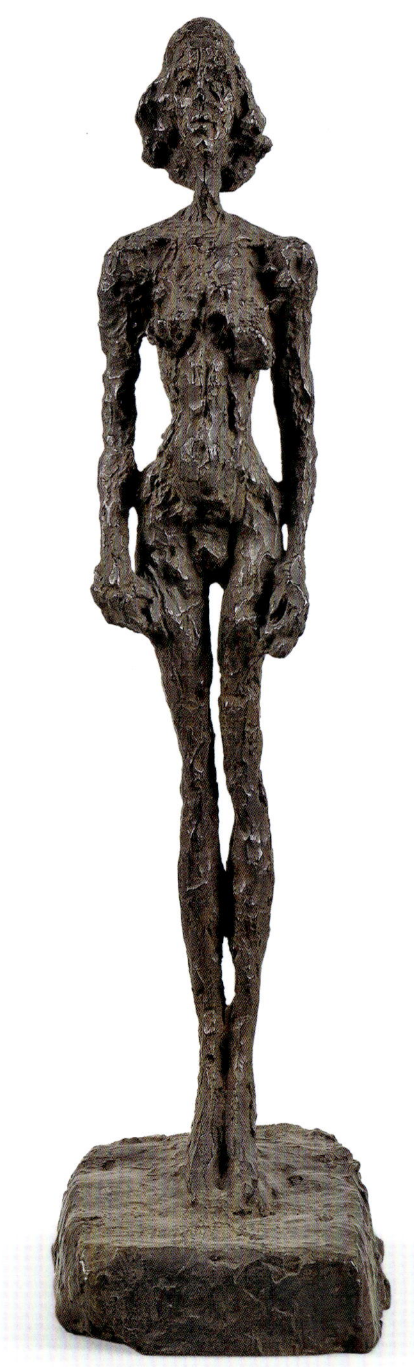

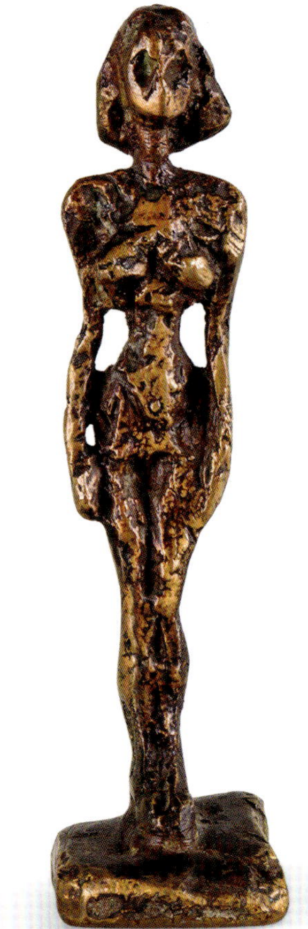

Fig. 130
Alberto Giacometti
Annette from Life
1954
Bronze, 54.1 × 14.3 × 20.1 cm (21 ¼ × 5 ⅝ × 8 in.)
Fondation Giacometti, Paris

Fig. 131
Alberto Giacometti
Annette Standing
c. 1954
Bronze, 11.5 × 2.9 × 3.4 cm (4 ½ × 1 ⅛ × 1 ⅜ in.)
Fondation Giacometti, Paris

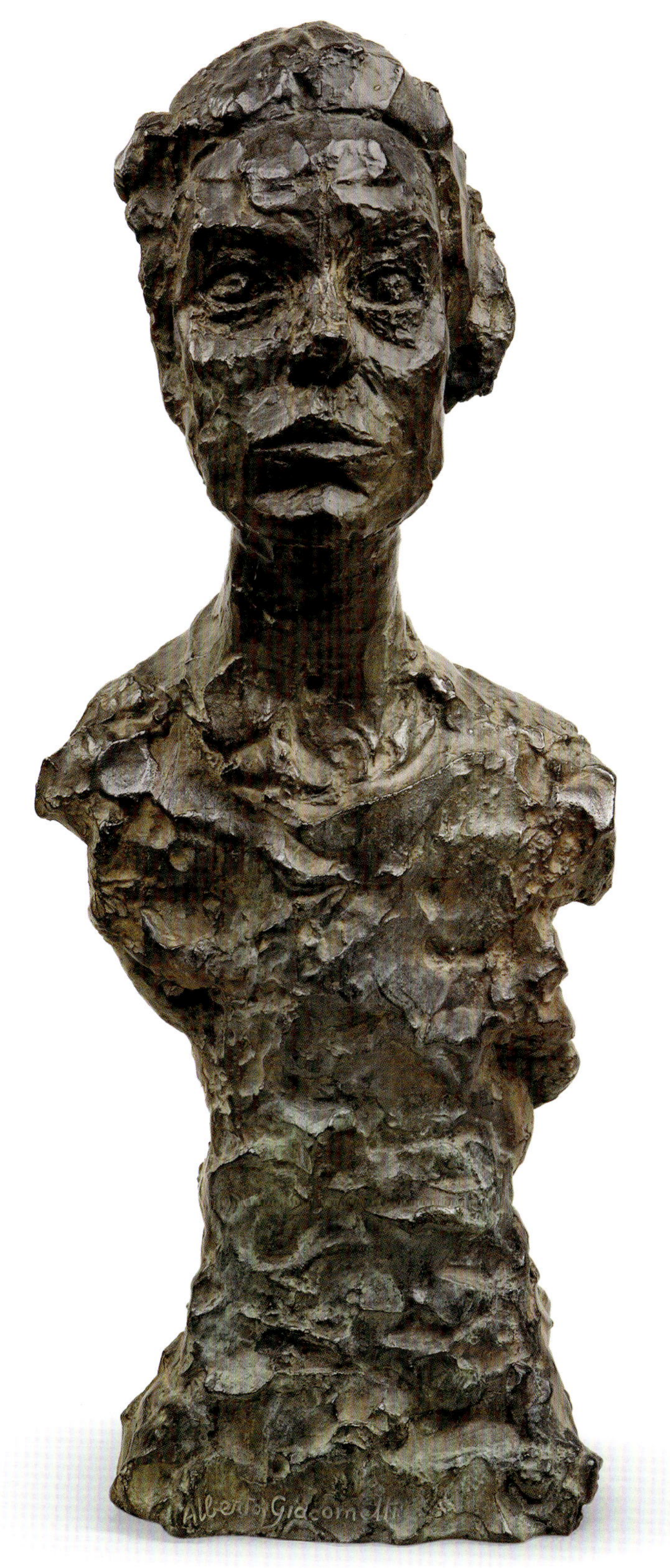

Fig. 132
Alberto Giacometti
Bust of Annette IX
1964
Bronze, 44.7 × 17.8 × 15 cm (17 ½ × 7 × 6 in.)
Fondation Giacometti, Paris

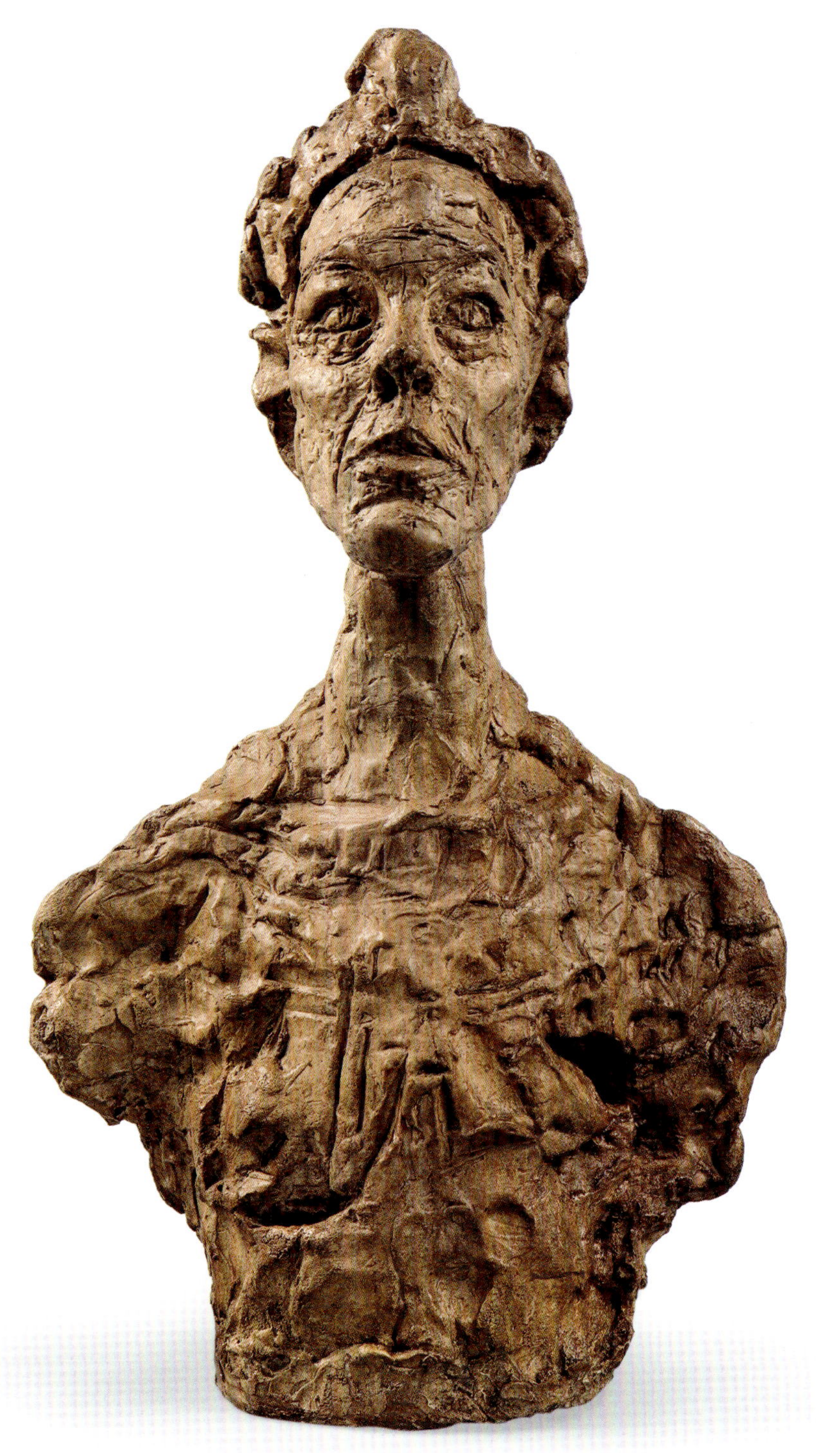

Fig. 133
Alberto Giacometti
Bust of Annette (Venise)
1962
Plaster, 47.3 × 27.5 × 16.4 cm (18 ⅝ × 10 ⅞ × 6 ½ in.)
Fondation Giacometti, Paris

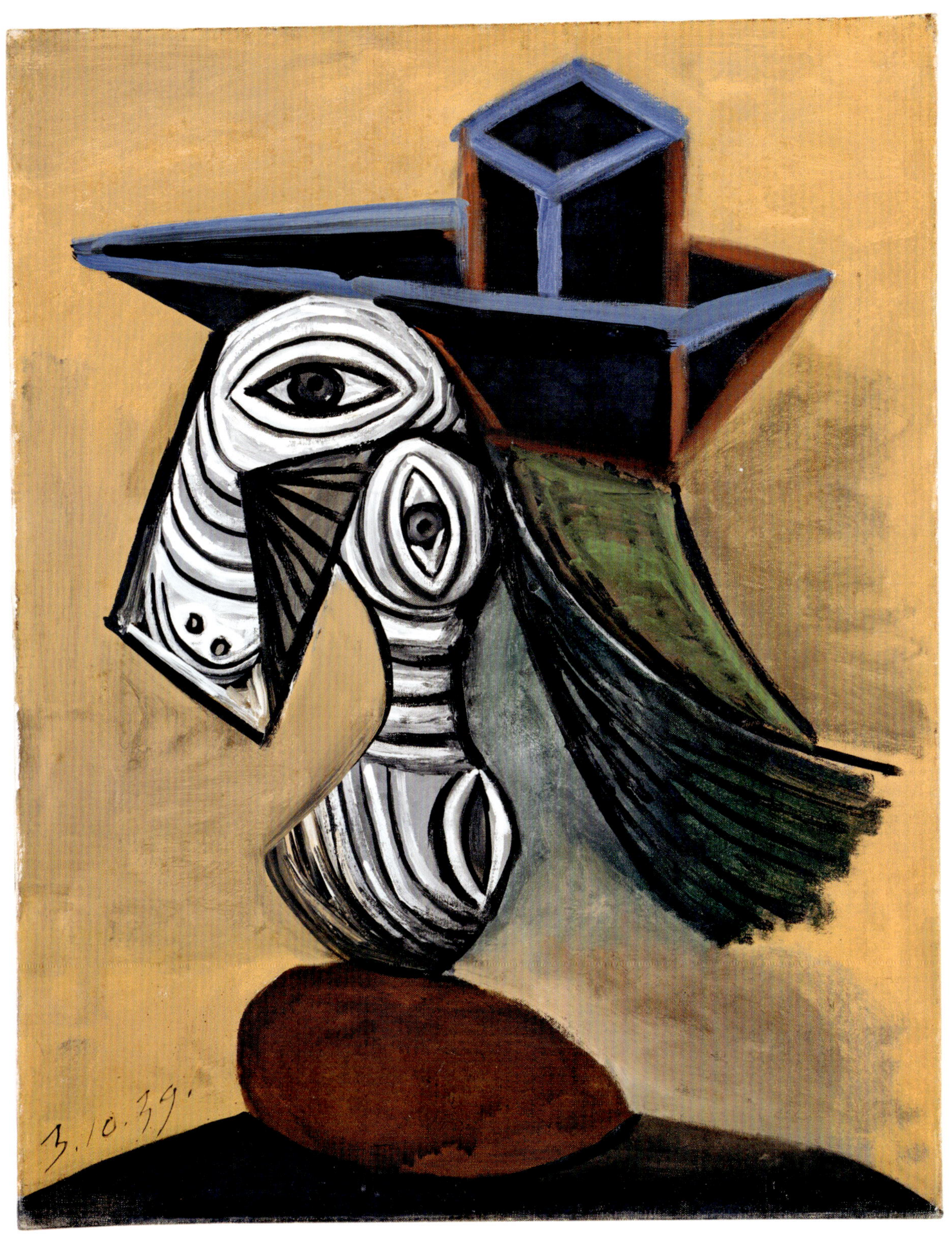

Fig. 134
Pablo Picasso
Woman with a Blue Hat
Royan, 3 October 1939
Oil on canvas, 65.5 × 50 cm (25 ¾ × 19 ⅝ in.)
Musée National Picasso-Paris
Dation Pablo Picasso, 1979. MP181

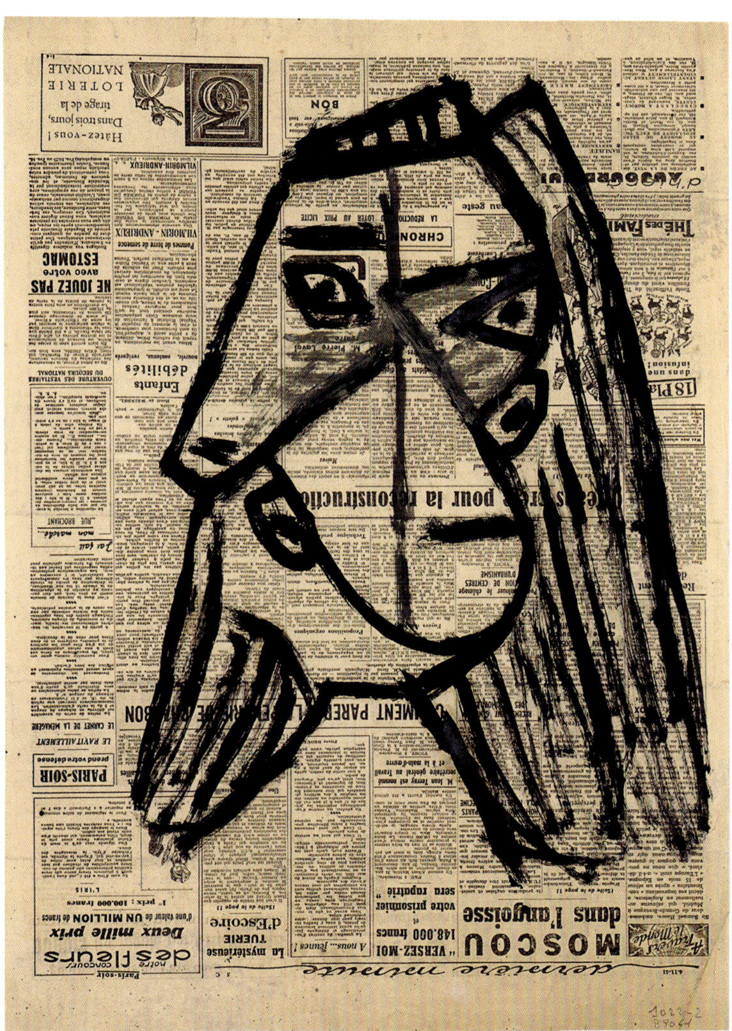

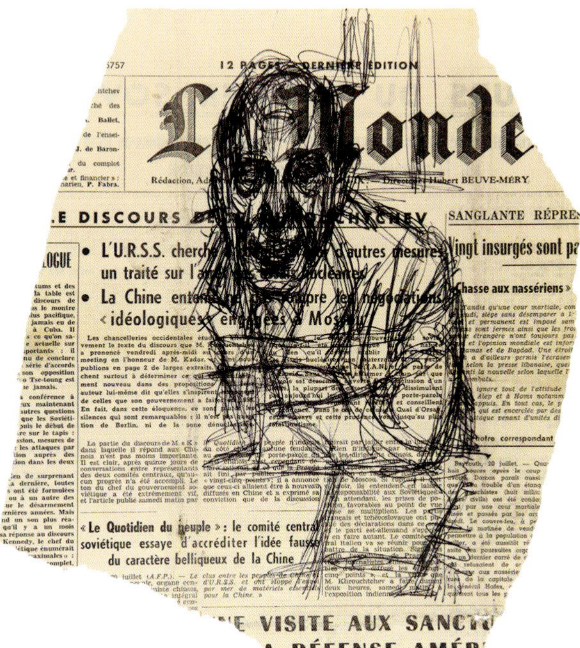

—
Fig. 135
Pablo Picasso
Head of a Woman
1941
Oil on newspaper, *Paris-Soir*,
60 × 43 cm (23 ⅝ × 16 ⅞ in.)
Musée National Picasso-Paris
Dation Jacqueline Picasso, 1990. MP1990-72
—
Fig. 136
Alberto Giacometti
Portrait of Théodore Fraenkel
After 1958
Black ballpoint pen on newspaper, *Le Monde*,
27.2 × 23.7 cm (10 ¾ × 9 ⅜ in.)
Fondation Giacometti, Paris
—

A Return to Realism

After the Second World War, the two artists returned to Paris, where they visited each other regularly. Their works from this period reconnect with the realism of everyday life. For Picasso, the overall composition of his pieces became oppressive and sombre, while Giacometti created frozen, motionless figures from rough, stone-like bronze. Their renewed link with 'the real' is also conveyed through works inspired by the natural world, such as fauna, landscapes and still lifes. To create his famous *Dog* (1957), Giacometti chose the slender frame of the Afghan hound that belonged to his friend Picasso. At this time, the question of creating a dramatised space lay at the heart of both artists' reflections, as seen in their solitary walking figures or sculpted groups such as *The Bathers* and *The Forest*.

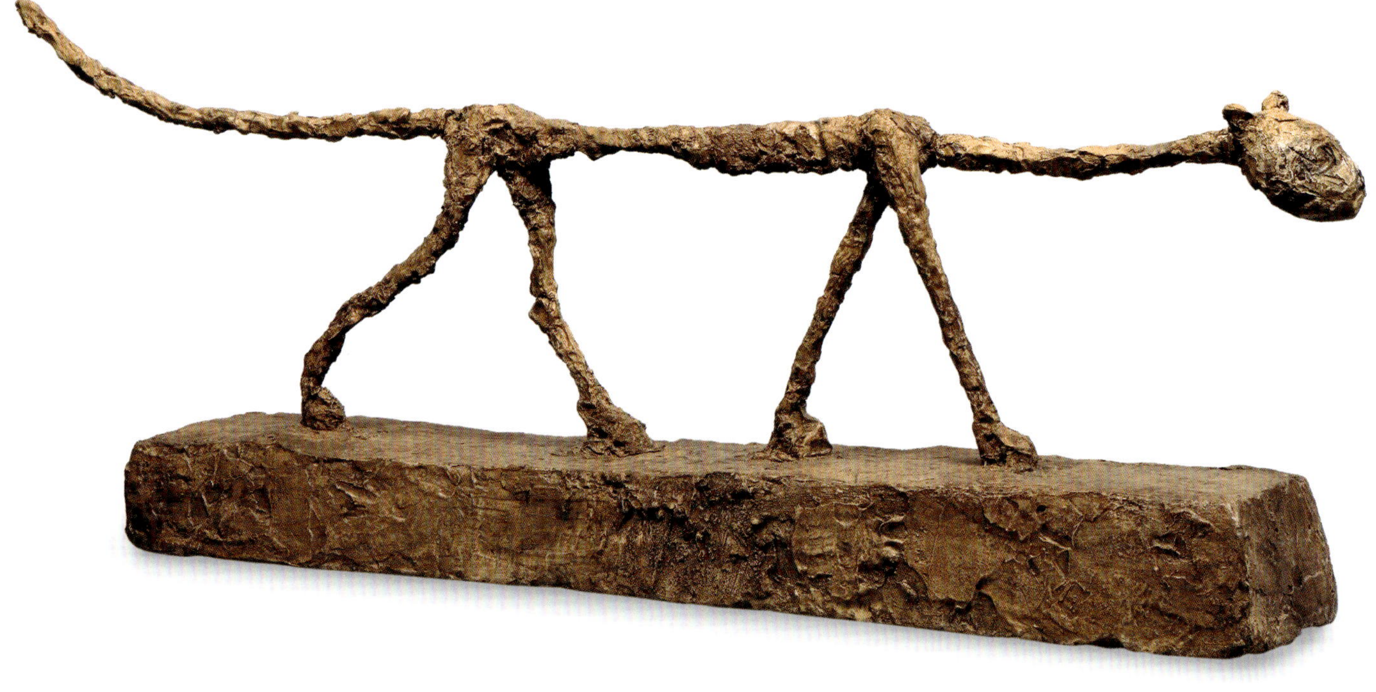

—

Fig. 137
Alberto Giacometti
The Cat
1951
Painted plaster, 32.8 × 81.3 × 13.5 cm (13 × 32 × 5 ⅜ in.)
Fondation Giacometti, Paris
—

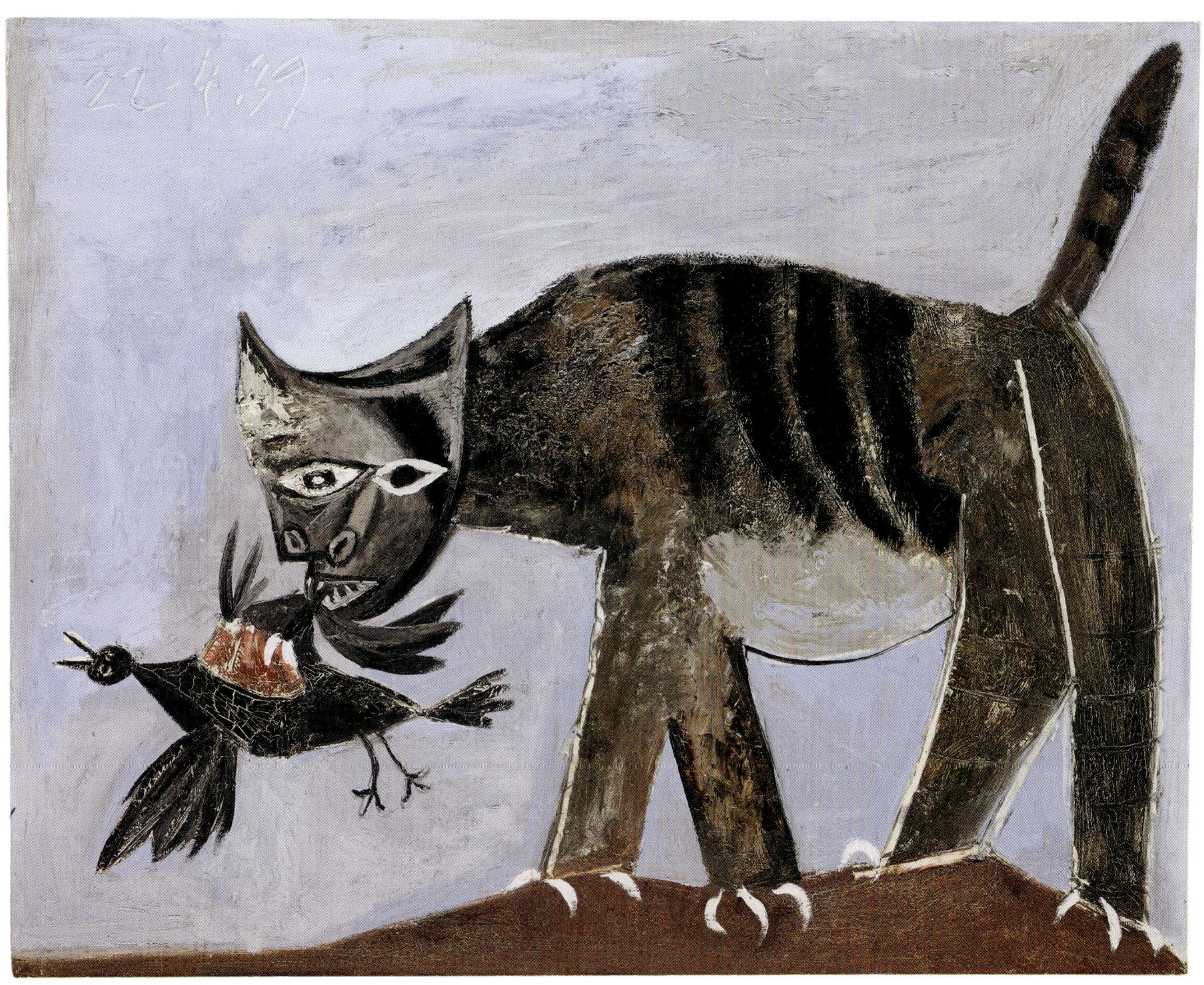

—
Fig. 138
Pablo Picasso
Cat Catching a Bird
Paris, 22 April 1939
Oil on canvas, 81 × 100 cm (2 ft. 8 in. × 3 ft. 3 ⅜ in.)
Musée National Picasso-Paris
Dation Pablo Picasso, 1979. MP178
—

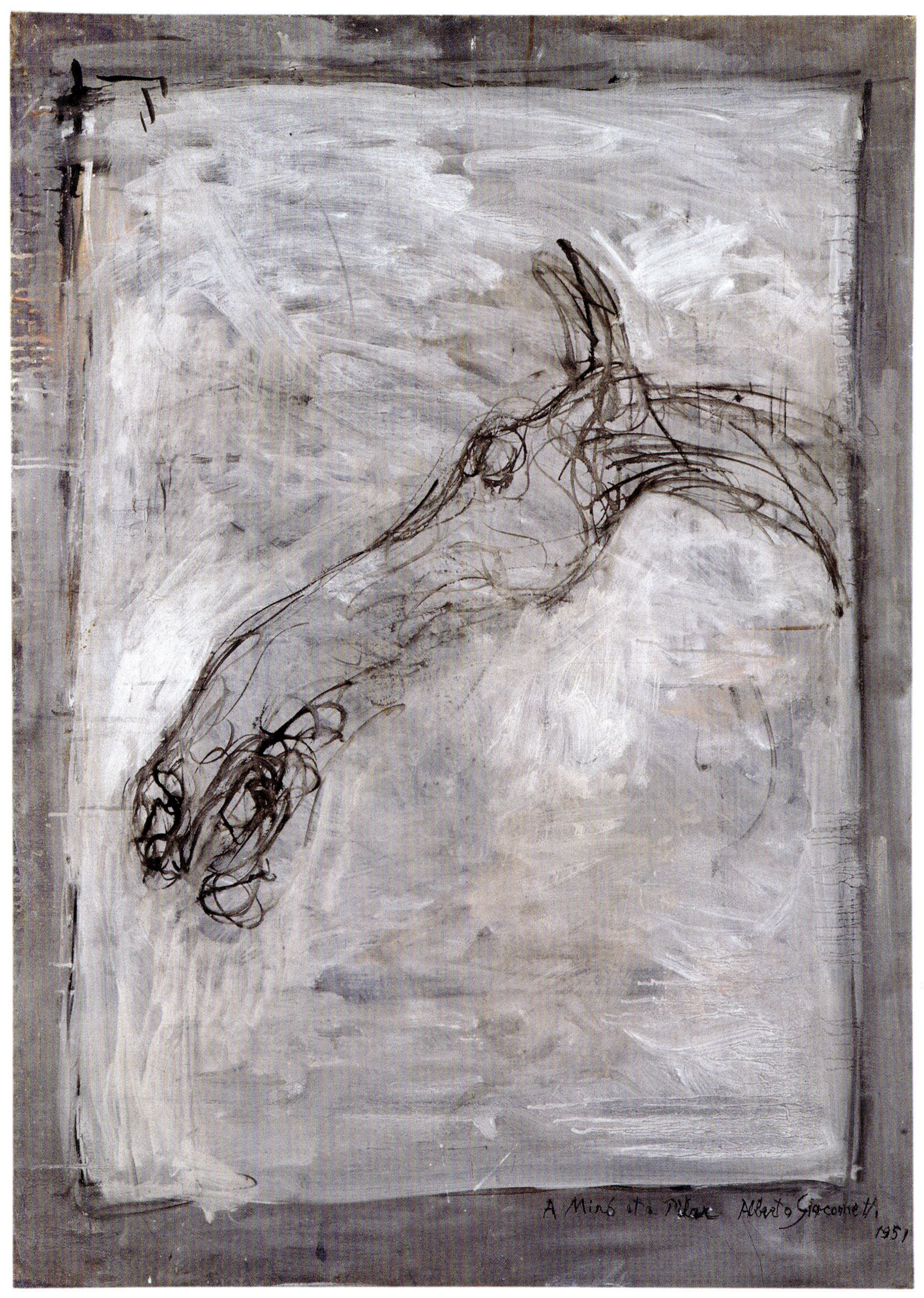

—

Fig. 139
Alberto Giacometti
Head of a Horse
1951
Oil on canvas, 91 × 63.5 cm (35 ⅞ × 25 in.)
Private collection, Palma de Mallorca (Spain)

—

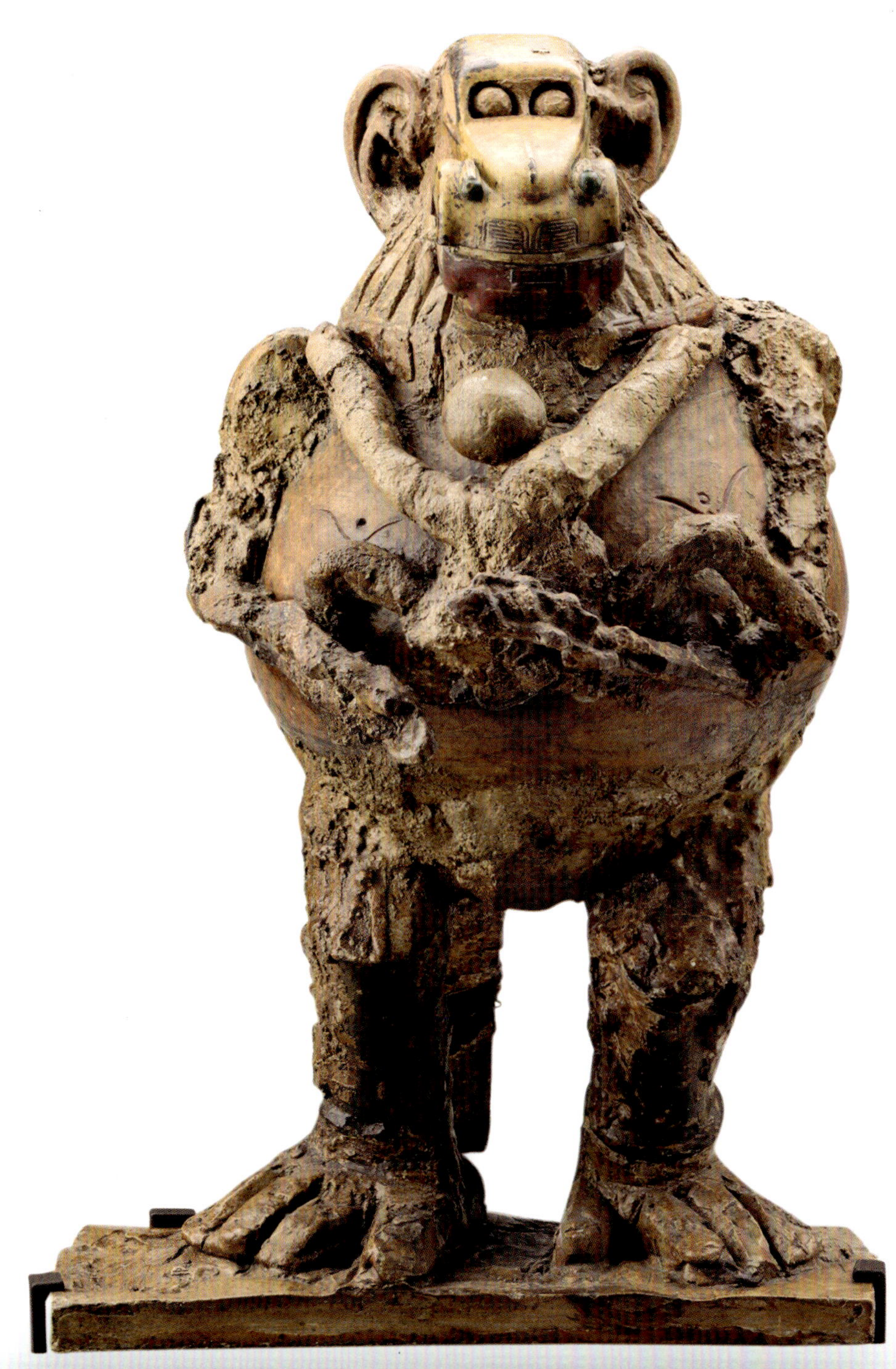

Fig. 140
Pablo Picasso
Baboon with Young
Vallauris, October 1951
Original: plaster, pottery, two model cars and metal,
56 × 34 × 71 cm (22 × 13 ⅜ × 28 in.)
Musée National Picasso-Paris
Dation Pablo Picasso, 1979. MP342

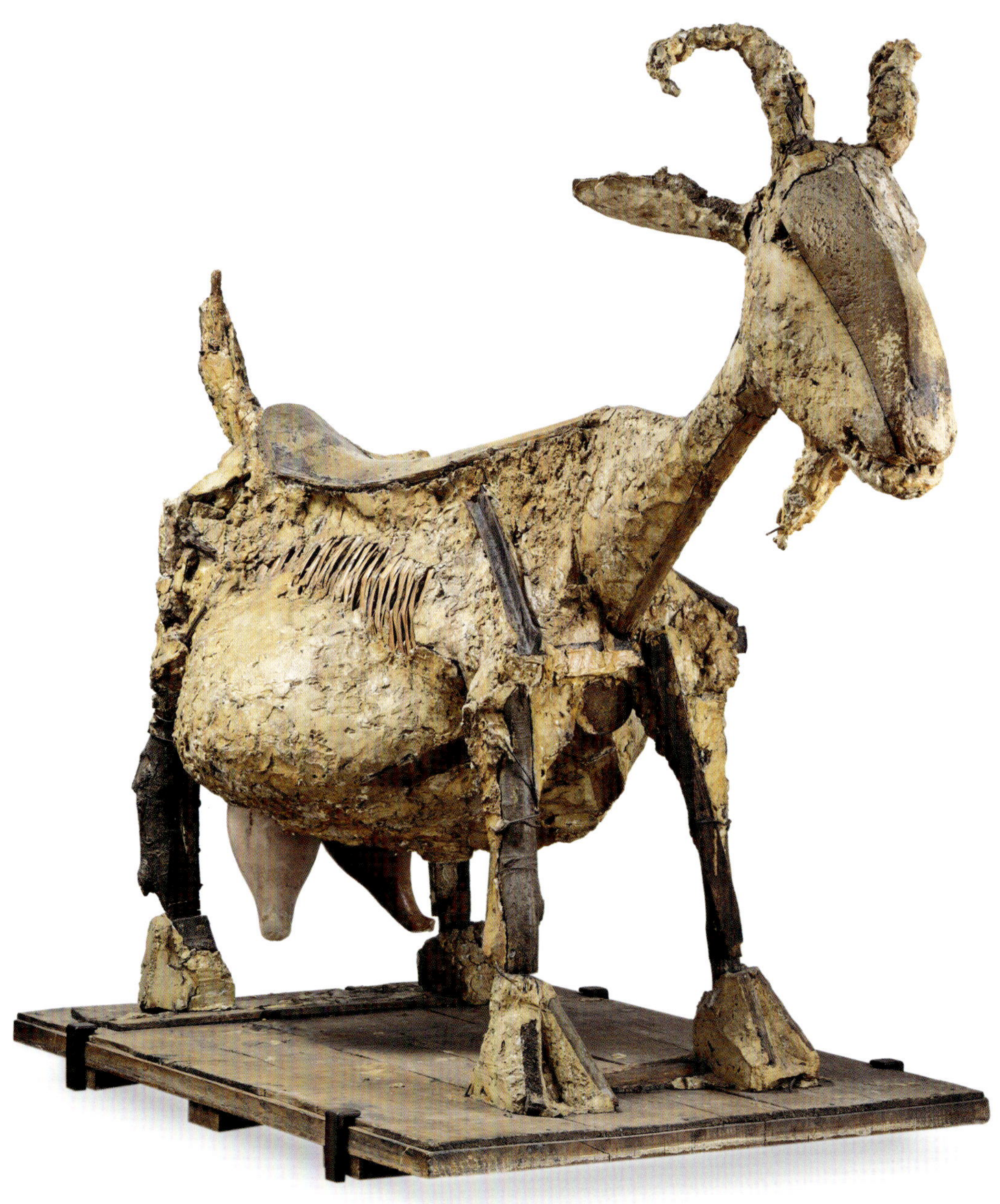

—

Pablo Picasso
The Goat
Vallauris, 1950
Original: plaster, wicker basket, ceramic pots, palm leaf, metal,
wood and cardboard, 120.5 × 72 × 144 cm (3 ft. 11 ⅜ in. × 2 ft. 4 ¼ in. × 4 ft. 8 ⅝ in.)
Musée National Picasso-Paris
Dation Pablo Picasso, 1979. MP339
—

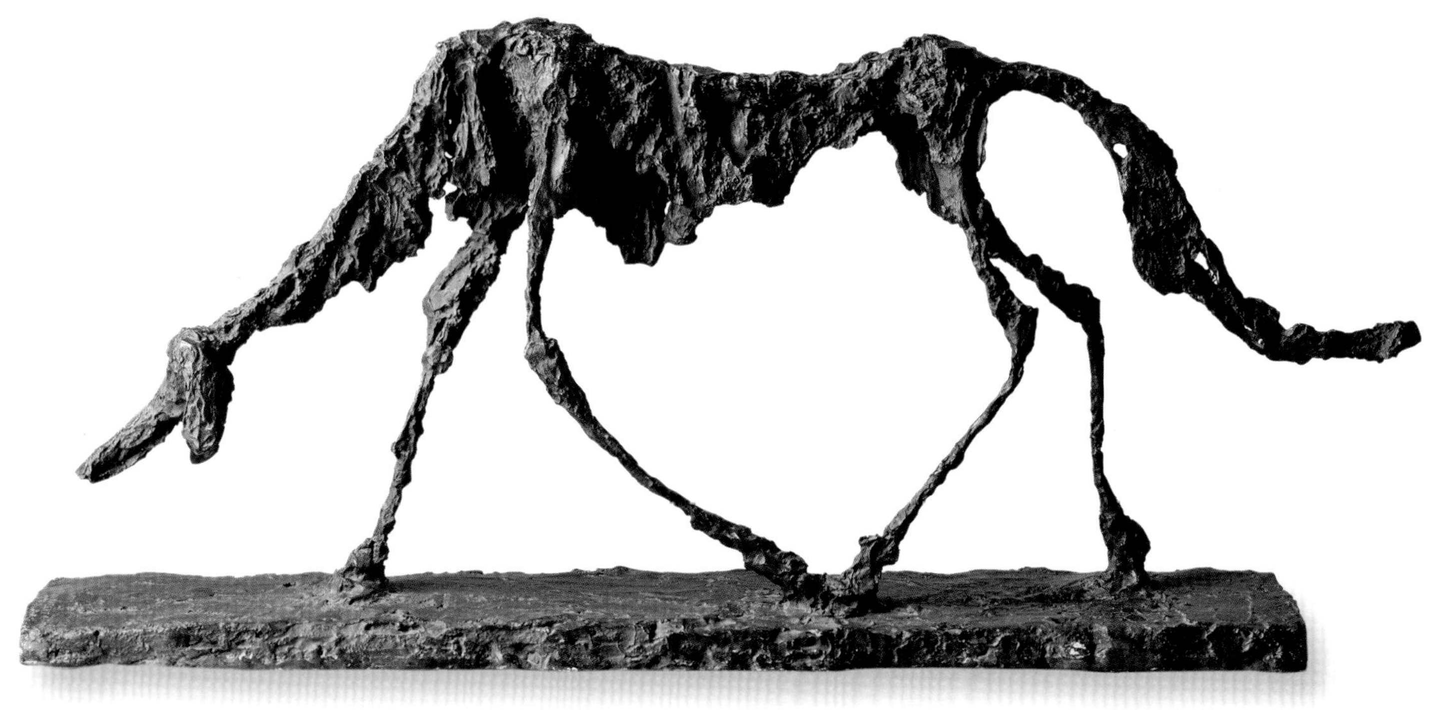

Fig. 142
Alberto Giacometti
The Dog
1951
Bronze, 47 × 100 × 15 cm (1 ft. 6 ½ in. × 3 ft. ⅜ in. × 6 in.)
Fondation Marguerite et Aimé Maeght collection,
Saint-Paul-de-Vence (France)

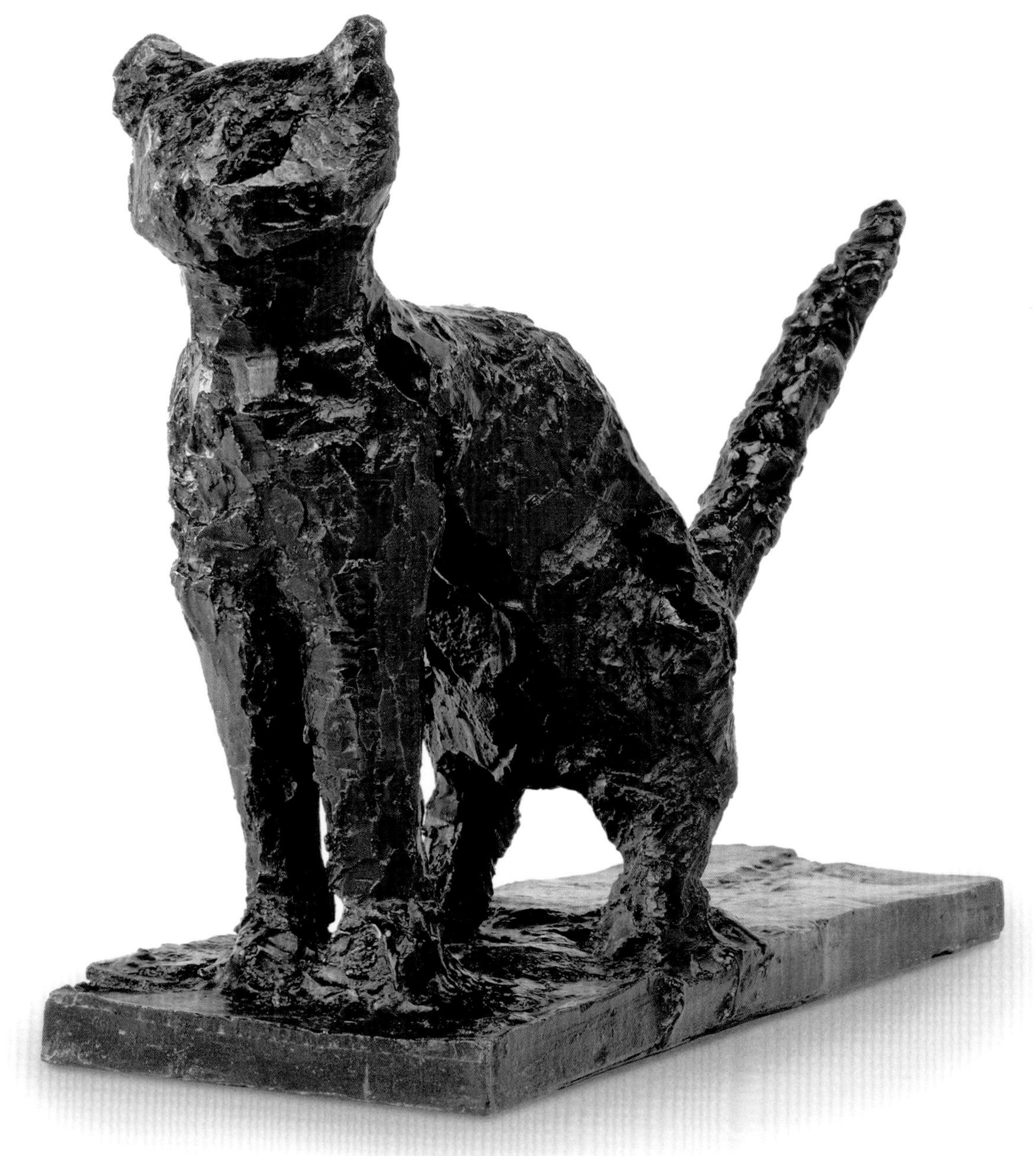

Fig. 143
Pablo Picasso
The Cat
Paris, 1943
Bronze, 36 × 18 × 55.5 cm (14 ⅛ × 7 × 21 ⅞ in.)
Musée National Picasso-Paris
Dation Pablo Picasso, 1979. MP324

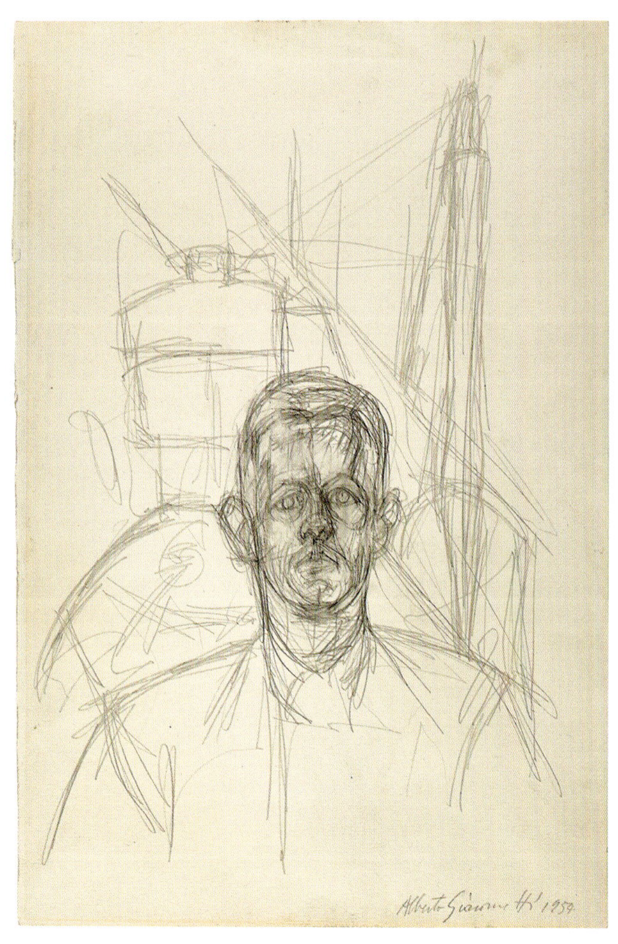

Fig. 144
Alberto Giacometti
Portrait of James Lord
1954
Graphite pencil on wove vellum paper,
50.5 × 32.5 cm (19 ⅞ × 12 ¾ in.)
Musée National Picasso-Paris
James Lord donation, 1992. MP1992-3

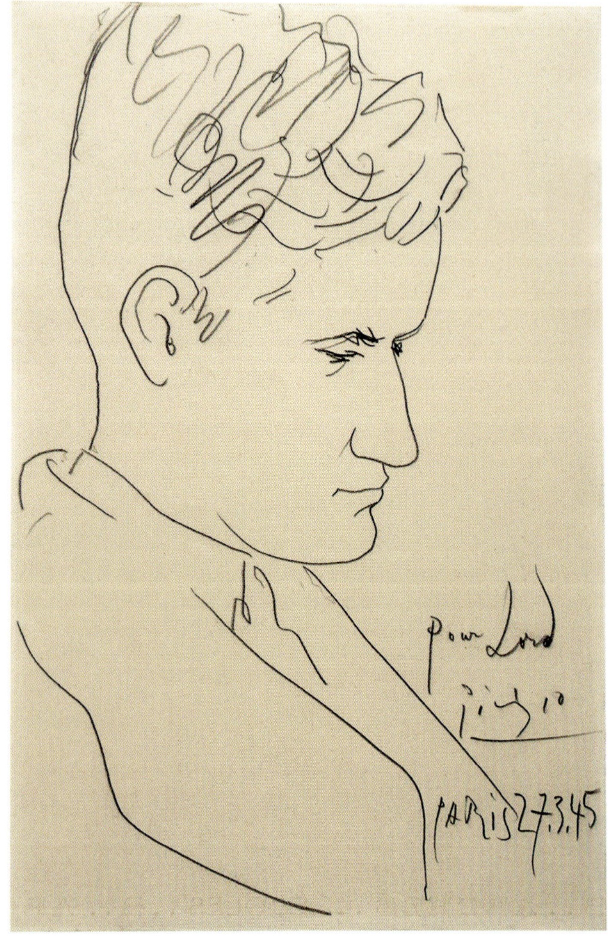

Fig. 145
Pablo Picasso
Portrait of James Lord
27 March 1945
Conté Crayon on wove vellum paper,
50.5 × 31.5 cm (19 ⅞ × 12 ⅜ in.)
Musée National Picasso-Paris
James Lord donation, 1992. MP1992-2

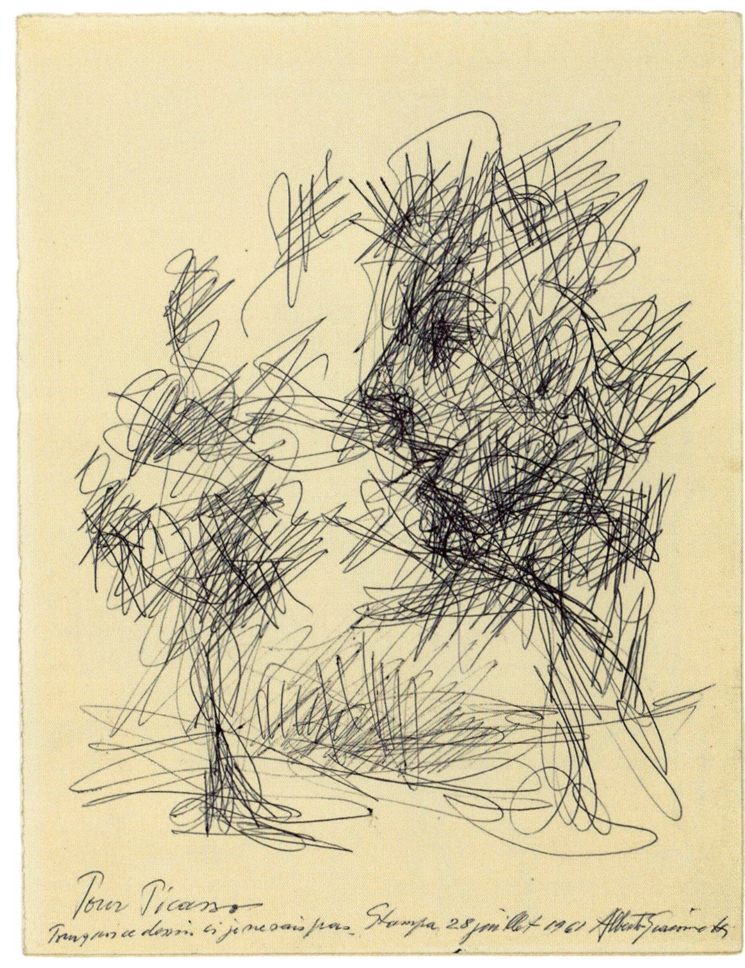

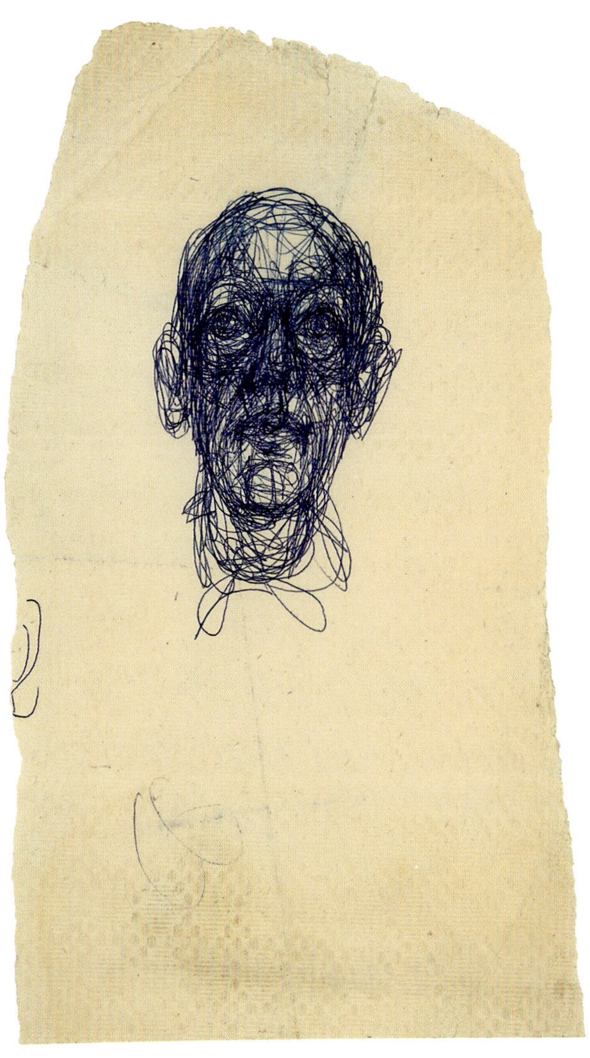

Fig. 146
Alberto Giacometti
Homage to Picasso [I]
1961
Blue ballpoint pen on wove drawing paper,
32.6 × 25 cm (12 ⁷⁄₈ × 9 ⁷⁄₈ in.)
Musée National Picasso-Paris
Gift of M. and Mme Jean Krugier, 1980. MP1981-1

Fig. 147
Alberto Giacometti
Man's Head from the Front
c. 1960
Blue ballpoint pen on paper tablecloth,
30 × 16.9 cm (12 ⅛ × 6 ⅝ in.)
Fondation Giacometti, Paris

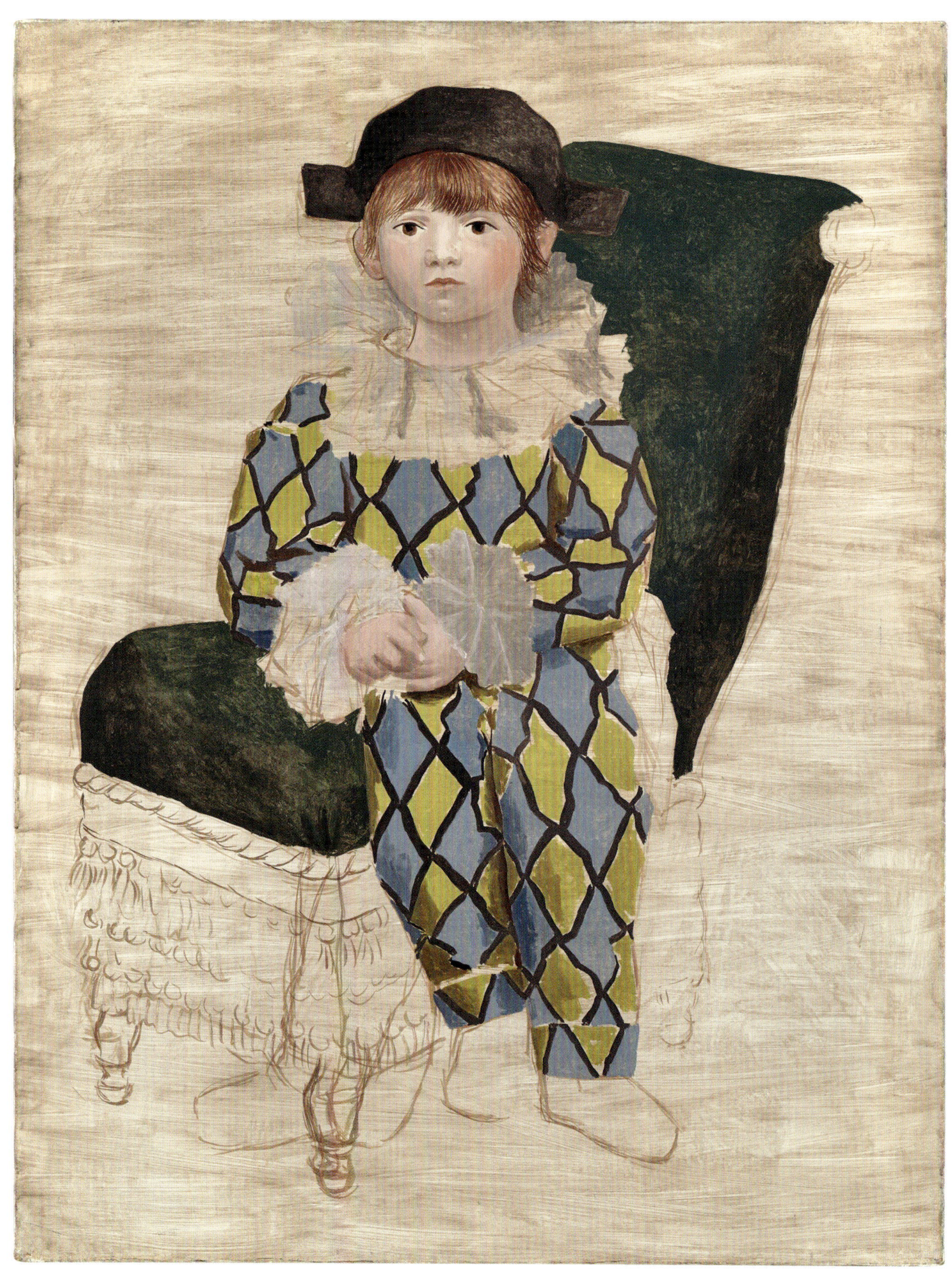

—
Fig. 148
Pablo Picasso
Paulo as Harlequin
Paris, 1924
Oil on canvas, 130 × 97.5 cm (4 ft. 3 ⅛ in. × 3 ft. 2 ⅜ in)
Musée National Picasso-Paris
Dation Pablo Picasso, 1979. MP83
—

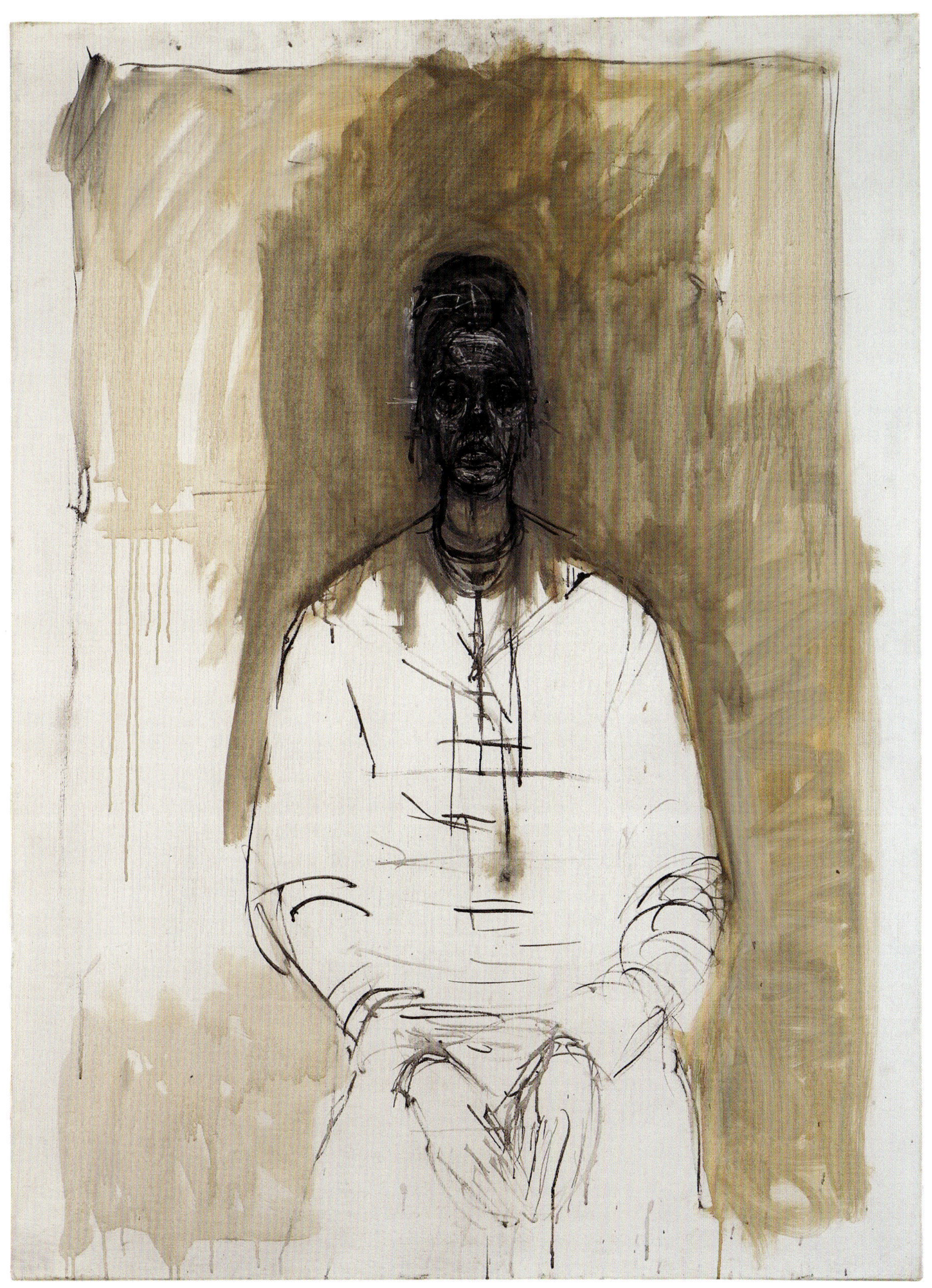

—
Fig. 149
Alberto Giacometti
Caroline in Tears
1962
Oil on canvas, 101 × 74 cm (3 ft. 3 ¾ in. × 2 ft. 5 ⅛ in)
Fondation Giacometti, Paris
—

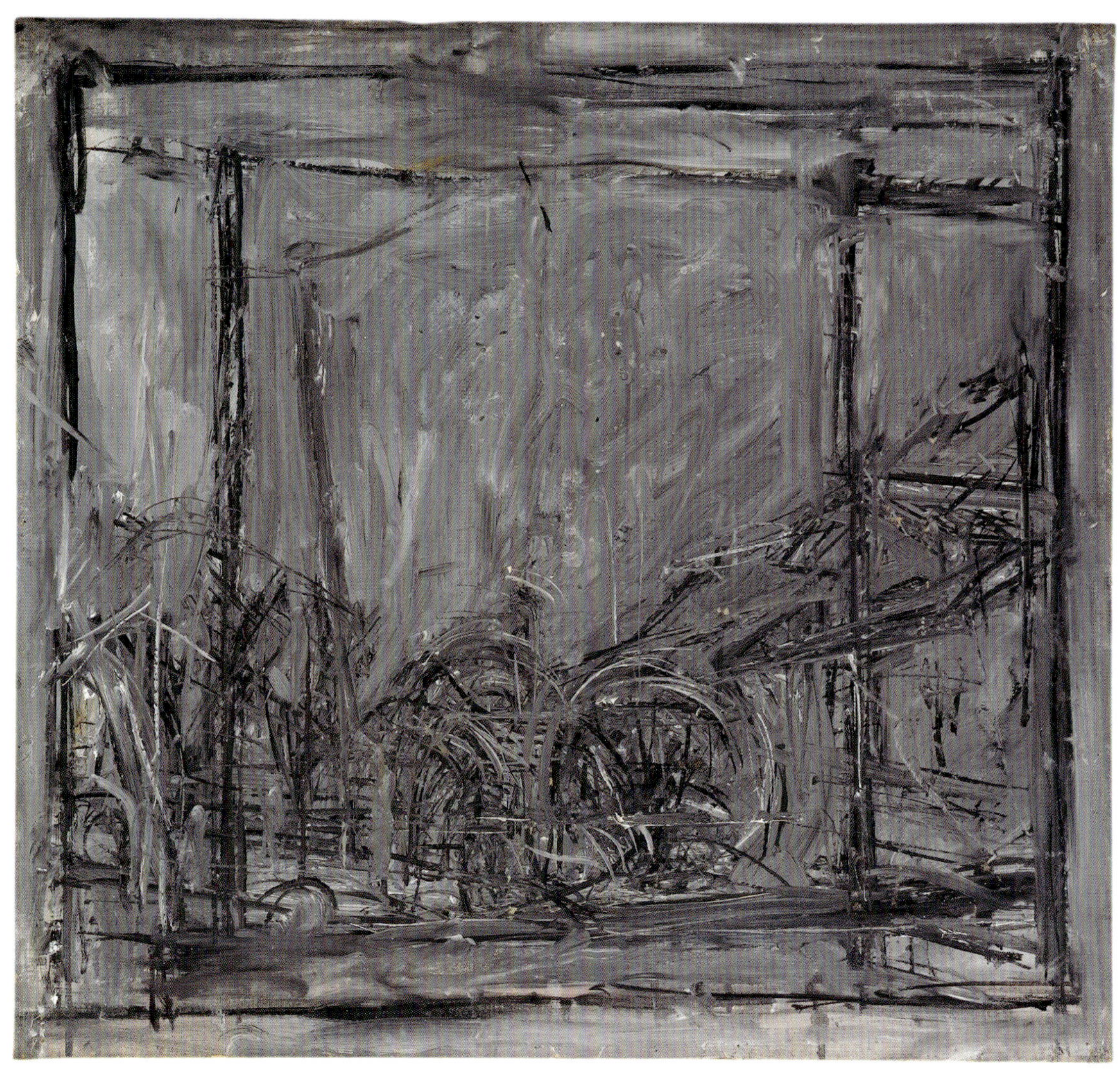

Fig. 150
Alberto Giacometti
Dark Landscape (Stampa)
1952
Oil on canvas, 51 × 54 cm (20 × 21 ¼ in.)
Fondation Giacometti, Paris

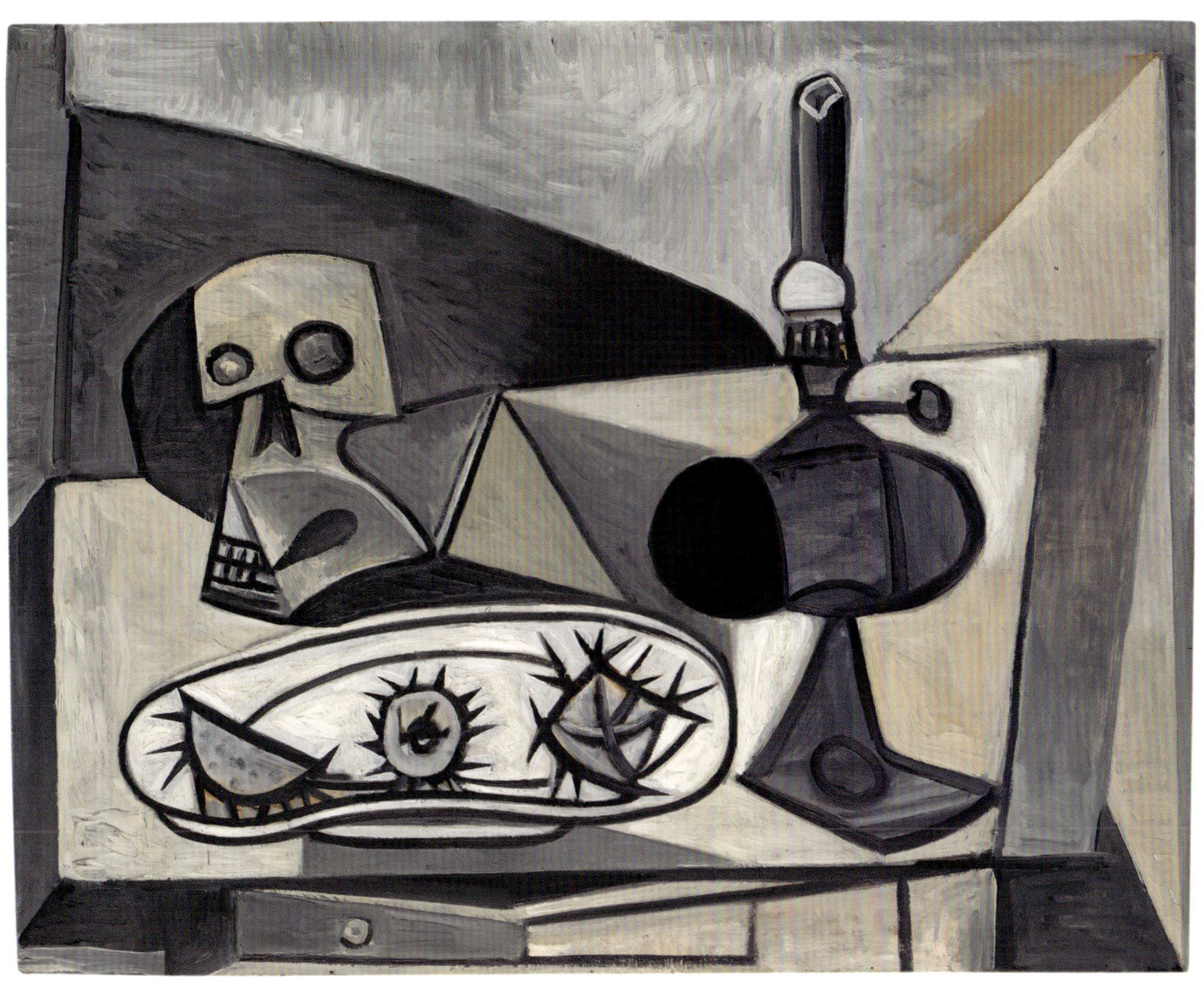

Fig. 151
Pablo Picasso
Skull, Sea Urchins and Lamp on a Table
[Antibes-Paris], 27 November 1946
Oil on plywood, 81 × 100 cm (2 ft. 8 in. × 3 ft. 3 ⅜ in)
Musée National Picasso-Paris
Dation Pablo Picasso, 1979. MP198

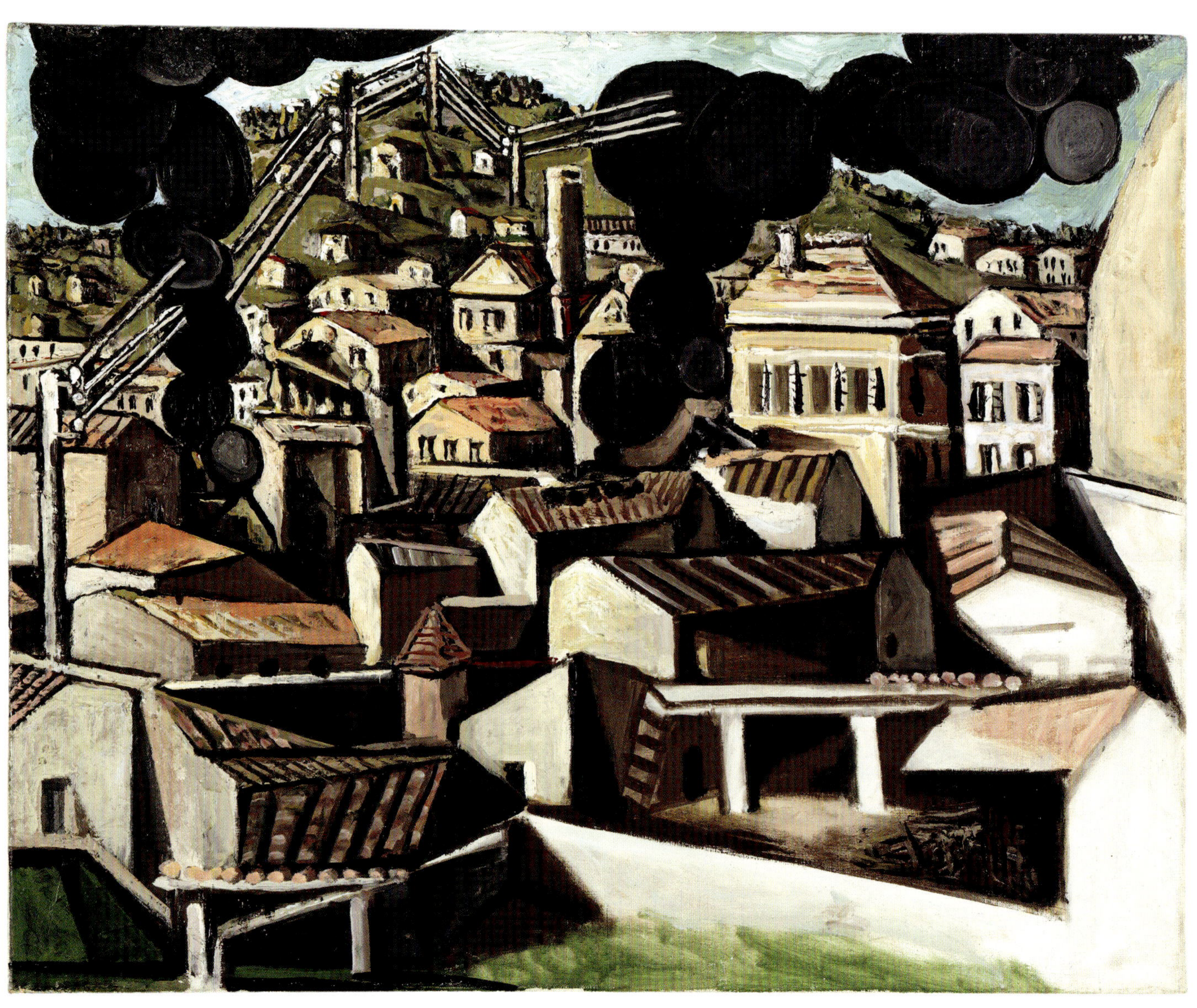

—
Fig. 152
Pablo Picasso
Smoke over Vallauris
Vallauris, 12 January 1951
Oil on canvas, 59.5 × 73.5 cm (23 ⅜ × 29 in.)
Musée National Picasso-Paris
Dation Pablo Picasso, 1979. MP202
—

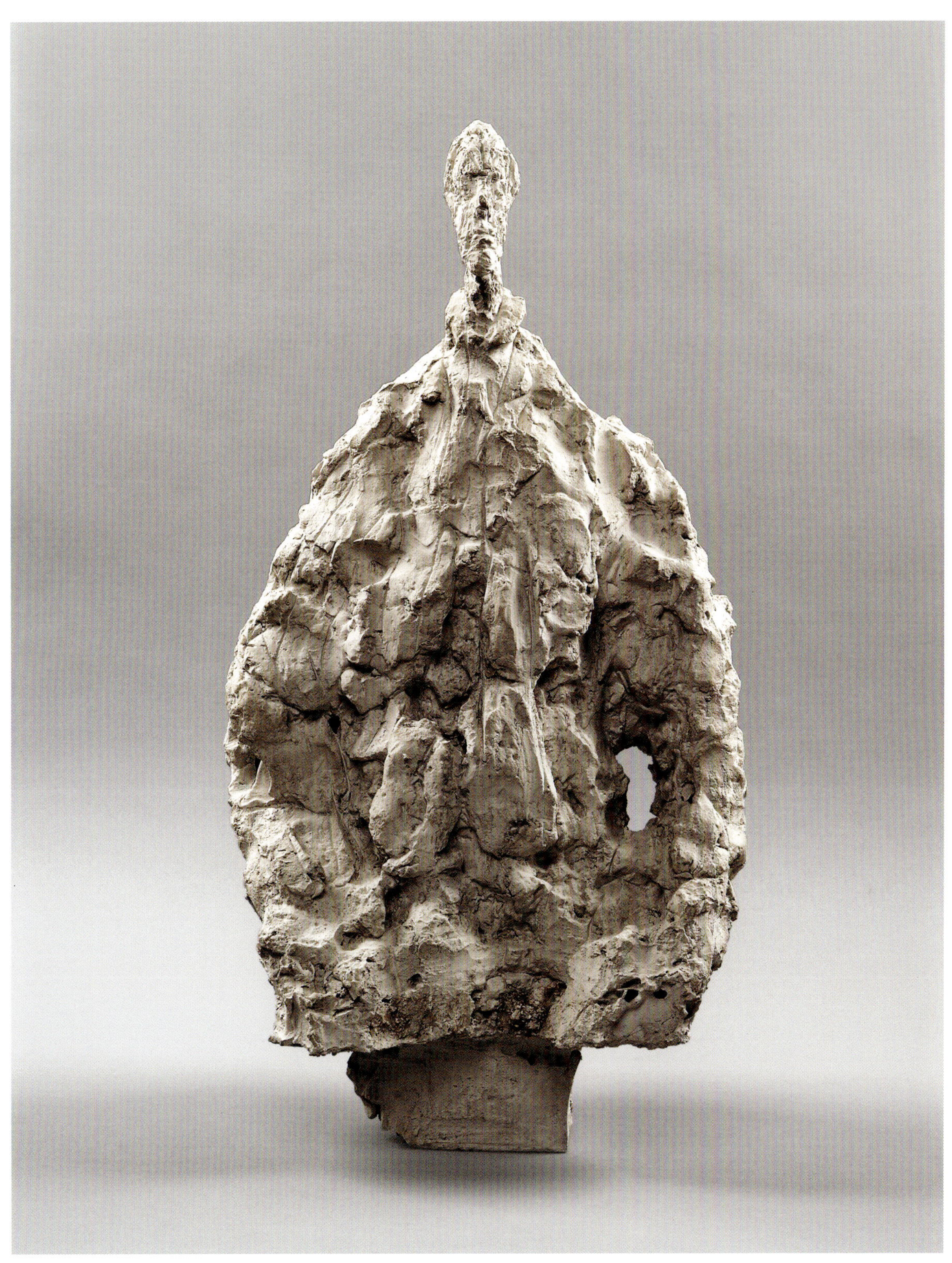

Fig. 153
Alberto Giacometti
Bust of a Man in a Pullover
c. 1953
Plaster, 54.5 × 27.7 × 21 cm (21 ½ × 11 × 8 ¼ in.)
Fondation Giacometti, Paris

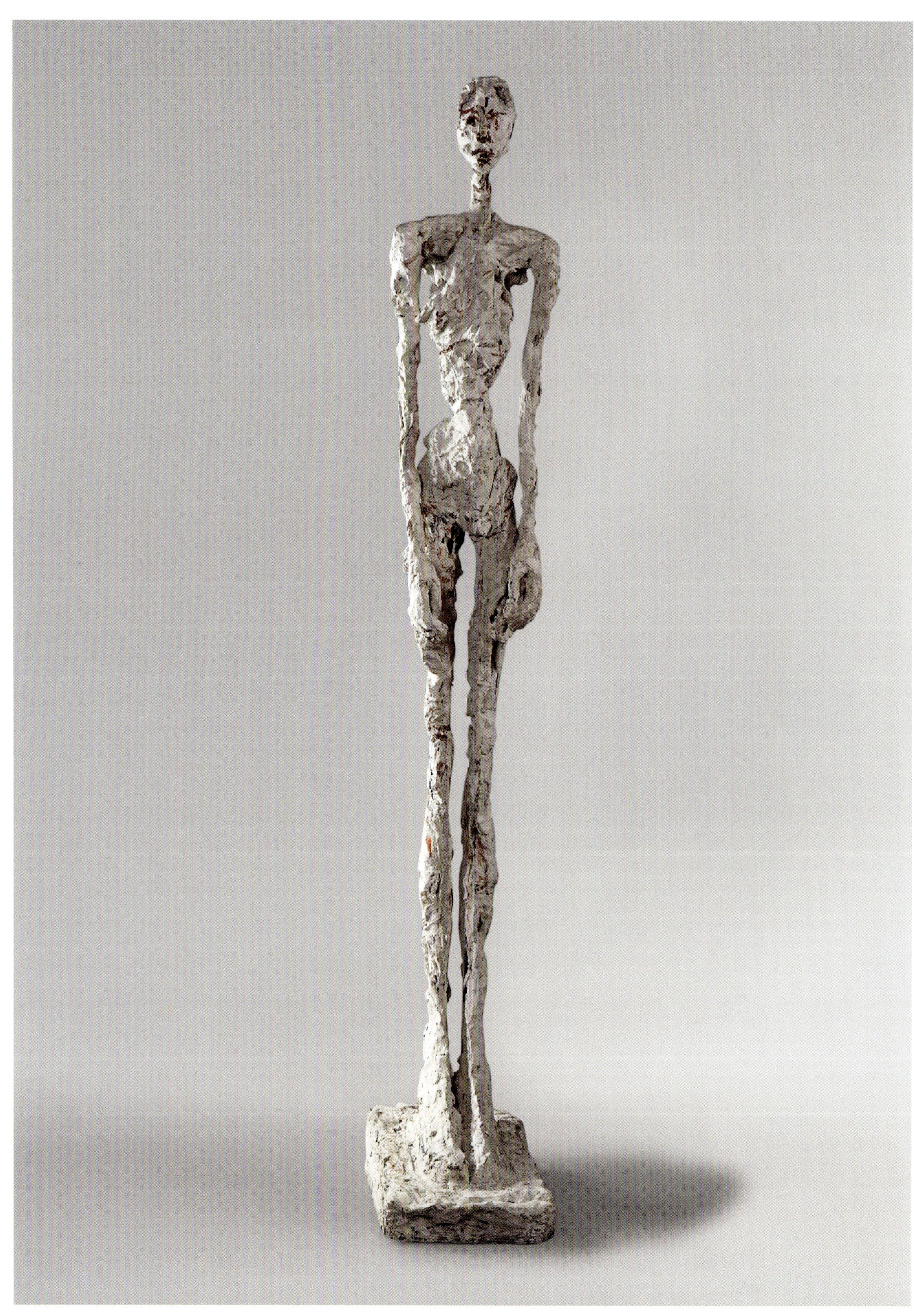

Alberto Giacometti
Large Woman
1958
Painted plaster, 188.3 × 28.8 × 40.9 cm
(6 ft. 2 ¼ in. × 11 ⅜ in. × 1 ft. 4 in.)
Fondation Giacometti, Paris

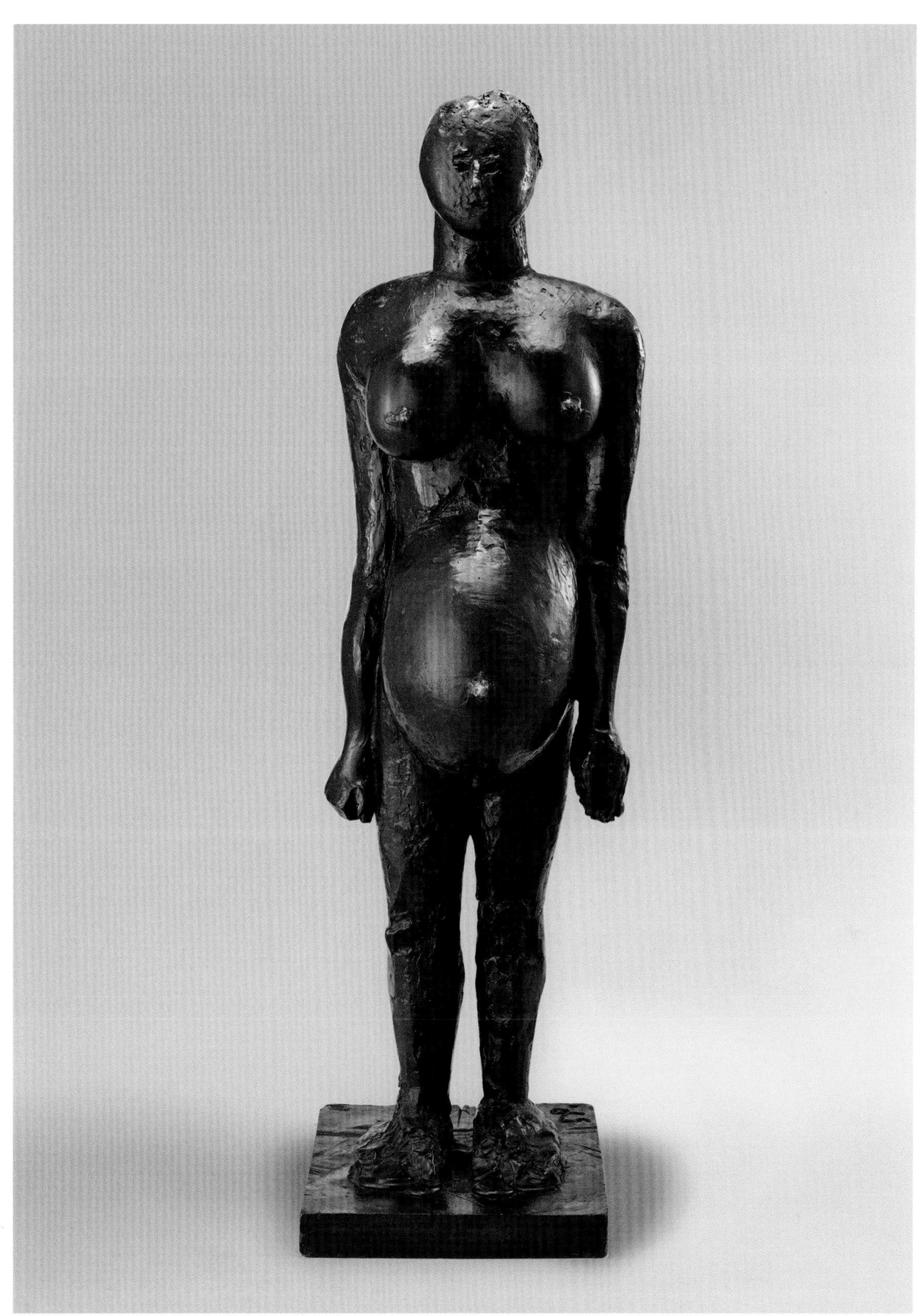

Fig. 155
Pablo Picasso
Pregnant Woman, 2nd State
Vallauris, 1950–15 March 1959
Bronze, 109 × 30 × 34 cm (3 ft. 7 in. × 12 in. × 13 ⅜ in.)
Musée National Picasso-Paris
Dation Pablo Picasso, 1979. MP338

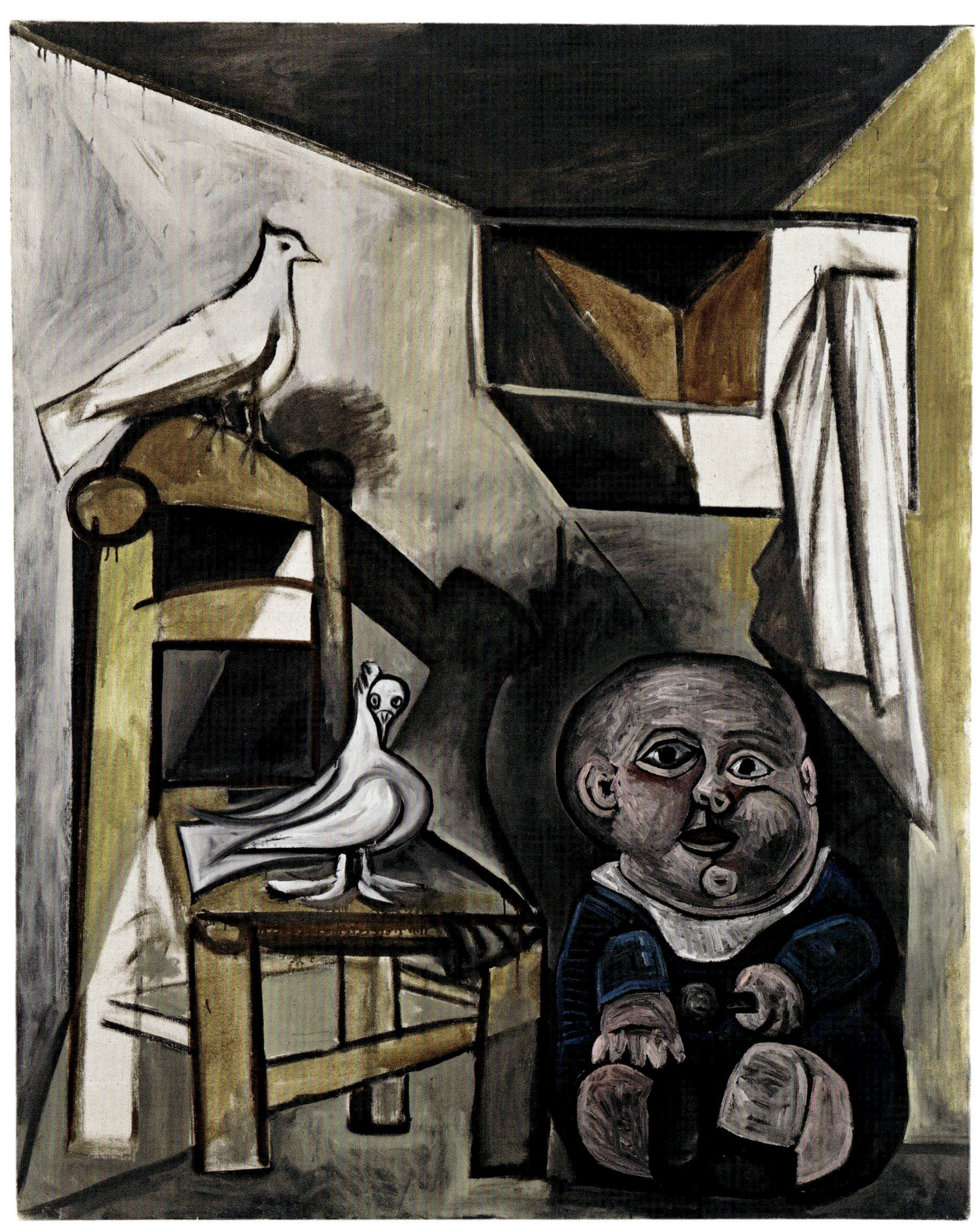

Fig. 156
Pablo Picasso
Child with Doves
Paris, 24 August 1943
Oil on canvas, 162 × 130 cm (5 ft. 3 ¾ in. × 4 ft. 3 ¼ in.)
Musée National Picasso-Paris
Dation Pablo Picasso, 1979. MP192

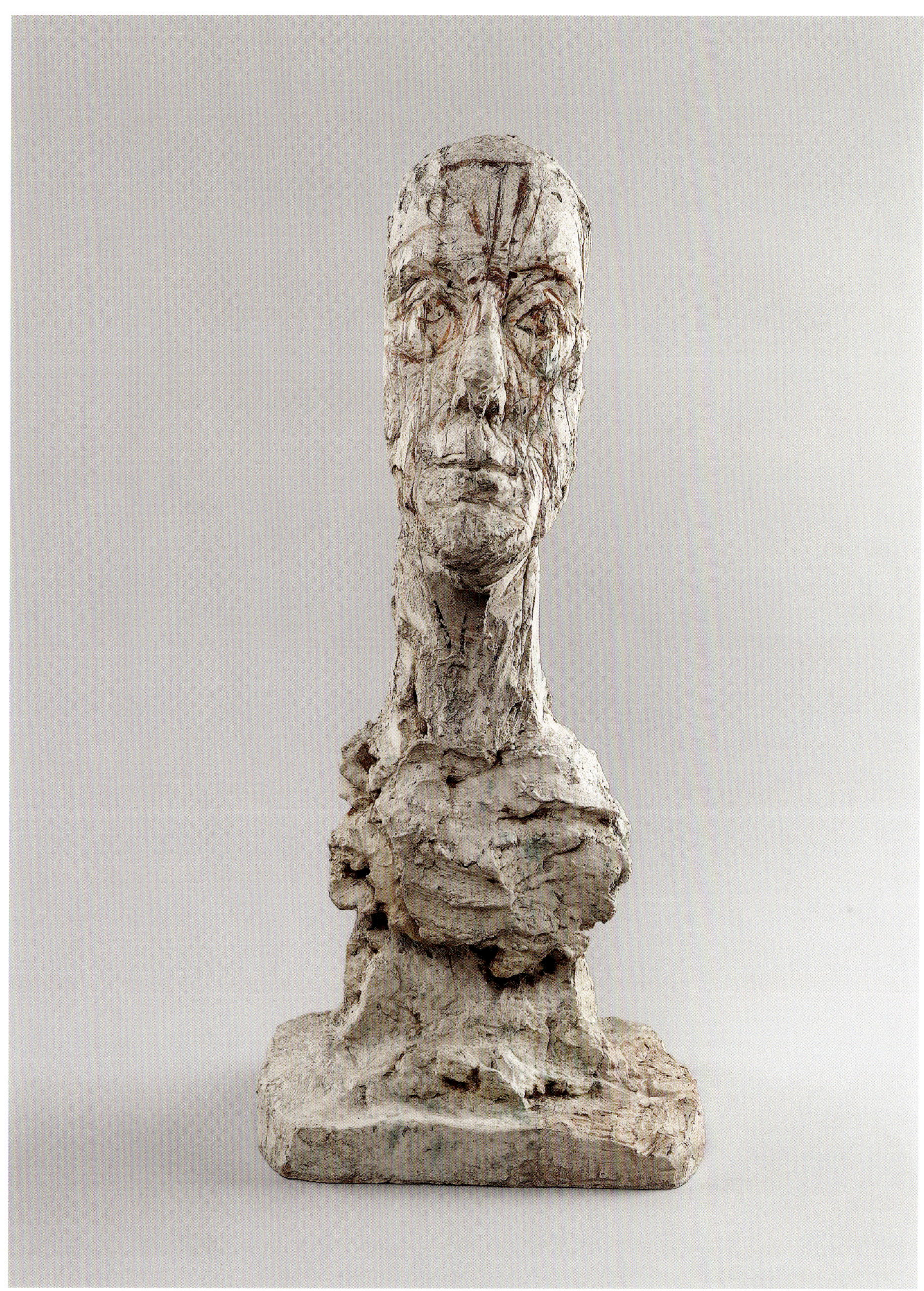

—
Fig. 157
Alberto Giacometti
Large Head
1958
Painted plaster, 58.1 × 26.4 × 22.5 cm (22 ⅞ × 10 ⅜ × 8 ⅞ in.)
Fondation Giacometti, Paris
—

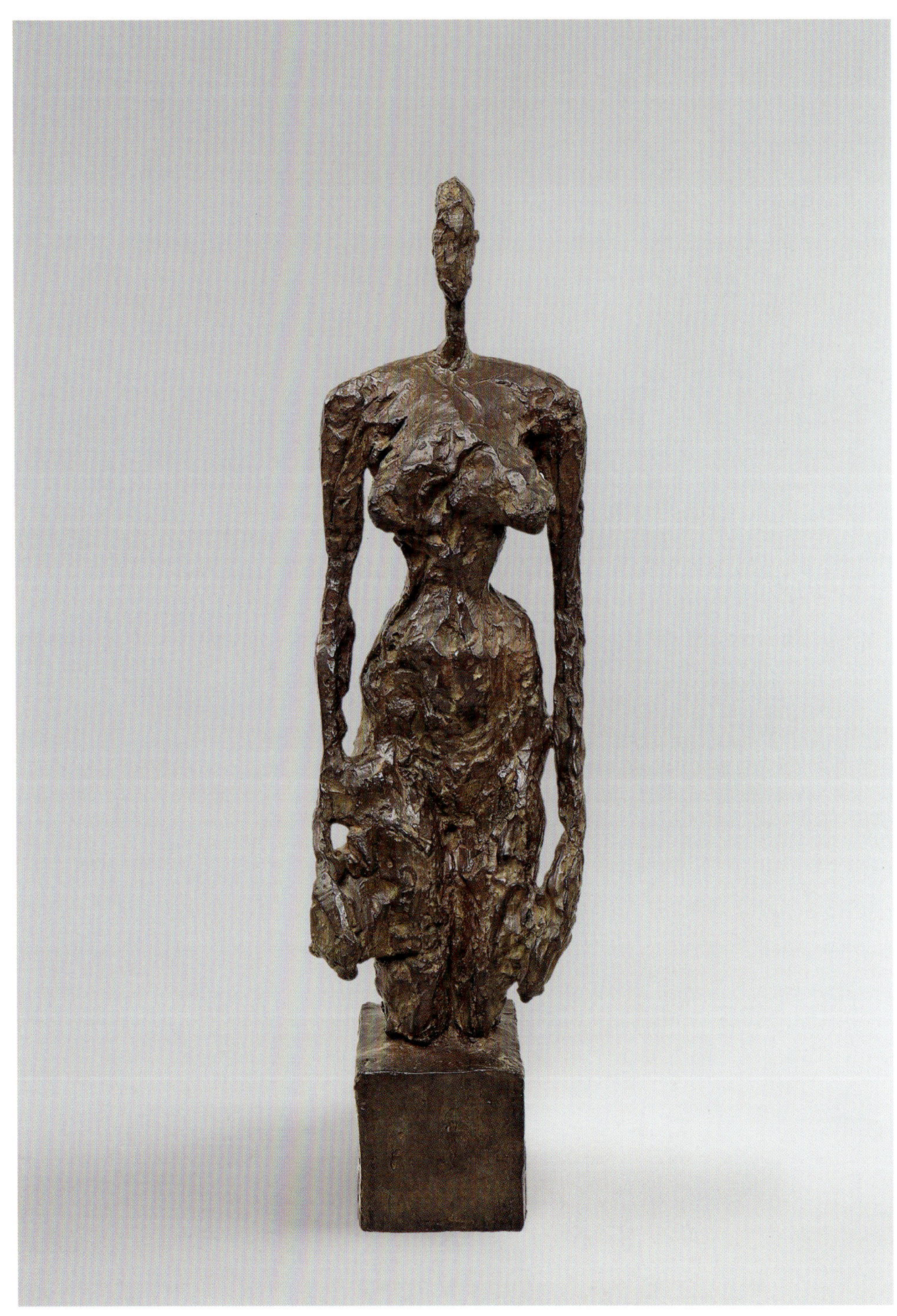

Fig. 158
Alberto Giacometti
Standing Nude on a Cubic Base
1953
Bronze, 43.2 × 11.4 × 10.5 cm (17 × 4 ½ × 4 ⅛ in.)
Fondation Giacometti, Paris

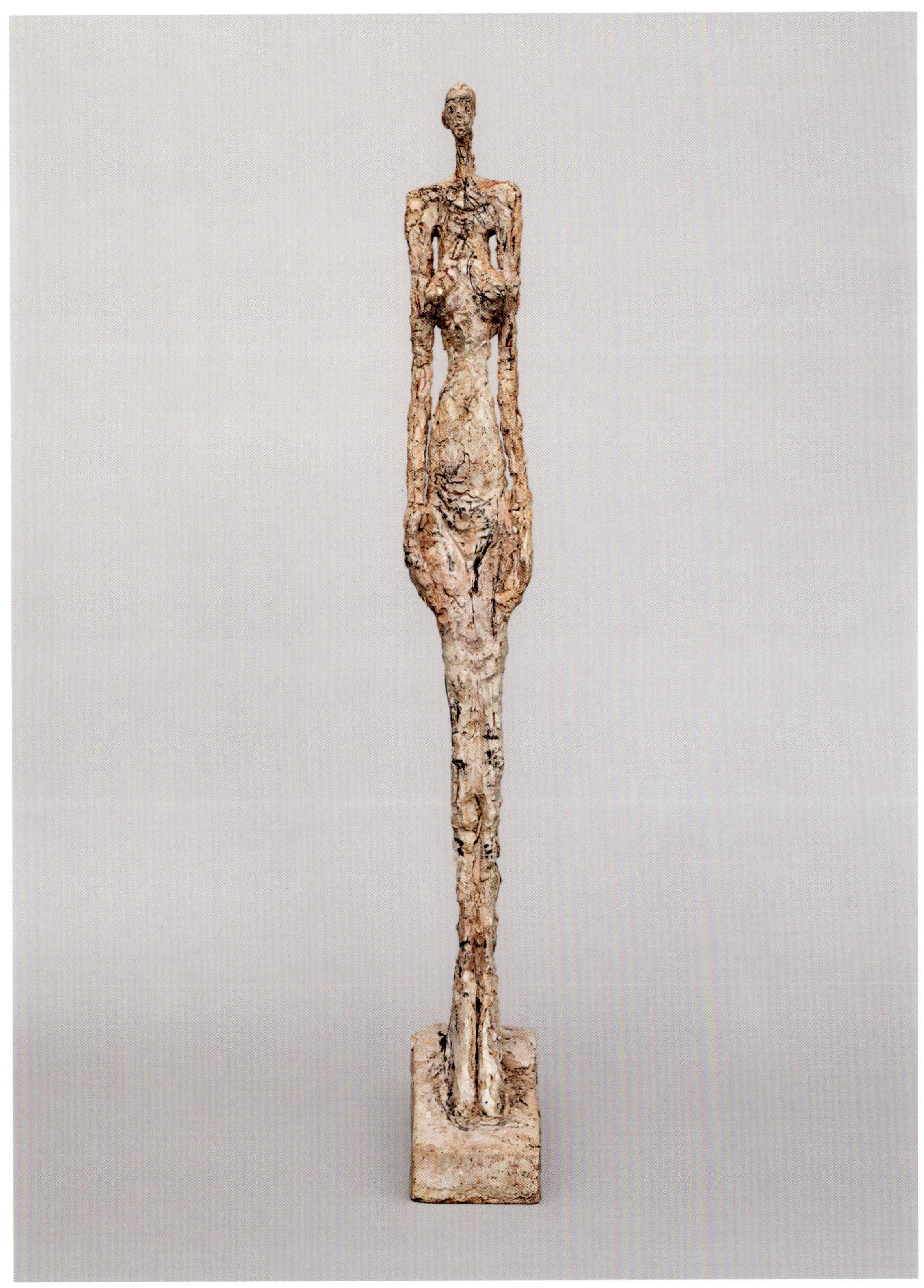

Fig. 159
Alberto Giacometti
Woman of Venice V
1956
Painted plaster, 113.5 × 14.5 × 31.8 cm
(3 ft. 8 ⅝ in. × 5 ¾ in. × 12 ½ in.)
Fondation Giacometti, Paris

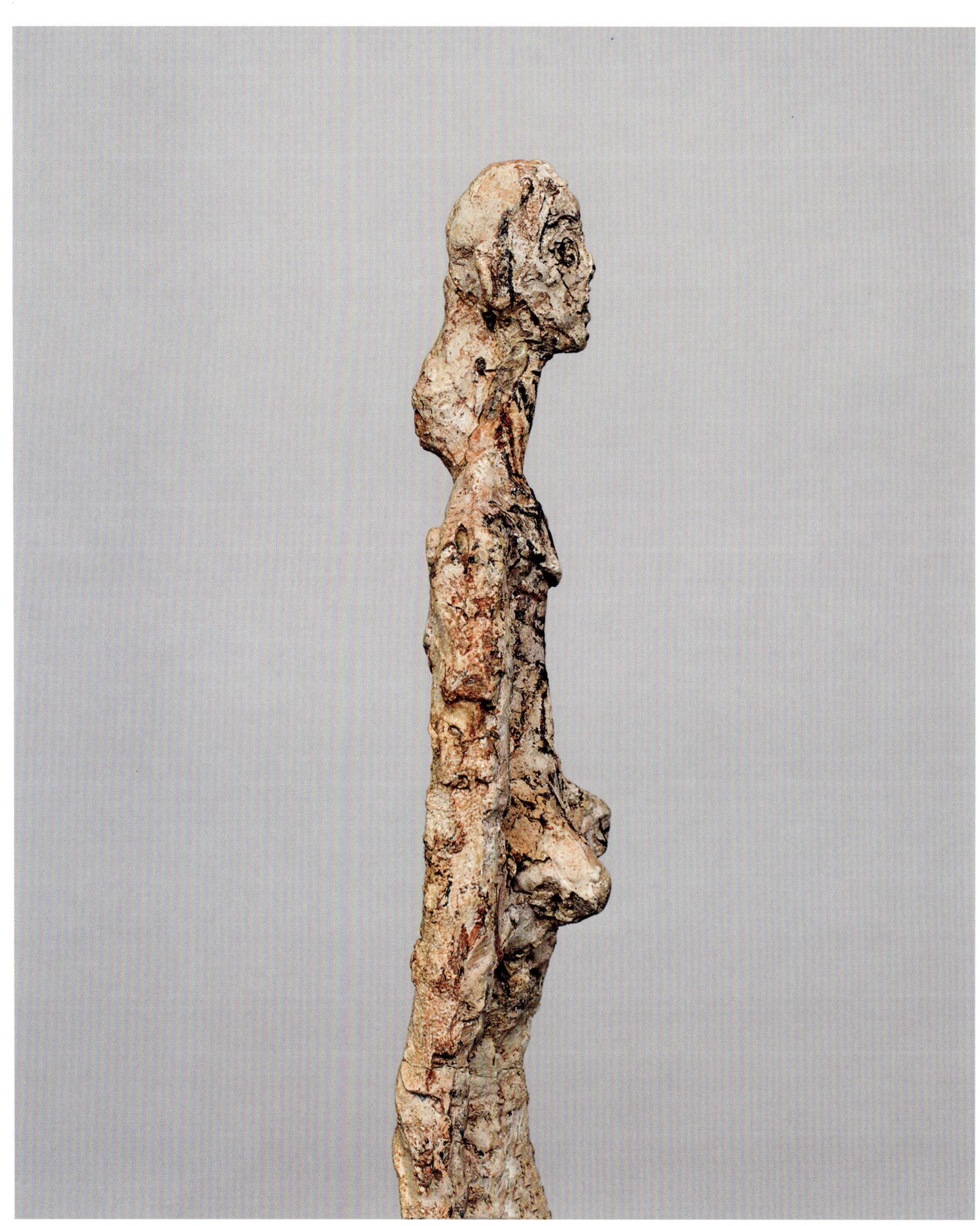

Fig. 160
Alberto Giacometti
Woman of Venice V (detail)
1956
Painted plaster, 113.5 × 14.5 × 31.8 cm
(3 ft. 8 ⅝ in. × 5 ¾ in. × 12 ½ in.)
Fondation Giacometti, Paris

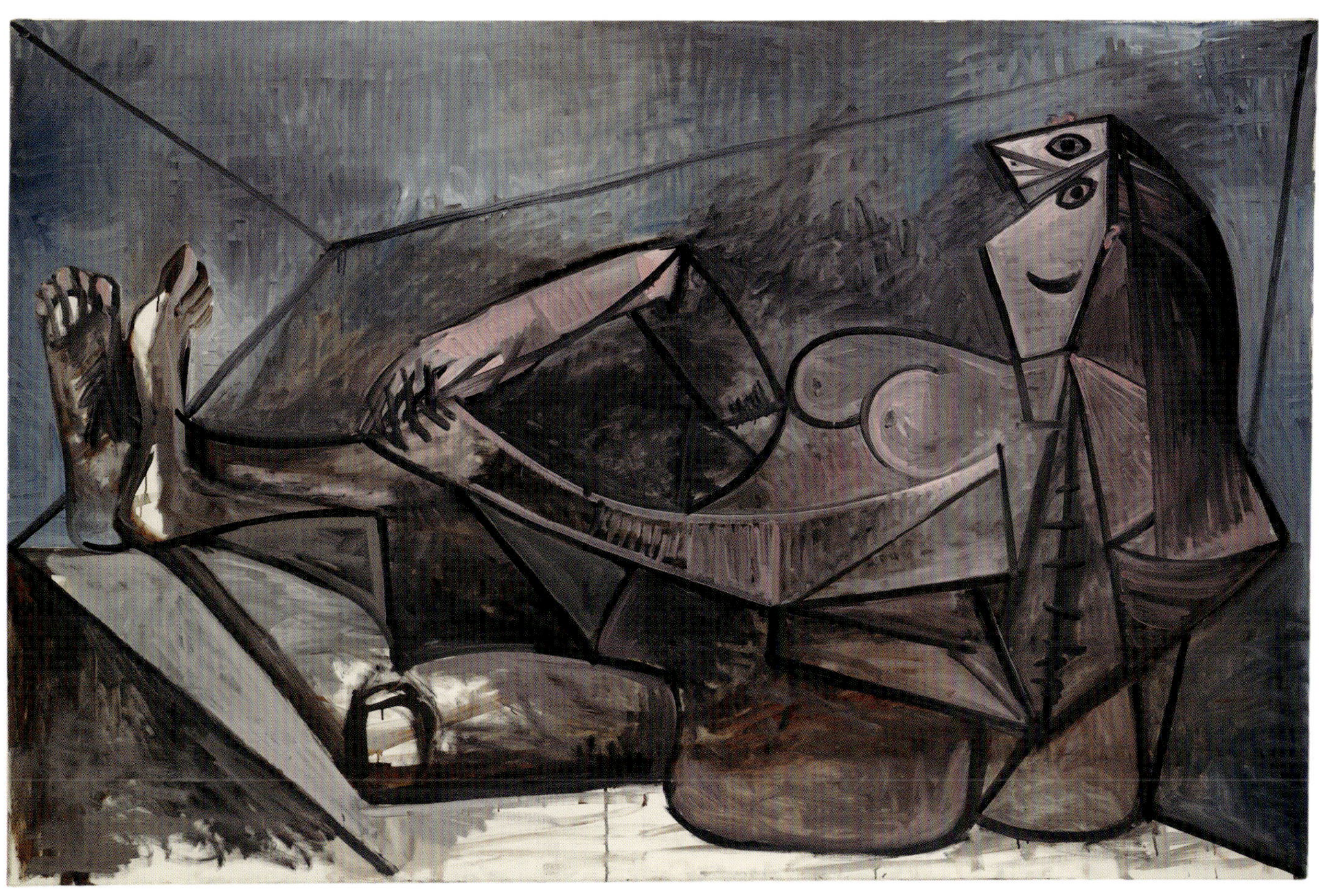

Fig. 161
Pablo Picasso
Large Reclining Nude
Paris, 28 June 1943
Oil on canvas, 130 × 195.3 cm (4 ft. 3 ¼ in. × 6 ft. 5 in.)
Musée National Picasso-Paris
Dation Pablo Picasso, 1979. MP191

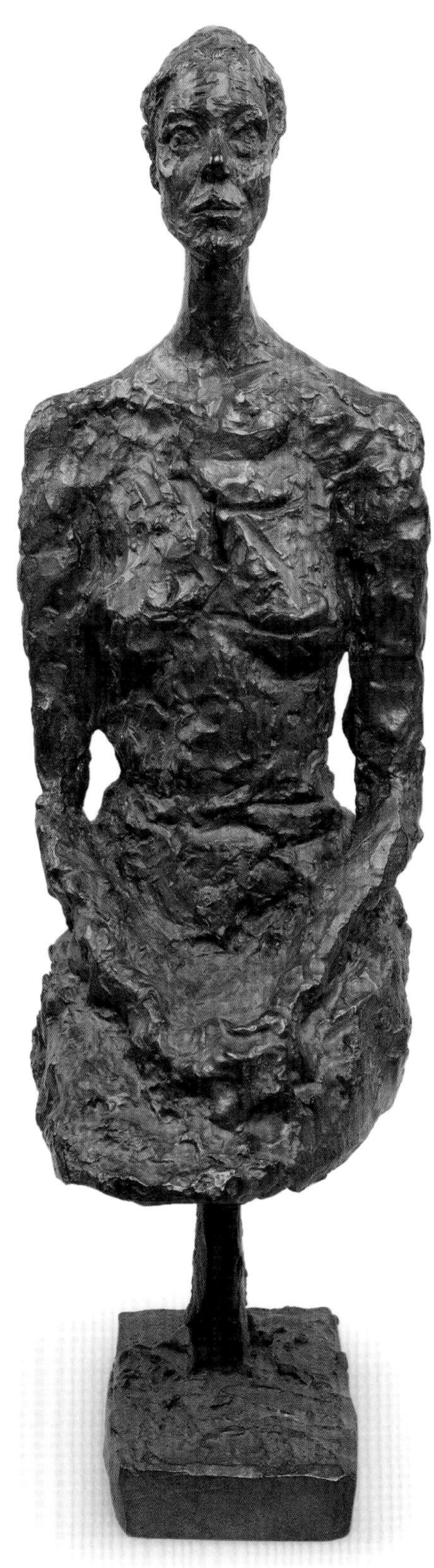

—
Fig. 162
Alberto Giacometti
Large Seated Woman
1958
Bronze, 80.5 × 22 × 30.5 cm (31 ¾ × 8 ⅝ × 12 in.)
Fondation Giacometti, Paris
—

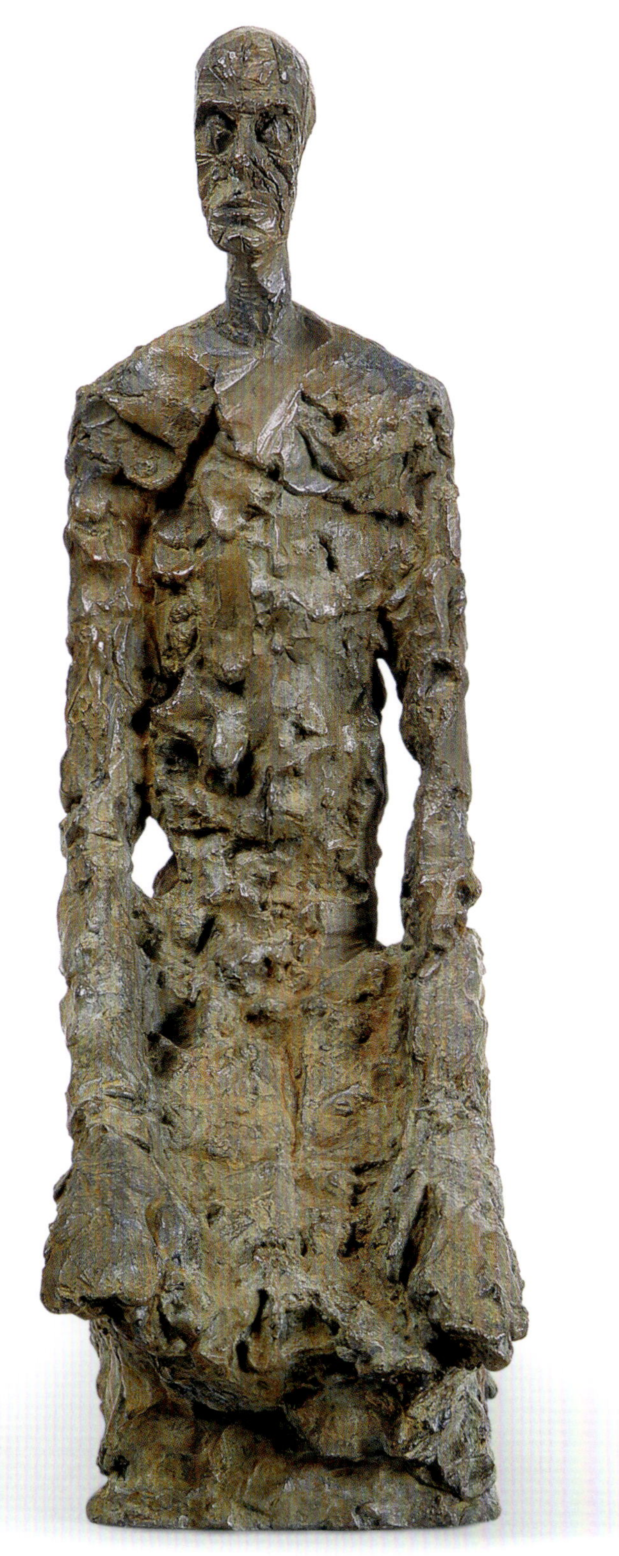

Fig. 163
Alberto Giacometti
Half-Length of a Man
1965
Bronze, 59.1 × 19 × 32.1 cm (23 ¼ × 7 ½ × 12 ⅝ in.)
Fondation Giacometti, Paris

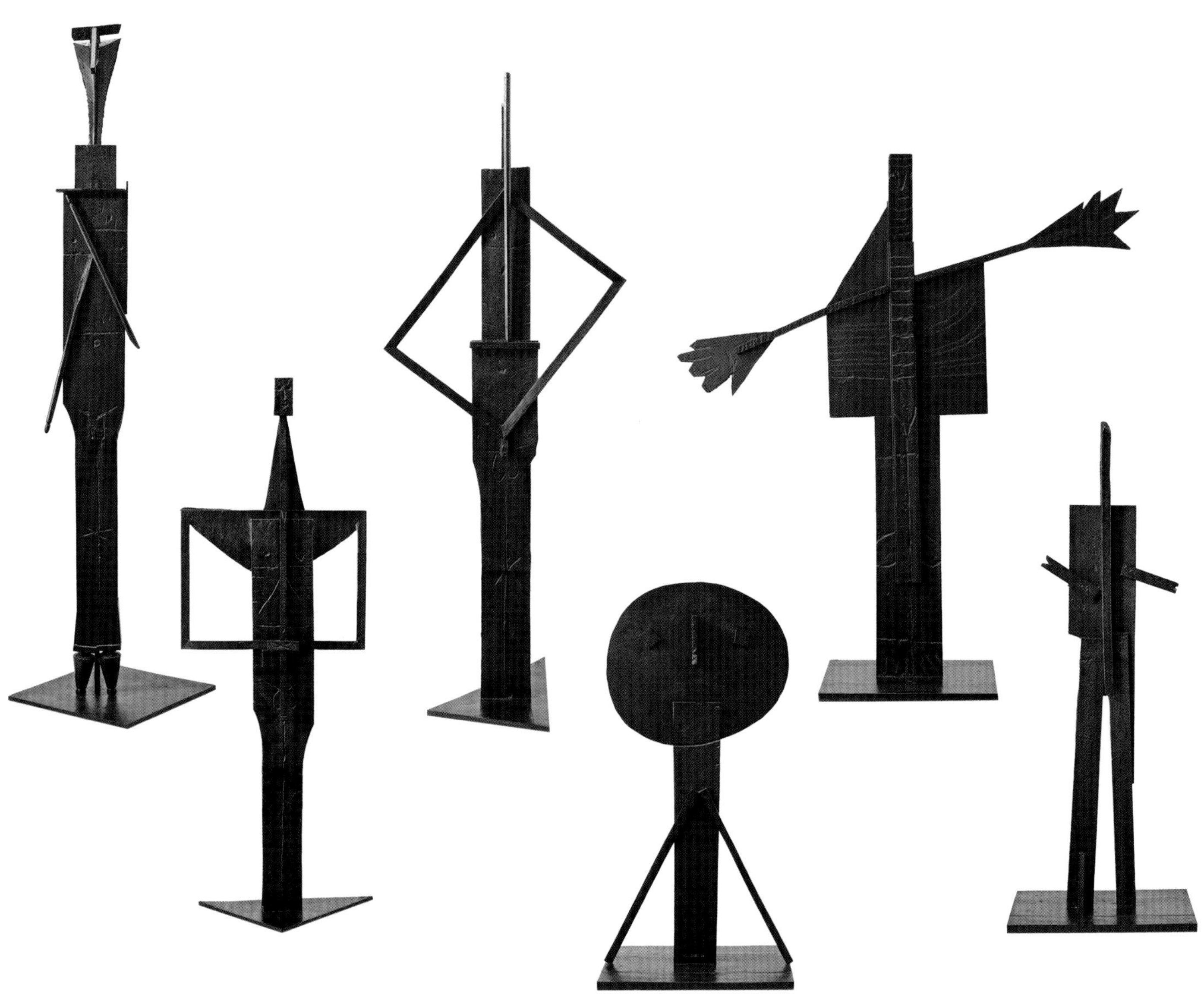

The Diver
264 × 83.5 × 83.5 cm
(8 ft. 8 in. × 2 ft. 8 ⅞ in. × 2 ft. 8 ⅞ in.)

Man with Clasped Hands
213.5 × 73 × 36 cm
(7 ft. × 2 ft. 4 ¾ in. × 1 ft. 2 ⅛ in.)

The Man-Fountain
228 × 88 × 77.5 cm
(7 ft. 5 ¾ in. × 2 ft. 10 ⅝ in. × 2 ft. 6 ½ in.)

The Child
136 × 67 × 46 cm
(4 ft. 5 ½ in. × 2 ft. 2 ⅜ in. × 1 ft. 6 ⅛ in.)

Woman with Outstretched Arms
198 × 174 × 46 cm
(6 ft. 6 in. × 5 ft. 8 ½ in. × 1 ft. 6 ⅛ in.)

The Young Man
176 × 65 × 46 cm
(5 ft. 9 ⅜ in. × 2 ft. 1 ½ in. × 1 ft. 6 ⅛ in.)

—
Fig. 164
Pablo Picasso
The Bathers
Cannes, summer 1956
Bronze
Musée National Picasso-Paris
Dation Pablo Picasso, 1979. MP352 to MP357
—

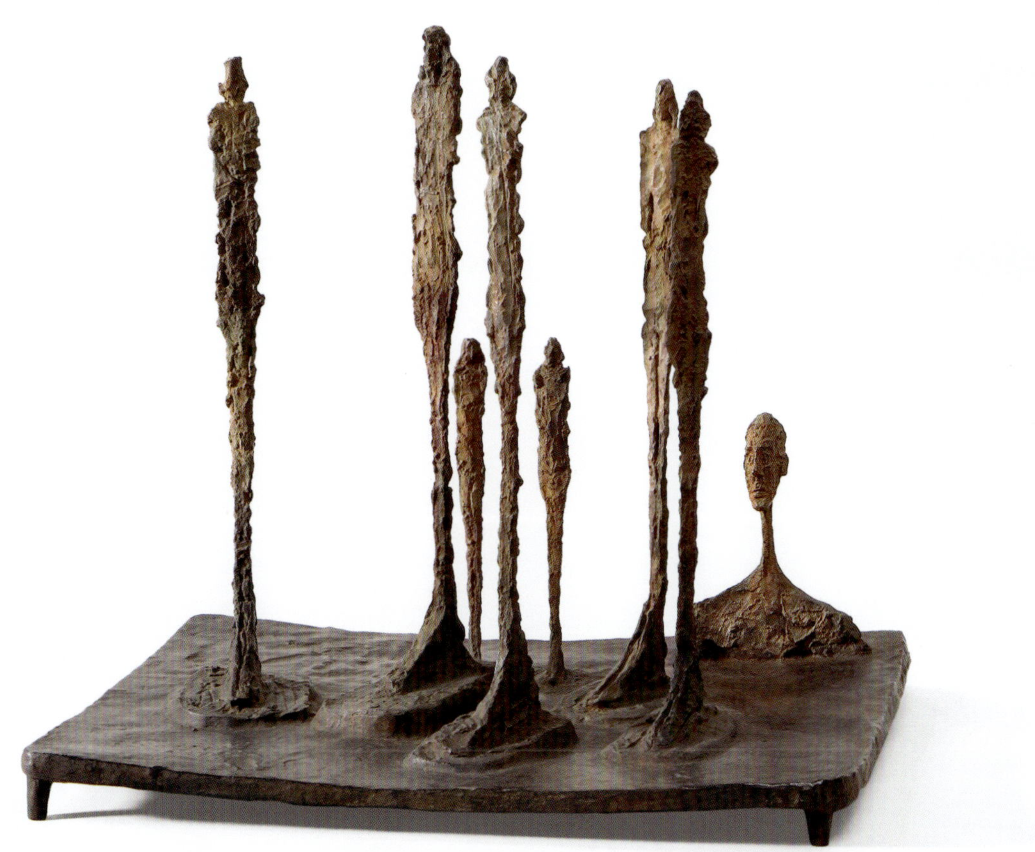

Fig. 165
Alberto Giacometti
The Forest
1950
Bronze, 57 × 61 × 47.3 cm (22 ½ × 24 × 18 ⅝ in.)
Fondation Giacometti, Paris

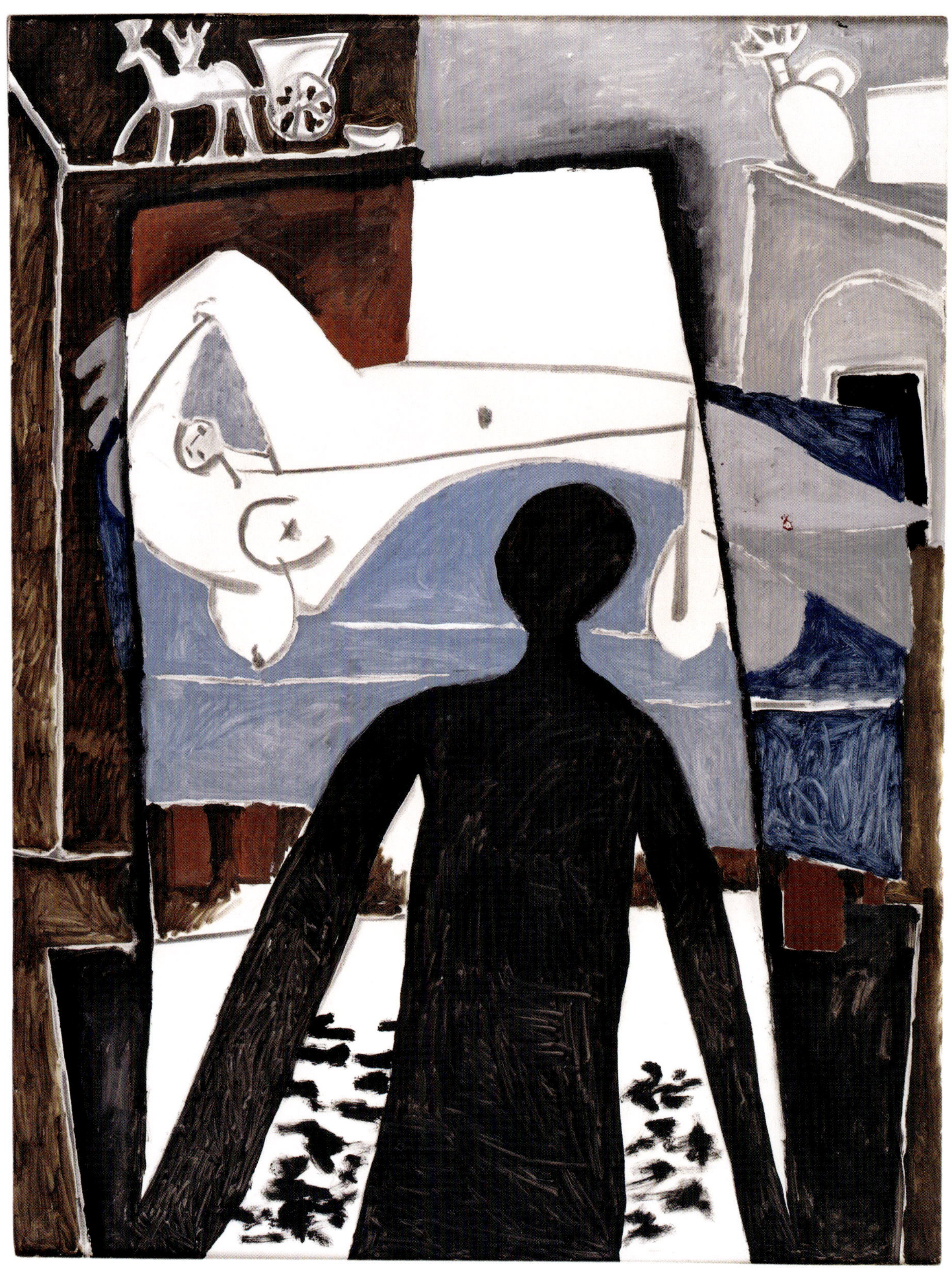

Fig. 166
Pablo Picasso
The Shadow
Vallauris, 29 December 1953
Oil and charcoal on canvas, 129.5 × 96.5 cm (4 ft. 3 in. × 3 ft. 2 in.)
Musée National Picasso-Paris
Dation Pablo Picasso, 1979. MP208

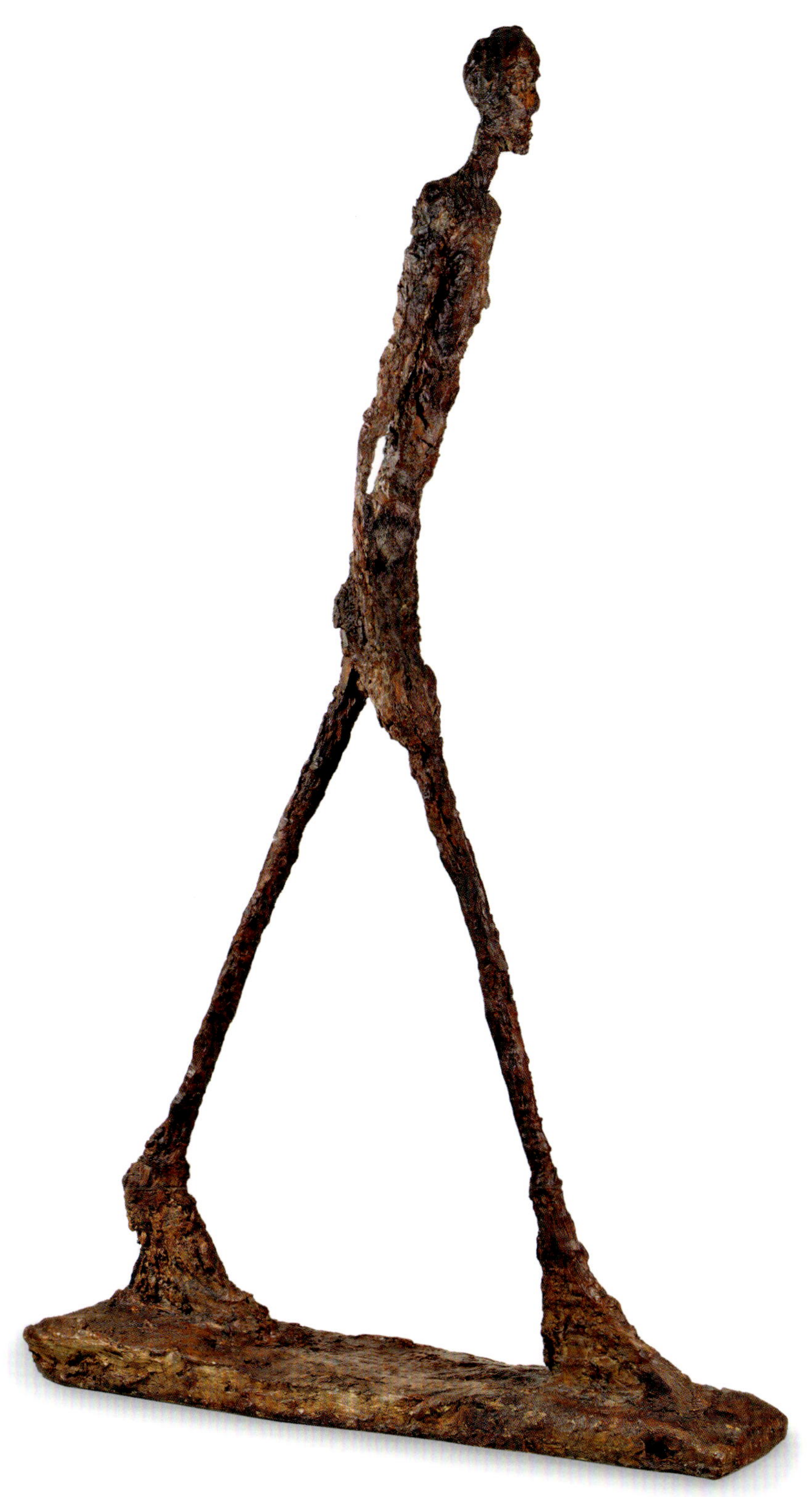

—
Fig. 167
Alberto Giacometti
Walking Man II
1960
Plaster, 188.5 × 29.1 × 111.2 cm
(6 ft. 2 ⅛ in. × 11 ½ in. × 3 ft. 7 ⅞ in.)
Fondation Giacometti, Paris
—

Constellation

Virginie Duchêne

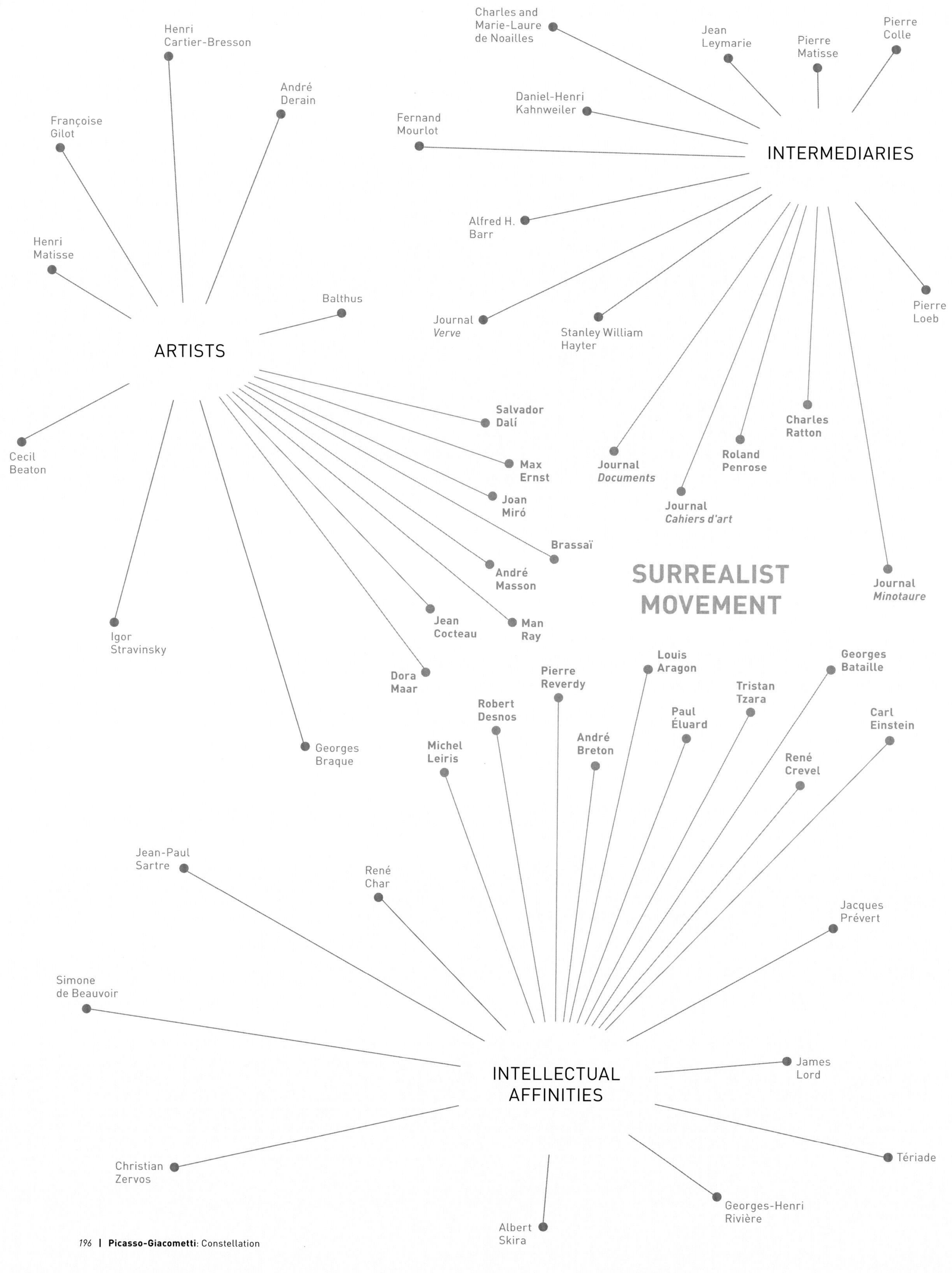

ARTISTS
INTERMEDIARIES
SURREALIST MOVEMENT
INTELLECTUAL AFFINITIES
Henri Cartier-Bresson
André Derain
Françoise Gilot
Henri Matisse
Balthus
Cecil Beaton
Igor Stravinsky
Georges Braque
Charles and Marie-Laure de Noailles
Jean Leymarie
Pierre Matisse
Pierre Colle
Daniel-Henri Kahnweiler
Fernand Mourlot
Alfred H. Barr
Pierre Loeb
Journal Verve
Stanley William Hayter
Charles Ratton
Salvador Dalí
Max Ernst
Joan Miró
Brassaï
André Masson
Man Ray
Jean Cocteau
Dora Maar
Journal Documents
Journal Cahiers d'art
Roland Penrose
Journal Minotaure
Louis Aragon
Georges Bataille
Pierre Reverdy
Tristan Tzara
Carl Einstein
Robert Desnos
Paul Éluard
René Crevel
Michel Leiris
André Breton
Jean-Paul Sartre
René Char
Jacques Prévert
Simone de Beauvoir
James Lord
Christian Zervos
Tériade
Albert Skira
Georges-Henri Rivière

Picasso and Giacometti: Recurrent Figures, Shared Influences

Alberto Giacometti's artistic career led him to cross paths with Pablo Picasso, his elder by twenty years, in the early 1930s. Against the backdrop of common influences and the major intellectual movements of the age, the two men were consequently to rub shoulders with an array of important figures in twentieth-century art. The links they forged with painters, poets, intellectuals and intermediaries soon drew them into an artistic network that made an enduring contribution to both the evolution and the visibility of their subsequent output.

A facet of the living frontier at which each of the two artists worked, this constellation turns the spotlight on these figures and on these connections, considering them from various angles, but with a special focus on artists of the Surrealist tendency and on the transitional period constituted by the early years of the movement proper. The density of the Surrealist spectrum testifies to its repercussions on the work of both men, while the presence of artists with links to Cubism recalls the proximity and influence of this seminal movement founded by Picasso and Georges Braque.

This panorama of creativity is completed by other galaxies: certain intellectual affinities demonstrate the crucial impact on both artists of the connections they maintained with thinkers, ethnologists, art historians and art critics. With respect to their perseverance and to the prominence of their oeuvre, the encouragement of many intermediaries often proved decisive.

Finally, the artists brought together painters, whose interest in and associations with Picasso and Giacometti never flagged, as well as photographers, whose images offer an invaluable testimony of creative moments captured in the studio and of the artists' work in progress.

Commentaries on the Constellation

Louis Aragon
He meets Picasso in 1919. Exchanges within the framework of Aragon's political activities, particularly in *Les Lettres françaises*. In 1929–30 he meets Giacometti, who in 1932–35 produces satirical drawings on political subjects for various reviews on which Aragon collaborates.

Balthus
In the mid-1930s, Balthus meets Picasso, who later collects his works. Around the same period, he meets Giacometti, forming a deep friendship with the artist with whom he shares an interest in realism and in the figure in space.

Alfred H. Barr
The first director of MoMA from 1939 to 1943. He acquires works by Picasso and Giacometti and organises landmark exhibitions.

Georges Bataille
Founder of the review *Documents*, Bataille writes about Picasso's unique status in his text 'Rotten Sun'. During the Surrealist years, Giacometti feels an affinity with Bataille's 'disturbing' visions. In 1946, he executes a sculpture portrait of Bataille's wife, illustrating *Histoire de rats* in 1947.

Cecil Beaton
Beaton has a long friendship with Picasso, whom he starts photographing in 1919. He takes photographs of Giacometti in his studio in 1956 and 1962.

Simone de Beauvoir
On 16 June 1944, Beauvoir is present at a reading of Picasso's play *Le Désir attrapé par la queue* in the Leiris household. She meets Giacometti with Sartre at the end of the 1930s. Giacometti makes a series of drawings and small heads of the writer in 1946.

Georges Braque
Founder of Cubism with Picasso, whom he meets in 1907. On his death in 1963, Picasso engraves a lithograph in homage to his friend, inscribing an epitaph consecrating the profound lifelong bond between the two artists, in spite of their divergences. Long friendship with Giacometti from 1930. On the artist's death, Giacometti publishes a tribute in 1964.

Brassaï (Gyula Halász, known as)
He meets Picasso in 1932 within the Surrealist movement and a long friendship ensues. In 1964, he publishes *Conversations with Picasso* which attests to their compatibility. He is one of the first to photograph Giacometti's studio in 1933 for the journal *Minotaure* and he collaborates with the sculptor on the review *Labyrinthe*.

André Breton
The leader of the Surrealist movement. He meets Picasso in 1918 and publishes 'Picasso in His Element' in the first issue of *Minotaure* in 1933. Giacometti's ties to the Surrealists and to Breton grow stronger in 1930. They become firm friends; Giacometti is a witness at Breton's wedding. He illustrates the collection composed by the poet on this occasion, *L'Air de l'eau*, with four prints.

Cahiers d'art (journal)
Founded by Christian Zervos in 1926, this review acts as a platform for information and critical analysis of Picasso's oeuvre. The journal devotes an important article to the discovery of Giacometti, who occasionally copies some of its illustrations.

Henri Cartier-Bresson
Cartier-Bresson photographs Picasso's studio on Rue des Grands-Augustins in 1952. He meets Giacometti in Paris in the 1930s, sparking a long friendship. In 1961, he follows Giacometti to Switzerland, taking photographs of the artist in the village where he was born.

René Char
He meets Picasso and Giacometti in the 1930s, in the Surrealist sphere. In 1954, Char pays tribute to Giacometti in the poem *Recherche de la base et du sommet*.

Jean Cocteau
He meets Picasso in 1915. Although their relationship wavers, for Picasso Cocteau remains an instigator of genius with a talent for bringing people together. The Spanish artist never fails to appreciate his creativity and is amused by his caprices. Cocteau meets Giacometti in 1929 at Jeanne Bucher's gallery. In 1930, the poet praises Giacometti's plaster sculptures in his book *Opium*.

Pierre Colle
He organises Giacometti's debut solo exhibition in 1932. Picasso is its first visitor.

René Crevel
Giacometti meets Crevel in Surrealist circles, engraving plates for his *Les Pieds dans le plat* (1933). Picasso also illustrates Crevel's poem *Nuit* in 1956.

Salvador Dalí
He meets Picasso in 1929, but Picasso breaks with him after Dalí supports Franco in 1936. Dalí associates with Giacometti within the Surrealist movement, defining *Suspended Ball* as the 'prototype of the symbolically functioning object'.

André Derain
He is friends from 1906 with Picasso, who collects his works and shares his taste for non-Western art. From 1936, Derain's work holds a genuine fascination for Giacometti that will never diminish.

Robert Desnos
A familiar of Picasso's since Dada. They are regularly seen together during the Occupation and meet up at Le Flore café or Le Catalan restaurant in Saint-Germain-des-Prés. He meets Giacometti in the Surrealist haunt on Rue Blomet in the 1930s.

Documents (journal)
Established in 1929, this magazine, which featured Giacometti and Picasso, is centred on Georges Bataille's thought. It is a transversal publication that rides roughshod over the frontiers between various disciplines.

Carl Einstein
Author of *Negerplastik* [Black African Sculpture] published in 1915, a book with a significant impact. He meets Picasso in 1906–7 and Giacometti in 1929, promoting the latter's work in his review *Documents*, following his career, and offering advice.

Paul Éluard
He enjoys a profound friendship with Picasso, from the 1930s to the poet's death. He meets Giacometti within the Surrealist movement, and the artist carries out a series of drawings entitled *Thinking of Paul Éluard* in 1952.

Max Ernst
He meets Picasso at the Galerie Pierre in 1925. They remain friends until Ernst leaves for the United States in 1941. Ernst visits Giacometti in Switzerland in 1934.

Françoise Gilot
Painter Gilot meets Picasso in 1943, becoming his model and sharing his life until the 1950s. In 1964, she publishes an important book of her memories of him. She meets Giacometti in the 1940s and remains in contact with him beyond her relationship with Picasso.

Stanley William Hayter
Founder of Atelier 17 in 1927. He invents new processes of burin engraving that interest Picasso. Hayter initiates Giacometti to copperplate engraving, providing him with a taste for experimentation in this field.

Daniel-Henry Kahnweiler
An important art dealer and promoter of Cubism. He signs a contract with Picasso in 1910 and remains very close to the artist. He reveals an interest in Giacometti's oeuvre on several occasions, but never becomes his dealer.

Michel Leiris
Leiris marries Kahnweiler's daughter in 1926 and joins Picasso's inner circle. His texts preface and accompany a great number of exhibitions and publications of Picasso's works. Leiris writes the first article devoted to Giacometti for the review *Documents* in 1929. A long friendship begins between the two men. After Leiris' suicide attempt in 1957, Giacometti draws portraits of him in his hospital bed.

Jean Leymarie
An art curator and writer, Leymarie battles against French museums' indifference to Picasso work. In 1966, he organises a retrospective of the artist at the Grand Palais. Director of the Musée de Grenoble, he buys Giacometti's *Cage* in 1952. He curates the Giacometti retrospective at the Orangerie, Paris, in 1969.

Pierre Loeb
Exhibiting Picasso and the Surrealists in the 1920s, this art dealer signs a contract with Giacometti in 1929. The artist drew many portraits of him.

James Lord
Lord presents himself at Rue des Grands-Augustins in 1944 in order to meet Picasso. He publishes *Picasso and Dora* in 1993. He meets Giacometti in 1952 at the Deux Magots café. He is the author of a biography of the artist and publishes *A Giacometti Portrait*. Lord has his portrait done by both artists.

Dora Maar (Henriette Theodora Markovitch, known as)
Maar meets Picasso in 1936–37, becoming his lover and muse. She inspires many key works, and her political convictions are one of the reasons why the artist takes sides against the Franco regime during the Spanish Civil War. Frequenting Giacometti in the Surrealist circle, she photographs *Invisible Object* which appears as an illustration for Breton's *L'Amour fou*.

Man Ray (Emmanuel Radnitzky, known as)
He meets Picasso at the beginning of the 1920s, probably within the Dadaist sphere. He takes numerous photographs of the Spanish artist, one of the most famous showing him in a bullfighter's costume. Associating with Giacometti in the Surrealist movement, he photographs the artist and his works.

André Masson
He exhibits with Picasso in the 1920s and 1930s. Giacometti meets Masson in 1929, collaborating with him to decorate the homes of Georges-Henri Rivière and Pierre David-Weill.

Henri Matisse
He meets Picasso in 1905–6. Their friendship is tinged with competitiveness. He is one of the painters best represented in Picasso's collection. Giacometti meets Matisse in 1951 and executes some thirty portraits of the artist in pencil in 1954.

Pierre Matisse
Son of Henri Matisse and a dealer in modern art, based in the United States. He is well acquainted with Picasso's oeuvre and keeps up a correspondence with him. In contact with Giacometti from 1936, he becomes a great friend and his US dealer, dedicating retrospectives to his work from 1948.

Minotaure (journal)
Surrealist magazine (1933–39) founded by Albert Skira and Tériade. Devoted to fiction, poetry and painting, the journal opens its pages to Picasso, who designs the front cover for the first issue. In 1933, it publishes photographs of Giacometti's studio by Brassaï.

Joan Miró
Picasso meets Miró in 1919 and collects his works. From summer 1929, he regularly sees Giacometti, and they remain close until his death. They both share the same art dealers.

Fernand Mourlot
Picasso's lithographer, producing in particular the famous *Dove*. One of the printer's masterpieces is the posthumous lithographs for Giacometti's *Paris sans fin* in 1969.

Charles and Marie-Laure de Noailles
Patrons close to the Surrealist movement. They are also collectors of works by Picasso and Giacometti. Between 1946 and 1948 the latter created a series of portraits of Marie-Laure.

Roland Penrose
Painter, writer and collector, close to the Surrealists. He meets Picasso in 1936, beginning a long friendship with the Spanish artist. Giacometti encounters Penrose within the Surrealist circle, visiting Picasso's studio with him in 1937 while the Spanish artist is painting *Guernica*.

Jacques Prévert
In 1925–26, he meets Picasso, to whom he dedicates the poem *Promenade de Picasso*. Giacometti puts him up in his studio in the 1930s. Their friendship lasts until Giacometti's death.

Charles Ratton
Dealer in 'primitive' art. Picasso and Giacometti visit his store on Rue de Rennes in Paris. In 1936, the *Surrealist Exhibition of Objects* features both artists.

Pierre Reverdy
He meets Picasso in 1910. In 1947, the Spanish artist illustrates his poetry collection *Le Chant des morts* with lithographs. He forms a friendship in the 1930s with Giacometti, who carries out a portrait tribute upon his death in 1960.

Georges-Henri Rivière
He meets Picasso at the Bœuf sur le Toit cabaret on 10 January 1922. Their paths cross again in the context of the famous 'Mission Dakar-Djibouti' ethnographic expedition, launched between 1931 and 1933 by the Musée d'Ethnographie du Trocadéro in Paris, the director of which is Rivière. He actively participates in the journal *Documents* between April 1929 and January 1931. In 1929, Giacometti produces a bas-relief for his Paris drawing room.

Jean-Paul Sartre
On 16 June 1944, he attends a reading of Picasso's play *Le Désir attrapé par la queue* at the Leiris residence. Giacometti meets Sartre in the late 1930s, and their friendship grows in the 1940s. In 1948, Sartre's essay *La Recherche de l'absolu* is published in the catalogue of the Giacometti exhibition at the Pierre Matisse Gallery in New York.

Albert Skira
He provides Picasso with the opportunity to illustrate literary works. He forms a profound friendship with Giacometti. In 1944, Skira's offices in Geneva launch the review *Labyrinthe*, with support from Giacometti and Balthus.

Igor Stravinsky
Picasso meets the composer in Rome in 1917 and draws his portrait. Giacometti meets the composer in October 1957, inviting him to pose for a series of portraits.

Tériade
Art director of the magazine *Minotaure* until 1936. He founds the journal *Verve* in 1937, and simultaneously publishes artist books such as Pierre Reverdy's *Le Chant des morts*, illustrated by Picasso. Giacometti and Tériade meet in 1927 at an exhibition at the Galerie Pierre, beginning a great friendship, as evidenced by portrait paintings and drawings of the publisher between 1946 and 1960.

Tristan Tzara
He meets Picasso in 1920 in the ambit of Dada. The two men encounter each other sporadically, particularly in the French Communist Party. He is close to Giacometti within the Surrealist movement, and after 1936 in the Association of Revolutionary Writers and Artists (AEAR).

Verve (journal)
Created in 1937, with Tériade as editor in chief. It features works by Picasso and Giacometti frequently.

Christian Zervos
An art historian, specialised in ancient Greek art. He meets Picasso in 1926. He heads the review *Cahiers d'art* and embarks on a catalogue raisonné of Picasso's work in 1932. He meets Giacometti in the sphere of his journal and Surrealist circles.

Anthology

Nathalie Leleu

Despite an age gap of some twenty years, Picasso and Giacometti shared a milieu and a circle of friends whose writings have proven extremely informative on both artists. In the 1930s, they feature almost simultaneously in texts by Christian Zervos, André Breton and Man Ray, who were at once witnesses to and facilitators of the two artists' intense activity. Yves Bonnefoy is the only author here to have compared them in a recent publication. Thanks to the alphabetical order of the anthology, an extract from the latter's essay opens this selection of texts in which reality spontaneously spawns fiction—a place of unspoken dialogue where one senses the authors reading over each other's shoulders, possibly even echoing one another's words through the only figures who remain silent: Picasso and Giacometti.

YVES BONNEFOY
(1923–2016)

It was during a lecture at the Musée Picasso in Antibes, in 1995, that the poet Yves Bonnefoy juxtaposed the names of Pablo Picasso and Alberto Giacometti. The relationship between the painter and his model is the sphere of a radical, violent alterity, in which each artist is, 'beneath the appearances, in a state of war with being'. A fervent biographer of Giacometti, Yves Bonnefoy carries out on Picasso the same intimate exercise in the dialectical analysis of a relationship with a father who was also an artist. Giacometti's 'anxious curiosity' concerning Picasso hovers between tradition and modernity, between the 'grand art' of presence and a refusal to engage with the other.

This anthology of texts devoted to Pablo Picasso and Alberto Giacometti begins with an essay by Yves Bonnefoy. This choice, made before the poet passed away on 1 July 2016, pays homage to the quality of his reflections on the oeuvre of both artists. Today, it celebrates the memory of a poet and an art critic whose quest was always for the 'mysterious fact' of presence.

Picasso and Giacometti

And I will observe only that this aptitude for perceiving and attesting to presence, as well as this discovery of the self and of his vocation, which occurred to him in reaction to the work of someone else—in this case, his father—may well explain, directly and profoundly, why Giacometti might at the same time think of himself as the polar opposite of Picasso, and yet be interested, if not fascinated, by his particular problem. He, for whom everything had seemed possible through drawing at a certain point in his adolescence, might readily understand the kind of trap the elder artist had fallen into. With respect to Picasso, he could feel both sympathetic and remote, with, lurking beneath, a concern that the kind of being-in-world and artistic project, which for his part he had left far behind, might perhaps have been suppressed rather than dissipating, and that therefore, if ever he lowered his guard, it might well come back to haunt his own destiny. Even if, by the time he came to Paris, Giacometti was not yet fully aware of his own potential, even if he was still trying to find himself in art as it is commonly understood, be it metamorphosed into the avant-garde, a sufficient number of dissatisfactions, of contradictions, and of imperceptible but inescapable intuitions had been stirred up in him for Picasso to become the object of his rapt attention, his anxious curiosity.

Moreover, in the 1920s, Picasso had attained the acme of his glory: hailed with enthusiasm, the very disparity of his output was at the time acclaimed for expressing an inventiveness that would pave the way for a new age that would transcend, by means of a playful, free art, the moralising and misleading language of the past. Hampered rather than emboldened by what was afoot within him, Alberto, however, did not yet know what he might achieve and was dogged by phases of disturbing sterility. Rather than performing a multitude of experiments like Picasso—who was prepared to reject them, hardly completed, strewing them about like aspects of a life-enhancing creativity—Alberto groped and destroyed, and it might have been said of him—as he himself stated—that he knew nothing and could do nothing. He had already experienced the intuition I'm trying to describe, as he says in his own account from a good while later. This gaze, which, by the mid-1930s, was to reinvigorate him, was still struggling up from his subconscious among all the ideas assailing him, be it in Bourdelle's studio, where he studied for a long time, or from post-Cubist sculpture, which benefitted in his eyes from the artistic and moral excellence of Henri Laurens. Giacometti could have nothing to set against Picasso. And he might fear that his strange dissatisfaction, something he experienced solely as a puzzle and a stumbling block, might be shown up as pointless, if not absurd, when compared with the interminable successes of the other artist against whom he was secretly protesting. It was his angst that kept him close to Picasso.

Nonetheless, one characteristic feature of Giacometti's first Paris period needs to be emphasised: all of the works and studies for works he attempted at this time, primarily in sculpture, in one way or another reveal a view that stands out forcefully against an environment that sometimes seems immaterial. Eyes, the gaze—this is what Picasso always avoided, as demonstrated by his *Painter and His Model* or the series of portraits of Dora Maar. On the contrary, in the portraits Giacometti made of his parents during those years and in his sculptures of 1925–27, a gaze turned directly on the artist clears a path through the signs, the simple artistic signs, with an intensity that verges on the mysterious. And this glance even tends to reduce other aspects of the work to naught, since it ends up almost alone in the flat sculptures of 1928–29, one of which is, moreover, entitled *Head Looking*.

What should be stressed is how in this manner and so soon, Giacometti, aware of the fact or no, was turning the very gaze Picasso could neither bear nor even catch into the chief axis of his research, into the supreme object of his desire, the ground on which his oeuvre would stand, and in any case into a challenge he was soon to take up with greater resolve. In fact, we now discover, Alberto harboured another reason to feel close to this Picasso who hid from the eyes of others, prepared to throw them a thousand facets of his outer self, each as misleading as it was picturesque, like a sop: it was the terrible experience he had had one night when just twenty years old, far from home, when he had found himself in a wretched hotel room alone with a dying old man. In this man's departing glance, a glance Giacometti had had to bear without offering any solace, he had perceived not only the presence of a person, but also his absence, not just the fact of being, but nothingness too, and consequently the fear had grown in him that henceforth every life, that of others, his own even, might mean no more for his troubled consciousness than this nothingness, than this irredeemable meaninglessness that one is tempted to elude.

Later on, in 1929 and 1930, he came across a number of no less terrible and traumatising pictures in Georges Bataille's review *Documents*—photographs, in particular, which nurtured and exacerbated his latent terror. This led to works like *The Cage* or *Woman with Her Throat Cut* that bespeak less of a cruel or sadistic temperament than they reflect a horror for the fragility of life, by its very nature blind violence, death, decomposition, and rejection of human debris in the decay and metamorphosis of all things. In such moments, art was for him no more than the irrepressible awakening of this fear.

At this time, at the end of the 1920s, Picasso was much vaunted by the group involved in *Documents* with which Giacometti had become associated. Georges Bataille, the intellectual guru of the circle, interpreted Picasso's recent works quite differently from the way I do, seeing them above all as a frenzied denunciation of the illusory character of all idealistic conceptions of reality, of life. In so doing, he focused on those paintings that demolish the human figure, such as the recent *Painter's Studio* of April 1929, and another dated 1927, but reproduced in 1930 in the same issue 3 of the review envisaged as a 'Homage to Picasso.' Thus, for

Giacometti, these works, and others of the time, naturally became food for thought, exerting a direct influence on his work. Some such 1929 painting by Picasso might well have inspired sculptures like *The Cage* of 1930-31 or *Three Figures Outside*, and much the same might be said of *Figures on the Seashore* painted by Picasso on 12 January 1931, and of *Woman Throwing a Stone*, from 8 March.

The painter and the sculptor were then extremely close and the interest Giacometti felt in the Picasso celebrated by *Documents* extended readily to other works from the same few years. It is thus easy to pass from Picasso's openwork sculpture of 1930 to Giacometti's lattice pieces; from the *Project for a Monument* to the 'object' that proved so decisive for Alberto's career, the *Suspended Ball*; and from the elongations of certain Picassos to the *Woman Who Walks* from 1932-34. It is impossible to understand Giacometti's 'Surrealist period' without keeping in mind all that Picasso's art offered him, in terms of daring suggestions on the use of form, and consequently in discovering solutions to express his obsessions plastically, of giving them free rein, but also of escaping them in the pleasure of inventing, astonishing, individualising himself.

It remains the case that, however Giacometti might strive to evade this fear of nothingness, he was nonetheless bent on defying and overcoming it, on finding a path along which his work, originating in that inaugural confrontation with the dying old man, might attain personal being. It was this which, in 1934, saw him create a large statue, *Invisible Object*—a figure of a woman, at once presence and absence, whose hands almost joining in the gesture of lifting up a child seemed to present him with the as yet untold work he still had to learn how to do. After which he abruptly abandoned the research he had been undertaking for the last few years related to dreams and barricaded himself in his workshop before a model, a young woman, his plan being to represent the human face, nothing more or less, but going well beyond mere resemblance. Harking back to and replenishing his previous intuition that had reappeared in the 'flat heads', his intention was now to capture in clay or plaster busts, which his friends would find academic, the absolute constituted by a being when it is there, before us, in its brief instant of presence.

And, patently, fixing as an outer appearance the fact—or better, the event—of this presence, that's what was difficult. And once again, for some length of time, the work made no headway, producing, it seemed, little more than 'banal little heads', as their creator was fond of calling them. In the months preceding the war, Giacometti was to embark on something quite different and genuinely unprecedented: extricated from a few ounces of plaster, tiny female figures appeared on his untidy turntable, scarcely an inch high and placed on what are in comparison gigantic plinths, endowing these figurines with a powerful sense of presence—the mystery of a goddess appearing at the frontier between the visible and the invisible. But so remote, in this wise, and so indistinct were these bodies of lumpy matter, with their arms stuck on their hips, that he seemed to have abandoned, if not the project of signifying being, then at least that of ever encountering it in a person on this earth.

Viewed generally, in this first period of his life ending in 1941, when he travelled to see his mother in Switzerland and found himself unable to return to a France occupied by the Germans, the artist about to create *Chariot* and *Man Pointing* had accomplished nothing to signal a break with the tradition embodied by his father or with the modernity represented by Picasso. On returning to Paris, Alberto Giacometti was no more than that young artist—although no longer as young as all that—who at the turn of the 1930s had produced some highly individual sculptures noticed only by writers and painters of the avant-garde, and who had gone on to disappoint this same circle, and his Surrealist friends in particular, by a return to the model which to them appeared incomprehensibly reactionary. His experimentation with small figures on large bases, undertaken a little later, did little to broaden his appeal.

'Picasso et Giacometti', *Remarques sur le regard: Picasso, Giacometti, Morandi, l'art en France entre les deux guerres* (Paris: Calmann-Lévy, 2002), pp. 103–12 (chapter 6).

ANDRÉ BRETON
(1896–1966)

In the space of one year, André Breton wrote two key texts in the history of Surrealism, with Picasso and Giacometti as their respective protagonists. Breton's article 'Picasso in His Element', accompanied by photographs taken by Brassaï in the artist's studio, inaugurated the review *Minotaure*. Starting from a butterfly that Picasso placed in a piece, Breton squares Picasso's universe with Surrealist doctrine in the exalted tone he relished when writing on the Spanish artist. On the other hand, in an article that posits the equation of the 'necessity' of encountering the *'objet trouvé'*, he incorporates Alberto Giacometti into an account of two 'finds' made at a flea market that are identified as catalysts for the creative process.

Picasso in His Element

Picasso is great in my eyes precisely because he has constantly remained on the defensive against these external things, including those he had drawn from himself, and has never taken them to be anything but *moments* of intercession between himself and the world. He has sought out the perishable and the ephemeral for themselves, going against the grain of everything that is usually the object of artistic delight and vanity. The twenty years that have washed over them have already yellowed those newspaper clippings, whose fresh ink contributed their fair share to the insolence of his magnificent collages from 1913. The light has faded, and humidity has stealthily lifted the corners of the great cutouts in blue and pink. And that's the way it should be. The stupefying guitars made of low-grade wood, makeshift bridges cast daily over the song, have not held up against the singer's headlong rush. But it's as if Picasso had already counted on this impoverishment, this weakening, even this dismembering. As if in this unequal struggle waged *nonetheless* by human creations against the elements, where there is no doubt about the outcome, he had wanted in advance to leave his options open, to reconcile everything precious (because ultra-real) with the process of its wasting away. Thus the stag-beetle, flying in oak forests on stormy June evenings with its face to the sun, despite its marvelous covering like that of some black prince, and after a hatching period lasting four or five years, enjoys no more than a month of existence in the open air—the same open air that the crow's piteous caw pierces for a hundred years. If there is room in nature for two beings presenting such an analogy of color, an opposition of structure, and a paradoxical difference in life span, it seems to me that a work of art should take it into account; that the artist, whose primary concern is to create a living thing, can do no less before attempting it than to weigh a bird feather against an insect's wing-sheath. I exult in the fact that while certain of Picasso's paintings take their solemn place in the museums of the world, he still makes ample room for everything that will never become an object of admiration or speculation of any sort other than intellectual. In this, too, the conception he has of his own work can seem absolutely dialectical. Now is the time to underline this, at the moment when a journal is gathering and presenting a large portion of his recent *extra-pictorial* production. A common plant—a fig tree, for instance—serves here not only as support but also as *justification* for an iron sculpture that is inseparable from it in the observer's mind. The sculpture is subjected to the same fate as the fig tree. So true is this that one can see that another image has deserted the area around the dead fig tree, whose roots spring from the earth, arch over, and mingle inextricably in a supreme convulsion, the grimace of an embrace. The total lignification of the stem, sheathed at its end with an animal horn; the absence of leaves compensated, in contrast, by the imperceptible trembling of a little red feather, are exploited in contradiction to anything that could possibly arouse a feeling of the real life of the bush. But this same idea of support or backing, with all the (once again) justificative value that clings to it, this idea reflecting upon itself demands reciprocity: if the sculpture is based on the plant, it is just as valid for extremely disparate objects to be based on it as well (so it is of dubious interest to wonder whether ivy was made for the wall, or the wall for ivy). In and of themselves, these objects—the cap of a street corner vizier, the little "Mickey Mouse" or the *marmosets* of local fairs, cheap toys—will never be too humble or too futile to attack the dignity of this cast-iron personage, who seems never to know what to do with his foot—which moreover is just a metal cobbler's mold. For anyone who would still feel entitled to cast doubt on the dialectical progression of that thought, I think it will be enough to point out how, during his exhibit last June at the Georges Petit galleries, Picasso placed on opposite sides of a long room two great ironworks—one of which seemed covered with rust and the other freshly coated with white paint—showing quite clearly that with their extremely dissimilar coverings he wanted the two to *answer each other* as visitors passed by. These two statues, twins beyond any doubt, exchanged all the remarks of a lightly ironic philosophy, remarks that become apt the moment one lets oneself raise the problem of fate.

If, as we have seen, Picasso the painter has no bias toward color, we might expect that Picasso the sculptor would not have any bias toward matter. Indeed, with a meaningful and charming complicity, he draws our attention to the slight imperfections that the frail creatures he invents, which come gilded from the foundry, draw from their original substance: some slip of the chisel, a few accidents in the wood. In his hands, moreover, these imperfections undeniably become so many visible perfections. Wood, wire, or plaster are used here one serially or together, by a man whose need for concretization is instantly renewed by its very gratification; a man who is, like all great inventors, continually prey to others' requests; for whom it is totally useless and, no doubt, totally impossible to see anything ahead of time. An elective attraction, excluding any previous elaboration, alone determines—through substances found literally *at hand*— the appearance of a body or a head. This matter is nevertheless cherished for itself, but only like matter in general, completely outside any consideration of its particular states. It is cherished as in Rimbaud's "Feasts of Famine":

> If I've a taste, it is alone
> For eating simply earth and stone.
> Dinn! dinn! dinn! dinn! So let us dine
> On air, and rock, and coal, and iron.

But, you may ask, why plaster as well? Why should we still be served up all that classic porridge of plaster? A chorus of young voices gathers around me, fascinated and irritated, shouting: enough plaster! The greedy Picasso has better things to do than ruin all that plaster! But I fear it is really *their* dialectical sense and not his that falls short. Since the external object, as I've tried to define it visually, is produced by the principle of darkness manifested in bright light, it is measured on the surface by color; so when it occurs in a three-dimensional mass, deprived of any support from color, it tries to make up for it by showing the appropriate relation of shadow to light. This relation does not require us to ponder that object *in a static position*—which would mean having to walk absurdly around the object to assure ourselves of its existence. Picasso was very explicit on the subject as early as 1906, when he painted his famous women with "noses shaped like a wedge of Brie," those faces seen both frontally and in profile where people liked to point out the preponderance of a sculptor's concerns. Of course it is ideally through the mediation of the docile and immaculate substance of plaster that these relations of shadow and light, implying all the quantitative shifts in volume—nothing in common with expressionist "distortions"—can be perceived in the infinite possibility of their variation. A real object: a head, a body whose light patches would replace shadows , and vice versa … perhaps that's the extreme case, but we'd still like to see it. To be able to reflect on the self in the work of art, not only knowing oneself to be other than oneself, but in wanting, in tolerating the contrary of oneself.…

'Picasso in His Element' in Break of Day, translated by Mark Polizzotti and Mary Ann Caws
(Lincoln, NE: University of Nebraska Press, 1999), pp. 115–120.

Equation
of the Found Object

At the forefront of discovery, from the moment when, for the first navigators, a new land was in sight to the moment when they set foot on the shore, from the moment when a certain learned man became convinced that he had witnessed a phenomenon, hitherto unknown, to the time when he began to measure the import of his observation—all feeling of duration abolished by the intoxicating atmosphere of *chance*—a very delicate flame highlights or perfects life's meaning as nothing else can. It is to the recreation of this particular state of mind that surrealism has always aspired, disdaining in the last analysis the prey and the shadow for what is already no longer the shadow and not yet the prey: the shadow and the prey mingled into a unique flash. Behind ourselves, we must *not let the paths of desire become overgrown.* Nothing retains less of desire in art, in science, than this will to industry, booty, possession. A pox on all captivity, even should it be in the interest of the universal good, even in Montezuma's gardens of precious stones! Still today I am only counting on what comes of my own openness, my eagerness to wander *in search* of everything, which, I am confident, keeps me in mysterious communication with other open beings, as if we were suddenly called to assemble. I would like my life to leave after it no other murmur than that of a watchman's song, of a song to while away the waiting. Independent of what happens, and what does not happen, the wait itself is magnificent.[1]

I had been talking about this a few days before with Alberto Giacometti when a lovely spring day in 1934 invited us to stroll near the Flea Market, described in *Nadja* (this repetition of the setting is excused by the constant and deep transformation of the place).[2] At this time Giacometti was working on the construction of the female figure…, and this figure, although it had appeared very distinctly a few weeks before and had taken form in plaster in a few hours, underwent certain variations as it was sculpted. Whereas the gesture of the hands and the legs leaning against the plank had never caused the slightest hesitation, and the eyes, the right one figured by an intact wheel, the left one by a broken wheel, endured without change through the successive states of the figure, the length of the arms, on which the relation of the hands and the breasts depended, and the angles of the face in no way settled upon. I had never ceased to be interested in the progress of this statue, which, from the beginning, I had considered the very emanation of the *desire to love and be loved,* in search of its real human object, in its painful ignorance. As long as it had not been quite exposed, the fragility, the dynamism contained, the air of being both trapped and giving thanks, by which this graceful being had so moved me, led me to fear that in the life of Giacometti at that time any feminine intervention was likely to be harmful. Nothing was better founded than this fear, if you realize that any such intervention, passing though it was, led one day to a regrettable lowering of the hands, consciously justified by the concern to show the breasts and, having, to my great surprise, as a consequence [of] the *disappearance of the invisible but present object* on which the interest of the figure centers, and that these hands are holding or holding up. With some slight modifications, they were reestablished the next day in their proper place. However, the head, although sketched out in its main lines, defined as to its general character, was almost alone in participating in the sentimental uncertainty from which I continue to think the work had sprung. Completely subject as it was to certain imprescribable givens—venomous, astonished, and tender—it clearly resisted individualization, this resistance, as that also of the breasts to their final specification, presenting various plastic pretexts for its existence. Nevertheless, the face, so clear, so striking today, was sufficiently slow in evolving from the crystal of its plane for us to wonder if it would ever reveal its expression, by which alone the unity of the natural and the supernatural world could be perfected, permitting the artist to go on to something else. There was lacking any reference to the real, something to lean on in the world of tangible objects. The term of comparison, even distant, which suddenly confers certainty was lacking.

The objects that, between the lassitude of some and the desire of others, go off to dream at the antique fair had been just barely distinguishable from each other in the first hours of our stroll. They flowed by, without accident, nourishing the meditation that this place arouses, like no other, concerning the precarious fate of so many little human constructions. The first one of them that really attracted us, drawing us as something we had *never seen*, was a half-mask of metal striking in its rigidity as well as in its forceful adaptation to a necessity unknown to us. The first bizarre idea we had was that of being in the presence of a highly evolved descendent of the helmet, letting itself be drawn into flirtation with the velvet mask. We were able, in trying it on, to convince ourselves that the eyeholes, lined with horizontal strips of the same substance differently angled, permitted a perfect visibility above and below as well as in front. The flatness of the actual face, outside of the nose, accentuated by the lines leading away, rapid and delicate, to the temples, joined to a second compartmentalization of the sight by strips perpendicular to the preceding ones, and narrowing gradually, starting from the curve, lent to the top of this blind face the haughty attitude, *sure of itself*, and unshakable, which had struck us from the start. Although the remarkably definitive character of this object seemed to escape the merchant who urged us to buy it, suggesting we paint it in a bright color and use it as a lantern, Giacometti, usually very detached when it came to any thought of possessing such an object, put it down regretfully, seemed as we walked along to entertain some fear about its next destination, and finally retraced his steps to acquire it. Some few boutiques later, I made just as elective a choice with a large wooden spoon, of peasant fabrication but quite beautiful, it seemed to me, and rather daring in its form, whose handle, when it rested on its convex part, rose from a little shoe that was part of it. I carried it off immediately.

We were debating about the meaning that [we] should attach to such finds, no matter how trivial they appear.[3] The two objects, which we had been given with no wrapping, of whose existence we were ignorant some minutes before, and which imposed with themselves this abnormally prolonged sensorial contact, induced us to think ceaselessly of their concrete existence, offering to us certain very unexpected prolongations from their life. So it is that the mask, losing little by little what we had agreed on assigning it as a probable use—we had first thought we were dealing with a German mask for saber fencing—tended to situate itself in the personal research of Giacometti, taking a place in it analogous to the one that the face statue I just spoke of occupied. Considering all the detail of its structure, we decided that it was somehow *included* between the *Head* reproduced in number 5 of the journal *Minotaur*, the last work he had finished and whose mold he had promised me, and this face, which had remained in a sketchy state. It remained, we saw, to lift the last veil: the intervention of the mask seemed to be intended to help Giacometti overcome his indecision on this subject. *The finding of an object serves here exactly the same purpose as the dream, in the sense that it frees the individual from paralyzing affective scruples, comforts him and makes him understand that the obstacle he might have thought insurmountable is cleared.*[4] A certain plastic contradiction, undoubtedly a reflection of a profound moral contradiction, observable in the first states of the sculpture, stemmed from the distinct manner in which the artist had treated the upper part—largely in planes, to flee, I suppose, certain depressing elements in the memory—and the lower part—very free, because surely unrecognizable—of the person. The mask, profiting from certain formal resemblances which must have caught our attention first (for example, as concerns the eye, the inevitable relation which can't be overlooked between the metallic trellis and the wheel), imposes, in the narrowest spatial limits, the fusion of these two styles. It seems to me impossible to underestimate its role, when I realize the perfect organic unity of this frail and imaginary body of a woman that we admire today.

'Equation of the Found Object' in *Mad Love*, translated by Mary Ann Caws
(Lincoln, NE: University of Nebraska Press, 1987), pp. 25–32.

---

1   *L'attente*: the state of waiting, of expectation, akin to André Gide's state of readiness, of the *disponibilité* Breton has just mentioned two sentences before. The readiness for an undefined event, in all its openness, permits the advent of the marvelous.

2   André Breton, *Nadja* (Paris: Gallimard, 1963), pp. 49–50, on the Flea Market of Saint-Ouen: "I go there often, looking for those objects not to be found anywhere else, out of fashion, in bits and pieces, useless, almost incomprehensible, really perverse in the sense I mean and love."

3   The found object, or the *trouvaille* … is invested with the sense of the marvelous, as one "hits on something."

4   Cf. *Les Vases communicants* (Denoël et Steele) [Breton's note].

MAN RAY

(1890–1976)

Providing him with an exercise in narrative synthesis, Man Ray's autobiography allowed him to contribute retrospectively to the public image of his inner circle and other contemporaries. The private part of the story, which is not always written down, had a tangible effect on the pages dedicated to Giacometti and especially to Picasso. If the portrait of Giacometti is brief, cautious and lacking in perspective, that of Picasso is thorough and articulate, nourished by an intimacy rooted in Man Ray's admiration for the Spanish artist. These revealing thumbnail sketches confirm the diverse views on both artists at the turn of the 1930s.

Self Portrait

Picasso gave me the impression of a man who was aware of all that was going on about him and in the world in general, a man who reacted violently to all impacts, but had only one outlet to express his feelings: painting. His short epigrammatic or enigmatic phrases which he let drop from time to time only emphasized his impatience with any other form of expression. And these words, almost exclusively concerned with painting, gave a clear indication, if one thought about it, of his philosophy and attitude to life.

My first meeting with him was for the purpose of photographing his recent works, in the early Twenties. As usual, when I had an extra plate, I made a portrait of the artist. It was nothing remarkable as a photograph, but showed the intense, intransigent look of the man, his black eyes sizing one up. He was a short stocky man, who never took any exercise, except that he liked to swim and walk with his dog. In town one could only see him right after lunch, before he took his lunch—he avoided definite appointments as much as possible. He detested dates and fixed rendezvous. I was invited for lunch, and brought my camera to make some pictures of his Russian wife, Olga, the ex-ballet dancer, and his little son Paolo....

Giacometti, the sculptor, always gave one the impression of a tortured soul. Always dissatisfied with his work, feeling that he had carried it not far enough, or perhaps too far, he'd abandon it in his heaped-up little studio and start on an entirely new formula. When he turned to painting for a while, his colorless line-searching figures seemed to express final resignation in a futile search of himself. Whatever the direction he took, the work was always a positive expression—a perfect reflection of the man. He could talk with lucid, voluble brilliance—on many subjects. I like to sit with him in a café and watch as well as listen to him. His deeply marked face with a grayish complexion, like a medieval sculpture, was a fine subject for my photographic portraiture. During my period of fashion photography I disposed of a budget for backgrounds; I got him to make some bas-reliefs, units of birds and fishes which were repeated over a surface. One motif which he submitted, four legs radiating from a center, reminded me too much of the Nazi's swastika—when I pointed this out, he destroyed the work. The others were taken up by an interior decorator, and it helped him to attract attention. I did a series of pictures of his more Surrealistic work, for publication in an art magazine. He rewarded me with pieces of sculpture of the period.

Self Portrait (Boston: Little, Brown and Company, 1963), pp. 223 and 252.

CHRISTIAN ZERVOS

(1889–1970)

The year 1932 was a significant one for Picasso and Giacometti, and Christian Zervos was one of its chief orchestrators. The Swiss artist's debut solo exhibition took place in Pierre Colle's gallery in Paris. Zervos, the editor of the journal *Cahiers d'art*, promised him an article, which appeared after the special issue devoted to Picasso. The first retrospective of the Spanish artist was held in the Georges Petit galleries in Paris, and Zervos published the first volume of the catalogue raisonné of his oeuvre covering 1895–1906. Zervos's empathy—dependence, even, with respect to the Picasso phenomenon—far outweighs his interest in Giacometti, although the latter's oeuvre nevertheless benefits from his research and critical acumen.

Picasso

One day I met Picasso on Rue La Boétie, and while we were talking I saw him halt in front of a shop window and gaze at it attentively. At first I thought his interest was directed at an object behind it, but I quickly realised that he was admiring the shape of a patch of condensation on the storefront glass. Recently, as he was working on his great sculpture, he spotted a horizontal crack on the wall running out from the head of a nail. Catching sight of some wire trailing on the floor, he hung it on the nail and made a dancer possessed of all the lyrical motion of dance.

Thus, for Picasso, everything that comes from Nature is an unhoped-for gift that he appreciates like Leonardo, but which he utilises better than the great Italian artist. And Picasso accepts what is man-made with no less eagerness. He has frequently been reproached for having assimilated and appropriated everything novel that the contemporary mind has created, but this ignores the fact that even the greatest genius would quickly reach his limits if he were obliged to draw everything from his own being. One day, I was talking about this to Picasso and he replied: 'copying others is necessary, but copying oneself, how pathetic!' An artist is obliged to attract to him everything that has been invented in his environment, so as to employ it for more elevated ends. It has been said of every true creator, and this also applies to Picasso, that he 'by no means owes his work to his wisdom alone, but to thousands of things and people outside him that provide its raw material'. At root, it is quite insane to want to discover whether a man sources things from inside himself or from others, if he acts on his own account or through some third party. The essential thing is to possess the personality necessary to carry it out better than anyone else. Was it not Goethe who, in his last letter, averred that 'the most blessed genius is the one who has absorbed everything, assimilated everything, all the while renewing himself and developing his every aptitude'?

This is why Picasso's goal—if he has one other than staying alive in order to work as long as possible—is to become aware of every human endeavour and to make it his own. Nothing attempted in the world of art escapes him, nothing leaves him indifferent. Hence his passionate love for art. For Picasso, art is not a second life: it *is* his life. He lives only for it and through it. This is no exaggeration. Any time of the day or night finds Picasso in a state of pictorial grace. He can set to work at any hour, at any time the demon possesses him. He has no fixed working hours. He is busy at mealtimes: he used to cover paper napkins in restaurants with drawings in pencil or with his fingernail. He works while he is taking a bath. It was from his bathtub that he noticed a floorcloth lying around, turning it into one of his first picture-objects, now familiar through its countless reproductions. Even when he is talking, Picasso does not let his hands remain inactive. If during the conversation a piece of paper is by chance within range, he will quickly cover it with drawings all the more extraordinary as he gives them so little thought.

More so even than his works, such drawings corroborate the fact that Picasso receives his impulses from a guardian genius that drives him unconsciously. Unlike those reductive artists whose perceptions are limited to sensible proportions—for whom the internal sounding of objects is replaced by their description, and techniques that should be flexible and fluid become mere pattern-making tools—Picasso's allotted task is invention more than combination. For him, the customary analytical tools yield the field to unmediated intuition. And surely it is to this intuitive ability that one must turn first if one wants to discover the starting point of Picasso's oeuvre, the seminal act behind the orientation and realisation of his work.

'Picasso', *Cahiers d'art*, no. 3–5, 1932, p. 86.

A Few Notes on Giacometti's Sculpture

When he discarded painting, Giacometti was, for the first time, able to give free rein to the qualities he was to develop later, honing and refining them in his subsequent output. Abandoning the literal description of things, he turned instead to their indispensable, essential indications. His unerring eye could thus come into its own, as could his faculty of distilling significant features from real things, seizing them and nothing else, so as to express the totality of their effects. The result is that, with no precise figuration, Giacometti's sculptures interest us in the way reality does. Eschewing forwardness and affectation, their poetry moves us profoundly. Far from contrived, it flows forth freely.

However, this has not prevented certain viewers from condemning Giacometti's works unthinkingly. If some treat them as yet another opportunity to repeat their claim that the artist lives entirely in his head, allowing himself to be carried away by an intoxication of the brain or by an uncontrolled outpouring of intellectual juices, others take it as a pretext to underscore the danger of conceptions they see as arbitrary and warn us against the illusions of an artist who fondly believes he is observing, when in fact he is just dreaming.

It must be admitted that some strange and contradictory ideas enter into the prevalent conception of what constitutes sculpture today. The oeuvre of sculptors who seek to keep their spirit not only free but honest is confronted by unheard-of prejudices, a consequence of the curiosity of an age that transcends and often uproots all the accepted rules. His sympathetic imagination allows the artist not only to reveal all the forms that man may marshal to express an emotion, but also to enter into all those forms without the ulterior motive of taking them back. Thanks, then, to this subtle sympathy, we have, in recent times, witnessed art venturing into uncharted territory.

'Quelques notes sur les sculptures de Giacometti', *Cahiers d'art*, no. 8–10, 1932, p. 338.

Appendices

Timeline
Pablo Picasso
(1881–1973)

1881

Born on October 25 in Málaga, Spain. His father, José Ruiz Blasco, conservator at the city museum, teaches drawing at the provincial school of fine arts.

1888–1889

Encouraged by his father, he starts to paint.

1900

First trip to Paris with his friend Casagemas: *Last Moments* (oil on canvas, 1899) is shown at the World's Fair. Picasso becomes interested in the changes affecting art in France at the turn of the century during a stay in Barcelona in the late 1890s.

1901

Embarking upon his Blue Period, he paints a *Self-Portrait*. Meets poet Max Jacob.

1904

Moves into Le Bateau-Lavoir in Montmartre. Meets poet and art critic Guillaume Apollinaire, with whom he maintains a fruitful friendship. He takes Fernande Olivier as his model, who will remain his partner for seven years. At the end of 1904, he begins his Rose Period.

1906

Summer sojourn with Fernande at Gósol, a remote village in the Catalan Pyrenees. The Rose Period attains its climax.

1907

Meets Georges Braque through Apollinaire: Braque will be his *compagnon de cordée*—a fellow mountaineer—in the conquest of Cubism. Visits the Musée d'Ethnographie du Trocadéro and finishes *Les Demoiselles d'Avignon.*

1910

Collector Daniel-Henry Kahnweiler, a significant promoter of Cubism and the avant-garde, becomes Picasso's official dealer until 1918. He will remain an attentive observer of Picasso's work and a friend.

1926

Publication of the first issue of *Cahiers d'art*, the review founded by Christian Zervos, which will regularly print articles on Picasso accompanied by reproductions.

1928

In tribute to his late friend Guillaume Apollinaire (who died in 1918), Picasso makes a group of four models entitled *Figures* that Daniel-Henry Kahnweiler calls 'drawings in space'.

1929

Paints *Large Nude in a Red Armchair*, in which the traditional theme of the nude is subverted by the virulence of the colours and a series of distortions. Publication of a text by Carl Einstein, *Pablo Picasso: Some Pictures of 1929*, in the first issue of *Documents*.

1930

Picasso buys the château at Boisgeloup in the Eure, setting up a sculpture workshop. Carries out heads and busts of his new partner, Marie-Thérèse Walter.

1931

Introduced to Alberto Giacometti by the Catalan painter Joan Miró. Their encounter marks the beginning of almost daily conversations between 1935 and 1942. Talks concerning their work are especially profitable, as Picasso's biographer Pierre Daix testifies. In these years that witnessed the flourishing of Surrealism, Picasso recognises Giacometti as possessing 'the same sexual brutality, the same plastic violence', as seen in *Reclining Woman Who Dreams* (1929), *Suspended Ball* (1930–1931) and *Disagreeable Object* (1931). They frequent the same circle of intellectuals and artists, including Georges Bataille, Carl Einstein, Michel Leiris, André Masson, Salvador Dalí and André Breton.

1932

Retrospective devoted to Picasso at Georges Petit's gallery in Paris, an expanded version of which then travels to the Kunsthaus in Zurich.

1933

Picasso takes part in the *Surrealist Exhibition* at the Galerie Pierre Colle, Paris.

1934–1935

Meets photographer Dora Maar, probably via poet Paul Éluard. She is also close to Giacometti. Picasso engages in the political and artistic activities of Surrealism and begins to visit André Breton's house at 42 Rue Fontaine, where the group meets. Picasso and Giacometti start seeing each other regularly in their studios or in cafés to discuss a return to realism in art.

1937

Paints the iconic *Guernica* which denounces the murderous bombardment of the eponymous village in the Spanish Basque Country ordered by General Franco. The canvas, whose genesis in the Rue des Grands-Augustins studio in Paris is chronicled in photographs by Dora Maar, embodies the horrors of the Civil War.

1939

Exhibition *Picasso: Forty Years of His Art*, organised by Alfred H. Barr at the Museum of Modern Art, New York. Picasso spends the entire war in Paris, in his studio on Rue des Grands-Augustins.

1942

From 1942 to 1945, Picasso does not see Giacometti, since the latter has moved to Switzerland, but he continues to benefit from his friend's advice. Pierre Daix states that it is under the influence of Giacometti that Picasso returns to sculpture in the 1940s. He works on small plaster figurines reminiscent of Giacometti's tiny female figures, as well as on pottery figurines and heads on rods, some of which are cast in bronze.

1944

An important Picasso retrospective at the Salon d'Automne in Paris causes violent reactions. On Giacometti's return to Paris in 1945, the two artists find themselves closer than ever before, and they continue their aesthetic discussions.

1946

Paints *Homage to the Spaniards Who Died for France*, which is unveiled with *The Charnel House* (1944–45), at the exhibition *Art and Resistance* held at the Musée National d'Art Moderne. He is now living with Françoise Gilot.

1947

Begins a period of intense activity as a ceramist at Ramié's pottery in Vallauris. In his paintings, fauns, centaurs and bacchantes recall a stay the previous year in Antibes, on the Mediterranean. Meetings with Giacometti become increasingly less frequent.

1950–1951

Picasso and Giacometti sever relations. When Giacometti visits him at Vallauris in 1951, Picasso allegedly gives him a cool reception, reproaching him for being a disloyal friend. Picasso also supposedly opposed Giacometti's entry into Louise Leiris's gallery in Paris, a mecca for the exhibition of modern art, with a very high profile. The two men are no longer on speaking terms.

A series of large plaster sculptures in which Picasso incorporates miscellaneous objects for their poetic or artistic significance, subverting their ordinary use: *Little Girl with a Skipping Rope; Woman with a Pushchair; Goat; Baboon and Young*. Continues the series of *Vanities* and his work in ceramic. Several retrospectives in Europe and elsewhere in the world (Paris, Rome, São Paulo).

1955

Buys a large turn-of-the-century villa in Cannes called La Californie, where he lives with his new partner, Jacqueline Roque. Henri-Georges Clouzot shoots the film *Le Mystère Picasso*, screened at the Cannes Film Festival the following year.

1959

Explores variations on *Le Déjeuner sur l'Herbe*, after Manet. They form part of a particular period in Picasso's work during which he reinterprets pictures by the great masters (Velázquez, Delacroix, etc.)

1961

Works in cut-out and painted sheet metal (*The Chair*, *Woman with Outstretched Arms*, *Seated Pierrot*, the *Footballers* series). Publication of *Picasso's Picassos* by David Douglas Duncan, showing works from the artist's personal collection, which will form the basis of the dation (gifts-in-lieu) presented to the Musée National Picasso. At the beginning of the 1960s, the tension between Picasso and Giacometti appears to ebb. Giacometti does a drawing for a special issue of the Swiss review *Du: Kulturelle Monatsschrift* entitled *Tribute to Picasso* for Picasso's eightieth birthday.

1963

Opening of the Museu Picasso in Barcelona. At Mougins, where he lives with Jacqueline, Picasso devotes much time to linocut, employing various techniques and mixed processes in the series of *Étreintes*, and then in *Painter and His Model*.

1966

Exhibition *Hommage à Picasso*, organised in Paris by Jean Leymarie at the Grand Palais and the Petit Palais, which reveals a large number of sculptures to the general public.

1967

Exhibition *Picasso: Sculptures, Ceramics, Graphic Work* at London's Tate Gallery, which subsequently travels to the Museum of Modern Art, New York.

1969

An intense period of painting, during which Picasso produces 176 canvases in a single year on the following subjects: portraits, couples, nudes, men with swords, smokers, still lifes.

1970

The Museu Picasso in Barcelona receives a donation of youthful works left behind with his family in Spain, as well as others carried out in 1917 during his period with the Ballets Russes. Exhibition *Picasso 1969–1970* at the Palais des Papes in Avignon stirs up a scandal. Picasso embarks on a series of large paintings that review all the major themes of his life's work, and continues working until his death in 1973.

1971

On the occasion of his ninetieth birthday, a selection of works from French public collections is shown in the Grande Galerie of the Louvre.

1973

Dies on 8 April in the farmstead of Notre-Dame-de-Vie in Mougins. *Pablo Picasso, 1970–1972 at the Palais des Papes in Avignon*, accompanied by a catalogue with a foreword by poet René Char, presents the last works selected by the artist for the exhibition.

Timeline
Alberto Giacometti
(1901–1966)

1901

Born on 10 October in Borgonovo (Stampa), a small village in Italian Switzerland. His father, Giovanni Giacometti, is a celebrated neo-Impressionist painter. Alberto has two brothers, Diego and Bruno, and a sister, Ottilia.

1914–1915

Taught drawing and painting by his father. Executes his first sculpture: a bust of Diego. First oil painting: *Still Life with Apples*.

1920

Studies at the school of fine arts and then at the technical school in Geneva. Produces several paintings in a neo-Impressionist style. During a trip to Italy, Giacometti discovers the great Italian masters, as well as Egyptian sculpture, two key elements in the development of his oeuvre.

1921

While travelling with Pieter Van Meurs, Giacometti witnesses first-hand his friend's death. He will often return to this traumatic experience of death in his work.

1922

Arrives in Paris, where he studies sculpture at the Académie de la Grande Chaumière, in the class of Antoine Bourdelle, remaining there until 1927. The first works by Picasso that Giacometti sees exhibited are neo-Ingresque paintings dating from the 1920s, together with Symbolist works from the Blue and Rose Periods.

1924

Takes an interest in Picasso's Cubist works at one of the latter's exhibitions, probably *Picasso: 100 Drawings*, at Paul Rosenberg's gallery.

1925

First participation in the Salon des Tuileries. Fosters his interest in the avant-garde, Cubism, and post-Cubism. Copies works by Picasso published in art magazines and seeks inspiration in so-called 'primitive' art. Learns much from the endeavours by reviews such as *Cahiers d'art* and *Documents* to juxtapose modern art with works by the peoples of Africa, the Pacific and the Cyclades.

1926

Moves into a studio at 46 Rue Hippolyte-Maindron, which he will continue to occupy until his death.

1927

Executes the sculpture *Spoon Woman*, revealing his interest in African art. Giacometti will assert that this work originated in what he learned from the work of Picasso and from the Cubists in general.

1928

Executes his first flat sculptures—the '*sculptures-plaques*'.

1929

Meets Max Jacob, a close friend of Picasso's. The series of *Flat Women* attracts attention from dealers and collectors. Michel Leiris devotes a debut article to him in the review *Documents*. The writer will remain a faithful friend of both Picasso and Giacometti. In December, Pierre Loeb offers him a contract with his gallery. Tériade includes two of his works in his *International Exhibition of Sculpture* at the Bernheim gallery. Giacometti is now a figure in the elite Parisian art world and his works start to enter renowned collections.

1930

Exhibition *Miró, Arp, Giacometti* at the Galerie Pierre. He presents *Suspended Ball*, much remarked upon by the Surrealists, in particular Salvador Dalí, who describes it as the prototype of 'symbolically functioning objects'. Giacometti collaborates with decorator Jean-Michel Frank to carry out his first decorative art objects.

1931

Meets Picasso through Joan Miró. They take part in the artistic explorations of Surrealism and orbit among the dissidents from the movement headed by Georges Bataille. From the 1930s, Giacometti and Picasso maintain strong artistic, intellectual, and personal bonds that survive the Second World War and are sustained until the early 1950s.

1932
Solo exhibition *Giacometti* at Pierre Colle's gallery. Picasso is its first visitor. *Suspended Ball* is enthusiastically acclaimed by the Spanish artist, who himself returns to the theme of the conjunction between a split ball and a crescent in compositions in the 1930s, most closely in his studies for *Woman Seated in a Red Armchair*. Giacometti makes copies of works in a sketchbook at a retrospective devoted to Picasso at the Kunsthaus, Zurich.

1933
The review *Minotaure* publishes photographs by Brassaï of the studios of both Giacometti and Picasso. Giacometti participates in the Surrealist exhibition at Pierre Colle's gallery, at which he sells *The Surrealist Table* to the de Noailles family. His father passes away on 25 June.

1934
Sculpts *Cube*. Meets the photographer Dora Maar, who will become Picasso's partner a year later. She immortalises *Invisible Object* in a series of photographs taken in the studio on Rue Hippolyte-Maindron. In December, Julien Levy's gallery dedicates a first solo exhibition to Giacometti's work in New York.

1935
Moving away from Surrealism, Giacometti returns to representation after the model. Embarks on a solitary exploration of the theme of the head, with Diego and Rita Gueyfier as models.

1936
Entrusts Pierre Matisse with representing his work in the United States. *The Palace at 4 a.m.* enters the collection of the Museum of Modern Art, New York; it is his first work to be acquired by a museum.

1937
Visits the studio on Rue des Grands-Augustins, where Picasso is working on *Guernica*, a canvas that impresses him immensely.

1939
Meets Jean-Paul Sartre and Simone de Beauvoir, with whom he will remain close.

1941
Frequent visits to Picasso, who is working on the large carved *Head* of Dora Maar. Picasso is always prepared to heed his friend's advice. Giacometti starts to work on a sculpture portrait of Picasso. It will never be completed. In December, Giacometti travels to Switzerland, where he will remain throughout the war.

1943
Meets Annette Arm, who will become one of his favourite models and whom he will marry in 1949.

1945
At the end of the war, Giacometti returns to Paris and joins up with his old acquaintances there. The circle of friends formed by Alberto and Annette Giacometti, Pablo Picasso and Françoise Gilot, and Michel and Louise Leiris meets up frequently.

1946
A series of portraits of personalities from the arts and from literature: Marie-Laure de Noailles, Simone de Beauvoir, Georges Bataille and a head of the Communist Resistant Rol-Tanguy. Publishes 'The Dream, the Sphinx, and the Death of T.' in the review *Labyrinthe*.

1947
Influence of Sartre's Existentialist thought that explores the concept of the 'universal man'. Conceives the first model of *Walking Man*. Returns to themes from the 1930s, such as the 'cages', implying the continuity of his output with his Surrealist period. In painting, many studies of busts and heads, including portraits (his mother, Annette, Diego).

1948
First monographic exhibition at the Pierre Matisse Gallery in New York. Sartre writes a foreword for the catalogue: *La Recherche de l'absolu*. The same gallery proceeds to devote solo shows to his work in 1950, 1958, 1961 and 1964. The studio, with or without a model, becomes an autonomous subject in both painting and drawing.

1949
Purchase of *Man Pointing* by the Tate Gallery; the first work to be acquired by a European museum.

1951

Break between Giacometti and Picasso. Combining his artistic explorations with an asceticism that is gradually turning into a way of life, Giacometti increasingly disapproves of Picasso's unabashed star status. Following rejection from the gallery of Louise Leiris, Giacometti signs up with the Maeght gallery in Paris, which holds a solo exhibition that same year.

1954

Meets the writer Jean Genet and paints or draws several portraits of him between 1954 and 1958.

1955

Earliest retrospectives in New York and London, as well as in Germany.

1956

Represents France at the Venice Biennial, exhibiting a group of sculptures: *Women of Venice*. Draws a cover for Jean Genet's book *Le Balcon*. Meets Japanese philosopher Isaku Yanaihara, who will return to pose for him over several summers.

1957

A text by Jean Genet entitled *Alberto Giacometti's Studio* appears in the journal *Derrière le miroir*.

1958

First monographic exhibition in Japan. Meets Caroline, who becomes his mistress and model.

1959

Invited to take part in the contest for the Chase Manhattan Plaza in New York; spends two years working on a group of figures. The project will never come to fruition. Creates *Tall Women* and *Walking Man*.

1961

At the request of writer and play-wright Samuel Beckett, he builds a plaster tree for the set of a production of *Waiting for Godot* at the Théâtre de l'Odéon.

1962

Invited to the Venice Biennial, where he receives the Grand Prix for sculpture. Major retrospective at the Kunsthaus, Zurich.

1964

Wins a Guggenheim International Award for painting. Inauguration of the Giacometti Room and Courtyard at the Fondation Maeght in Saint-Paul-de-Vence.

1965

Three retrospectives in London, New York and Copenhagen. Awarded the Grand Prix National des Arts de France.

1966

Death of Alberto Giacometti on 11 January. Jacqueline Picasso, in a letter of condolence addressed to his widow, Annette, recalls 'the immense friendship Picasso had, still has' for Alberto. Towards the end of his life, Picasso said that, if it were possible, he would have liked to see only two people again: André Malraux and Alberto Giacometti.

Pablo Picasso:
Selected Bibliography

Jeanne-Yvette Sudour

REFERENCE WORKS

BAER, Brigitte, and Bernhard GEISER. *Picasso, peintre-graveur.* 7 vols. and addendum. Bern: Kornfeld, 1986–96.

BLOCH, Georges. *Pablo Picasso, catalogue de l'œuvre gravé céramique.* Vol. 2, 1949–71. Bern: Kornfeld & Klipstein, 1972.

BLOCH, Georges. *Pablo Picasso, catalogue de l'œuvre gravé et lithographié.* Vol. 1, 1904–67. Bern: Kornfeld & Klipstein, 1968.

BLOCH, Georges. *Pablo Picasso, catalogue de l'œuvre gravé et lithographié.* Vol. 2, 1966–69. Bern: Kornfeld & Klipstein, 1971.

BLOCH, Georges. *Pablo Picasso, catalogue de l'œuvre gravé et lithographié.* Vol. 4, 1970–72. Bern: Kornfeld & Klipstein, 1979.

CRAMER, Patrick, Sebastian GOEPPERT, and Herma GOEPPERT-FRANK. *Pablo Picasso, catalogue raisonné des livres illustrés.* Geneva: Patrick Cramer, 1983.

CZWIKLITZER, Christophe. *Les Affiches de Pablo Picasso.* Basel/Paris: Art-C.C., 1970.

DAIX, Pierre, and Joan ROSSELET. *Le Cubisme de Picasso, catalogue raisonné de l'oeuvre peint 1907–1916.* Neuchâtel: Ides et Calendes, 1979.

DAIX, Pierre, Georges BOUDAILLE, and Joan ROSSELET. *Picasso, 1900–1906, catalogue raisonné de l'oeuvre peint.* 1966. New edition, Neuchâtel: Ides et Calendes, 1988.

DUNCAN, David Douglas. *Picasso's Picasso.* London: Ballantyne, 1968.

FAIRWEATHER, Sally. *Picasso's Concrete Sculptures.* New York: Hudson Hills Press, 1982.

GEISER, Bernhard. *Picasso, peintre-graveur, catalogue illustré de l'œuvre gravé et lithographié.* Vol. 1, 1899–1931, Bern: B. Geiser, 1933; Vol. 2, 1932–1934, Bern: Kornfeld & Klipstein, 1968.

MCCULLY, Marilyn. *Céramiques de Picasso.* Illustrations by Éric Baudouin. Paris: Images Modernes, 1999.

MOURLOT, Fernand. *Picasso lithographe.* 4 vols. Monte-Carlo: André Sauret, 1949–64.

RAMIÉ, Alain. *Picasso, catalogue de l'œuvre céramique édité, 1947–71.* Vallauris: Madoura, 1988.

RAMIÉ, Georges. *Céramique de Picasso.* Paris: Cercle d'Art, 1974.

SPIES, Werner, and Christine PIOT. *Picasso: The Sculptures.* Ostfildern: Hatje Cantz, 2000.

ZERVOS, Christian. *Pablo Picasso.* 33 vols. Paris: Éditions des Cahiers d'Art, 1932–78.

MONOGRAPHS AND FIRST-HAND ACCOUNTS

ALBERTI, Rafael. *Picasso en Avignon.* Paris: Cercle d'Art, 1971.

ALBERTI, Rafael. *Picasso, le rayon ininterrompu.* Paris: Cercle d'Art, 1974.

ARAGON, Louis. *Écrits sur l'art moderne.* Edited by Jean Ristat. Paris: Flammarion, 2011.

AUBERT, Raphaël. *Malraux & Picasso, une relation manquée.* Gollion (Switzerland): Infolio, 2013.

AXIONOV, IVAN. *Picasso et alentours.* Foreword by Natalia Adaskina. Translated into French by Gérard Conio. Paris: Infolio, 2012.

BACHOLET, Raymond, Pierre DAIX, Gérard GOSSELIN, and Jean-Pierre JOUFFROY. *Picasso et la presse, un peintre dans l'histoire.* Paris: L'Humanité/Cercle d'Art, 2000.

BERGER, John. *Success and Failure of Picasso.* Harmondsworth: Penguin, 1965.

BONNEFOY, Yves. *Remarques sur le regard, Picasso, Giacometti, Morandi.* Paris: Calmann-Lévy, 2002.

BOUDAILLE, Georges, Marie-Laure BERNADAC, and Marie-Pierre GAUTHIER. *Picasso.* Paris: Nouvelles Éditions Françaises, 1985.

BRASSAÏ. *Conversations with Picasso.* Translated by Jane Marie Todd. Chicago: University of Chicago Press, 1999.

BRETON, André. *Œuvres complètes, IV, écrits sur l'art et autres textes.* Edited by Étienne-Alain Hubert. Paris: Gallimard, 1988.

BUTOR, Michel. *Les Ateliers de* Picasso. Paris: Images Modernes, 2003.

CABANNE, Pierre. *Le Siècle de Picasso.* 1975. New edition, Paris: Gallimard, 1992.

CHAR, René. *Œuvres complètes.* Paris: Gallimard, 1983.

CLAIR, Jean. *Une leçon d'abîme, neuf approches de Picasso.* Paris: Gallimard, 2005.

CLARK, T. J. *Picasso and Truth: From Cubism to Guernica.* Princeton: Princeton University Press, 2013.

COCTEAU, Jean. *Picasso.* Paris: Stock, 1923. Reprinted in *Entre Picasso et Radiguet.* Paris: Hermann, 1967.

COOPER, Douglas. *Picasso, Theatre.* New York: Harry H. Abrams, 1968.

COWLING, Elizabeth. *Style and Meaning.* London: Phaidon, 2002.

COWLING, Elizabeth. *Visiting Picasso: The Notebooks and Letters of Roland Penrose.* London: Thames & Hudson, 2008.

CSATÓ GASMAN, Lydia. *War and the Cosmos in Picasso's Texts, 1936–1940.* Lincoln NE: Universe Inc., 2007.

DAGEN, Philippe. *Picasso.* New York: Monacelli Press, 2009.

DAGEN, Philippe. *Picasso.* Paris: Hazan, 2008.

DAIX, Pierre. *Le nouveau dictionnaire Picasso.* Paris: Robert Laffont, 2012.

DAIX, Pierre. *Picasso.* Paris: Tallandier, 2007. New edition, Paris: Pluriel, 2014.

DESNOS, Robert. *Écrits sur les peintres.* Paris: Flammarion, 1984.

ÉLUARD, Paul. *À Pablo Picasso.* Geneva: Les Trois Collines, 1944.

FERMIGIER, André. *Picasso.* Paris: Librairie générale française, 1969.

FITZGERALD, Michael C. *Making Modernism: Picasso and the Creation of the Market for Twentieth-Century Art.* New York: Farrar, Straus, and Giroux, 1995.

FITZGERALD, Michael C., and William H. ROBINSON. *Picasso: The Artist's Studio.* Hartford: Wadsworth Atheneum Museum of Art/ New Haven, Yale University Press, 2001.

GALASSI, Susan Grace. *Picasso's Variations on the Masters: Confrontations with the Past.* New York: Harry N. Abrams, 1996.

GALLWITZ, Klaus.
Picasso, 1945–1973.
Essay by José Bergamin.
Paris: Denoël, 1985.

GEELHAAR, Christian.
*Picasso Wegbereiter und
Förderer seines Aufstiegs
1899–1939.* Zurich: Palladion
Verlag, 1993.

GERVEREAU, Laurent.
*Guernica, autopsie d'un
chef-d'œuvre.* Paris: Paris-
Méditerranée, 1996.

GILOT, Françoise.
Dans l'arène avec Picasso.
Montpellier: Indigène
Éditions, 2004.

**GILOT, Françoise,
and Carlton LAKE.**
Life with Picasso. Charleston,
S.C.: Nabu Press, 2011.

GIRAUDY, Danièle.
*Picasso, la mémoire du
regard.* Paris: Cercle d'Art,
1986.

**GLIMCHER, Marc,
and Arnold B. GLIMCHER.**
*'Je suis le cahier, les carnets
de Picasso'.* Paris: Grasset,
1986.

GOLDING, John.
*Cubism: A History and an
Analysis 1907–1914.* 1959.
New edition, Berkeley:
University of California
Press, 1988.

GOMEZ DE LA SERNA, Ramon.
*Completa y verídica historia
de Picasso y el cubism.* Turin:
Chiantore, 1945.

GREEN, Christopher.
Life and Death in Picasso.
London: Thames & Hudson,
2009.

GREEN, Christopher.
*Picasso: Architecture and
Vertigo.* New Haven/London:
Yale University Press, 2005.

JOUFFROY, Alain.
*XXᵉ siècle, essais sur l'art
moderne et d'avant-garde.*
Lyon: Fage, 2008.

KAHNWEILER, Daniel-Henry.
Confessions esthétiques.
Paris: Gallimard, 1963.

KAHNWEILER, Daniel-Henry.
*Mes galeries et mes peintres,
entretiens avec Francis
Crémieux.* 1961. New edition,
Paris: Gallimard, 1998.

KARMEL, Pepe.
*Picasso and the Invention
of Cubism.* New Haven/
London: Yale University
Press, 2003.

KRAMAR, Vincenc.
Le Cubisme. Edited by
Hélène Klein and Erika
Abrams. Paris: École
Nationale Supérieure
des Beaux-Arts, 2002.

KRAUSS, Rosalind.
The Picasso Papers. London:
Thames & Hudson, 1998.

**LÉAL, Brigitte, Christine PIOT,
and Marie-Laure BERNADAC.**
*Picasso, la monographie,
1881– 1973.* Paris: La
Martinière, 2000.

LEIGHTEN, Patricia Dee.
*Re-ordering the Universe:
Picasso and Anarchism,
1897–1914.* Princeton:
Princeton University Press,
1989.

LEIRIS, Michel.
Écrits sur l'art. Paris:
CNRS Éditions, 2011.

LEYMARIE, Jean.
*Picasso, métamorphoses et
unité.* Geneva: Skira, 1971.

LINARÈS, Serge.
Picasso et les écrivains.
Paris: Citadelles et Mazenod,
2013.

LORD, James.
Picasso and Dora: A Memoir.
London: Weidenfeld and
Nicolson, 1993.

MADELINE, Laurence.
Picasso devant la télé. Dijon:
Les Presses du Réel, 2013.

MALRAUX, André.
La Tête d'obsidienne. Paris:
Gallimard, 1974.

MCCULLY, Marilyn.
*A Picasso Anthology:
Documents, Criticism,
Reminiscences.* London: The
Arts Council of Great Britain/
Thames & Hudson, 1981.
Revised edition, Princeton:
Princeton University Press,
1997.

MILI, Gjon.
*Picasso et la troisième
dimension.* Paris: Triton,
1970.

OLIVIER, Fernande.
Picasso and His Friends.
Translated by James Miller.
1933. New edition, New York:
Appleton-Century, 1965.

OLIVIER, Fernande.
Souvenirs intimes. Paris:
Calmann-Lévy, 1988.

PALAU I FABRE, Josep.
*Picasso 1917–1926, des
ballets au drame.* Cologne:
Könemann, 1999.

PALAU I FABRE, Josep.
Picasso, cubisme, 1907–1917.
Paris: Albin Michel, 1990.
New edition, Cologne:
Könemann, 1998.

PALAU I FABRE, Josep.
*Picasso vivant, enfance
et première jeunesse, un
démiurge, 1881–1907.* Paris:
Albin Michel, 1981. New
edition, Cologne: Könemann,
1998.

PARMELIN, Hélène.
*Picasso dit suivi par Picasso
sur la place.* Paris: Les
Belles Lettres, 2013.

PARMELIN, Hélène.
Picasso says… Translated
by Caroline Trollope. 1966.
New edition, London: George
Allen & Unwin, 1969.

PARMELIN, Hélène.
Voyage en Picasso. Paris:
Robert Laffont, 1980. New
edition, Paris: Christian
Bourgois, 1994.

PARVU, Ileana.
*La Peinture en visite, les
constructions cubistes
de Picasso.* Bern/Berlin/
Brussels: Peter Lang, 2007.

PENROSE, Roland.
Picasso: His Life and Work.
London: Victor Gollancz,
1968.

*Picasso, Guernica, histoire,
élaboration, signification.*
Herschel B. Chipp, in
collaboration with Javier
Tusell. Paris: Cercle d'Art,
1992.

Picasso, l'objet du mythe.
Edited by Laurence
Bertrand-Dorléac. Paris:
ENSBA, 2005.

PICASSO, Pablo.
Écrits. Foreword by Michel
Leiris. Edited by Marie-
Laure Bernadac and
Christine Piot. Translated by
Albert Bensoussan. Paris:
Gallimard/RMN, 1989.

PICASSO, Pablo.
*Picasso on Art: A Selection
of Views.* New York: Da Capo
Press, 1996.

**PICASSO, Pablo,
and Gertrude STEIN.**
Correspondance. Edited by
Laurence Madeline. Paris:
Gallimard, 2005.

**PICASSO, Pablo,
and Guillaume APOLLINAIRE.**
Correspondance. Edited
by Pierre Caizergues and
Hélène Seckel. Paris:
Gallimard/RMN, 1992.

**PICASSO, Pablo,
and Max JACOB.**
Correspondance. Edited by
Hélène Seckel. Paris: RMN,
1994.

PICON, Gaëtan.
*La Chute d'Icare de Pablo
Picasso.* Geneva: Skira, 1971.

PLEYNET, Marcelin.
*Essais et conférences, 1987–
1998.* Paris: Beaux-Arts de
Paris Les Éditions, 2012.

PODOKSIK, Anatoli.
Picasso, la quête perpétuelle.
Paris: Cercle d'Art, 1989.

PONGE, Francis.
Picasso évidemment. Edited
by Gérard Farasse. Paris:
Galilée, 2005.

PRÉVERT, Jacques.
Portraits de Picasso.
Photographs by André
Villers. Paris: Ramsay, 1981.

QUINN, Edward.
*Picasso avec Picasso, textes
et photographies.* Paris:
Pierre Bordas et Fils, 1987.

RAYNAL, Maurice.
Picasso. Geneva: Skira, 1953.

READ, Peter.
Picasso and Apollinaire: The Persistence of Memory. Berkeley: University of California Press, 1998.

REVERDY, Pierre.
Pablo Picasso. Paris: Nouvelle Revue Française, 1924. New edition, Paris: Mercure de France, 1999.

RICHARDSON, John.
A Life of Picasso: The Triumphant Years 1917–1932. New York: Alfred A. Knopf, 2007.

RICHARDSON, John.
A Life of Picasso. Vol. II, 1907–1917. London: Jonathan Cape, 1996.

ROY, Claude.
La Guerre et la paix. Paris: Cercle d'Art, 1954.

RUBIN, William Stanley, Pierre DAIX, and Judith COUSINS.
Picasso and Braque: Pioneering Cubism. New York: Museum of Modern Art, 1989.

SABARTÉS, Jaime.
Picasso: An Intimate Portrait. New York: Prentice-Hall, 1948.

SABARTÉS, Jaime.
Picasso, documents iconographiques. Geneva: Pierre Cailler, 1954.

SALMON, André.
Souvenirs sans fin, 1903–1940. 1955. New edition, Paris: Gallimard, 2004.

SCHAPIRO, Meyer.
The Unity of Picasso's Art. New York: George Braziller, 2000.

SOLLERS, Philippe.
Picasso, le héros. Paris: Cercle d'Art, 1996. Reprinted in *Éloge de l'infini.* Paris: Gallimard, 2001.

SPIES, Werner.
Un inventaire du regard, écrits sur l'art et la littérature. 10 vols. Paris: Gallimard, 2011.

STEIN, Gertrude.
Picasso. London: Batsford, 1948.

STEINBERG, Leo.
Other Criteria: Confrontations with Twentieth-Century Art. Chicago: University of Chicago Press, 2007.

STEPAN, Peter.
Picasso's Collection of African and Oceanic Art: Masters of Metamorphosis. Munich/Berlin/London/New York: Prestel, 2006.

TINTEROW, Gary.
Picasso in the Metropolitan Museum of Art. New York: The Metropolitan Museum of Art/Yale University Press, 2010.

TZARA, Tristan.
Œuvres complètes. T. IV, 1947–1963. Edited by Henri Behar. Paris: Flammarion, 1980.

UHDE, Wilhelm.
Picasso et la tradition française, notes sur la peinture actuelle. Paris: Les Quatre-Chemins, 1928.

UHDE, Wilhelm.
Von Bismarck Bis Picasso. Zurich: Oprecht, 1938.

UTLEY, Gertje.
Picasso: The Communist Years. New Haven: Yale University Press, 2000.

VALLENTIN, Antonina.
Picasso. Paris: Albin Michel, 1957.

WARNCKE, Carsten-Peter, and Ingo F. WALTHER.
Pablo Picasso, 1881–1973. 2 vols. 1992. New edition, Cologne: Taschen, 2007.

WEISNER, Ulrich.
Picasso. Bielefeld: Kerber, 1997.

WILSON, Sarah.
Picasso/Marx and Socialist Realism in France. Liverpool: Liverpool University Press, 2015.

WOLF, Laurent, and Androula MICHAEL.
Pablo Picasso. Paris: Les Cahiers de l'Herne, 2014.

ZERVOS, Christian.
Dessins de Picasso, 1892–1948. Paris: Cahiers d'Art, 1949.

ZERVOS, Christian.
Picasso, œuvres de 1920 à 1926. Paris: Cahiers d'Art, 1926.

COLLECTION CATALOGUES

RICHET, Michèle.
The Picasso Museum, Paris: Drawings, Watercolours, Gouaches, and Pastels. Translated by Augusta Audubert. London: Thames & Hudson, 1988.

RICHET, Michèle, Marie-Laure BESNARD-BERNADAC, Hélène SACKEL, and Laurence MARCEILLAC.
Musée Picasso, Catalogue of the Collections: Paintings; Papiers collés; Picture Reliefs; Sculptures; and Ceramics. Introduction by Dominique Bozo. Translated by Alexander Lieven. London: Thames & Hudson, 1986.

EXHIBITION CATALOGUES

BALDASSARI, Anne.
La Collection du musée national Picasso-Paris. Paris, Musée Picasso, 2015. Paris: Musée National Picasso/Flammarion, 2014.

BALDASSARI, Anne.
Le Miroir noir, Picasso, sources photographiques, 1900–1928. Paris, Musée Picasso, 1997. Paris: RMN, 1997.

BALDASSARI, Anne.
Picasso et la photographie, à plus grande vitesse que les images. Paris, Musée Picasso, 1995. Paris: RMN, 1995.

BALDASSARI, Anne.
Picasso: Life with Dora Maar. Paris: Musée Picasso, 2006; Melbourne: National Gallery of Victoria, 2006. Paris: Flammarion/RMN, 2006.

BALDASSARI, Anne, and CARTIER-BRESSON, Anne.
Picasso photographe, 1901–1916. Paris, Musée Picasso, 1994. Paris: RMN, 1994.

BALDASSARI, Anne, and Sylvie FRESNAULT.
Brassaï-Picasso, conversations avec la lumière. Paris, Musée Picasso, 2000. Paris: RMN, 2000.

BALDASSARI, Anne, Marie-Laure BERNARDAC, and Susan Grace GALASSI.
Picasso et les maîtres. Paris, Galeries Nationales du Grand Palais, Musée du Louvre, Musée d'Orsay, 2008–2009. Paris: RMN, 2008.

BEZZOLA, Tobia, Simonetta FRAQUELLI, Christian GEELHAR, and Michael C. FITZGERALD. *Picasso, sa première exposition muséale de 1932.* Zurich, Kunsthaus, 2010–2011. Munich, Berlin, and London: Prestel, 2010.

COWLING, Elisabeth, Anne BALDASSARI, John GOLDING, John ELDERFIELD, Isabelle MONOD-FONTAINE, and Kirk VARNEDOE. *Matisse-Picasso.* London, Tate Modern, 2002; Paris, Galeries Nationales du Grand Palais, 2002–2003; New York, Museum of Modern Art, 2003. London: Tate Publishing; Paris: RMN and Centre Pompidou, Musée National d'Art Moderne/Centre de Création Industrielle, 2002.

GAUDICHON, Bruno, and Joséphine MATAMOROS. *Picasso et les arts et traditions populaires.* Marseille, MuCEM, 2016. Paris: Gallimard; Marseille: MuCEM, 2016.

KELLER, Mariah, Simonetta FRAQUELLI, Elizabeth COWLING, Dominique H. VASSEUR, and Kenneth E. SILVER. *Picasso: The Great War, Experimentation, and Change.* Philadelphia, Barnes Foundation, 2016; Columbus Museum of Art, 2016. New York: Scala Arts Publishers, 2016.

Le Dernier Picasso, 1953–1973. Edited by Marie-Laure Bernadac and Isabelle Monod-Fontaine. Paris, Musée National d'Art Moderne, 1988; Paris, Musée Picasso, 1988; London, Tate Gallery, 1988. Paris: Centre Pompidou, 1988.

Les Demoiselles d'Avignon. Edited by Hélène Seckel. Paris, Musée Picasso, 1988; Barcelona, Museu Picasso, 1988. Paris: RMN, 1988.

MADELINE, Laurence. *Les Archives de Picasso, 'On est ce que l'on garde!'* Paris, Musée Picasso, 2003–2004. Paris: RMN, 2003.

MCCULLY, Marilyn. *Picasso, 1900–1907, les années parisiennes.* Amsterdam, Van Gogh Museum, 2011; Barcelona, Museu Picasso, 2011. Brussels: Fonds Mercator, 2011.

PERDRISOT, Virginie, and Cécile GODEFROY. *Picasso Sculptures.* Paris, Musée National Picasso, 2016; Brussels, Palais des Beaux-Arts (BOZAR), 2016. Paris: Musée National Picasso; Brussels: Palais des Beaux-Arts (BOZAR)/Somogy, 2016.

¡Picasso! Paris, Musée National Picasso, 2015. Paris: Musée National Picasso/RMN, 2015.

Picasso, œuvres reçues en paiement des droits de succession. Edited by Dominique Bozo. Grand Palais, 1979–1980. Paris: RMN, 1979.

REGNIER, Gerard. *Picasso, une nouvelle dation.* Paris, Galeries nationales du Grand Palais, 1990–1991. Paris: RMN, 1990.

RUBIN, William, Anne BALDASSARI, Pierre DAIX, Michael C. FITZGERALD, et al. *Picasso et le portrait.* New York, Museum of Modern Art, 1996; Paris, Galeries Nationales du Grand Palais, 1996–1997. Paris: Flammarion/RMN, 1996.

SECKEL-KLEIN, Hélène, and Emmanuelle CHEVRIERE. *Picasso collectionneur.* French edition of the catalogue of the Musée Picasso published to coincide with the exhibition *Picasso und seine Sammlung*, Munich, Kunsthalle der Hypo-Kulturstiftung, 1998. Paris: RMN, 1998.

SPIES, Werner, and Christine PIOT. *Picasso sculpteur, catalogue raisonné des sculptures.* Paris, Centre Pompidou, Musée National d'Art Moderne/Centre de Création Industrielle, 2000. Paris: Centre Pompidou, 2000.

SUTHERLAND BOGGS, Jean, and Marie-Laure BERNADAC. *Marie Picasso et les choses, les natures mortes.* The Cleveland Museum of Art, 1992; The Philadelphia Museum of Art, 1992; Paris, Galeries Nationales du Grand Palais, 1992. Paris: RMN, 1992.

TEMKIN, Anne, and Anne UMLAND. *Picasso Sculpture.* New York, MoMA, 2015. New York: MoMA, 2015.

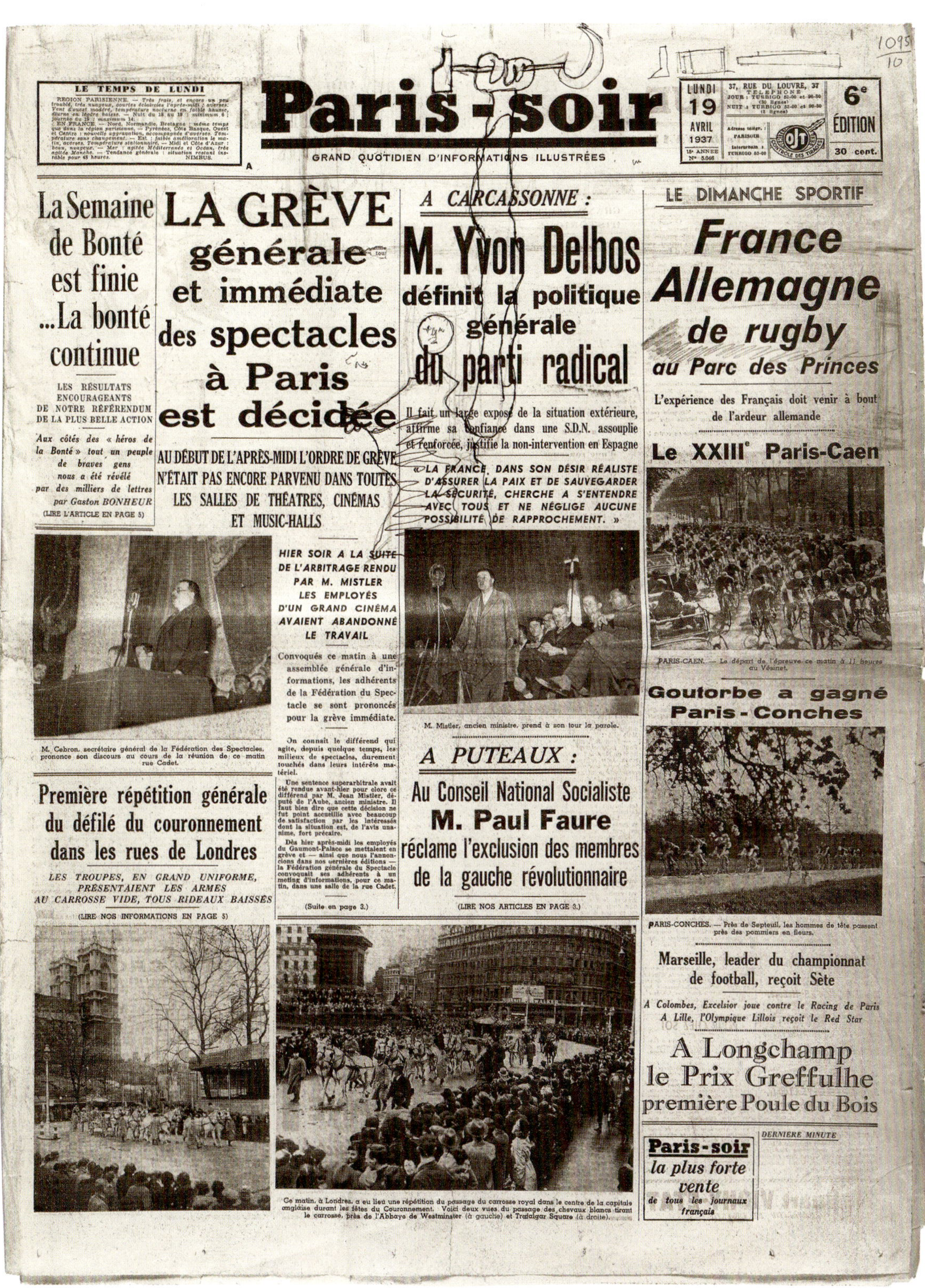

Fig. 168
Pablo Picasso
Figure Holding a Hammer and Sickle
[Paris, Le Tremblay-sur-Mauldre], 1937
Graphite pencil, pen and black ink on the front page of the newspaper
Paris-Soir dated 19 April 1937, 60 × 43 cm (23 ⅝ × 16 ⅞ in.)
Musée National Picasso-Paris
Dation Pablo Picasso, 1979. MP1177

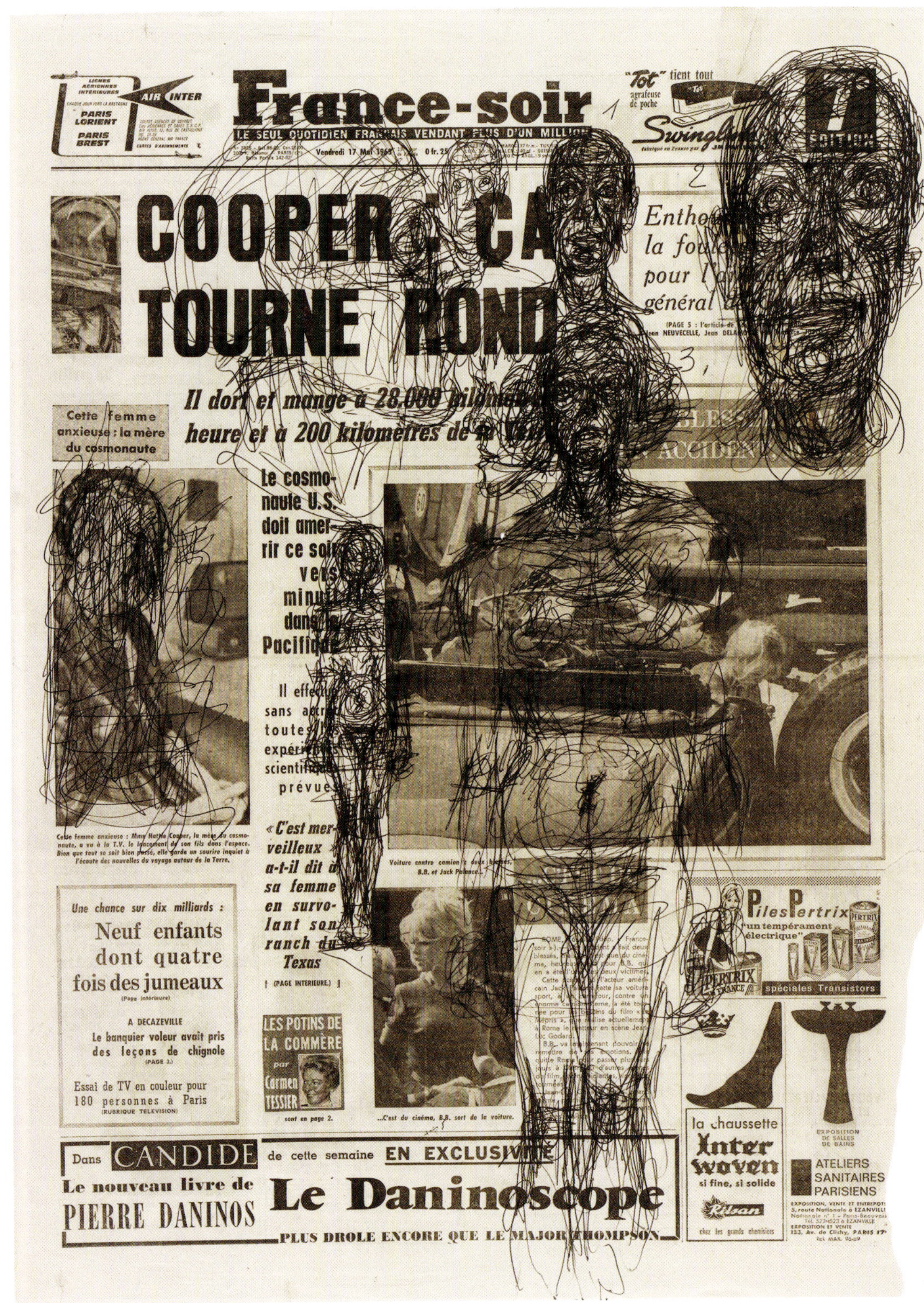

—
Fig. 169
Alberto Giacometti
Heads of Diego and *Annette Full-Length*
c. 1963
Black ballpoint pen on a page of the newspaper *France-Soir*,
60.5 × 42.5 cm (23 ⅞ × 16 ¾ in.)
Fondation Giacometti, Paris
—

Alberto Giacometti:
Selected Bibliography

Serena Bucalo-Mussely

**MONOGRAPHS
AND FIRST-HAND
ACCOUNTS**

BELLONY, Alice.
Une soirée avec Giacometti.
Paris: L'Échoppe, 2007.

BEN JELLOUN, Tahar.
*Giacometti, la rue d'un
seul, suivi de Visite fantôme
de l'atelier.* Paris: NRF
Gallimard, 2006.

BONNEFOY, Yves.
*Alberto Giacometti:
A Biography of His* Work.
Paris: Flammarion, 1991.

BRENSON, Michael.
*The Early Work of Alberto
Giacometti: 1925–1935.*
Baltimore: The Johns
Hopkins University, 1974.

BUCARELLI, Palma.
Giacometti. Rome: Editalia
Edizioni d'Italia, 1962.

CAROLA, Paola.
*Monsieur Giacometti,
je voudrais vous
commander mon buste.*
Paris: Léo Scheer, 2008.

CLAIR, Jean.
Le Nez de Giacometti.
Paris: Gallimard, 2000.

CLAIR, Jean.
*Le Résidu de la
ressemblance,
un souvenir d'enfance
d'Alberto Giacometti.* Paris:
L'Échoppe, 2000.

CREVEL, René.
*Mais si la mort n'était
qu'un mot.* Paris:
L'Échoppe, 2007.

DEL PUPPO, Alessandro.
Alberto Giacometti.
Rome: Gruppo Editoriale
L'Espresso, 2005.

DIDI-HUBERMAN, Georges.
*The Cube and the Face:
Around a Sculpture by
Alberto Giacometti.* Zurich:
Diaphanes, 2015.

DU BOUCHET, André.
Alberto Giacometti, dessins.
1969. New edition, Paris:
Maeght, 1991.

DUFRÊNE, Thierry.
*Alberto Giacometti, les
dimensions de la réalité.*
Geneva: Skira, 1994.

DUFRÊNE, Thierry.
*Giacometti, Genet: masques
et portrait moderne.* Paris:
L'Insolite, 2006.

DUFRÊNE, Thierry.
Le Journal de Giacometti.
Paris: Hazan, 2007.

DUPIN, Jacques.
Alberto Giacometti. Tours:
Farrago/Léo Scheer, 1999.

DUPIN, Jacques.
*Alberto Giacometti,
textes pour une approche.*
Paris: Fourbis, 1991.

DUPIN, Jacques,
and Ernst SCHEIDEGGER.
*Alberto Giacometti, éclats
d'un portrait.* Marseille:
André Dimanche, 2007.

FINK, Michèle.
*Giacometti et les poètes:
'Si tu veux voir, écoute.'* Paris:
Hermann, 2012.

FLETCHER, Valérie.
*Alberto Giacometti:
The Paintings.* New York:
Columbia University, 1994.

GENET, Jean.
L'Atelier d'Alberto Giacometti.
1958. Paris: Gallimard, 2007.

GIACOMETTI, Alberto.
Écrits. Edited by the
Fondation Alberto et Annette
Giacometti. Paris:
Hermann, 2007.

GIACOMETTI, Alberto.
Les Copies du passé. Cecilia
Braschi, Luigi Carluccio, and
Véronique Wiesinger. Paris:
Fage/Fondation Alberto et
Annette Giacometti, 2012.

GIACOMETTI, Alberto,
and Isabel NICHOLAS.
Correspondances. Lyon:
Fage, 2007.

GONZALEZ, Angel.
*Alberto Giacometti, œuvres,
écrits, entretiens.* Paris:
Hazan, 2006.

HOHL, Reinhold.
*Giacometti: A Biography
in Pictures.* Ostfildern:
Hatje Cantz, 1998.

JEDLICKA, Gotthard.
*Alberto Giacometti als
Zeichner.* Olten: Vereinigung
Oltner Bücherfreunde, 1960.

KLEMM, Christian.
*Die Sammlung der Alberto
Giacometti-Stiftung.* Zurich:
Zürcher Kunstgesellschaft,
1990.

KLEMM, Christian,
and Franziska LENTZSCH.
*Die neuen Räume: Alberto
Giacometti im Kunsthaus
Zürich.* Zurich: Zürcher
Kunstgesellschaft, 2002.

LA BEAUMELLE, Agnès de.
*À la rencontre d'Alberto
Giacometti.* Saint-Étienne:
Musée d'Art Moderne et
Contemporain, 1999.

LEIRIS, Michel.
'*Pierre pour un Alberto
Giacometti': Derrière le
miroir,* June–July 1951,
no. 39–40. New edition,
Paris: L'Échoppe, 1991.

LORD, James.
A Giacometti Portrait.
New York: Museum
of Modern Art, 1965.

LORD, James.
Giacometti: A Biography.
London: Faber & Faber,
1986.

MATTER, Mercedes,
Herbert MATTER,
Louis FILKENSTEIN,
and Andrew FORGE.
Alberto Giacometti.
New York: Harry N.
Abrams Inc., 1987.

NATSUME-DUBE, Sachiko.
*Giacometti et Yanaihara, la
catastrophe de novembre
1956.* Paris: L'Échoppe, 2003.

PLEYNET, Marcelin.
Giacometti, le jamais vu.
Paris: Éditions Dilecta, 2007.

READ, Peter,
and Julia KELLY.
Giacometti: Critical Essays.
Farnham:
Ashgate Publishing, 2009.

RÜTIMANN, Donat.
*Alberto Giacometti,
écrire la déchirure.* Paris:
L'Harmattan, 2006.

RÜTIMANN, Donat.
*Alberto Giacometti, le Rêve,
le Sphinx et la Mort de T.*
Zurich: Scheidegger &
Spiess, 2005.

SCHEIDEGGER, Ernst.
*Alberto Giacometti:
Traces of a Friendship.*
Zurich: Scheidegger &
Spiess, 2001.

SCHEIDEGGER, Ernst,
and Christian KLEMM.
*Alberto Giacometti: Sculpture
in Plaster: Photographs.*
Zurich: Scheidegger
& Spiess, 2006.

SCHNEIDER, Pierre.
*Alberto Giacometti,
'Un pur exercice optique'.*
Paris: Hazan, 2007.

SOAVI, Giorgio.
*Alberto Giacometti, il sogno
di una testa.* Milan: Edizioni
Gabriele Mazzotta, 2000.

SOAVI, Giorgio.
Mon Giacometti. Venice:
Basilissa, 2001.

SOLDINI, Jean.
La somiglianza introvabile.
Milan: Jaca Book, 1998.

SYLVESTER, David.
Looking at Giacometti.
London: Chatto & Windus,
1994.

USAMI, Eiji.
Mittsu no kotoba. Tokyo:
Misuzu Shobo, 1983.

WIESINGER, Véronique.
Giacometti, la figure au défi.
Paris: Gallimard, 2007.

WILSON, Laurie.
*Alberto Giacometti: Myth,
Magic, and the Man.*
New Haven; London: Yale
University Press, 2003.

YANAIHARA, Isaku.
Avec Giacometti. Paris:
Allia, 2015.

YANAIHARA, Isaku.
Dialogues avec Giacometti.
Paris: Allia: 2015.

EXHIBITION CATALOGUES

Alberto Giacometti. Edited by Catherine Grenier. Istanbul, Pera Müzesi, 2015. Istanbul: Suna ve İnan Kıraç Vakfi/ Pera Müzesi, 2015.

Alberto Giacometti. Edited by Catherine Grenier, Christian Alandete, and Cecilia Braschi. Fonds Hélène et Édouard Leclerc, 2015. Paris: Fondation Alberto et Annette Giacometti, 2015.

Alberto Giacometti, le peintre et le modèle. Aix-en-Provence, Galerie d'Art du Conseil Général of the Bouches-du-Rhône, 2007. Marseille: André Dimanche, 2007.

Alberto Giacometti, rétrospective. Edited by Catherine Grenier. Rabat, Musée Mohammed VI d'Art Moderne et Contemporain de Rabat, 2016. Rabat: Fondation Nationale des Musées du Maroc; Paris Fondation Alberto et Annette Giacometti, 2016.

BALVANYOS, Anna, and Christian KLEMM. *Alberto Giacometti 1901–1966: Works from the Alberto Giacometti Stiftung Zürich, and Other Collections.* Budapest, Szépművészeti Múzeum (The Budapest Museum of Fine Arts), 2004. Budapest: Szépművészeti Múzeum, 2004.

BAUMANN, Felix, and Poul Erik TØJNER. *Cézanne & Giacometti: Paths of Doubt.* Ostfildern: Hatje Cantz, 2008.

BELLASI, Pietro, Marco OBRIST, and Chasper PULT. *Giacometti, la valle, il mondo.* Milan, Fondazione Antonio Mazzotta, 2000. Milan: Gabriele Mazzotta, 2000.

BEZZOLA, Tobia. *Alberto Giacometti, Henri Cartier-Bresson, une communauté de regards.* Paris, Fondation Henri Cartier-Bresson, 2005; Zurich, Kunsthaus, 2005. Zurich: Scalo Verlag, 2005.

BONNEFOY, Yves. *Alberto Giacometti, sculptures, peintures, dessins.* Paris, Musée d'Art Moderne de la Ville de Paris, 1991–1992. Paris: Paris-Musées, 1991.

BRUGUIERE, Pierre, Jean STAROBINSKI, Hendel TEICHER, Christian DEROUET, and Casimiro Di CRESCENZO. *Alberto Giacometti: Early Work in Paris (1922–1930).* New York, Yoshii Gallery, 1994. New York: Yoshii Gallery, 1994.

CASTELLANI, Valentina, and Andrea CRANE. *Isabel and Other Intimate Strangers: Portraits by Alberto Giacometti and Francis Bacon.* New York, Gagosian Gallery, 2008. New York: Gagosian Gallery, 2008.

CRESCENZO, Casimiro Di. *Alberto Giacometti: sculture, dipinti, disegni.* Milan, Palazzo Reale, 1995. Florence: Artificio, 1995.

CRESCENZO, Casimiro Di, and Franco MONTEFORTE. *Alberto Giacometti, percorsi lombardi.* Sondrio, Museo Valtellinese di Storia e Arte, 2005. Sondrio: Credito Valtellinese, 2005.

CRESCENZO, Casimiro Di, and Marilena PASQUALI. *Alberto Giacometti, disegni, sculture e opere grafiche.* Bologna, Museo Morandi, 1999. Milan: Gabriele Mazzotta, 1999.

CRESCENZO, Casimiro Di, and Simone SOLDINI. *Alberto Giacometti, dialoghi con l'arte.* In collaboration with Jean Soldini. Mendrisio, Museo d'Arte, 2000. Mendrisio: Museo d'Arte, 2000.

FENOSA, Nicole. *Giacometti, Fenosa, concordances.* El Vendrell, Fundació Apelles Fenosa, 2005. Barcelona: Mediterrània, 2005.

Giacometti. Edited by Catherine Grenier, Serena Bucalo, Grazia Livi, and Giorgio Soavi. Milan, 24 Ore Cultura et Galleria d'Arte Moderna, 2014. Milan: 24 Ore Cultura et Galleria d'Arte Moderna; Paris: Fondation Alberto et Annette Giacometti, 2014.

Giacometti e la montagna. Stampa, Museum Ciäsa Granda, 2006; Laufenburg, Museum Rehmann, 2006. Stampa: Museum Ciäsa Granda, 2006.

Giacometti & Maeght: 1946–1966. Edited by Isabelle Maeght. Saint-Paul-de-Vence, Fondation Marguerite et Aimé Maeght, 2010. Saint-Paul-de-Vence: Fondation Marguerite et Aimé Maeght, 2010.

Giacometti, la scultura. Edited by Anna Coliva and Christian Klemm. Rome, Galleria Borghese, 2014. Milan: Skira, 2014.

Giacometti: Pure Presence. Edited by Paul Moorhouse. London, National Portrait Gallery, 2015. London: National Portrait Gallery Publications, 2015.

Giacometti, retour à la figuration, 1933–1947. Geneva, Musée Rath, 1986; Paris, Musée National d'Art Moderne, 1986–1987. Paris: Centre Pompidou/ Musée National d'Art Moderne/Centre de Création Industrielle, 1986.

Giacometti: Sculptures, Prints & Drawings from the Maeght Foundation. Edited by Edmund Capon Sydney. Art Gallery of New South Wales, 2006; Christchurch, Art Gallery Te Puna o Waiwhetu, 2006. Sydney: Art Gallery of New South Wales, 2006.

GRENIER, Catherine. *Giacometti, el hombre que mira.* Madrid, Fundación Canal, 2007. Madrid: Fundación Canal; Paris: Fondation Alberto et Annette Giacometti, 2007.

GRENIER, Catherine, and Christian ALANDETE. *Giacometti.* Shanghai, Yuz Museum, 2016. Paris: Dilecta/Fondation Alberto et Annette Giacometti, 2016.

HOLDIUS, Gabriele. *Giorgio Morandi, Alberto Giacometti: Ein Dialog.* Schwäbisch Gmünd, Museum im Prediger, 2008; Paderborn, Städtische Galerie in der Reithalle, 2009. Schwäbisch Gmünd (Germany): Museum im Prediger, 2008.

KLEMM, Christian. *Alberto Giacometti. Moja rzeczywistosc. Paryż bez końca, późne litografie.* Kraków, Galeria Starmach, 2003–2004. Kraków: Galeria Starmach, 2003.

KLEMM, Christian, and Dietrich WILDUNG. *Giacometti: Der Ägypter.* Berlin, Ägyptisches Museum und Papyrussammlung, 2008; Zurich, Kunsthaus, 2009. Munich and Berlin: Deutscher Kunstverlag, 2008–2009.

KLEMM, Christian, and Gottfried BOEHM. *La Mamma a Stampa, Annetta: Gesehen von Giovanni und Alberto Giacometti.* Coire, Bündner Kunstmuseum, 1991; Kuntshaus Zürich, 1990–1991. Coire: Bündner Kunstmuseum; Zurich: Kuntshaus Zürich, 1990.

KLEMM, Christian, Tobia BEZZOLA, Carolyn LANCHNER, and Anne UMLAND. *Alberto Giacometti.* Zurich, Kunsthaus, 2001; New York, Museum of Modern Art, 2001–2002. New York: Museum of Modern Art, 2001.

KÜSTER, Ulf. *Giacometti.* Riehen, Basel, Beyeler Foundation, 2009. Ostfildern: Hatje Cantz, 2009.

LA BEAUMELLE, Agnès de. *Alberto Giacometti: La collection du Centre Georges Pompidou.* Saint-Étienne, Musée d'Art Moderne, 1999. Paris: Éditions du Centre Georges Pompidou, 1999.

LA BEAUMELLE, Agnès de.
Alberto Giacometti, le dessin à l'œuvre. Paris, Musée National d'Art Moderne, 2001. Paris: Gallimard/ Éditions du Centre Pompidou, 2001.

LANGE, Christiane.
Alberto Giacometti: Sammlung Klewan. Altötting, Stadtgalerie Altötting, 2004. Bonn: Bild Kunst, 2004.

**LORD, James,
and Michael F. BRENSON.**
Alberto Giacometti (1901– 1966): A Loan Exhibition. New York, Acquavella Galleries, 1994. New York: Acquavella Galleries, 1994.

**NASH, Steven,
and Louise TOLLIVER DEUTSCHMANN.**
The Women of Giacometti. New York, Pace Wildenstein, 2005; Dallas, Nasher Sculpture Center, 2005–2006. New York: Pace Wildenstein, 2005.

SCHNEIDER, Nadia.
Alberto Giacometti. Geneva, Musée d'Art et d'Histoire, 2009–2010. Zurich: JRP Ringier, 2009.

Seeing. Feeling. Being: Alberto Giacometti.
Singapore, Singapore Art Museum, 2008. Singapore: Singapore Art Museum, 2008.

SPADONI, Claudio.
Alberto Giacometti. Ravenne, Loggetta Lombardesca, 2004–2005. Milan: Gabriele Mazzotta, 2004.

STUTZER, Beat.
Alberto Giacometti, Stampa-Paris. Coire, Bündner Kunstmuseum, 2000. Zurich: Scheidegger & Spiess, 2000.

**VAN LINGEN, Charlotte, Emily ANSEK,
and Véronique WIESINGER.**
Alberto Giacometti. Rotterdam, Kunsthal, 2008. Harderwijk: Uitgeverij d'Jonge Hond; Paris: Fondation Alberto et Annette Giacometti, 2008.

WIESINGER, Véronique.
Alberto Giacometti, colección de la Fundación Alberto y Annette Giacometti. Buenos Aires: Fundación Proa; Paris: Fondation Alberto et Annette Giacometti, 2012.

WIESINGER, Véronique.
En perspective, Giacometti, Georg Baselitz, Jean-Pierre Bertrand, Louise Bourgeois... Caen, Musée des Beaux-Arts, 2008. Lyon: Fage; Paris: Fondation Alberto et Annette Giacometti, 2008.

WIESINGER, Véronique.
Giacometti. São Paulo, Pinacoteca do Estado de São Paulo, 2012. São Paulo: Cosac Naify, Base 7; Paris: Fondation Alberto et Annette Giacometti, 2012.

WIESINGER, Véronique.
Giacometti in Switzerland. Geneva, Gagosian Gallery, 2010. Geneva: Gagosian Gallery, 2010.

WIESINGER, Véronique.
Giacometti, Leiris et Iliazd, portraits gravés. Caen, Musée des Beaux-Arts, 2008. Lyon: Fage; Paris: Fondation Alberto et Annette Giacometti, 2008.

WIESINGER, Véronique.
L'atelier d'Alberto Giacometti, collection de la Fondation Alberto et Annette Giacometti. Paris, Centre Georges Pompidou, Musée National d'Art Moderne/Centre de Création Industrielle, 2007–2008. Paris: Éditions du Centre Georges Pompidou/ Fondation Alberto et Annette Giacometti, 2007.

**WIESINGER, Véronique,
and Bo NILSSON.** *Alberto Giacometti. Bror Hjorth.* Stockholm: Liljevalchs Konsthall, 2006.

**WIESINGER, Véronique,
and Gottlieb LEINZ.** *Alberto Giacometti: Die Frau auf dem Wagen: Triumph und Tod.* Munich: Hirmer; Paris: Fondation Alberto et Annette Giacometti, 2010.

**WIESINGER, Véronique,
and José LEBRERO STALS.**
Alberto Giacometti, una retrospective. Museo Picasso Malaga, 2011–2012. Barcelona: Poligrafa, 2012.

**WIESINGER, Véronique,
and Toshio YAMANASHI.**
Alberto Giacometti, Isaku Yanaihara. Kamakura & Hayama Museum of Modern Art, 2006; Hyogo, Hyogo Prefectural Museum of Art, 2006; Kawamura, Kawamura Memorial Museum of Art, 2006. Tokyo: The Tokyo Shimbun, 2006.

**WIESINGER, Véronique,
Szeto LAP, and Shen YUAN.**
Giacometti: Without End. Hong Kong, Gagosian Gallery, 2014. Hong Kong: Gagosian-Rizzoli, 2014.

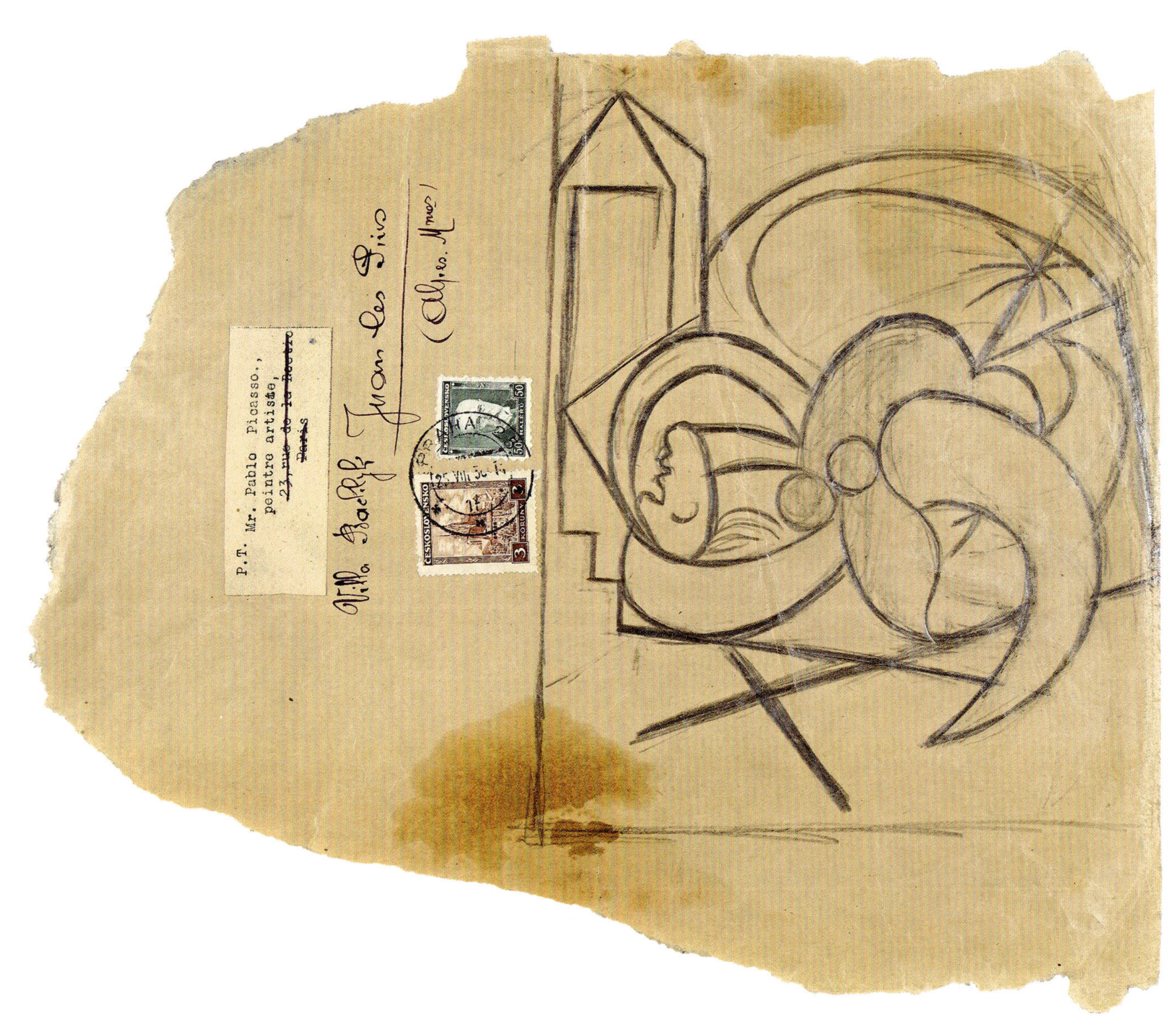

Fig. 170
Pablo Picasso
Bather with a Parasol
Juan-les-Pins, September 1930
Pencil, 23.5 × 28.3 cm (9 ¼ × 11 ⅛ in.)
Musée National Picasso-Paris
Dation Pablo Picasso, 1979. MP1061

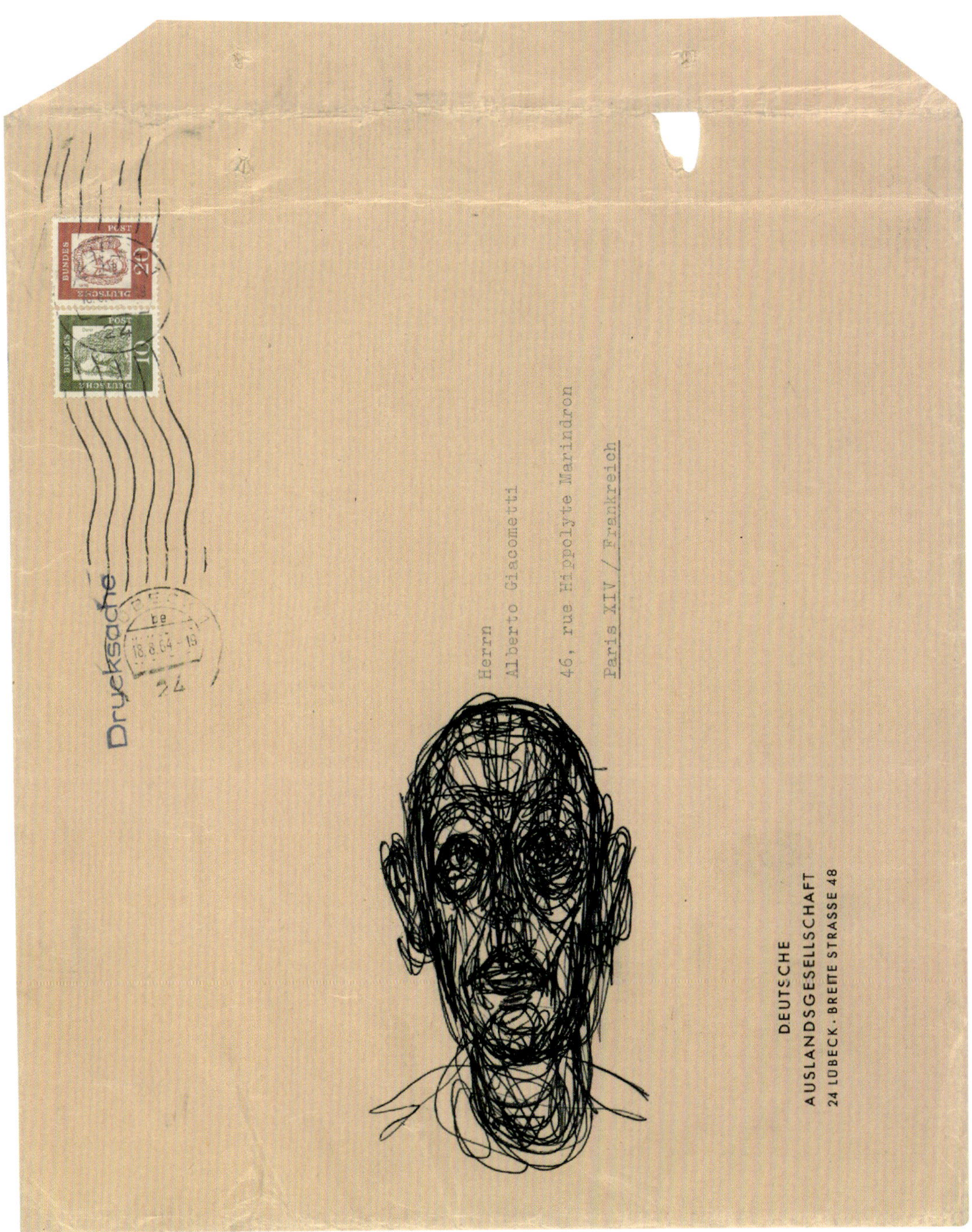

Fig. 171
Alberto Giacometti
Head
After 1964
Black ballpoint pen on an envelope, 29.1 × 22.8 cm (11 ½ × 9 in.)
Fondation Giacometti, Paris

Authors

Serena Bucalo-Mussely
Associate curator at Fondation Giacometti, where she is in charge of the *catalogue raisonné* of paintings, Serena Bucalo-Mussely has also been the associate curator for several Giacometti retrospectives, including at the Galleria d'Arte Moderna in Milan, Italy, and the Musée Mohammed-VI in Rabat, Morocco. She followed up her master's degree in art history from the Università degli Studi di Messina in Italy with a diploma from the École du Louvre in Paris.

Virginie Duchêne
Associate heritage curator Virginie Duchêne is responsible for publications and merchandising at the Musée National Picasso-Paris.

Catherine Grenier
Heritage curator and art historian Catherine Grenier has been the director of the Fondation Giacometti since 2014. Formerly associate director of the Musée National d'Art Moderne, Centre Pompidou in Paris, she has curated over thirty exhibitions showcasing the work of a series of modern and contemporary artists. Since her arrival at the foundation, she has organised outstanding exhibitions of Giacometti's work in Milan, Madrid, Istanbul, Landerneau, Shanghai and Rabat. She has published numerous essays on modern and contemporary art, including *Salvador Dalí: The Making of an Artist* (Flammarion, 2012) and *Annette Messager* (Flammarion, 2013).

Agnès de La Beaumelle
Honorary chief heritage curator at the Musée National d'Art Moderne, Centre Pompidou in Paris, where her responsibilities include overseeing the graphic art department, Agnès de La Beaumelle has curated a wide range of exhibitions, including, at the Centre Pompidou, *Leiris & Co* in 2015; *Joan Miró 1917–1934: La naissance du monde* in 2004; *Alberto Giacometti: Le dessin à l'oeuvre* in 2001; and *André Breton: La beauté convulsive* in 1991.

Nathalie Leleu
Researcher at the Musée National Picasso-Paris, Nathalie Leleu previously held posts at the Musée National d'Art Moderne and at the Bibliothèque Kandinsky–Centre Pompidou, Paris. Since 2001, she has been on the teaching staff for the Master 2 'Contemporary Art and Its Exhibition' course at the Université Sorbonne–Paris-IV, and, since 2011, the Master 2 'Art History and the Museum Profession' course at the Université Paris-Sorbonne Abu Dabi.

Virginie Perdrisot
Heritage curator at the Musée National Picasso-Paris, where she is in charge of the painting collections (1922–1937), sculptures and ceramics, Virginie Perdrisot was the associate curator for the *Picasso Sculpture* exhibition at the MoMA in New York from 2015 to 2016, prior to curating the *Picasso Sculptures* exhibition held at the Musée National Picasso-Paris in 2016, then at the Palais des Beaux-Arts in Brussels (BOZAR) from 2016 to 2017.

Jeanne-Yvette Sudour
Since 1987, Jeanne-Yvette Sudour has run the library at the Musée National Picasso-Paris. She has contributed to various publications by the museum, in particular *Picasso, la passion du dessin*, as well as to exhibitions catalogues devoted to Picasso abroad, including *Picasso: The Love and the Anguish – The Road to Guernica* (National Museum of Modern Art, Kyoto) and *Picasso: Mão erudita, olho selvagem* (Instituto Tomie Ohtake, São Paulo).

Sarah Wilson
Professor of contemporary art at the Courtauld Institute of Art, part of the University of London, Sarah Wilson's publications include *The Visual World of French Theory: Figurations* (Yale University Press, 2010) and *Picasso/Marx and Socialist Realism in France* (Liverpool University Press, 2013). She curated the exhibition *Paris: Capital of the Arts, 1900–1968* (Royal Academy, London; Guggenheim Museum, Bilbao, 2002), and has written an authoritative essay on Giacometti's work, 'Giacometti in Fez', in *Giacometti: The Anxious Body* (Ashgate Press, 2009).

Figs. 1–8 (pp. 1–8)

Fig. 1
DORA MAAR (Henriette Theodora Markovitch, known as) (1907–1997)
Standing Woman, plaster sculpture in the Grands-Augustins studio, Paris, c. 1941
Vintage print, gelatin silver print, 6.4 × 6.4 cm (2 ½ × 2 ½ in.)
Musée National Picasso-Paris
Estate of Dora Maar, 1998. MP1998-286

Fig. 2
DORA MAAR (Henriette Theodora Markovitch, known as) (1907–1997)
Alberto Giacometti [c. 1936]
Film negative, 24 × 18 cm (9 ½ × 7 ⅛ in.)
Image obtained using reversal process from the original negative
Centre Georges Pompidou, Musée National d'Art Moderne/Centre de Création Industrielle, Paris
Inv. 2004-0163 (206)

Fig. 3
DORA MAAR (Henriette Theodora Markovitch, known as) (1907–1997)
Portrait of Pablo Picasso in Dora Maar's studio at 29 Rue d'Astorg, Paris, winter 1935–1936
Film negative, 12 × 9 cm (4 ¾ × 3 ½ in.)
Image obtained using reversal process from the original negative
Centre Georges Pompidou, Musée National d'Art Moderne/Centre de Création Industrielle, Paris
AM2004-163 (205N)

Fig. 4
BRASSAÏ (Gyula Halász, known as) (1899–1984)
Open door to the sculpture studio at Boisgeloup, with Tériade and Bob the dog, Gisors, 1932
Printed c. 1950
Gelatin silver print, 29.2 × 23.4 cm (12 × 9 ¼ in.)
Musée National Picasso-Paris
Purchase, 1986. MP1986-5

Fig. 5
HENRI CARTIER-BRESSON (1908–2004)
Tall Woman IV, plaster in the studio courtyard, 1961
Magnum Paris
Inv. PAR1905

Fig. 6
BRASSAÏ (Gyula Halász, known as) (1899–1984)
Head of a Woman, plaster sculpture with other plaster works in the studio at Boisgeloup, Gisors, 1932
Printed c. 1960
Gelatin silver print, 29.5 × 22.8 cm (11 ⅝ × 9 in.)
Musée National Picasso-Paris
Purchase, 1986. MP1986-7

Fig. 7
DORA MAAR (Henriette Theodora Markovitch, known as) (1907-1997)
Alberto Giacometti's studio (*The Invisible Object*), 1934
Flexible negative, 18 × 13 cm (7 ⅛ × 9 ⅛ in.)
Image obtained using reversal process from the original negative
Centre Pompidou, Musée National d'Art Moderne/Centre de Création Industrielle, Paris
Inv. AM 2004-0163 (954)

Fig. 8
ÉMILE SAVITRY (1903–1967)
Alberto Giacometti's studio, 1945
Gelatin silver print, 25.7 × 32.6 cm (10 ⅛ × 12 ⅞ in.)
Fondation Giacometti, Paris

Figs. 172–179 (pp. 249–256)

Fig. 172
HENRI CARTIER-BRESSON (1908–2004)
Head with a Helmet, Head of a Woman, Woman in a Long Dress, Bust of a Woman, Bather and *Woman Leaning on Her Elbow*, sculptures in the Grands-Augustins studio, Paris, 1944
Undated print
Gelatin silver print, 18 × 23.2 cm (7 × 9 ⅛ in.)
Musée National Picasso-Paris
Museum's documentation MPPH2588

Fig. 173
CECIL BEATON (1904–1980)
Woman in a Long Dress, Head with a Helmet, Bust of a Woman, sculptures in the Grands-Augustins studio, Paris, 1945
Undated contact sheet
Gelatin silver print, 6 × 6 cm (2 ⅜ × 2 ⅜ in.)
Musée National Picasso-Paris
Museum's documentation
Contact sheet MPPH2880

Fig. 174
EMMY ANDRIESSE (1914–1953)
Alberto Giacometti's studio, 1948
Gelatin silver print, 27.7 × 26 cm (11 × 10 ½ in.)
Fondation Giacometti, Paris

Fig. 175
DORA MAAR (Henriette Theodora Markovitch, known as) (1907–1997)
Small sculpture and *Head of a Woman (Dora Maar)* in the Grands-Augustins studio, Paris, c. 1941
Vintage gelatin silver print, 6.4 × 6.4 cm (2 ½ × 2 ½ in.)
Musée National Picasso-Paris
Estate of Dora Maar, 1998
MP1998-295

Fig. 176
ISAKU YANAIHARA (1918–1989)
Alberto Giacometti working in his studio, Paris, 1959
Gelatin silver print, 15.5 × 11.2 cm (6 ⅛ × 4 ⅜ in.)
Fondation Giacometti, Paris

Fig. 177
SABINE WEISS (born 1924)
Alberto Giacometti in his studio, Paris, 1954
Gelatin silver print 23.6 × 16.3 cm (9 ½ × 6 ⅜ in.)
Fondation Giacometti, Paris

Fig. 178
CECIL BEATON (1904–1980)
Pablo Picasso with his sculpture *Head of a Woman (Dora Maar)* in the Grands-Augustins studio, Paris, 1945
Undated print
Gelatin silver print, 25.5 × 25 cm (10 × 9 ⅞ in.)
Musée National Picasso-Paris
Museum's documentation
MPPH358

Fig. 179
ANONYMOUS
Figurine
Undated
Gelatin silver print, 6.9 × 9.8 cm (2 ¾ × 3 ⅞ in.)
Fondation Giacometti, Paris

Credits

COPYRIGHT HOLDERS

Despite the Publisher's best efforts, certain authors and copyright holders have not been able to be identified and located. We would ask any authors or rights holders we may have inadvertently omitted to accept our apologies and ask them to contact us. Any errors or omissions referred to the Publisher will be corrected in subsequent printings.

For the name, image and works of Pablo Picasso © Succession Picasso, 2017

For the name, image and works of Alberto Giacometti © Alberto Giacometti Estate (Fondation Alberto et Annette Giacometti + ADAGP), Paris 2017

FOR THE WORKS:

pp. 1, 2, 3, 7, 56, 62, 252: © ADAGP, Paris, 2017
pp. 4, 6: © Estate Brassaï – RMN – Grand Palais
pp. 5, 249: © Henri Cartier-Bresson/Magnum Photos
p. 8: © Photo Émile Savitry courtesy Sophie Malexis
p. 14: © Peter Scheier
p. 35: © Photo Marc Vaux
pp. 39, 256: © All rights reserved
p. 45: © MAN RAY TRUST/ ADAGP, Paris, 2017
pp. 250, 255: © The Cecil Beaton Studio Archive at Sotheby's
p. 251: © 2017 Emmy Andriesse
p. 253: © Photo by Isaku Yanaihara/© Suki Yanaihara/ Permission granted through Misuzu Shobo, Ltd. Tokyo
p. 254: © Sabine Weiss 1945–2016 – All rights reserved.

FOR THE TEXTS:

pp. 203–206: © Calmann-Lévy, 2002.
pp. 208–210: Reprinted from *Break of Day* by André Breton, translated by Mark Polizzotti and Mary Ann Caws, by permission of the University of Nebraska Press. Originally published as *Point du jour*, copyright 1934, 1970 by Éditions Gallimard. English translation copyright 1999 by Mark Polizzotti and Mary Ann Caws.
pp. 211–213: Reprinted from *Mad Love* by André Breton, translated by Mary Ann Caws, by permission of the University of Nebraska Press. Originally published as *L'Amour fou*, copyright 1937 by Éditions Gallimard. English translation copyright 1987 by the University of Nebraska Press.
p. 215: From *Self Portrait* by Man Ray. Copyright © 1963 by Man Ray. Used by permission of Little, Brown and Company. All rights reserved.
pp. 217–219: © Éditions Cahiers d'Art.

PHOTOGRAPHIC CREDITS

© 2016 Digital Image, The Museum of Modern Art, New York/Scala, Florence: pp. 19, 55, 61
© All rights reserved: pp. 14, 51
© Photo Claude Germain – Archives Fondation Marguerite et Aimé Maeght, Saint-Paul-de-Vence (France): p. 169
© Courtesy Éditions Cahiers d'Art: p. 24
© Photo: Éric Baudouin: p. 81
© Fondation Pierre Gianadda: p. 87
© Henri Cartier-Bresson/ Magnum Photos: pp. 5, 249
© Jean-Pierre Lagiewski: pp. 40, 75, 79, 80, 89, 90, 101, 103, 105, 107, 108, 110, 113, 114, 119, 121, 122, 132, 136, 143, 148, 150, 153, 157, 158l, 159, 160, 164, 175, 176, 179, 180, 183, 184, 188, 191
© Marc Domage: pp. 76, 82, 93, 95, 97, 128
© Marco Illuminati: pp. 139, 185, 186, 193
© MNAM-CCI, Centre Pompidou, Dist. RMN-Grand Palais/All rights reserved: pp. 18, 45 / Image MNAMCCI, Centre Pompidou: pp. 2, 3, 7 / Jean-Claude Planchet: p. 39
© Museu Picasso, Barcelona. Fotografía, Gasull Fotografia: pp. 74, 77
© RMN-Grand Palais/ Béatrice Hatala: p. 109
© RMN-Grand Palais/ René-Gabriel Ojéda: p. 142
© RMN-Grand Palais (Musée National Picasso-Paris)/ Adrien Didierjean: pp. 52, 91, 118, 168, 174, 177, 187, 190 / Adrien Didierjean-Mathieu Rabeau: pp. 44, 67, 78 / All rights reserved: pp. 42, 172l, 233 / Franck Raux: pp. 1, 4, 6, 125t, 252 / Béatrice Hatala: pp. 59, 65, 70, 92, 94, 100, 104, 124t, 162 / Daniel Arnaudet: pp. 146t, 250 / Hervé Lewandowski: p. 255 / Jean-Gilles Berizzi: pp. 16, 137, 142, 172r / Mathieu Rabeau: pp. 73, 88, 102, 106, 111, 112, 115, 120, 123, 129, 130, 133, 135, 138, 140, 145, 149, 151, 152, 156, 161, 165, 167, 171, 181, 182, 190, 192 / Michèle Bellot: p. 64 / René-Gabriel Ojéda: pp. 155, 178 / Thierry Le Mage: pp. 52, 84b, 98b, 116t, 126, 173t, 238
© Thierry Pautot: p. 134.

This English-language edition
is based on the catalogues
accompanying the exhibition
Picasso–Giacometti, held at
the Musée National Picasso-
Paris from 4 October 2016
to 5 February 2017 and
at The Fire Station, Doha,
from 22 February 2017 to
21 May 2017.

CATALOGUE

A Musée National Picasso-Paris /
Flammarion co-edition

Scientific Direction
Serena Bucalo-Mussely (Fondation
Giacometti)
Virginie Perdrisot (Musée National
Picasso-Paris)

**Editorial Direction and Coordination
of the French Edition**
Julie Rouart, Editorial Director
(Flammarion)
Delphine Montagne, General
Administration (Flammarion)
Marion Doublet and Mélanie Puchault,
Editors (Flammarion)

Émilie Bouvard (Musée National
Picasso-Paris)
Céline Moulard, Freelance
Publishing Adviser for the Musée
National Picasso-Paris

In collaboration with Christian Alandete
(Fondation Giacometti), with the
assistance of Victoria Giovannoni

Design
M et Moi Studio

**Editorial Direction and Coordination
of the English Edition**
Kate Mascaro, Editorial Director
(Flammarion)
Helen Adedotun, Editor (Flammarion)

Translated from the French by
Mot.tiff Inside, Paris (Philippa
Bowe-Smith and Justin Hillier)
and David Radzinowicz

Typesetting
Thierry Renard

Proofreading
Lindsay Porter

Production
Corinne Trovarelli

Color Separation
Reproscan, Italy

Authors
Serena Bucalo-Mussely
Virginie Duchêne
Catherine Grenier
Agnès de La Beaumelle
Nathalie Leleu
Virginie Perdrisot
Jeanne-Yvette Sudour
Sarah Wilson

EXHIBITION

Head Curator of the Exhibition
Catherine Grenier (Fondation
Giacometti)

Associate Curators
Serena Bucalo-Mussely (Fondation
Giacometti)
Virginie Perdrisot (Musée National
Picasso-Paris)

Project Manager
Audrey Gonzalez (Musée National
Picasso-Paris)

MUSÉE NATIONAL PICASSO-PARIS

President
Laurent Le Bon

Director-General
Erol Ok

**Director of Communications and
Partnerships**
Leslie Lechevallier

Director of Collections and Production
Claire Garnier

**Director of Audiences
and Cultural Development**
Guillaume Blanc

Director of Resources and Budget
Matthieu Chapelon

**Director of Facilities, Security and
Information Systems**
Guillaume Gaillard

FONDATION GIACOMETTI, PARIS

Director
Catherine Grenier

Deputy Director
Sabine Longin

Executive PA
Sarah Oliver

Head of Exhibitions and Editions
Christian Alandete

Exhibition Project Manager
Alban Chaine

Head of Research
Thierry Pautot

Head of Publics and Partnership
Camille Guerin

Collection Manager for Paintings
Serena Bucalo-Mussely

Collection Manager for Sculptures
Michèle Kieffer

Collection Manager for Graphic Arts
Mathilde Lecuyer

Collection Manager for Decorative Arts
Thierry Pautot

Collections and Exhibitions Registrars
Stéphanie Barbé-Sicouri
Alban Chaine

Associate Registrar
Marion Buffaut

Assistant Registrar
Laetitia Bailly

Registrar Intern
Clara Gibertoni

**Head of Legal Affairs
and Intellectual Property**
Emilie Le Mappian

ACKNOWLEDGEMENTS

The Musée National Picasso-Paris would particularly like to thank the Gagosian Gallery for its generous support

GAGOSIAN GALLERY

The Musée National Picasso-Paris also thanks the Embassy of Switzerland for its support

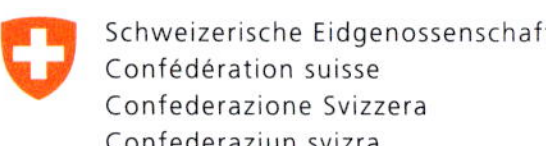

and Mr and Mrs François-Xavier, as well as Natasha de Mallmann.

The Musée National Picasso-Paris and the Fondation Giacometti hereby express their gratitude to the members of the Picasso family for their invaluable assistance.

Both institutions would like to thank Almine and Bernard Ruiz-Picasso, together with the Fundación Almine y Bernard Ruiz-Picasso para el Arte (FABA), for their generous backing.

They also offer their thanks to the teams of the Picasso Administration, first and foremost Claude Ruiz-Picasso, as well as to Christine Pinault.

They would like to express their appreciation to Alexandre Colliex for his involvement at the beginning of this project and to Françoise Gilot for her precious memories.

They acknowledge their gratitude to Philippe Büttner, Christian Klemm, Olivier Kaeppelin, Léonard Gianadda and Serena Cattaneo Adorno for their unfailing support during preparations for the exhibition.

They would also like to thank the authors of the present volume for their contributions.

The museums, institutions and collectors whose generous loans helped make the exhibition a reality are also hereby warmly thanked:

**Centre Pompidou, Paris,
Musée National d'Art Moderne/
Centre de Création Industrielle**
Serge Lasvignes, President
Denis Berthomier, Director-General
Jack Lang, President of the Association for the Development of the Centre Pompidou
Didier Grumbach, President of the Société des Amis du Musée National d'Art Moderne
Bernard Blistène, Director of the Musée National d'Art Moderne
Brigitte Leal, Deputy Director of the Musée National d'Art Moderne, Head of Collections
Olga Makhroff, Head of Loans and Deposits Service
Stéphane Guerreiro, Director of Production
Hélène Vassal, Chief Registrar
Marion Julien, Registrar
Rania Moussa Morin, Collections Assistant

Fondation Pierre Gianadda Collection, Martigny, Switzerland
Léonard Gianadda, President

**Fondation Marguerite et Aimé Maeght,
Saint-Paul-de-Vence, France**
Adrien Maeght, President of the
Fondation Marguerite et Aimé Maeght,
Honorary President of the Société
des Amis de la Fondation Marguerite
et Aimé Maeght
Olivier Kaeppelin, Director of the
Fondation Marguerite et Aimé Maeght
François de Rancourt, President of
the Société des Amis de la Fondation
Marguerite et Aimé Maeght
Cathy Cordova, Assistant to the Director

**Fundación Almine y Bernard Ruiz-
Picasso para el Arte (FABA)**
Almine and Bernard Ruiz-Picasso,
Co-Founders and Co-Presidents
François Bellet, Curator
Marie Brisson, Secretary
Iro Biehler, Assistant
Thomas Chaineux, Archivist/Librarian
Claire Guérin, Restorer

**Kunsthaus Zürich,
Alberto Giacometti-Stiftung**
Dr. Christoph Becker, Director
Dr. Philippe Büttner, Curator
Karin Marti, Registrar

Musée des Beaux-Arts, Lyon
Sylvie Ramond, Director,
Chief Heritage Curator
Patricia Viscardi, Secretary-General
Maryse Bertrand, Assistant to the
Director and Loans Coordinator

**Museo Nacional Centro de Arte
Reina Sofía, Madrid**
Manuel Borja-Villel, Director
Michaux Miranda, Deputy Director
General
João Fernandes, Artistic Deputy
Director
Teresa Velázquez, Director of
the Exhibitions Department
Belén Díaz de Rábago, General
Coordinator of Exhibitions
Rosario Peiró, Director of Collections
Paula Ramírez, General Coordinator
of Collections
Carmen Cabrera, Chief Registrar
Victoria Fernández-Layos Moro,
Registrar
Jorge García, Head of Restoration

Museu Picasso Barcelona
Emmanuel Guigon, Director
Esther Calvo de Haro, Assistant
to the Director
Malén Gual, Heritage Curator
Claustre Rafart, Heritage Curator
Isabel Cendoya and Mariona Tió
de Gispert, Directors of Exhibitions
Anna Fàbregas Sauret, Anna Rodríguez,
and Anna Anglès, Registrars
of the Collections
Reyes Jiménez and Anna Vélez,
Heads of Restoration and Preventive
Conservation

Museo Picasso Málaga
Guillermo Peiró Posadas,
Director-General
José Lebrero Stals, Artistic Director
Begoña Mendoza Pérez, Assistant
to the Director

We would like to sincerely thank all
those lenders who wish to remain
anonymous.

And finally we extend our warm thanks
to Pascal Abel, Damarice Amao,
Bernardo Laniado-Romero and
Perrine Renaud, who, in various ways,
did so much to prepare the exhibition.

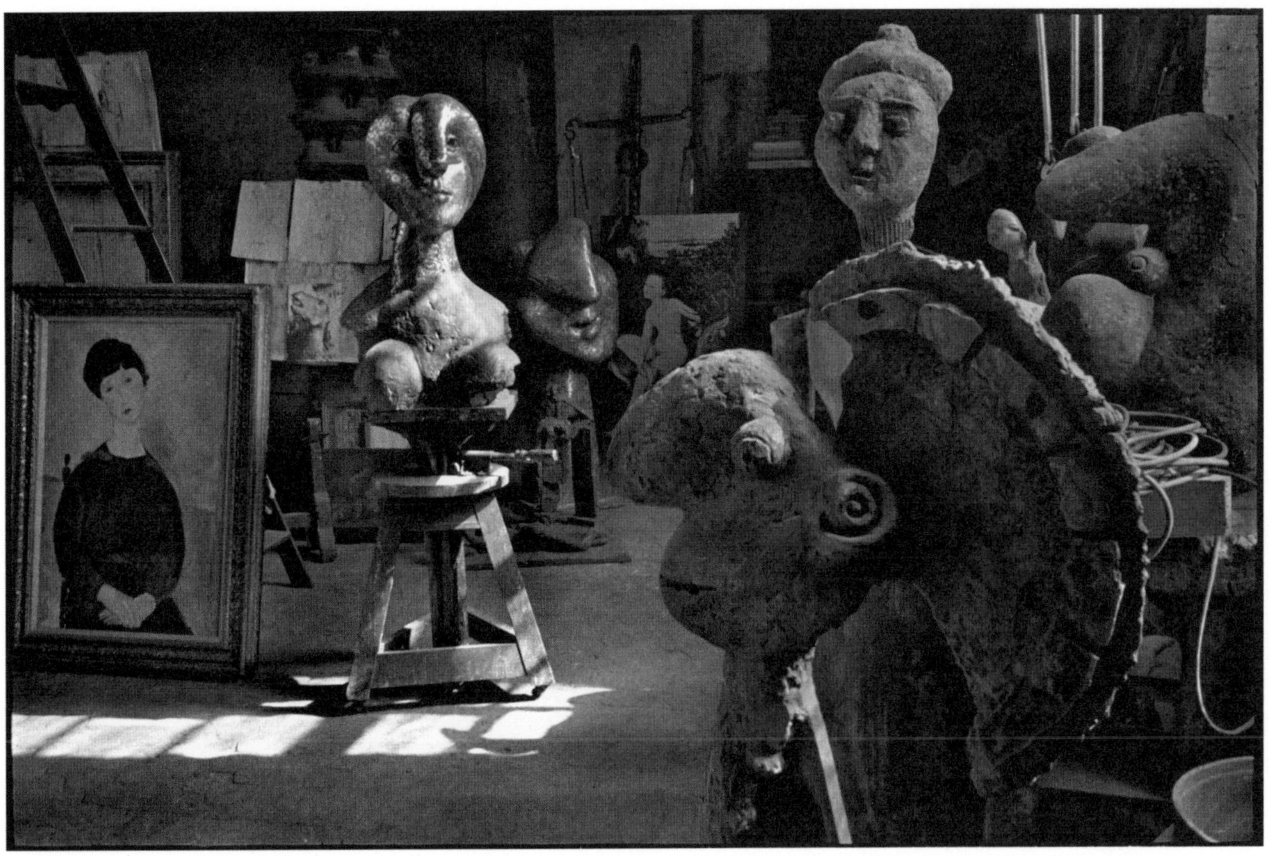

Fig. 172

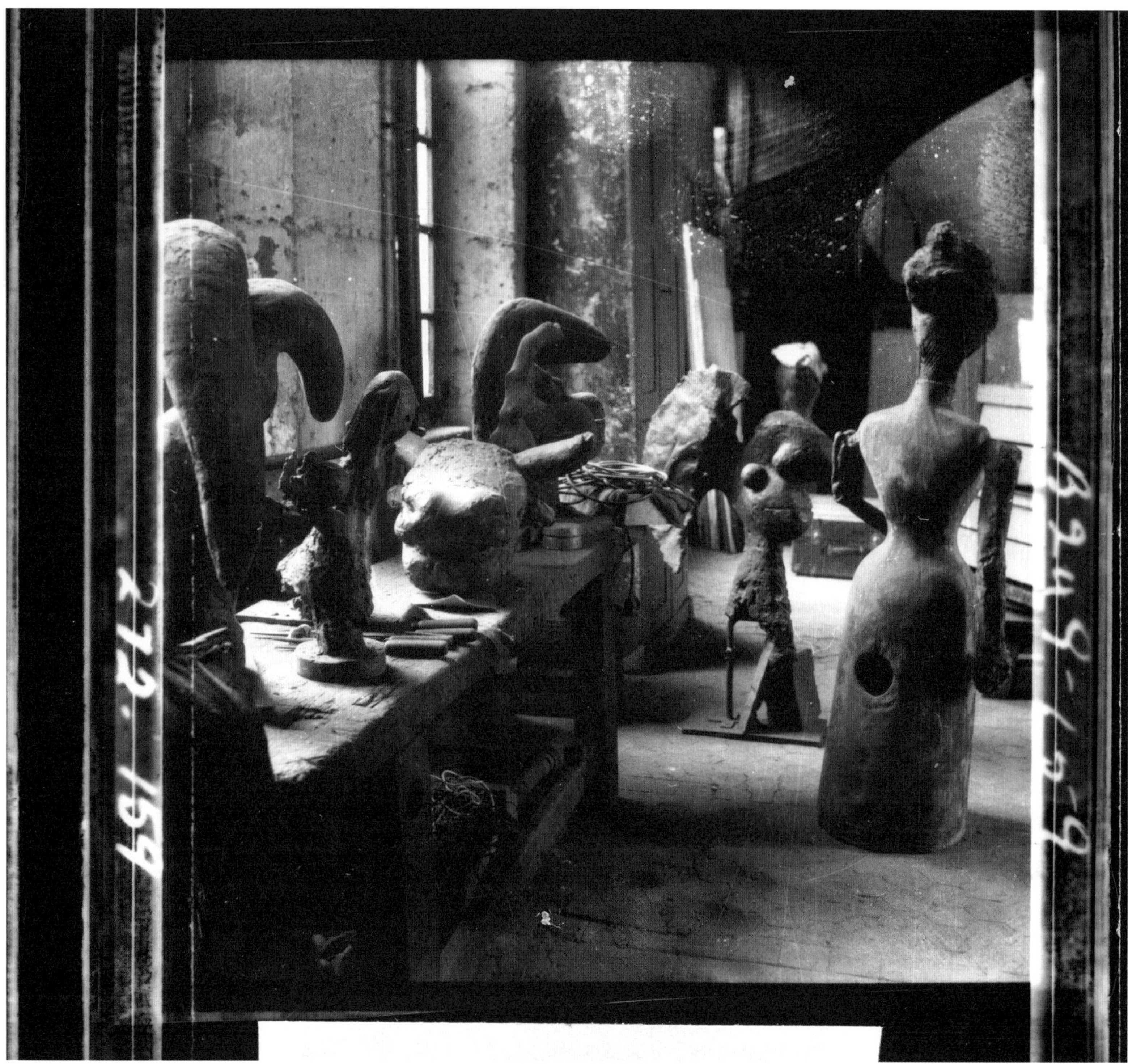

Fig. 173

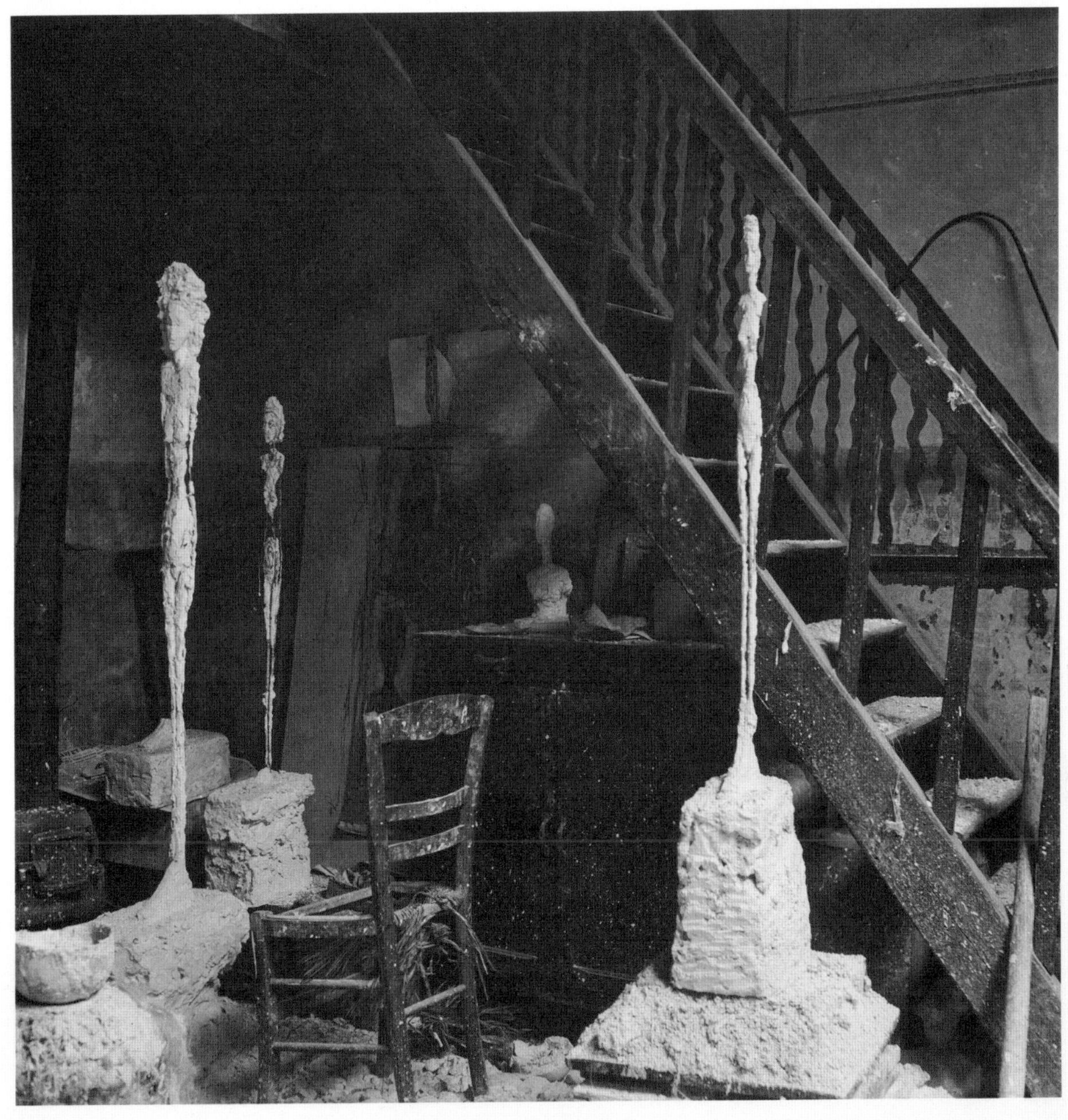

Fig. 174

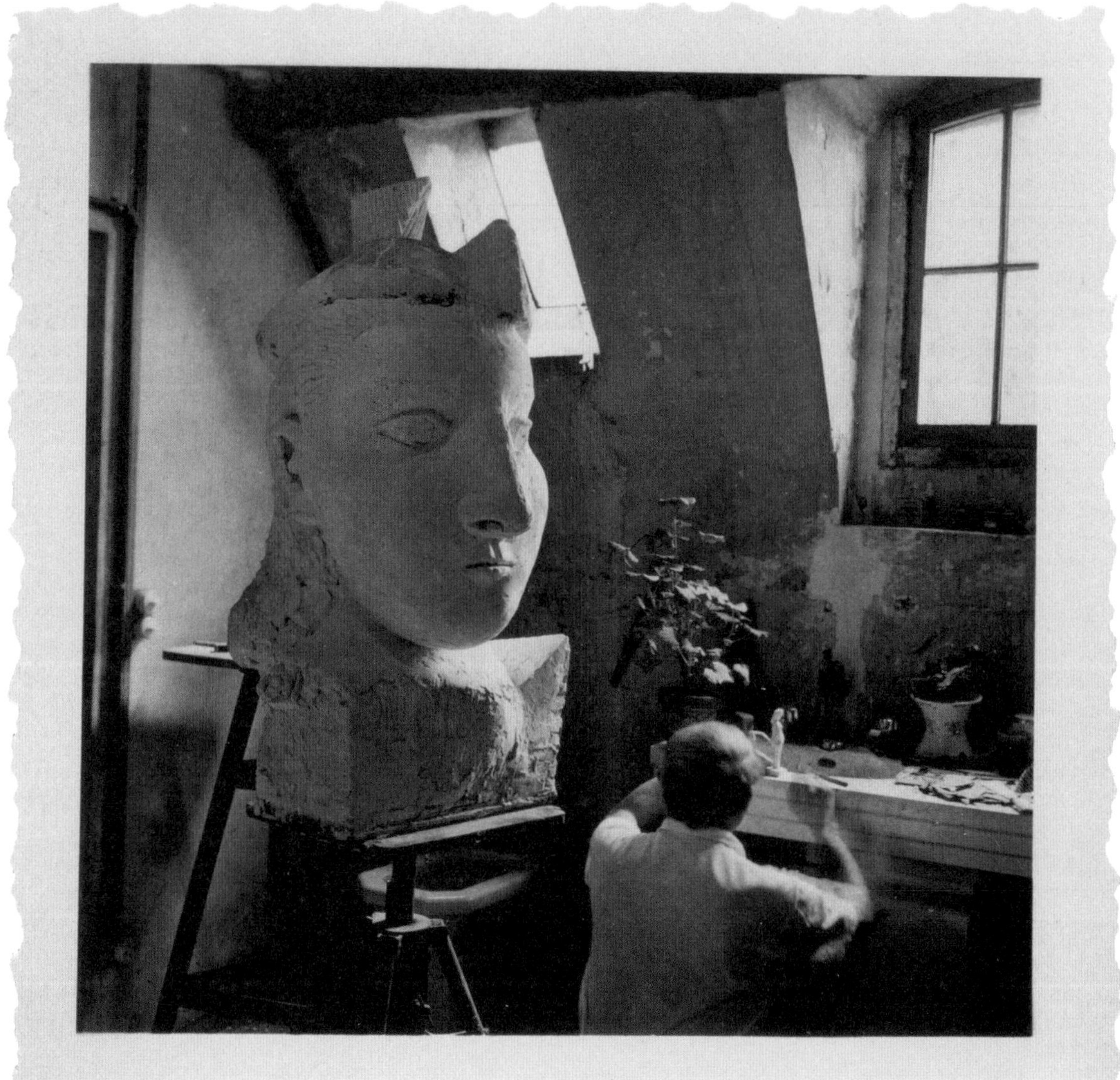

Fig. 175

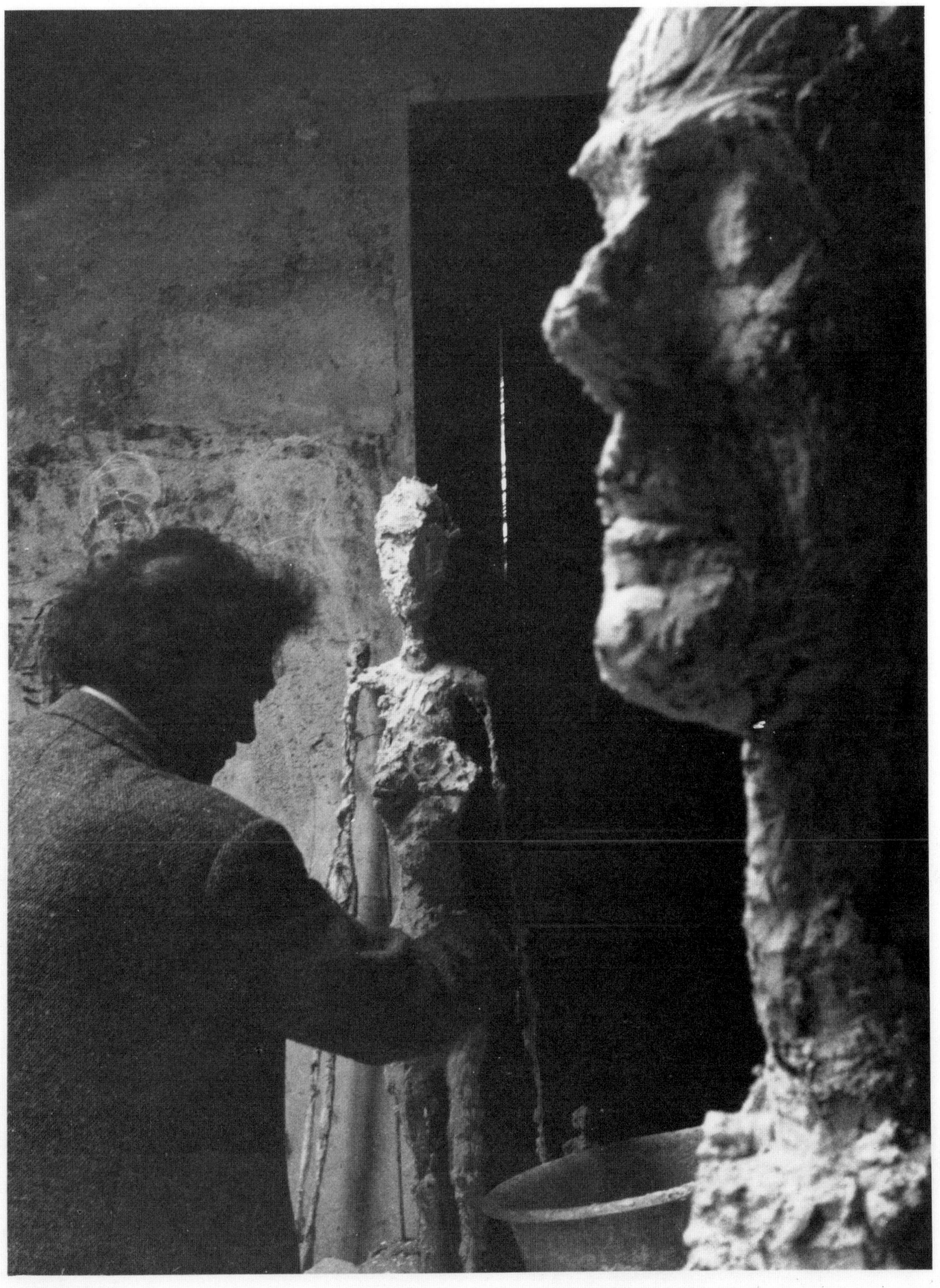

Fig. 176

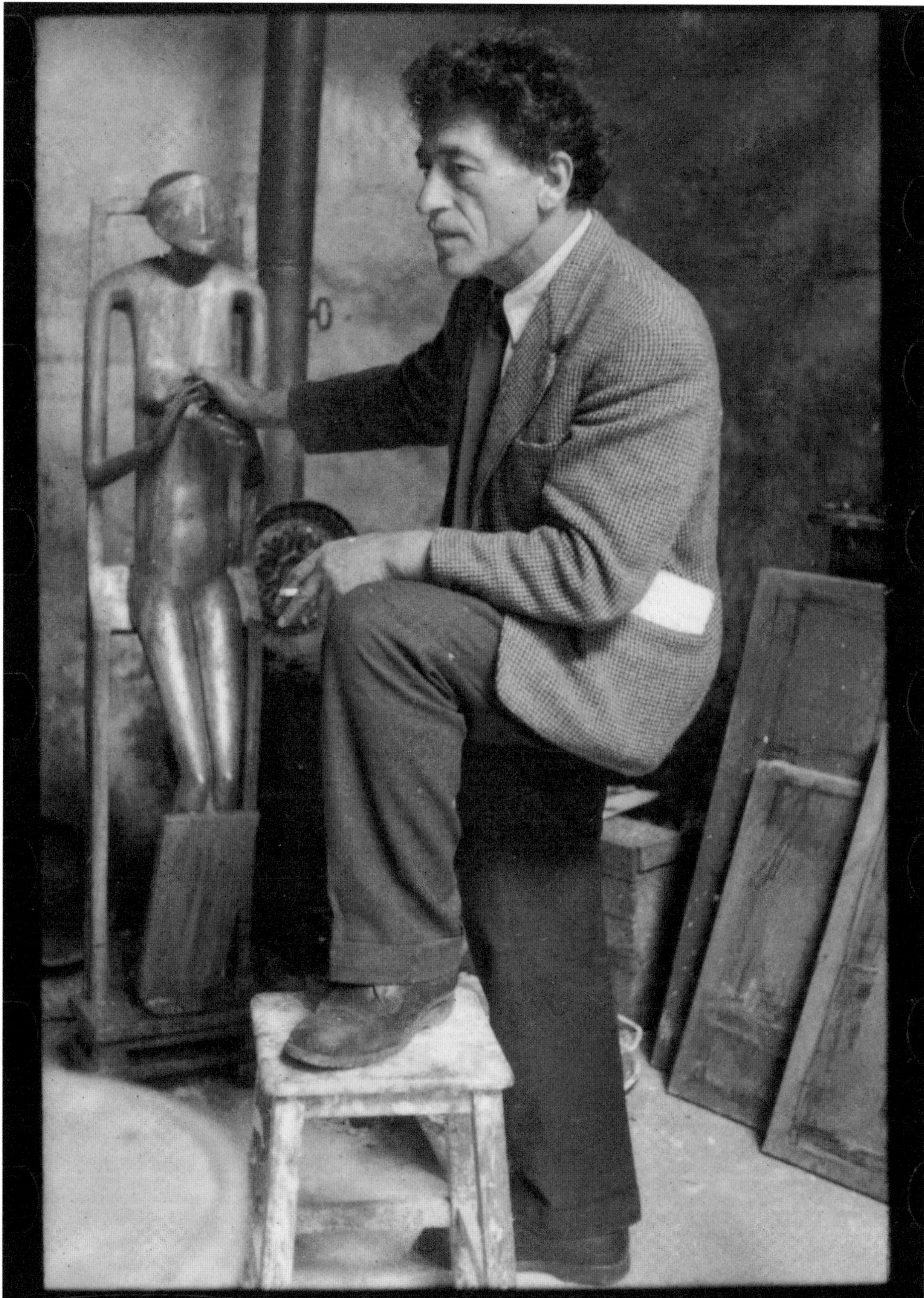

Fig. 177

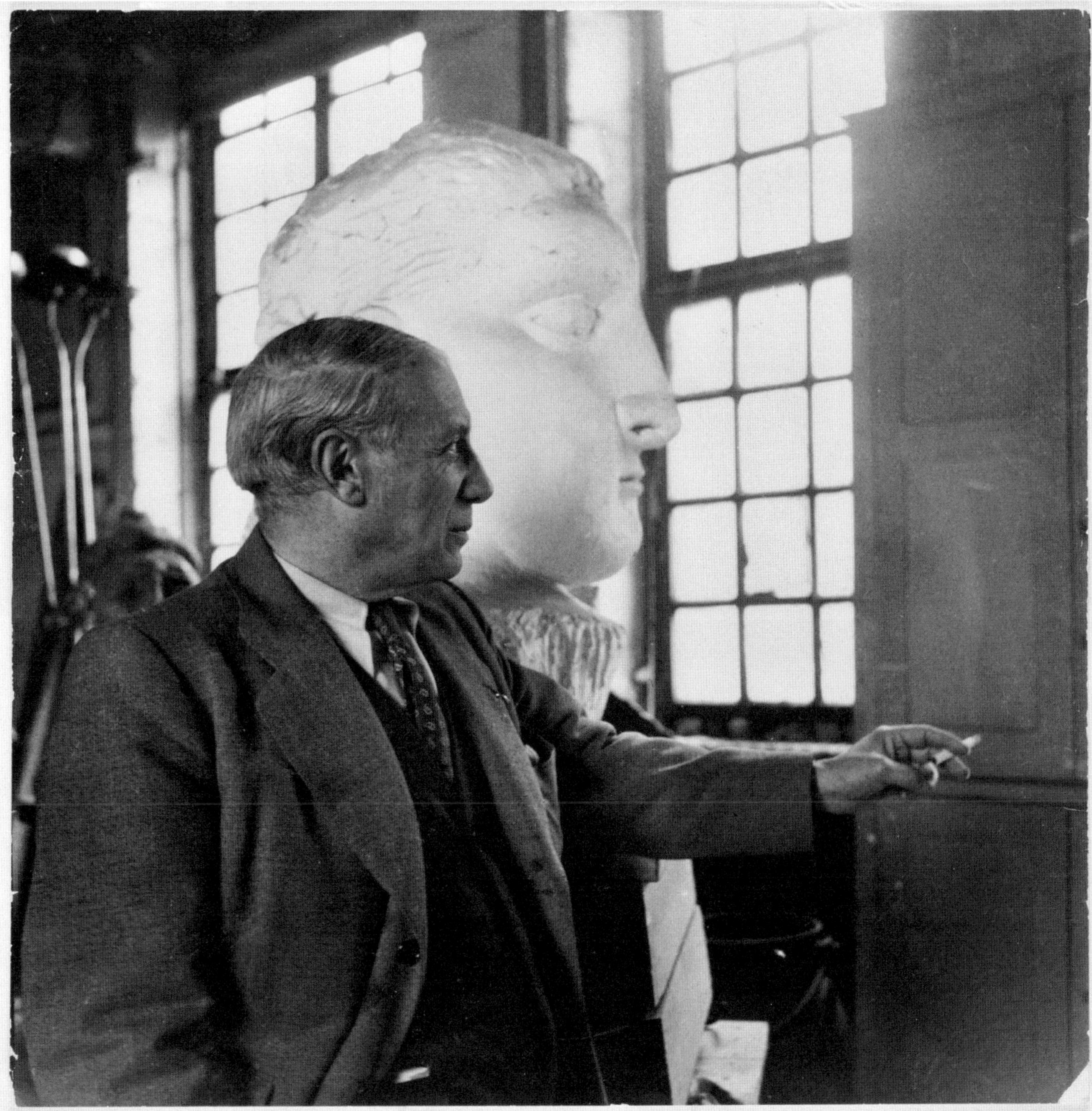

Fig. 178

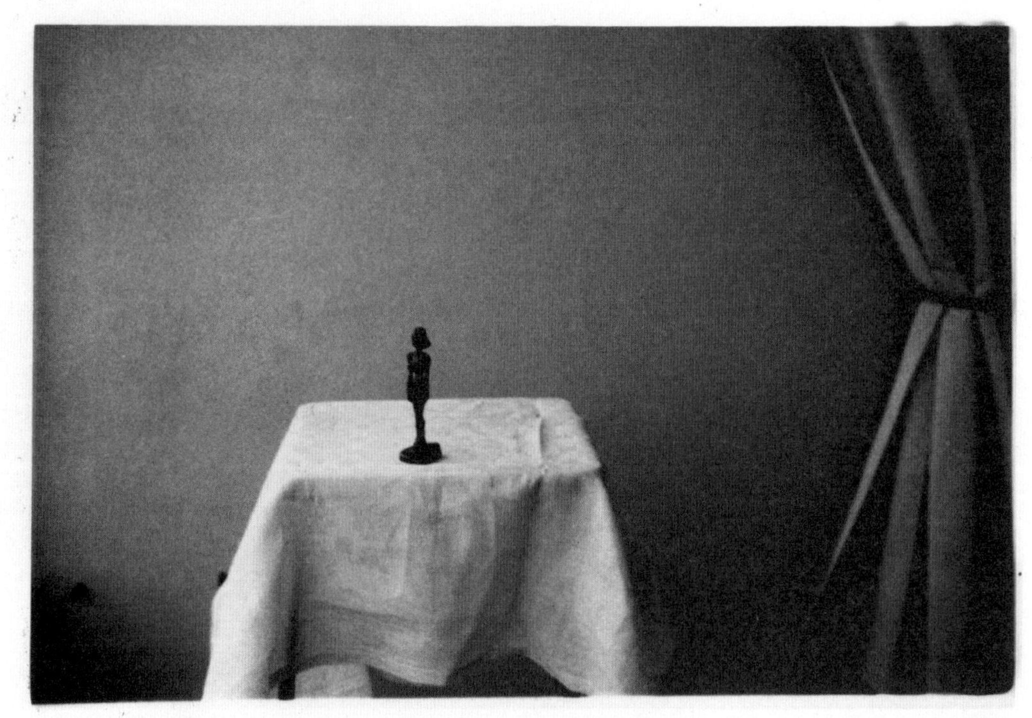

Fig. 179